Introducing the
World of Education

DEDICATION

to the memory of
Paul Huo-Chin Yin and Loo Yuin How Yin

Introducing the World of Education

A Case Study Reader

Editor

Robert K. Yin
COSMOS Corporation

SAGE Publications
Thousand Oaks ▪ London ▪ New Delhi

For information:

Sage Publications, Inc.
2455 Teller Road
Thousand Oaks, California 91320
E-mail: order@sagepub.com

Sage Publications Ltd.
1 Oliver's Yard
55 City Road
London EC1Y 1SP
United Kingdom

Sage Publications India Pvt. Ltd.
B-42, Panchsheel Enclave
Post Box 4109
New Delhi 110 017   India

Printed in the United States of America

Library of Congress Cataloging-in-Publication Data

Introducing the world of education: A case study reader / edited by Robert K. Yin.
    p. cm.
Includes bibliographical references and index.
ISBN 1-4129-0667-9 (pbk.)
1. Education—Social aspects—United States—Case studies.
2. Education—Social aspects—Cross-cultural studies. I. Yin, Robert K.
LC191.4.I59 2005
306.43′2—dc22   2005002335

This book is printed on acid-free paper.

05   06   07   08   10   9   8   7   6   5   4   3   2   1

Acquisitions Editor:	Lisa Cuevas Shaw
Editorial Assistant:	Karen Wong
Production Editor:	Denise Santoyo
Copy Editor:	Gillian Dickens
Typesetter:	C&M Digitals (P) Ltd.
Indexer:	Pamela Van Huss
Cover Designer:	Michelle Lee Kenny

Contents

Preface   ix

Acknowledgments   xi

Introduction   xiii

PART I: TEACHING AND LEARNING   1

1. Student Teaching   3
   Kidder, Tracy. (1989). *Among Schoolchildren*
   (pp. 3–11 and 114–132). Boston: Houghton Mifflin.

2. Vignette of a Fifth-Grade Teacher   23
   Shaw, Kenneth L., & Etchberger, Mia Lena. (1993).
   "Transitioning Into Constructivism: A Vignette
   of a Fifth Grade Teacher." In Kenneth Tobin (Ed.),
   The Practice of Constructivism in Science Education
   (pp. 259–266). Washington, DC: AAAS Press.

3. A Commitment to Children   33
   White, Merry. (1987). "Elementary Schools: Harmony
   and Cooperation." In *The Japanese Educational
   Challenge: A Commitment to Children* (pp. 110–133).
   New York: Free Press.

PART II: THE DIVERSITY OF EDUCATIONAL LIFE   57

4. Culturally Diverse Families and Schools   59
   Valdés, Guadalupe. (1996). *Con Respeto: Bridging
   the Distances Between Culturally Diverse Families
   and Schools* (pp. 1–8). New York: Teachers College Press.

5. Educating Students With Disabilities   69

Cambone, Joseph. (1994). *Teaching Troubled Children: A Case Study in Effective Classroom Practice* (pp. 37–43 and 191–196). New York: Teachers College Press.

6. School Inequality: Federal Courts   83

Kozol, Jonathan. (1991). "The Dream Deferred, Again, in San Antonio." In *Savage Inequalities: Children in America's Schools* (pp. 206–233). New York: Crown.

7. School Inequality: State Courts   101

Anyon, Jean. (1997). "Class, Race, Taxes, and State Educational Reform, 1970–1997." In *Ghetto Schooling: A Political Economy of Urban Educational Reform* (pp. 134–148). New York: Teachers College Press.

PART III: SCHOOLS   119

8. The Good High School   121

Lawrence-Lightfoot, Sara. (1983). "George Washington Carver High School: Charismatic Leadership—Building Bridges to a Wider World." In *The Good High School: Portraits of Character and Culture* (pp. 29–55). New York: Basic Books.

9. Low- and High-Performing Schools Serving Native American Students   149

Epp, Walter, & Epp, Juanita Ross. (2002). "North America—Canada." In David Reynolds, Bert Creemers, Sam Stringfield, Charles Teddlie, & Gene Schaffer (Eds.), *World Class Schools: International Perspectives on School Effectiveness* (pp. 85–95). London: Taylor & Francis.

10. Schools on Probation   165

Mintrop, Heinrich (with Curtis, Kim, & Plut-Pregelj, Lea). (2004). "Schools Moving Toward Improvement." In *Schools on Probation: How Accountability Works (and Doesn't Work)* (pp. 76–86). New York: Teachers College Press.

11. Public School Choice   177

Teske, Paul, Schneider, Mark, Roch, Christine, & Marschall, Melissa. (2000). "Public School Choice: A Status Report." In Diane Ravitch & Joseph P. Viteritti (Eds.), *Lessons From New York City Schools* (pp. 313–338). Baltimore: Johns Hopkins University Press.

PART IV: DISTRICTS AND STATES   205

12. The Superintendency   207
Yee, Gary, & McCloud, Barbara. (2003). "A Vision
of Hope: A Case Study of Seattle's Two Nontraditional
Superintendents." In Larry Cuban & Michael
Usdan (Eds.), *Powerful Reforms With Shallow Roots:
Improving America's Urban Schools* (pp. 54–76).
New York: Teachers College Press.

13. Reforming Urban Districts   233
Cuban, Larry, & Usdan, Michael. (2003).
"What Happened in the Six Cities?" In Larry Cuban &
Michael Usdan (Eds.), *Powerful Reforms With Shallow
Roots: Improving America's Urban Schools* (pp. 147–170).
New York: Teachers College Press.

14. State Departments of Education   261
Lusi, Susan Follett. (1997). "Methodology."
In *The Role of State Departments of Education
in Complex School Reform* (pp. 183–192).
New York: Teachers College Press.

15. State Education Standards   273
Wu, Hung-Hsi. (2000). "The 1997 Mathematics
Standards War in California." In Sandra Stotsky (Ed.),
*What's at Stake in the K–12 Standards Wars:
A Primer for Educational Policy Makers*
(pp. 3–31). New York: Peter Lang.

PART V: COMMUNITY AND SCHOOL BOARD ACTION   289

16. An Urban Youth Program   291
Stake, Robert E. (1986). *Quieting Reform:
Social Science and Social Action in an Urban
Youth Program* (pp. ix–xvii and 3–15). Urbana:
University of Illinois at Urbana-Champaign.

17. School–Community Collaboration in Starting a New School   305
Stuart, Lee. (2000). "The Bronx Leadership
Academy High School: The Challenges of Innovation."
In Diane Ravitch & Joseph P. Viteritti (Eds.), *Lessons
From New York City Schools* (pp. 117–137). Baltimore:
Johns Hopkins University Press.

18. Educational Programs and the Local
    Community Power Structure 327
    Soto, Lourdes Diaz. (1997). "Media Accounts."
    In *Language, Culture, and Power: Bilingual Families
    and the Struggle for Quality Education* (pp. 65–81).
    Albany: State University of New York Press.

19. School Board Leadership 349
    McAdams, Donald R. (2000). "The Wonderful
    Cacophony of a Free People Disagreeing." In *Fighting
    to Save Our Urban Schools . . . and Winning!
    Lessons From Houston* (pp. 104–121). New York:
    Teachers College Press.

20. A Post-9/11 Perspective on U.S. Education 369
    Burkett, Elinor. (2001). *Another Planet:
    A Year in the Life of a Suburban High School*
    (pp. 323–332). New York: HarperCollins.

APPENDIX: Doing Case Studies in Education 379
    Yin, Robert K. (2005). "Case Study Methods." In Judith
    Green, Gregory Camilli, & Patricia Elmore (Eds.),
    Complementary Methods for Research in Education
    (3rd ed.). Washington, DC: American Educational
    Research Association.

Index 399

About the Editor 407

Preface

This collection of readings represents a new venture for me, not without risks.

My earlier books have been directed at people intent on learning about the case study method, as part of their graduate training or professional work. Although the pertinent academic subjects might have varied—from education to urban planning to management science to the core disciplines of political science and sociology and the practice fields of public administration, nursing, and social work—the unifying theme has been a common interest in doing case studies. As a result, I have shared much lore about case study research and design with people in all these different fields.

This book, however, is mainly aimed at people in one field—education. In this field, the book is intended to serve both undergraduates and graduates. Rather than emphasizing case studies as a research method, the main purpose of the collection of readings is to reveal the breadth of experiences in what I call "the world of education." It happens that all of the selections are from case studies in education, for reasons explained in the introduction. But the vision for the entire collection remains an education vision, not a research or research methods vision.

Wherein lie the risks. My own training and background, although in related fields, are not in education. I have taught at the university level but never in a K–12 system—not for a single day or even for a single class. So the vision for this book, represented mainly by its five parts but also by the selection of the readings themselves, may not suit the visions of those in the system, whether you may be taking an education course, studying to become a teacher, actually teaching, or even serving as a principal or other administrator.

The underpinnings for my vision come from doing K–12 education research. One way or the other, I have been doing such research for nearly 30 years. The earliest years emphasized technological innovations in education, highlighted by computer-assisted instruction (remember that?) and even the introduction of closed-circuit television into classrooms (remember that, too?). I spent many years doing research on special education, covering a broad range of issues involving prereferrals and early childhood education, individualized education plans (IEPs), transition to work, the use of technology and media, and what then was called the "mainstreaming" of students with disabilities (including "categorical" and "noncategorical" programs). More recently and for the past several years, my research has covered education reform, comprehensive school reform, urban education, related initiatives in mathematics and science education, and public school choice.

In doing this research, I have collected data, based on direct field experiences, from numerous schools, school districts, and state departments of education. I have site visited and studied the informal science education that takes place in science museums and related institutions. I and the research teams under my leadership also have done extensive work on community youth programs, including major efforts on substance abuse prevention, juvenile gang prevention, and violence prevention—all of which have involved collaboration with schools. So I guess I have been "around the block," if not in the classroom.

Well, by now you should be able to figure out both the risks and even the possible benefits from using this book. Its vision reflects those facets important from experiences and findings in education research, not necessarily from practicing education. You will be the best judge in deciding whether the vision appeals to the education field.

Acknowledgments

In the Chinese culture, any devotion to education inevitably comes from one's parents. My upbringing was no exception, and this volume is dedicated to the memory of my parents, Huo-Chin (Paul) Yin and Loo Yuin How Yin. To them, education was not a choice. It was an imperative—and also an opportunity. One was a fool for thinking otherwise. Both parents had the good fortune to pursue postcollege studies in the United States, having attained their initial bachelor's degrees in China. Both made sure that I and my two siblings, all born in the United States, had the best possible education, through K–12 and well beyond.

I also have been fortunate to have participated in educational research for nearly 30 years, starting with grants from the U.S. Department of Education (National Institute of Education) and continuing from a variety of federal and nonfederal sources to this day. The research has been directed at practical issues, covering the use of technology in education, the education of students with disabilities, informal science education, mathematics and science education, education reform, and public school choice. In these endeavors, key colleagues to whom I owe thanks have been Carol Weiss, Marty Kaufman, Karen Seashore Louis, Michael Kane, Rolf Lehming, Dave Roessner, Irwin Feller, and, more recently, Hank Levin, Bob Stake, Bernice Anderson, and Kenneth Wong. Earlier, I had the pleasure of working with education colleagues at the Rand Corporation, who included Milbrey McLaughlin, Paul Berman, and Lorraine McDonnell, but the work at COS-MOS Corporation with its staff for the past 25 years has been even more rewarding. At COSMOS, we have completed numerous education research projects, interacted with many expert panels and consultants, and made multiple presentations at annual meetings of the American Education Research Association and other meetings.

A panel of education advisers, specifically organized to guide the development of this anthology and overseen by Margo Crouppen at Sage Publications, also provided invaluable guidance. Serving on the panel were

Jennifer Greene
University of Illinois at Urbana–Champaign

Ming Fang He
Georgia Southern University

James Jackson
George Washington University

Holly Kreider
Harvard Family Research Project

George W. Noblit
University of North Carolina at Chapel Hill

Festus E. Obiakor
University of Wisconsin–Milwaukee

Sharon Rallis
University of Connecticut

Gretchen Rossman
University of Massachusetts–Amherst

Jeanne Shay Shumann
University of Miami, Coral Gables

I thank you all for reviewing my initial outlines and ideas about the book. In response to a query, several of you also nominated case studies, though I did not always take your suggestions.

Finally, I am indebted to the editors at Sage, and especially Lisa Cuevas Shaw, who has been instrumental in identifying the anthology's potential contribution and then in encouraging me to start and complete it.

Although I bear the sole responsibility for this book, I hope that it will be seen as a token of thanks to all of you with whom I have collaborated, inside and outside of COSMOS, over the years.

Introduction

Welcome to the world of education. Our nation's public schools educate more than 50 million students a year, from kindergarten to Grade 12 (K–12). The schools employ 3 million teachers and occupy 100,000 school buildings, involving expenditures of roughly $500 billion per year. The entire enterprise is aimed at providing free and public education to every American child.

The pervasiveness of the enterprise means that most of us have had public school experiences and may even have fond memories of our classroom days. However, other than what we might read in the popular press, we actually may know little about how public schools work, how school systems are organized, or about the diversity of what contemporary students are being taught to learn. For instance, school systems are units of government, not simply administrative agencies, but most of us probably cannot remember the last time we voted for a school board member or the names of the current members serving our communities—even if our own children may now be attending a public school.

The complexity of school systems adds to our difficulties in learning more about public education. First, any given school system has many different kinds of schools. Second, detailed but obscure collective bargaining contracts may define specific education conditions for teachers and principals. Third, within the same school may be found a bewildering variety of courses, educational programs, and teaching specialists. However, adding most to the complexity, public education varies by locale. K–12 education is not organized as a single national enterprise but operates differently in different states and communities. The local variations mean that, when we relocate to a different community, we need to start all over again in understanding our local schools and the content of their public education.

In fact, learning about education and how it occurs in this country may assume the proportions of a formal research inquiry, rather than a quick surf across various Web sites. The depth and extent of the inquiry will be dictated by each person's own motives and curiosity. Aspiring educators are likely to go farther than most, but everyone has to start somewhere.

Purpose of This Anthology

This anthology is intended to help you start your own inquiry, introducing you to the world of education. The anthology is organized according to five parts. They start with teaching and learning in the classroom and then move to increasingly broader but nevertheless critical (and little understood) contexts, including school districts, communities, and states.

One way of starting your inquiry would have been to amass a lot of statistics about schools, such as the modest ones at the outset of this introduction. The size of the public education enterprise lends itself to such statistics. But statistics is not what education is really about. Starting to understand the world of education means bringing to life what goes on in classrooms and in schools and how both are connected to a broader panoply of real-life school districts, state agencies, communities—and educational controversy.

Case studies eminently fill this need. Properly done, they can provide both descriptive richness and analytic insight into people, events, and passions as played out in real-life environments. As a result, this anthology consists entirely of a set of readings from selected case studies. Make no mistake, however. In nearly every instance, the selected reading is only a portion of the original case study. You may have to retrieve and read the entire case study before you reach any final conclusions. In this sense, a case study anthology can only be an *introduction* to the case studies on a given subject such as education (see Yin, 2004, for a similar anthology, but covering case studies on a variety of subjects).

Besides illuminating real-life experiences, the use of case studies to begin your inquiry has another, possibly invaluable bonus. The selected readings do not just inform you about the world of education. They also illustrate how case studies have been used to study topics in education. Thus, although the initial motive for your inquiry might have merely been to learn more about education, the readings also expose you to a methodological tool useful for doing your own study. Doing your own case study may not have crossed your mind, but it enables you to make your own contribution to research. Alternatively, you may actually *need* to do a case study to complete class assignments or degree requirements (including a term paper, master's thesis, or doctoral dissertation).

This added bonus of learning how to do case studies is highlighted in the introductions to each selection. The introductions start with the educational significance of the selection and what it might reveal about the world of education. They then briefly describe the relevant features of the case study method as also illustrated by the selection, on the chance that you might want to (or have to) do a similar kind of case study in your own work. To enhance the value of the added bonus, the different selections highlight different aspects of the case study method. The final selection, appearing in the Appendix, then gives you a comprehensive operational guide for using case studies to do educational research.

Advice for Choosing Among the Anthology's Selections

Selecting Readings on the World of Education. Regarding topics in education, the anthology is organized to be used either from cover to cover or selectively. From cover to cover, the anthology's five parts shift from the most immediate educational environment (i.e., a classroom) to increasingly complex environments (e.g., communities). You may feel familiar with the classroom selections (Parts I and II). They emphasize teaching and learning and other educational processes in everyday terms. The final selections in these first two parts (Chapters 6 and 7) also point to a continuing challenge—the potentially inequitable distribution of resources and opportunities as found from school to school or district to district in our decentralized system of schools.

In the later selections (Parts III, IV, and V), the everyday terms diminish, and you may be less familiar with the concepts used in characterizing the role of the superintendent and education's connections with larger organizational and community entities. The connections are nevertheless worth knowing because they all are part of the governance of schools and can affect what occurs in the classroom. For instance, the working of state agencies, especially in setting educational standards, has not been fully appreciated by the literature, and hence the selections in Chapters 14 and 15 may be quite helpful to you. By the time you get to Chapter 20's pointed commentary on the average American student's sparse knowledge of global matters and international affairs, you should have a good idea of some of the basic features of education in this country.

If you want to be selective instead of going from cover to cover, Table 1 helps by listing three common dimensions for such selectivity—each selection's dominant topic (or academic subject), grade level, and geographic locale. By perusing the last three columns in Table 1, you will quickly see the

Table 1 Guide to the Selections in This Anthology

Chapter/Title in This Book	Author/Title of Original Work	Yr. of Pub.	Locale	Grade Level	Academic Subject
PART I: TEACHING AND LEARNING					
1. Student Teaching	Kidder, *Among Schoolchildren*	1989	Holyoke, Massachusetts	5th grade	student teaching
2. Vignette of a Fifth Grade Teacher	Shaw & Etchberger, *Transitioning Into Constructivism*	1993	nonspecific	5th grade	science
3. A Commitment to Children	White, *The Japanese Educational Challenge*	1987	international	elem. school	classroom culture
PART II: THE DIVERSITY OF EDUCATIONAL LIFE					
4. Culturally Diverse Families and Schools	Valdes, *Con Respeto*	1996	community near U.S.-Mexico border	1st grade	bilingual ed.
5. Educating Students With Disabilities	Cambone, *Teaching Troubled Children*	1994	suburban Massachusetts	special ed. program	special ed.
6. School Inequality: Federal Courts	Kozol, *The Dream Deferred, Again, in San Antonio*	1991	San Antonio, Texas	district	equity
7. School Inequality: State Courts	Anyon, *Ghetto Schooling*	1997	New Jersey	state	equity
PART III: SCHOOLS					
8. The Good High School	Lawrence-Lightfoot, *The Good High School*	1983	Atlanta, Georgia	high school	school culture
9. Low- and High-Performing Schools Serving Native American Students	Epp & Epp, *North America—Canada*	2002	international	gr.1-6 school & preK-11 school	effective schools
10. Schools on Probation	Mintrop, *Schools on Probation*	2004	Maryland	middle school	student achievement
11. Public School Choice	Teske, *Public School Choice*	2000	NYC District 4	district	public school choice

Chapter/Title in This Book	Author/Title of Original Work	Yr. of Pub.	Locale	Grade Level	Academic Subject
PART IV: DISTRICTS AND STATES					
12. The Superintendency	Yee & McCloud, *A Vision of Hope*	2003	Seattle, Washington	district	superintendency
13. Reforming Urban Districts	Cuban & Usdan, *What Happened in the Six Cities?*	2003	Boston, Memphis, NYC Dist. 2, San Antonio, San Fran. & Seattle	district	reform initiatives
14. State Departments of Education	Lusi, *The Role of State Departments of Education in Complex School Reform*	1997	Kentucky & Vermont	state	case study methodology
15. State Education Standards	Wu, *The 1997 Mathematics Standards War in California*	2000	California	state	mathematics
PART V: COMMUNITY AND SCHOOL BOARD ACTION					
16. An Urban Youth Program	Stake, *Quieting Reform*	1990	Atlanta, Georgia; Indianapolis, Indiana; & New York City	street academies	evaluation research
17. School-Community Collaboration in Starting a New School	Lee, *The Bronx Leadership Academy High School*	2000	Bronx, New York	a new high school	community-district relations
18. Education Programs and the Local Community Power Structure	Soto, *Language, Culture, and Power*	1997	industrial city, Pennsylvania	bilingual program	bilingual education
19. School Board Leadership	McAdams, *The Wonderful Cacophony of a Free People Disagreeing*	2000	Houston, Texas	district	school board leadership
20. A Post-9/11 Perspective on U.S. Education	Burkett, *Another Planet*	2001	international	high school	social studies
APPENDIX					
Doing Case Studies in Education	Yin, *Case Study Methods*	2005	nonspecific		case study methods

diversity of the selections. They cover a variety of geographic locales, grade levels, and academic subjects. At the same time, space in an anthology always is limited, and do not be surprised to find some omissions that you might have cared about.

More sophisticated users will find other ways of being selective. For instance, if you are interested in comprehensive school reform and the surge of interest in school accountability later given heightened attention by the No Child Left Behind Act of 2001, you may have figured out that selection numbers 9, 10, 12, and 13—which happen also to represent more recent publications among all of the selections—all deal with this topic.

Selecting Readings According to the Case Study Method. You also may want to be selective because you need to identify different aspects of the case study method. You can get started on this path by recalling some of the distinctive features of case study research. It can enable you to get a close-up view of an important phenomenon (the "case"), examine a phenomenon from different perspectives, appreciate the importance of the contextual conditions surrounding the case, compare multiple cases as part of the same case study, or try to derive broader generalizations going beyond your single or multiple cases (see Yin, 2003, for a detailed presentation of the case study method). One or more of these functions, in any combination, may be the main motive underlying your own case study.

Table 2 helps you to identify the present set of selections according to their case study characteristics. The table is divided into two parts: situational characteristics (those pertaining to the topic of the case) and methodological characteristics (those pertaining to a particular case study tactic or strategy). From the table, you can see that many of the selections in this anthology cover individual persons as cases or within case studies. In addition, in a good number of selections, the author has brought some personal experience to the case study. These personal experiences include having worked at the scene of the case study or having been an actual participant in the case. If you have had some highly relevant educational experience pointing to a possible case study, you will find these latter cases to be solid and helpful examples.

Table 2 also shows how several of the characteristics are represented by only a single selection or a small number of selections. Remember that this does not have anything to do with the proportion of the case studies in the field at large. For instance, many evaluations have relied on the case study method. However, this anthology might only have one example because the cases were deliberately chosen to cover diverse characteristics.

Table 2   Case Study Characteristics of Selections in This Anthology

Case Study Characteristic	Chapter
Situational:	
Close-Up, Intimate View of Everyday Life	1, 2, 3, 4
Controversy as Case	6, 7, 15, 18
Extended Period of Years Covered by Case	7
Group and Organizational Dynamics as Case	17, 19
Individual Person as Case or within Case Study	1, 2, 3, 4, 5, 8, 12
Methodological:	
Anonymity of Case Study	5, 10
Author Brings Personal Experience to Case Study	3, 4, 5, 18, 19
Contrasting Cases within Same Case Study	9, 14
Documents Cited as Evidence	7, 12, 15, 19
Evaluation	16
Methodology of Case Study Described	4, 5, 14, 16
Multiple-Case Study	9, 13, 14
Qualitative Analysis and Use of "Word Tables"	9, 13
Quantitative Analysis within a Case Study	11
Reflections about Case	20

How the Selections Were Chosen

The selections in this anthology are not necessarily models or exemplars of any sort. All represent some type of empirical investigation—usually based on fieldwork, or the analysis of available documents and archival data, or both. However, the selections favor no particular "style" of doing case studies. All were chosen because they were reasonably well written (and hence more interesting for you to read)—and because they helped to cover the diversity of education and case study topics just discussed. Overall, making the final selections was a subjective task constrained by space limitations.

Nor are the final selections intended to be a commentary on the quality or worthiness of those case studies that were omitted. The initial search for case studies was exhaustive, if not systematic—covering reading lists, publishers' lists, journals, and works nominated by others in the education field. Typical reasons for omitting candidates (formally cited in the references so you can find them if needed) were as follows.

Some works covered similar topics and were hence redundant with existing selections in the anthology (e.g., case studies of high schools, of urban schools, or of school choice—Ancess, 2003; Corwin, 2000; Hill, Campbell, &

Harvey, 2000; Kozol, 2000; Maran, 2000; Perrone & Associates, 1985; Peterson & Noyes, 1997; Powell, Farrar, & Cohen, 1985; Ravitch & Viteritti, 1997). Other works deliberately reflected a particular educational program or practice such as the Comer schools, too narrow to be included (e.g., Chubb, 1997; Freedman, Simons, Kalnin, Casareno, & The M-Class Teams, 1999; Jervis, 1996; Noblit, Malloy, & Malloy, 2001). Yet other works covered situations deemed either too specialized or exotic (e.g., Chamoiseau, 1994; Elmore, 2003; Elmore, Abelmann, & Fuhrman, 1996; He, 2003) or works mainly motivated by guidance rather than systematic study (e.g., Lortie, 1975; Macrorie, 1984; Sirotnik & Goodlad, 1988; Willie, Edwards, & Alves, 2002). Some works were relevant but just didn't have a suitable portion of text that could easily be extracted as a self-standing selection (e.g., Fuller, 2000; Martin, 2003; Michie, 1999; Obiakor, 2001; Whitford & Jones, 2000). Finally, three other works already have appeared in my (Yin, 2004) general case study anthology (Bryk, Bebring, Kerbow, Rollow, & Easton, 1998; Gross, Giacquinta, & Bernstein, 1971; Zigler & Muenchow, 1992).

Entering the World of Education

Today, more than ever, K–12 public education needs your bright mind (and hard work). Educators know more about the learning process than they ever have. Students, given their demonstrated prowess in conquering today's electronic games, probably bring greater talents into the classroom than they ever have. State and local governments, despite fiscal setbacks, invest more into education than they have. Nevertheless, running good classrooms, schools, and school systems entails greater uncertainties than we might like.

One remedy is to get people like yourself more informed about the world of education. Whether you are now a part of the K–12 system, hope eventually to enter it, or remain outside as a highly supportive citizen, today, more than ever, you can make a meaningful contribution.

Figure it out. Where can you best contribute? The selections in this anthology are a way of starting to think about this challenge. It's therefore time to get started. You can use this anthology independently, reading some or all of its selections. Alternatively, you can map the selections onto your related texts or ongoing education studies. Whichever your approach, be prepared to be entertained but also sobered by the world of education that you will encounter.

References

Ancess, J. (2003). *Beating the odds: High schools as communities of commitment.* New York: Teachers College Press.

Bryk, A. S., Bebring, P. B., Kerbow, D., Rollow, S., & Easton, J. Q. (1998). *Charting Chicago school reform: Democratic localism as a lever for change.* Boulder, CO: Westview.

Chamoiseau, P. (1994). *School days* (L. Coverdale, Trans.). Lincoln: University of Nebraska Press.

Chubb, J. (1997). Lessons in school reform from the Edison Project. In D. Ravitch & J. P. Viteritti (Eds.), *New schools for a new century* (pp. 86–122). New Haven, CT: Yale University Press.

Corwin, M. (2000). *And still we rise: The trials and triumphs of twelve gifted inner-city students.* New York: HarperCollins.

Elmore, R. F. (2003). *Knowing the right thing to do: School improvement and performance-based accountability.* Washington, DC: NGA Center for Best Practices, National Governors Association.

Elmore, R. F., Abelmann, C. H., & Fuhrman, S. H. (1996). The new accountability in state education reform: From process to performance. In H. F. Ladd (Ed.), *Holding schools accountable: Performance-based reform in education* (pp. 65– 98). Washington, DC: The Brookings Institution.

Freedman, S. W., Simons, E. R., Kalnin, J. S., Casareno, A., & The M-Class Teams. (1999). *Inside city schools: Investigating literacy in multicultural classrooms.* New York: Teachers College Press.

Fuller, B. (Ed.). (2000). *Inside charter schools: The paradox of radical decentralization.* Cambridge, MA: Harvard University Press.

Gross, N., Giacquinta, J. B., & Bernstein, M. (1971). *Implementing organizational innovations: A sociological analysis of planned educational change.* New York: Basic Books.

He, M. F. (2003). *A river forever flowing: Cross-cultural lives and identities in the multicultural landscape.* Greenwich, CT: Information Age Publishing.

Hill, P. T., Campbell, C., & Harvey, J. (2000). *It takes a city: Getting serious about urban school reform.* Washington, DC: The Brookings Institution.

Jervis, K. (1996). *Eyes on the child: Three portfolio stories.* New York: Teachers College Press.

Kozol, J. (2000). *Ordinary resurrections: Children in the years of hope.* New York: HarperCollins.

Lortie, D. C. (1975). *Schoolteacher.* Chicago: University of Chicago Press.

Macrorie, K. (1984). *Twenty teachers.* New York: Oxford University Press.

Maran, M. (2000). *Class dismissed: A year in the life of an American high school, a glimpse into the heart of a nation.* New York: St. Martin's.

Martin, B. (2003). *Wayside attractions: The negotiation of aspirations and careers among African-American adolescent males in an urban alternative school.* Cresskill, NJ: Hampton.

Michie, G. (1999). *Holler if you hear me: The education of a teacher and his students.* New York: Teachers College Press.

Noblit, G. W., Malloy, W. W., & Malloy, C. E. (Eds.). (2001). *The kids got smarter: Case studies of successful Comer schools.* Cresskill, NJ: Hampton.

Obiakor, F. E. (2001). *It even happens in "good" schools: Responding to cultural diversity in today's classrooms.* Thousand Oaks, CA: Corwin.

Perrone, V., & Associates. (1985). *Portraits of high schools.* Lawrenceville, NJ: The Carnegie Foundation for the Advancement of Teaching, Princeton University Press.

Peterson, P., & Noyes, C. (1997). Under extreme duress, school choice success. In D. Ravitch & J. Viteritti (Eds.), *New schools for a new century* (pp. 123–146). New Haven, CT: Yale University Press.

Powell, A. G., Farrar, E., & Cohen, D. K. (1985). *The shopping mall high school: Winners and losers in the educational marketplace.* Boston: Houghton Mifflin.

Ravitch, D., & Viteritti, J. P. (Eds.). (1997). *New schools for a new century: The redesign of urban education.* New Haven, CT: Yale University Press.

Sirotnik, K. A., & Goodlad, J. I. (Eds.). (1988). *School-university partnerships in action: Concepts, cases, and concerns.* New York: Teachers College Press.

Whitford, B. L., & Jones, K. (Eds.). (2000). *Accountability, assessment, and teacher commitment: Lessons from Kentucky's reform efforts.* Albany: State University of New York Press.

Willie, C. V., Edwards, R., & Alves, M. J. (2002). *Student diversity, choice, and school improvement.* Westport, CT: Bergin & Garvey.

Yin, R. K. (2003). *Case study research: Design and methods* (3rd ed.). Thousand Oaks, CA: Sage.

Yin, R. K. (Ed.). (2004). *The case study anthology.* Thousand Oaks, CA: Sage.

Zigler, E., & Muenchow, S. (1992). *Head Start: The inside story of America's most successful educational experiment.* New York: Basic Books.

PART I

Teaching and Learning

1

Student Teaching*

editor's introduction:

Classroom Life and the Challenges of Being a Student Teacher. This selection, like many others in this anthology, comes from a larger case study that fills an entire book. The case study illustrates how education takes place in a fifth-grade classroom, over the course of an entire academic year. The book's chapters are organized according to the months of the school year.

The specific selection for this anthology comes from two different parts of the case study. The first part is the beginning of the book and introduces the fifth-grade teacher, several of the students, and a student teacher who has joined the class for the fall semester. The second part highlights the challenges confronting the student teacher, especially in light of a difficult student (whose behavior tests both teachers' patience). The selection illustrates how a common educational process—student teachers having their first classroom experience and learning to cope with classroom discipline, as well as the fifth-grade teacher's stress in trying not to intervene—can be expressed in highly personal and particularistic terms. As part of the scene, other students also assume lifelike proportions.

The classroom scene seems to be a common part of American public education. How teachers can cope with and be productive in this environment is the theme of the case study. The school serves an economically declining neighborhood, in a city—Holyoke, Massachusetts—that also was undergoing industrial decline at the time of the case study. The student population had become increasingly Puerto Rican, and about two-thirds of the children in the fifth-grade classroom were in the

---

*Kidder, Tracy. (1989). *Among Schoolchildren* (pp. 3–11 and 114–132). Boston: Houghton Mifflin.

free and reduced-price lunch program—an indicator of their families' low-income status. As with other schools in similar settings, referrals to special education classes are a common way of dealing with children with disciplinary problems.

Also, many of the children were coping with a new language environment. In the fifth-grade classroom, at least one child benefited from an inspired school psychologist. This child, described elsewhere in the original case study, could hardly read or speak English, but the psychologist had the foresight to administer a test often administered to stroke victims who have lost their language—a test calling for sophisticated pattern recognition abilities. The student scored in the near-genius range.

Relevance of Case Studies: Recreating Everyday School Life. The case study gives you a sense of what it is like to live through a school year and the daily circumstances confronted by teachers and students in many contemporary classrooms. The case study also conveys the richness and complexity of everyday life in a school, in a manner not readily emulated by other social science methods. The depth and breadth of the selection delve into the personalities of the actual participants while covering a broad range of topics, such as the teacher's relationships with the students and other adults, the challenges of maintaining order and discipline in the classroom, the teacher's own home and family life (including her grading of homework), and the broader neighborhood setting in which the teacher lives.

Overall, the case study helps you feel like an unobtrusive observer in the life of the classroom, at close proximity. Possibly reflecting what must be done to produce such a sense of intimacy, the author spent the entire school year with the fifth-grade class. At the same time, the particularism and intimacy do not lead to an idiosyncratic or unique case. In the hands of a Pulitzer Prize–winning author, the book demonstrates a core strength of the case study method: to examine an individual or an event within its real-life context, but to lay the basis for a more general understanding though only being exposed to a single case.

September

Mrs. Zajac wasn't born yesterday. She knows you didn't do your best work on this paper, Clarence. Don't you remember Mrs. Zajac saying that if you didn't do your best, she'd make you do it over? As for you, Claude, God forbid that you should ever need brain surgery. But Mrs. Zajac hopes that if you do, the doctor won't open up your head and walk off saying he's almost done, as you just said when Mrs. Zajac asked you for your penmanship, which, by the way, looks like you did it and ran. Felipe, the reason you have hiccups is, your mouth is always open and the wind rushes in. You're in fifth grade now. So, Felipe, put a lock on it. Zip it up. Then go get a drink of water. Mrs. Zajac means business, Robert. The sooner you realize she never said everybody in the room has to do the work except for Robert, the sooner you'll get along with her. And . . . Clarence. Mrs. Zajac knows you didn't try. You don't just hand in junk to Mrs. Zajac. She's been teaching an awful lot of years. She didn't fall off the turnip cart yesterday. She told you she was an old-lady teacher.

She was thirty-four. She wore a white skirt and yellow sweater and a thin gold necklace, which she held in her fingers, as if holding her own reins, while waiting for children to answer. Her hair was black with a hint of Irish red. It was cut short to the tops of her ears, and swept back like a pair of folded wings. She had a delicately cleft chin, and she was short—the children's chairs would have fit her. Although her voice sounded conversational, it had projection. She had never acted. She had found this voice in classrooms.

Mrs. Zajac seemed to have a frightening amount of energy. She strode across the room, her arms swinging high and her hands in small fists. Taking her stand in front of the green chalkboard, discussing the rules with her new class, she repeated sentences, and her lips held the shapes of certain words, such as "homework," after she had said them. Her hands kept very busy. They sliced the air and made karate chops to mark off boundaries. They extended straight out like a traffic cop's, halting illegal maneuvers yet to be perpetrated. When they rested momentarily on her hips, her hands looked as if they were in holsters. She told the children, "One thing Mrs. Zajac expects from each of you is that you do *your* best." She said, "Mrs. Zajac gives homework. I'm sure you've all heard. The old meanie gives homework." *Mrs. Zajac.* It was in part a role. She worked her way into it every September.

At home on late summer days like these, Chris Zajac wore shorts or blue jeans. Although there was no dress code for teachers here at Kelly School, she always went to work in skirts or dresses. She dressed as if she were applying for a job, and hoped in the back of her mind that someday, heading for job interviews, her students would remember her example. Outside school, she wept easily over small and large catastrophes and at sentimental movies, but she never cried in front of students, except once a few years ago when the news came over the intercom that the Space Shuttle had exploded and Christa McAuliffe had died—and then she saw in her students' faces that the sight of Mrs. Zajac crying had frightened them, and she made herself stop and then explained.

At home, Chris laughed at the antics of her infant daughter and egged the child on. She and her first-grade son would sneak up to the radio when her husband wasn't looking and change the station from classical to rock-and-roll music, "You're regressing, Chris," her husband would say. But especially on the first few days of school, she didn't let her students get away with much. She was not amused when, for instance, on the first day, two of the boys started dueling with their rulers. On nights before the school year started, Chris used to have bad dreams: Her principal would come to observe her, and her students would choose that moment to climb up on their desks and give her the finger, or they would simply wander out the door. But a child in her classroom would never know that Mrs. Zajac had the slightest doubt that students would obey her.

The first day, after going over all the school rules, Chris spoke to them about effort. "If you put your name on a paper, you should be proud of it," she said. "You should think, This is the best I can do and I'm proud of it and I want to hand this in." Then she asked, "If it isn't your best, what's Mrs. Zajac going to do?"

Many voices, most of them female, answered softly in unison, "Make us do it over."

"Make you do it over," Chris repeated. It sounded like a chant.

"Does anyone know anything about Lisette?" she asked when no one answered to that name.

Felipe—small, with glossy black hair—threw up his hand.

"Felipe?"

"She isn't here!" said Felipe. He wasn't being fresh. On those first few days of school, whenever Mrs. Zajac put the sound of a question in her voice, and sometimes before she got the question out, Felipe's hand shot up.

In contrast, there was the very chubby girl who sat nearly motionless at her desk, covering the lower half of her face with her hands. As usual, most of their voices sounded timid the first day, and came out of hiding gradually. There were twenty children. About half were Puerto Rican. Almost two-thirds of the twenty needed the forms to obtain free lunches. There was a lot of long and curly hair. Some boys wore little rattails. The eyes the children lifted up to her as she went over the rules—a few eyes were blue and many more were brown—looked so solemn and so wide that Chris felt like dropping all pretense and laughing. Their faces ranged from dark brown to gold, to pink, to pasty white, the color that Chris associated with sunless tenements and too much TV. The boys wore polo shirts and T-shirts and new white sneakers with the ends of the laces untied and tucked behind the tongues. Some girls wore lacy ribbons in their hair, and some wore pants and others skirts, a rough but not infallible indication of religion—the daughters of Jehovah's Witnesses and Pentecostals do not wear pants. There was a lot of prettiness in the room, and all of the children looked cute to Chris.

So did the student teacher, Miss [Pam] Hunt, a very young woman in a dress with a bow at the throat who sat at a table in the back of the room.

Miss Hunt had a sweet smile, which she turned on the children, hunching her shoulders when they looked at her. At times the first days, while watching Chris in action, Miss Hunt seemed to gulp. Sometimes she looked as frightened as the children. For Chris, looking at Miss Hunt was like looking at herself fourteen years ago.

The smell of construction paper, slightly sweet and forest-like, mingled with the fading, acrid smell of roach and rodent spray. The squawk box on the wall above the closets, beside the clock with its jerky minute hand, erupted almost constantly, adult voices paging adults by their surnames and reminding staff of deadlines for the census forms, attendance calendars, and United Way contributions. Other teachers poked their heads inside the door to say hello to Chris or to ask advice about how to fill out forms or to confer with her on schedules for math and reading. In between interruptions, amid the usual commotion of the first day, Chris taught short lessons, assigned the children seat work, and attended to paperwork at her large gray metal desk over by the window.

For moments then, the room was still. From the bilingual class next door to the south came the baritone of the teacher Victor Guevara, singing to his students in Spanish. Through the small casement windows behind Chris came sounds of the city—Holyoke, Massachusetts—trailer truck brakes releasing giant sighs now and then, occasional screeches of freight trains, and, always in the background, the mechanical hum of ventilators from the school and from Dinn Bros. Trophies and Autron, from Leduc Corp. Metal Fabricators and Laminated Papers. It was so quiet inside the room during those moments that little sounds were loud: the rustle of a book's pages being turned and the tiny clanks of metal-legged chairs being shifted slightly. Bending over forms and the children's records, Chris watched the class from the corner of her eye. The first day she kept an especially close eye on the boy called Clarence.

Clarence was a small, lithe, brown-skinned boy with large eyes and deep dimples. Chris watched his journeys to the pencil sharpener. They were frequent. Clarence took the longest possible route around the room, walking heel-to-toe and brushing the back of one leg with the shin of the other at every step—a cheerful little dance across the blue carpet, around the perimeter of desks, and along the back wall, passing under the American flag, which didn't quite brush his head. Reaching the sharpener, Clarence would turn his pencil into a stunt plane, which did several loop-the-loops before plunging in the hole.

The first morning, Chris didn't catch one of the intercom announcements. She asked aloud if anyone had heard the message. Clarence, who seemed to stutter at the start of sentences when he was in a hurry to speak, piped up right away, "He he say to put the extra desks in the hall." Clarence noticed things. He paid close attention to the intercom. His eyes darted to the door the moment a visitor appeared. But he paid almost no attention to her lessons and his work. It seemed as if every time that she glanced at Clarence he wasn't working.

"Take a look at Clarence," Chris whispered to Miss Hunt. She had called Miss Hunt up to her desk for a chat. "Is he doing anything?"

The other children were working. Clarence was just then glancing over his shoulder, checking on the clock. Miss Hunt hunched her shoulders and laughed without making a sound. "He has such huge eyes!" she said.

"And they're looking right through me," said Chris, who lifted her voice and called, "Clarence, the pencil's moving, right?" Then Chris smiled at Miss Hunt, and said in a half whisper, "I can see that Clarence and I will have a little chat out in the hall, one of these days."

Miss Hunt smiled, gulped, and nodded, all at once.

Chris had received the children's "cumulative" records, which were stuffed inside salmon-colored folders known as "cumes." For now she checked only addresses and phone numbers, and resisted looking into histories. It was usually better at first to let her own opinions form. But she couldn't help noticing the thickness of some cumes. "The thicker the cume, the more trouble," she told Miss Hunt. "If it looks like *War and Peace*. . ." Clarence's cume was about as thick as the Boston phone book. And Chris couldn't help having heard what some colleagues had insisted on telling her about Clarence. One teacher whom Chris trusted had described him as probably the most difficult child in all of last year's fourth-grade classes. Chris wished she hadn't heard that, nor the rumors about Clarence. She'd heard confident but unsubstantiated assertions that he was a beaten child. These days many people applied the word "abused" to any apparently troubled student. She had no good reason to believe the rumors, but she couldn't help thinking, "What if they're true?" She wished she hadn't heard anything about Clarence's past at this early moment. She found it hard enough after thirteen years to believe that all fifth-graders' futures lay before them out of sight, and not in plain view behind.

She'd try to ignore what she had heard and deal with problems as they came. Clarence's were surfacing quickly. He came to school the second morning without having done his homework. He had not done any work at all so far, except for one math assignment, and for that he'd just written down some numbers at random. She'd try to nip this in the bud. "No work, no recess," she told Clarence late the second morning. He had quit even pretending to work about half an hour before.

Just a little later, she saw Clarence heading for the pencil sharpener again. He paused near Felipe's desk. Clarence glanced back at her. She could see that he thought she wasn't looking.

Clarence set his jaw. He made a quick, sharp kick at Felipe's leg under the desk. Then he stalked, glancing backward at Chris, to the pencil sharpener. Felipe didn't complain.

Maybe Felipe had provoked the kick. Or maybe this was Clarence's way of getting even with her for threatening to keep him in from recess. It wasn't a pleasant thought. She let the incident pass. She'd have to watch Clarence carefully, though.

The afternoon of that second day of class, Chris warned Clarence several times that she would keep him after school if he didn't get to work. Detention seemed like a masochistic exercise. Sometimes it worked. It was a tool she'd found most useful at the beginning of a year and after vacations. In her experience, most children responded well to clearly prescribed rules and consequences, and she really didn't have many other tangible weapons. The idea was to get most of the unpleasantness, the scoldings and detentions, out of the way early. And, of course, if she threatened to keep Clarence after school, she had to keep her word. Maybe he would do some work, and she could have a quiet talk with him. She didn't plan to keep him long.

The other children went home, and so did Miss Hunt. Chris sat at her desk, a warm late-summer breeze coming through the little casement window behind her. She worked on her plans for next week, and from under cover of her bowed head, she watched Clarence. The children's chairs, the plastic backs and seats of which came in primary colors, like a bag full of party balloons, were placed upside down on the tops of their desks. Clarence sat alone at his desk, surrounded by upended chairs. He had his arms folded on his chest and was glaring at her. The picture of defiance. He would show her. She felt like laughing for a moment. His stubbornness was impressive. Nearly an hour passed, and the boy did no work at all.

Chris sighed, got up, and walked over to Clarence.

He turned his face away as she approached.

Chris sat in a child's chair and, resting her chin on her hand, leaned her face close to Clarence's.

He turned his farther away.

"What's the problem?"

He didn't answer. His eyelashes began to flutter.

"Do you understand the work in fifth grade?"

He didn't answer.

"I hear you're a very smart boy. Don't you want to have a good year? Don't you want to take your work home and tell your mom, 'Look what I did'?"

The fluorescent lights in the ceiling were pale and bright. One was flickering. Tears came rolling out of Clarence's eyes. They streaked his brown cheeks.

Chris gazed at him, and in a while said, "Okay, I'll make a deal with you. You go home and do your work, and come in tomorrow with all your work done, and I'll pretend these two days never happened. We'll have a new Clarence tomorrow. Okay?"

Clarence still had not looked at her or answered.

"A new Clarence," Chris said. "Promise?"

Clarence made the suggestion of a nod, a slight concession to her, she figured, now that it was clear she would let him leave.

Her face was very close to his. Her eyes almost touched his tear-stained cheeks. She gazed. She knew she wasn't going to see a new Clarence tomorrow. It would be naive to think a boy with a cume that thick was going to change overnight. But she'd heard the words in her mind anyway. She had to keep alive the little voice that says, Well, you never know. What was the alternative? To decide an eleven-year-old was going to go on failing, and there was nothing anyone could do about it, so why try? Besides, this was just the start of a campaign. She was trying to tell him, "You don't have to have another bad year. Your life in school can begin to change." If she could talk him into believing that, maybe by June there *would* be a new Clarence.

"We always keep our promises?" Chris said.

He seemed to make a little nod.

"I bet everyone will be surprised. We'll have a new Clarence," Chris said, and then she let him go. . . .

Discipline

Ancient Greek and Roman schoolmasters adopted various instruments for classroom management, such as ferrules, switches, and taws, which nineteenth-century English pedagogues found useful. In some of Germany's nineteenth-century Latin schools, children passed by whipping posts on their way to class, and when they got in trouble had to visit the Blue Man, the official in charge of punishments—the Blue Man always wore a blue coat, under which he concealed his tools. Although the practice has been greatly reduced, formal beatings of schoolchildren still happen in America; most states still permit them, though not Massachusetts, at least in theory. Some medieval European and some colonial American schoolmasters probably thought they were doing their students a favor by literally beating the Devil out of them. Historical records make it plain that some teachers and school administrators enjoyed having licenses for their tempers, and perhaps some still do. But a central fact in most sorts of schools has always been the fear of the Lilliputian mob. In America, corporal punishment began to wane around the time when elementary education was becoming universal and compulsory—around the time, that is, when keeping order probably became more difficult. One sociologist of teaching describes the situation as "dual captivity": the children *have* to be there, and the teacher has to take the children sent to her.

The problem is fundamental. Put twenty or more children of roughly the same age in a little room, confine them to desks, make them wait in lines, make them behave. It is as if a secret committee, now lost to history, had made a study of children and, having figured out what the greatest number were least disposed to do, declared that all of them should do it.

Some people think it must be easy to manage a room full of children, but if that were the case, it wouldn't often be said that adults who have been behaving badly have been behaving like children. A man recently out of college came to Kelly School one day that fall to try his hand at substitute teaching. It wasn't even noon when [principal] Al [Laudato], making his third visit to restore order in that substitute's room, told the man that he might as well give up and go home. The screams of his pupils had broadcast his failure throughout the classroom wing. He left with his collar loosened, his necktie askew. He had to go down the main hallway to get out of there, and he walked as fast as a man can without running, and kept his eyes lowered, avoiding the looks from the teachers, mostly women, whom he passed.

Classroom management, as Mrs. Zajac practiced it, required an enlargement of senses. By now Chris could tell, without seeing, not only that a child was running on the stairs but also that the footfalls belonged to Clarence, and she could turn her attention to curing one child's confusion and still know that Clarence was whispering threats to Arabella. She was always scanning the room with her eyes without moving her head, seeing without being seen. Peripheral vision gave her that glimpse of Judith squinting at the board. And there had developed in Chris a sense not easily accounted for— like a hunter's knack for spotting a piece of furry ear and inferring a deer standing in a thicket—so that, for example, she could sit at the slide projector, pausing in a film strip to lecture the class on the Iroquois, and know that, behind her, Robert wasn't paying attention. In fact, Robert was playing baton with his pencil, noiselessly flipping it in the air. Chris didn't stop talking to the class or even turn around. Extending her left hand back toward Robert, she snapped her fingers once. Robert stopped flipping his pencil and, as usual, blushed.

Once when Chris was busy on the other side of the room, Dick, the quiet boy from the Highlands who loved social studies, leaned over to a classmate and, inclining his head toward Mrs. Zajac, said, "She knows every trick in the book."

At the end of a day in October, Pam said to Chris, "I don't know how you do it." Pam looked sad. "You just come in and they're quiet.". . .

That fall, Chris ran the class and Pam practiced on them for a while every day. For the first several weeks Chris sat in on Pam's lessons, and afterward gave her advice. Pam tried to cover too much ground; Chris showed her how to plan against the clock. Pam spoke too softly. "We need to give you a mean, horrid voice like mine," Chris told her. All in all, Chris felt pleased about Pam's teaching. She liked the way Pam enfolded her lessons in games for the children. She could tell that Pam labored over her lesson plans. Pam came from Westfield State, which was Chris's alma mater. Chris imagined her planning at night in her dormitory room, just as Chris had done in her own practice-teaching days. One time Chris told Pam, "Jimmy loves you," and Pam replied, "I think I'd rather have him hate me and do his work." Chris felt pleased. Pam had the right instincts, Chris thought.

Above all, Chris approved of the emotion that Pam brought to the job. In Chris's philosophy, a brand-new teacher needed to feel strong affection for her first students in order to sustain her. The first days of school, when Pam merely sat as an observer in the back of the room, Chris spied on her, including Pam in the searchlight sweeps she made of the room. She saw Pam gazing fondly at the children. Some, especially Clarence and Felipe, kept turning around at their desks to smile at Pam. Pam hunched her shoulders and smiled back, a smile she might have used to entertain a baby in a crib. Pam was falling in love with these children, Chris thought, and the gentle spectacle took her back to her own first class, to a time when she had felt that there never were more fetching children than the ones placed in her care, and she had indulged herself by crying a little at night, in her room at her parents' house, over her first deeply troubled student—the boy who had stolen the class's goldfish. That boy had possessed so little sense of right and wrong that when the fish had been extracted, gasping, from his pockets, he had declared indignantly, "I didn't hurt 'em. They're still breathin.' "

Chris felt confident that Pam had all the equipment to become a good teacher. She needed only to learn how to control a classroom. "The discipline part," Chris thought. "She's got all the rest of it."

At the end of her sixteen weeks of practice, Pam would have to teach the class for three entire days without Chris in the room. After the third week of school, to start breaking Pam in, Chris left her alone for a half hour to teach spelling. The first couple of times, Pam's spelling went well. On a Friday, however, Clarence struck.

Pam was trying to administer the weekly spelling test. Robert, Felipe, Arnie, and Clarence kept telling each other to shut up. As Mrs. Zajac had advised, Pam gave them all warnings, and then she wrote the next offender's name on the board: Robert. That meant he was in for recess. Robert shrugged. Then Pam wrote Clarence's name on the board, explaining that he was not to disturb the rest of the class anymore.

"So?" said Clarence, glaring.

"If you don't care, then go out and stand in the hall," said Pam. Mrs. Zajac had said to put him out there if he was disturbing the class and wouldn't stop.

"No," said Clarence.

"Yes," said Pam. But she didn't make him go. She wasn't sure how to do so. If she laid hands on the boy, he'd make a fuss, Pam thought. So, instead, she told him, "You're not impressing anyone by having that attitude. Clarence, get up and go sit at this front desk. Clarence, right now."

He obeyed, but he banged chairs as he went.

"I feel bad for the people who want to take the test and do a good job."

"So?" said Clarence angrily.

"Don't answer me back!"

She turned her back on him and read the next spelling word. Behind her, Clarence muttered, making faces at her. She wheeled around. "Clarence, get up and go stand in the hall!"

She lowered her voice. "Please."

She stood over him and said softly, "Please move your body into the hallway."

Clarence jumped up. He made a small cry. In the doorway, he turned back and said to Pam, "I'll punch you out! I'll punch you in the face!"

"All right!" Her voice hit her upper register. "You can say that to [the principal] Mr. Laudato!"

Mrs. Zajac had said that you need to know your ultimate threat, which at Kelly was usually Mr. Laudato, but that you should never go to it right away. And as Pam explained later, "The reason I get wishy-washy, part of me wants to yell at him, and another part wants to wait until he's cooled down a little and I can talk to him." Now she obeyed the second impulse. She didn't take Clarence to Mr. Laudato.

Behind her, Robert was chortling. "He said he'd punch her!" Robert squirmed in his seat. Julio and Jimmy grinned at each other.

Pam returned to stand in front of the class. Behind her, Clarence edged himself around the doorjamb. He peeked in. Several children giggled. Pam turned. Clarence vanished. "Clarence, I don't want to see your face!" Pam turned back to the class to read the next spelling word. Clarence's face came back around the doorjamb, mouthing silently at her back, "Fuckin' bitch. Gonna get you." The class giggled. Clarence began to grin.

Pam went to the door. Clarence's face disappeared. She closed the door and said to the class, "I hope you'll just ignore him." But in that contest of personalities, hers as a teacher still unformed and divided, she was bound to lose.

The door was closed, but Clarence's face now appeared in the small, rectangular, gun-slit window in the door, his nose and lips distended as he pressed them against the glass. Even Judith ducked her head and shook with the giggles. Others laughed openly. "I'd appreciate it if you'd ignore him and not laugh. You're making things worse," said Pam. But how could they help it? School days were long and this was something new.

Clarence was making faces in the window, bobbing up and down in it. The sound of his drumming on the door—*bang, bang, bang*—accompanied Miss Hunt's reading of the words for the remainder of the test.

The dénouement was predictable by then. Pam tried to talk to Clarence in the hall, and he wouldn't look at her. So she held his chin in her hand, to make him, and a few minutes later he got even with her by sneaking up behind Felipe—in the hallway, on the way to reading. Quickly thrusting both arms between Felipe's legs, Clarence lifted his friend up and dumped him, face down, on the hallway carpet. Felipe arose weeping. Clarence got suspended. Pam spent the afternoon worrying about his mother punishing him.

Chris stayed after school with Pam that day. They sat at the front table. Pam told Chris the whole story. Chris said, "You've got to remember there are twenty other kids, and you *are* getting to them. Clarence may be beyond us. We'll do our best, but don't let him ruin your time here. It's not your fault. He walked in like this. You've got to take your little advances and try to forget things like this."

Pam nodded and smiled. She had a confession to make. "The thing is, I almost cried, and then he'd know he'd gotten to me, and I'm thinking, 'He's only ten years old. I can't let him make me cry.'"

Chris went home worried. She told Billy the story. When she got to the end, she said, "Oh, God. If she had cried . . ."

Chris didn't want to preside over the destruction of a promising career. She worried that Pam would lose her enthusiasm if being alone with this class turned into torture. Chris wanted Pam to taste success, so from time to time Chris continued to sit in on some of her lessons. The children always behaved on those occasions. It was obvious why. They kept glancing at

Mrs. Zajac. "If I stay in the room, she won't learn how to discipline," Chris thought. Within months Pam would become a certified teacher. Next year, probably, she would have her own class. Then there'd be no Mrs. Zajac to intervene and help out. Pam had to learn how to control a class now. So for the most part, when it was Pam's turn to teach, Chris gathered up her books and went out to the hall, and told herself as she left, "You have to sink a few times before you learn."

Chris did her own practice teaching in the old West Street School, where, war stories had it, the staff wore mittens indoors in the winter and often got bruised when breaking up fights on the playground. Chris's supervising teacher eventually left Chris alone, to teach her lessons in a dank, decrepit basement room—one day the blackboard fell off the wall. Chris found herself with a class of thirty-four children, many of whom didn't speak much English. Chris remembered coming into that room one day and finding the class bully perched on a chair with one chair leg planted on the stomach of a writhing classmate. She didn't do much real teaching, she thought, but in truth she always could manage, almost from the start, to get a class under control. Chris's skills had grown. Now she could make discipline into a game, as on the day this fall when, apparently looking elsewhere, she noticed some girls passing a piece of paper down the back row during reading. "I'm not even going to ask you for that note," Chris said ten minutes later. The girls' mouths fell open in astonishment. Chris smiled at them. "Teachers have eyes *all around* their heads," she said. She leaned down to get her face close to the girls' faces and drew her fingers all the way around her head, as if encircling it with a scarf. "That's why I don't cut my hair shorter. I *hide* them."

Chris knew that confidence is the first prerequisite for discipline. Children obeyed her, she knew, because she expected that they would. But that kind of confidence can't be invented. Pam would have to find it herself. Chris tried to help. For an hour on Wednesday afternoons, during art and music, Chris and Pam would sit down on the brown vinyl sofa in the balcony corridor between Room 205 and the boys' lavatory. Then, and also after school, the two women would sit facing each other, both dressed in clothes fit for church, the elder looking old only in comparison to the neophyte, the rookie teacher eyeing the veteran respectfully. Pam compressed her lips and nodded as Chris gave her tips:

- No college course prepares you for the Clarences and Roberts, so don't think that you should have known how to handle them when you got here. You are doing a good job, at least as good a one as the other practice teachers in the building.

- Don't let yourself imagine that you are a cause of a troubled student's misbehavior. If you do, you become entangled in the child's problems. You must cultivate some detachment. You have to feel for troubled children, but you can't feel too much, or else you may end up hating children who don't improve.
- When teaching a lesson, don't only call on the ones with their hands up.
- While you teach, scan the room with your eyes for signs of incipient trouble.
- Don't put a child in a situation where he, for the sake of his pride, has to defy you.
- If a child starts getting "hoopy," call on him at once. Stand beside his desk while you teach the class.
- If he acts up anyway, send him to the hall. You must not allow one child to deprive the others of their lessons.
- Before you even start a lesson, wait until all the children have taken their seats. Don't try to teach until all of them have stopped talking.

That was easy for Mrs. Zajac to say. Before starting a lesson, she would simply fold her arms and, leaning a shoulder against the front chalkboard, stare at the class. The children would scurry to their desks. They'd stop talking at once. But what if Pam did that and some of them just went on talking and wandering around the room? What should she do then?

Pam wanted the class to do some work at their desks, quietly. She was trying to get Clarence to sit down first. He was walking around the room backwards. She touched his arm. He threw her hand aside and proceeded, walking backwards. She turned to Robert, who was making choking, chuffing sounds. "Robert!"

"My motor run out of gas," Robert explained.

She turned again, and there were Felipe and Arnie wrestling on the carpet. She ordered them to stop, but while she was doing that, Courtney had gotten up from her desk and had gone over to Kimberly's to gossip.

"Courtney, go back to your desk."

"Wait a minute," said Courtney, who had never talked back before.

"No, I'm not waiting!"

Robert was babbling. "That cold. Cheat. Cheat. Cheat. Five-dollar food stamps." He stood up as Pam approached, and did a shimmy in front of her, his big belly jiggling. He was protesting that he couldn't get to work. "I don't have no book," he said.

Mrs. Zajac walked in. The sentries had failed.

"Then you go over there and get one!" thundered Mrs. Zajac.

Robert froze. His face turned pink.

Pam was trying to show a film strip about colonial days, but Clarence kept putting his hand in the beam. Then Robert put his hand in the beam. Then the usually well-behaved Julio tried it, too. Then Clarence put his hand on the rump of the colonial maid on the screen. Felipe leaned way back in his chair, laughing and laughing.

Pam stopped the film strip. She put the names Clarence, Robert, and Felipe on the board, which meant they couldn't go outside after lunch. As the class arose for lunch, Clarence said, right in front of Pam but as though she weren't there, "Lunch! I'm goin' outside."

"*I'm* goin' outside," said Robert.

As for Felipe, he refused to get up and go to lunch at all. He had his arms folded. He pouted.

"Felipe, you are going to lunch," said Pam.

"No, I ain't!"

"Yes, you are!"

"Read my lips!" said Felipe. "I'm stayin' here!"

"Tsk, tsk, tsk," said Robert.

"Because we were laughin', then she had to put my name down. I hate her! I'm sick of her!" yelled Felipe as Pam, twisting her mouth, decided to leave him there and get help.

One day, when sent to the hall, Clarence stood in the doorway, pointed a finger at Pam, and declared, "I ain't stayin' after school either." Then he watched Pam wrangle with Robert. He cheered Robert on, saying, "Crunch her, crunch her."

Pam said, "Okay, Robert, would you get up and go down the hall to the office?"

"No, please. I wanta stay," said Robert, smirking up at her.

"Robert, get up," she said. "Robert, get up."

"I wanta stay here."

"If you're going to stay here, you have to be good."

"See dat?" said Clarence from the doorway. "She doesn't make Robert go. She prejudice, too. See, she didn't get Robert."

"Shut up, Clarence," said Robert.

"Robert, go to the office," said Pam.

"No," said Robert, smirking.

Another time, Pam said to Clarence, "Shut your mouth!"

Clarence replied, "No. It's *my* mouth."

Pam said to Robert, "You can work on your story now."

"No, I can't," said Robert. "I don't know what to write."

"Use your brain," said Pam.

"My brain gooshed out," said Robert. Then he looked up at her and began beating on his cheeks, a popping sound. Then he gnawed on his hand. Then he slapped his own wrist.

"I don't want any more foolish comments!" she thundered. "Do you under-*stand*?"

Clarence watched. "She not human," he said.

Pam turned to Clarence. "You don't disturb twenty other people."

"There aren't twenty people," said Clarence. "There's . . ." He started counting.

"He knows how to count," said Robert.

Chris returned to find Pam sitting at the teacher's desk, staring out the window, with her jaw misaligned.

It wasn't as if Pam did no teaching. The children would sidle up to her table throughout the day, bringing her pictures they'd drawn and asking for help. She tutored many individually. Some of the lessons she taught without Chris in the room went smoothly. Once in a while when Miss Hunt was teaching, Judith or Alice or Arabella spoke up and told Clarence and Robert to be quiet and stop making trouble. But usually that just egged the boys on, especially Clarence. Some of those boys' responses to Pam's efforts to tame them seemed surprisingly sophisticated, as if they themselves had read handbooks on classroom management. Once, for instance, Pam turned her back on Robert, and Robert called to her, "That's right. Just ignore me."

As for Clarence, he often wrote his name and Judith's on the board, as if to claim her, but that didn't give Judith any special power over him. He told her once that she needed someone "to pop her cherry." One time, after he had been especially nasty to Pam, Judith told him, "You have the brain of a caterpillar."

Without hesitation—the lines seemed to have been already planted—Clarence replied, "I'll take yours out and put it in your hand and make you eat it." Clarence made his slow, threatening nod at Judith.

Judith looked skyward. She said to Alice, "How did God make such a mistake? He had no choice but to put Clarence on earth. He didn't want him up *there*."

On one of those bad days that fall, on the way to lunch, Judith said softly to Pam, "Are you reconsidering your decision to become a teacher?"

"No, Judith," said Pam, and she smiled. "*You* make it all worthwhile."

Judith herself had begun reconsidering her embryonic plans for becoming a teacher. She wondered why Pam kept coming back, and didn't even take a sick day. Judith believed that Pam had to be a very strong and admirable person, but even as the days of Pam's travails wore on and Clarence's antics lost their novelty, Judith still couldn't help laughing when Clarence, banished to the hall, did a soft-shoe routine for the class in the doorway. As Robert indignantly pointed out—"Hey, the teacher's laughin', you're not sposed to laugh"—even Pam couldn't always hide her amusement. For example, the day when she told the class that primates have tails, and Clarence stood up, poked out his rear end, patted it, and said, "Check out mines."

Chris didn't witness those scenes. Leaving Pam alone in the room for a period, Chris would go out to the sofa in the hall and try to work on her plans for next week's lessons. She had a hard time concentrating. She'd hear distant, muffled sounds of commotion, then Pam's voice, high and angry, then more commotion. Chris would flinch. She'd get up and peer down the corridor, to see if Pam had put Clarence out in the hall. One time, when Pam had put him out there, Chris waylaid a passing teacher and said, "Give Clarence a dirty look when you go by, okay?" When boys came by on the way to the bathroom, she waylaid them. "Felipe, come here, please. What's going on in the room?"

"Miss Hunt is in a bad mood," said Felipe. "Clarence was talking back to her, and everybody laughed. He wrote on the board, 'Miss Hunt is a jerk.' She kicked him out, and he wanted to come back, and she yelled at him, and he's mad."

"Okay. Thank you."

Felipe moved on. Chris sat on the couch, fuming. "Children can be so cruel when they sense a weakness. I'd like to go in there and . . ." She bared her teeth.

On the bulletin boards in the hallways, Halloween displays lingered almost until Thanksgiving. Most of the displays were store bought or inspired by books of ideas for bulletin boards, on sale at all stores that cater to teachers. No child would have recognized his fears in the black cats, toothy pumpkins, and witches on broomsticks. They all looked much too benign. But some of the witches' faces that hung in the classroom, over the closets and under the clock, had malevolence, especially high-strung Felipe's. His witch's face was long and distended, like an El Greco, and her mouth suggested an appetite for little children. And Clarence had acquired a pair of plastic fangs, painted red, which he wore for the class during one of Pam's lessons.

As November wore on, Pam taught more and more. Chris grew increasingly restive out on the couch in the hall. Now and then Chris felt a little consternation at Pam. One afternoon, she stood on a chair just outside the door, taking down an old bulletin board display. While she pulled staples, Chris eavesdropped. A fair amount of noise came out of the room. "Does it always sound like this?" Chris muttered under her breath.

From the room came Pam's voice. "Felipe! Why are you out of your chair?"

"That's a good question, Miss Hunt," muttered Chris. "Why is he?"

Sometimes rivalry develops between a practice teacher and the one whose class she borrows. Neither Pam nor Chris committed any rivalrous deeds, though. Chris really liked Pam. She ached for Pam while she sat on the sofa imagining trouble back in the room. But Chris had more on her mind than Pam's travail. In December, the real test began, both for Pam and Chris. Pam took over the class for three whole days in a row. Chris couldn't sit still. She roamed the olive-carpeted halls like an expectant father. Two days went by. Finally, Chris sat down on the sofa. "Oh!" she exclaimed. "I want my class back!"

* * *

A dusting of snow covered the playground. Heavy coats filled the closets. Out in the hall, just before Pam's last grammar lesson, one of the last lessons she would teach the class, Chris said, "Well, Pam, are you ready to slam down the book, and close the door, and let 'em have it?"

Pam looked at Chris, and then Pam hunched her shoulders and smiled.

Chris went to the sofa. In a moment, she arose and sneaked up to the door of Room 205. She peeked through the gun-slit window. "Oh, good. Pam just threw down the book. I wish I could hear what she's saying. I told her to get right up to Robert's face with her teacher finger."

Chris went back to the sofa. From there, she could hear Pam's voice, not the words, but the form of it, loud and angry but confident. In a moment, all was still. This time, quiet endured.

Afterward, Pam told Chris that the class behaved well after she slammed down the book and let Clarence have it. Pam said she felt better. She said she believed that the class had been waiting for her to do that, and that they felt better, too.

"She's learning," said Chris after school that day.

They gave Pam her farewell party on a day in mid-December. Chris, Judith, Alice, and Mariposa organized it. Chris sent Pam on an errand so they could hang up crepe streamers. Felipe got so excited during the preparations that Chris had to send him out to the hall. "So you can calm down."

When Felipe came back in, Clarence, now on his best behavior, looked at him and said, "You still ain't calmed down."

On the front table was apple juice and a cake inscribed "Good Luck." Pam had brought each child a candy cane and now laid them on the desks. Robert refused even to touch his. He refused to get into the class picture that Pam took. He sat at his desk, and while the other children scurried around and chattered, Robert pulled his sweatshirt up over his mouth, to his nose.

Then he clawed at his eyelids. Then he began slapping himself, harder and harder, in the face.

Chris stared at Robert from her desk. "Look at him! I gotta get him out of here."

She took Robert down to the office to see the counselor, but the counselor was busy, as usual. So she sat Robert down on one of the bad-boy chairs outside Al's office. "Why didn't you want to make a card for Miss Hunt?"

Robert shrugged. "I didn't have no paper," he said in a squeaky voice.

"Don't give me that!" said Chris. She lowered her voice. "What's wrong, Robert?"

"Nuttin'!"

She left him there. Maybe the counselor could get something out of him. Probably not. Later, she'd wish that she had asked Robert, "You're sad Miss Hunt is leaving, aren't you?" At the moment, though, Chris had to get back to the party.

Pam gave Chris a new, larger bookbag and a note that concluded, "You are a very special person and a dear teacher."

Chris had decided that she missed Pam already. So had the children, including most of her tormentors. They were putting on their coats.

"Bye, Miss Hunt," said Jimmy.

"We'll remember you," said Felipe.

Pam smiled and gulped.

The time arrived for the walkers to leave. Judith pulled Arabella back by the collar and delivered her to Pam. Arabella hugged Pam. So Felipe had to hug her, too. Judith, who had said she'd like to give Pam a present but couldn't think of anything except maybe earplugs, gave Pam a casual, one-armed hug. Last was Clarence. He hugged Pam hard for a long time, burying his face in her dress.

"Bye, Miss Hunt."

"Goodbye, Clarence. Be good and do all your work."

"I *will!*"

Then it was Chris's turn. Walking Pam to the door of the room, she said, "I think you'll do well. I really do. I hope you have an easier class. And remember, the first day it's gotta be *grrrr.*"

All of the children except Robert had made cards for Pam. Clarence's was the longest and most elaborate. He had decorated the outside with hearts, inside which he had written, "Spelling BEST" and "Teaching is the BEST." Inside, in very neat lettering, he had written:

Dear Miss Hunt

I am sorry you are leaving Today and I now how i been bad to you but i Want to say something before you leave That here it is I Love you And thank you for all the help i needed Thank you Miss Hunt?

Merry Christmas

Your Friend
Clarence by!

Once again, Chris felt moved by Clarence's note. But when, several weeks later in the Teachers' Room, someone said that Westfield State should pay part of Pam's tuition to Chris, Chris remarked, "Actually, they should pay Clarence." She added, "Pam took Clarence 202."

2

Vignette of a Fifth-Grade Teacher*

editor's introduction:

Teaching to Meet "World-Class" Standards. "Constructivism" is a philosophy of learning that became increasingly popular starting in the late 1980s. The constructivist philosophy of teaching, especially in mathematics and science, has been associated with the quest to get American students to perform at the level of "world-class" standards. On international tests, our students have characteristically performed worse than those in many other countries, and changed teaching methods have been one of the attempted remedies.

The constructivist goal is to have students learn by forming ("constructing") their own reality, rather than having new knowledge presented to them through realities defined by textbooks or teachers. A needed shift in a teacher's orientation is from worrying about finding better ways to teach to worrying about understanding and promoting better ways for students to learn.

For instance, in traditional science teaching, teachers present factual material, the students receive or intake this material, and the students then demonstrate their knowledge of the material on some test or exercise. However, the process can appear to have been successful even though the factual material may have had little meaning to the student—therefore leaving only a shallow level of understanding and not necessarily any recall of the material weeks later. By comparison, the challenge to

*Shaw, Kenneth L., & Etchberger, Mia Lena. (1993). "Transitioning Into Constructivism: A Vignette of a Fifth-Grade Teacher." In Kenneth Tobin (Ed.), *The Practice of Constructivism in Science Education* (pp. 259–266). Washington, DC: AAAS Press.

the constructivist teacher is to become an enabler of the student's learning, not a dispenser of knowledge against a backdrop of assumed reality. Students' learning in their own terms would then be claimed to produce a deeper understanding that also is longer lasting.

Relevance of Case Studies: Gaining Insight Into a Teacher's Thinking. This selection vividly captures the teacher's challenge and tells you how a single teacher overcame the challenge. As with the first selection, this one also happens to focus on a fifth-grade teacher. However, the case study is mainly concerned with an important transition in the teacher's method for teaching science.

The selection captures the teacher's changed practices as well as her thinking—and her qualms. Despite the fact that she already had been a successful teacher and had received several awards for her exemplary practices, she had observed that her students might not have been learning as well as she had expected. With "much fear and trembling" and "severe struggle," she embarked on new ways of teaching. A particular strength of the case study is its ability to render an individual's transformation—in this case, the teacher's own "re-conceptualization of teaching and learning."

Again, although focusing on a single person, the selection is still able to raise and air more general issues. These have to do with the needed changes in vision, commitment, and attitude when starting a new classroom teaching practice. The case study therefore provides you with another example of how substantive insights can go beyond the specific experiences of the single case that was studied.

J essica, a self-contained fifth-grade teacher, is considered by her district to be a successful elementary teacher. She received the District Science Council's Outstanding Elementary School Science Teacher Award in 1990 and the Teacher of the Year Award from her school for the 1988–1989 school year. Yet, while the awards were encouraging, Jessica realized something was lacking in the students' abilities to conceptualize or formulate knowledge. During the 1989–1990 school year, she realized she and her students were but playing a "game" and calling it school. She contemplated her past two years of teaching and realized she taught quite traditionally; she felt she was no different from the ordinary teacher. She became aware of a disturbing pattern emerging in her students. They would memorize certain bits of information, sets of facts, or operational procedures and algorithms, and repeat them back on a test. When she asked her students what meaning they had for the information, sets of facts, or operational procedures and algorithms, most were unable to adequately explain what they had learned. With few exceptions, a few weeks or months later, they were unable to converse about a previously studied concept. They could not or would not relate that information and use it in any meaningful way. The game essentially was as follows: teacher dispenses information; student receives information; student transmits information back to the teacher. Most students played the game well, as evidenced by their grades, but Jessica began asking the question, "Were they learning?"

Jessica was very perplexed by what was taking place in her classroom and by what was taking place in classrooms within her school and county. What could she do to make a difference? This perplexity was heightened because of her colleagues' perceptions that she was a successful teacher. This chapter will endeavor to capture the epistemological and methodological struggles of Jessica and will describe the resulting reconceptualizations of how she made sense of her own instruction and her students' learning as she came to understand constructivism.

Grades and Knowledge

The realization that good grades do not necessarily indicate students' understanding of concepts caused Jessica to begin a process of rethinking her position, ideology, role, and purpose in the field of education. She was thoroughly disturbed that children did not "know." As a result of this perturbation, she decided she must do something to help children know. Jessica resolved that she must not continue in her old pattern of teaching, which was strongly bound to textbooks and scope-and-sequence curriculum plans. She realized she needed to change, but did not know where to begin.

This initial overriding and ever-present perturbation led Jessica to begin searching for a new way to teach. This led her back to school to complete her master's degree in Elementary Education. What she found instead of new ways to teach was a new way of viewing the entire learning process. She began to formulate a vision of possibility which was nonexistent prior to her return to college.

Realizing something had to change was not enough for Jessica. Committing to change empowered her to search for an alternative. She could not envision an alternative, but knew it must be "out there" somewhere. She did not have a clear vision, just a general hope that there was something better.

When Jessica began reading and looking into case studies, she discovered that teachers found it more helpful to focus on helping students learn by enabling them to form their own knowledge, rather than to focus on learning new teaching methods. Instead of focusing on teaching and better ways to teach, Jessica began to focus on learning and better ways to learn. Constructivism became the alternative through which she was able to generate an initial vision of how she could change what she was doing to help children come to know. She perceived that she needed to change her metaphor of teaching and learning from that of teacher-dispenser, student-receiver to that of teacher-enabler, student-constructor. This led her to another dilemma.

Teaching From a Constructivist Perspective

Jessica asked herself, "How do I take concepts, information, and other people's knowledge, and arrange them in such a way as to allow students to construct their own knowledge?" Jessica wanted a quick answer to this question. She was not aware of any textbooks, programs, or people that could show her how to take her next week's science lessons and make the activities constructivist in nature. She began at ground zero, with much fear and trembling. She was very comfortable with her textbook and felt safe as she answered questions, showed films, did preset projects and demonstrations, and reviewed for the test. She was familiar with this approach and so were her students. Furthermore, this was the way she learned when she attended elementary school. Even though she was on unfamiliar ground, she decided to create her first constructivist activity. Just thinking about it raised several questions in her mind: "How can I be sure they will learn or come upon the concept themselves? How much do I need to tell them? How much is too much? Do I tell them anything at all?"

It was a severe struggle, and Jessica lacked confidence in her ability to produce a truly constructivist environment, but her vision propelled her to try. She began in science, the one subject in which she believed students would readily construct knowledge. She arranged her students into groups, believing that cooperative groups were the perfect vehicle for optimum construction to occur. Indeed, her vision at that time saw cooperative groups as necessary and intrinsic to the process of knowledge construction; they were inseparable. She gave students a few ground rules for working together because they were used to working individually and sitting in rows: (1) Be kind to each other, (2) Respect everyone's opinions, (3) Allow all students to have their say, and (4) Everyone is equal—no leaders. Jessica had no experience in cooperative grouping, so this too was uncharted territory for her. She commented that "the only way to begin is to begin, so we all jumped in head first."

Following the scope-and-sequence, they were on the unit for the study of invertebrates. The lesson she chose to use was ants, as those were the next creatures in the book. Jessica's confidence was heightened as a result of a recent group activity she experienced in her college class, the subject being ants. The student groups were told very generally to go outside, find some ants, and watch them. She told the students to "write down everything they could about them, try to copy their motions, draw pictures . . . ANYTHING." Then they would come back to the room and share what they had found. Their energy, excitement, and total absorption in the activity would have been enough to convince Jessica to change forever, but there was much more. They came back to the room bubbling over with information about ants. They filled three chalkboards full of their observations and drawings; Jessica even learned new things about ants. In the process, the class covered all of the information that the book covered (three body parts, six legs, etc.) and much more. The students talked with authority and conviction because of their experience. They KNEW about those ants. That was in October, 1989. The following May, they still knew about ants and had added to their knowledge as they read and interacted further with others and made additional observations of ants.

Experiencing the exuberance of true knowledge construction and innate motivation of her students, Jessica was propelled to further reflection and strengthened commitment to further change. Her vision became broader. Together, she and her students explored concepts and relationships, learned how to work together, and increased their own knowledge. However, the transition from a teacher-dominated environment to a student-centered one was not, by any means, smooth.

When the Novelty Wore Off

When Jessica's science class began learning in groups, the students were focused and motivated. It was novel; it was something innovative and unique. The activities and situations in which they were involved were stimuli enough to keep them interacting, discussing, arguing, negotiating, and searching for meaning and understanding. But it became apparent that the initial novelty was wearing off after about a week into their new learning environment. Students were fighting and refusing to work with others; they were arguing about things such as who would record information, who would present it, and who was not doing anything. This was taking a lot of class time and detracting from any construction that could be taking place. It was a very real problem to the children and it took precedence over everything else.

This led Jessica to a commitment to try new groupings and to learn more about cooperative groups. She envisioned a room of happy cooperative children constructing knowledge together without conflict. She asked them what could be done and discerned a new way of solving problems: "Let

THEM solve the problems!" They made lists on the board of things they did not like about groups and things they did like. The class talked about all of the items and discussed ways to improve the groups.

What they came up with was a highly flexible system of grouping. Jessica had been assigning them to work in groups of four. They wanted to choose their own groups, give themselves jobs to do, and switch jobs for each new activity. They also wanted to switch group members from time to time; so that is what they did. The first time, the class ended up with one group of five, two groups of four, three groups of three, and one set of partners. As time went by, Jessica occasionally saw the need to group them heterogeneously for certain activities and in groups of six or four because of materials constraints. In the meantime, Jessica became familiar with the research on cooperative learning and discovered that her students had constructed much of their own knowledge about successful cooperative groups, information that was reflected in the literature. The class did it through trial, reflection, and re-trial. They continued to have class discussions whenever a problem arose, and they searched for acceptable alternatives.

Jessica learned something. The children were undergoing their own perturbations, commitments, and visions as well. They saw that group learning was a much better way to understand. Realizing that, they committed to change their method of learning and generated a new vision of what school science was all about.

This was not true for all the children. Some of them liked the individual rows and the quiet room; they liked the way it used to be. The first year that Jessica was incorporating constructivist cooperative groups, she did not allow anyone to work by themselves in science class. She was convinced they would not have experiences as enriching as they could have if they were in groups. But as she reflected over the summer and continued her studies, she became disturbed about those few children who just could not function in a group. Her understanding of constructivism at that time involved interaction with others. She did not see how successful negotiation of meaning could occur without group processing.

Knowledge Construction

What Jessica discovered the following year (1990–1991) was that students do not have to be in a group in order to construct their own knowledge. However, she recognized that students' knowledge would be richer, fuller, and more intricate if they did confer with others. Broader relationships would emerge as a result of interaction.

For example, the following fall, Jessica allowed several students to observe ants individually. They came back with several good observations; however, the number of observations was less, and they tended to see only one aspect (i.e., legs, antennae, body parts, or patterns of movement). Jessica struggled with how to handle those students that suffered in group situations or caused groups to suffer in some way by their lack of involvement and/or behavior problems. Her vision at that time was of successful constructivist situations being group-oriented and problematic in nature, with her role being the questioner and prodder, never quite "giving away" the concept. However, when she began to pull students out of groups or allowed students to work by themselves, she realized that they were constructing knowledge every time they related the problem to something they knew, and they were able to understand and utilize the concept. One of Jessica's students, working with molecules in the form of colored marshmallows and toothpicks, put two blues and one green together to form H_2O, and discerned that the numbers indicated how many atoms of each element a molecule contained. She was able to come up with that relationship herself. But without interaction with others, she was not forced to prove or disprove it; discussion, amplification, clarification, and consensus were not available to her. But Jessica did see that she grasped a major concept in molecular construction for herself.

Because of her realization that individuals construct their own knowledge, Jessica began to relax somewhat about her role as information source. She realized that along with activities and situations, books and printed material, audio and video, she, too, could be a source of information for the students. Initially, she desperately attempted to remove herself from the position of information-giver but realized if she could provide some information they could not "come upon" themselves in order to help them solve some problem, then she should provide it for them. This proved to be further enriching for them, as long as she guarded against moving into the familiar lecture format.

Group learning, which allows rich constructions to occur, was working so well in science that she began to become perturbed about other subjects as well. So, during the second year, she began quite another chapter in her development as a constructivist teacher and attempted to overhaul her mathematics program as well (Etchberger and Shaw, in press).

Components of Reconceptualization

As we noticed Jessica wrestling with her new epistemology, we have noticed several recurring components that have affected her reconceptualization of teaching and learning.

Perturbation. Change cannot occur without some perturbation. This is analogous to Newton's first law of motion, "A body at rest or in uniform motion will remain at rest or in uniform motion unless some external force is applied to it." A teacher will continue teaching in a similar way unless perturbed by something or someone. Perturbations often cause frustration, discomfort, and a great deal of reflection. For Jessica, the perturbation of seeing children listen intently to the teacher, relaying the information back on a test, and then promptly forgetting the material was a significant perturbation that caused her to rethink what she was doing in her classroom, and more broadly, what education should be. Her readings when she began her master's degree of constructivism and cooperative learning also caused a perturbation in how she believed students learn. Prior to her graduate studies, she spent little time thinking of how students learn and a great deal of time thinking about how to teach more effectively. Now she believes students' thinking is vitally important to consider in every aspect of teaching.

Commitment. Commitment is a personal decision to make a change as a result of one or more perturbations. After Jessica made a commitment to change her instruction to a more constructivist approach, many perturbations arose. For example, she asked herself: "What do I do about grades? How do I assess students' knowledge? How do I teach in a constructivist manner? How do students learn?" Shaw and Jakubowski (1991) suggest when a perturbation disrupts a mental state of equilibrium, teachers tend to deal with the perturbation in one of three ways: (1) they block out the perturbation, thus stifling the opportunity to learn or change; (2) they develop a rationale for not dealing with the perturbation; or (3) they plan to make a change. With each perturbation, Jessica committed to make a change.

Vision. For teachers to change, they need to construct a personal vision of what teaching and learning should be like in their classrooms. Jessica needed alternative images to replace the traditional views of teaching. She had constructed a vision: students should be responsible for their own learning; the learning environment should be conducive to students being responsible for their own learning; and students learn best when they negotiate, conjecture, test, evaluate, and justify their thinking with other students. Even though this vision was not totally in focus, it, nevertheless, was a vision. She had a level of confidence in what she wanted in her classroom. This vision became more focused as she experienced changes in her classroom and as she had further dialogue with her colleagues and instructors.

Cultural Environment. The cultural environment for each teacher is different. Geertz (1973) stated that a "man is an animal suspended in webs of significance he himself has spun" (5). For Jessica, she noticed distinctive elements of the culture that affected her change process. These were support, time, resources, and beliefs about taboos and customs. Jessica believed that she was on her own in making changes in her classroom. For teachers to make veritable change, Rogers (1969) stressed that when teachers are making changes, they need support that is genuine and laden with respect, unconditional acceptance, sensitivity, and understanding. When new teaching strategies are incorporated into a traditional classroom, students' routines are sometimes abruptly changed, and dissonance is often the result. This classroom dissonance can easily influence teachers to return to the traditional way of teaching if they have received no other support. Fortunately for Jessica, the opposite was true; students overwhelmingly enjoyed the cooperative activities and thus strengthened her belief that the changes she was implementing were worthwhile.

Her recent readings of constructivism were coupled with the awareness of a need to change, and so Jessica set out to make changes in her classroom. She frequently inquired of her instructors what a fifth grade constructivist science classroom should look like. Her intense desire to have viable alternatives was not adequately met. Nevertheless, she decided to "jump in head first." She looked for curricular materials that would best fit her newly held beliefs about learning, but was unsuccessful, and so she created her own lessons. Resources are essential for teachers to gain alternative images of what can occur in their classrooms. Jessica was quite exceptional in that the constraints of not having what she considered appropriate resources did not overwhelm her into returning to her normal teaching routines.

Within the culture of school, teachers hold certain beliefs about existing taboos and customs. For Jessica, one custom was that teachers should strictly follow their textbooks, and students should sit in rows and remain quiet during class. When a reconceptualization of an epistemology to constructivism occurs, it is necessary that customs and taboos be questioned. It is also necessary to question routines and reflect on if and how they need to be modified. This is not an easy task since routines may be formed and reinforced over many years.

Reflection. Reflective thinking means "turning a subject over in the mind and giving it serious and consecutive consideration" (Dewey 1933, 3). Reflection is integral throughout any change process. Because Jessica's change process was gradual, it required time and understanding and necessitated that she give serious consideration to her daily decisions. Becoming aware that change was needed was a product of reflection on the congruence between her beliefs and practices. Making a personal commitment to change required Jessica to reflect upon the possible costs and benefits of the change. The creation of a vision required considerable reflection and deliberation of possible viable alternatives. The social negotiation of the vision among other teachers enhanced her reflections. The reflection process was important as Jessica constructed a vision and projected herself into a vision of teaching from a constructivist perspective.

Conclusion

For successful and positive change to occur, teachers need to be perturbed, to be committed to do something about the perturbation, to establish a vision of what they would like to see in their classrooms, to develop a plan to implement this vision, and to have the support to carry out their vision. Change is a slow, arduous process that requires patience, persistence, and respect. Respect is shown when the teachers are given the ownership of what they are changing.

The implication of the case of Jessica to educational reform is that teachers must be actively involved in the planning phases of any innovation. However, even teachers who are part of the first levels of planning may hold deeply rooted beliefs that may cause them much mental dissonance when they return to their classrooms. But through collaboration with other teachers, they can discuss, deal with, and support each other with their personal dilemmas and successes. The collaboration will also give teachers alternatives. Jessica is now more empowered: she has taken full responsibility for what happens in her classroom in terms of curricular and pedagogical decisions. She is now aware of the importance of the relationship between student empowerment and learning. She realizes that they, too, should take full responsibility for their own learning.

References

Dewey, J. *How We Think, a Restatement of the Relation of Reflective Thinking to the Educative Process.* Boston: D.C. Heath, 1933.

Etchberger, M. L., and K. L. Shaw (in press). "Teacher Change as a Progression of Transitional Images: A Chronology of a Developing Constructivist Teacher." *School Science and Mathematics.*

Geertz, C. *The Interpretation of Cultures.* New York: Basic Books, 1973.

Rogers, C. *Freedom to Learn.* Columbus, OH: Merrill, 1969.

Shaw, K. L., and E. H. Jakubowski. "Teachers Changing for Changing Times." *Focus on Learning Problems in Mathematics,* 13(4), (1991): 13–20.

3

A Commitment to Children*

editor's introduction:

An Example of Teaching and Learning Outside of the United States. As a specific example of U.S. students' international performance, over many years and through many international comparisons, American students have been chronically outperformed by Japanese students. During the latter part of the 20th century, how Japan organized its schools and how its schooling took place therefore became of great interest to those in American education.

The present selection comes from a book that described the Japanese experience as of the late 1980s, continually contrasting it with American practices. The contrasts point to some misleading preconceptions Americans might have had about Japanese schooling. Among these might be the longstanding stereotype that Japanese students only behave in rigid and proscribed patterns and that they are not encouraged to pursue creative problem solving—which may at first appear to produce disorderly classrooms. The selection finds both creativity and orderliness in the Japanese schools.

The selection draws from one of the book's 10 chapters. It describes everyday life at the classroom level (again happening to be at the elementary school level), from the perspective of students, parents, and teachers, but also attending to the relationship between schooling and cultural conditions such as child-rearing practices and beliefs—an important dimension in any comparison to American education. The author personalizes the case study by focusing on illustrative but concrete daily interactions involving student, parent, and teacher. Within the selection also

---

*White, Merry. (1987). "Elementary Schools: Harmony and Cooperation." In *The Japanese Educational Challenge: A Commitment to Children* (pp. 110–133). New York: Free Press.

are embedded instances of individual Japanese students—a third-grader and a sixth- grader. Note how these vignettes come at the end of the selection, to illustrate the school life that has been the main case study. Unlike the attention given to individual teachers in the first two selections in this anthology, the two individual students are not themselves the main subjects of the case study.

Relevance of Case Studies: Recalling Earlier Educational Conditions. American interest in Japan's educational practices also appeared to have peaked during the 1980s and 1990s. Educators have now benefited from a broader appreciation of a diverse array of practices internationally, not just those coming from a single country like Japan. From this perspective, the value of case studies can be to capture historic and not just contemporary conditions, as in the first two selections.

The entire case study, again unlike the first two selections, also shows how case studies may be developed from a blend of experience and evidence, collected over a large number of years—and not necessarily based on a single, formal study. Instead, the author, formally trained in anthropology and sociology, notes that her book is based on "years of experience and observation in Japan," including "observation, interview analysis, and vignettes of individual children at various grade levels." You may have had a similarly extensive experience and therefore need not have to do a formal study in order to design your own case study.

Harmony and Cooperation

When Kenichi is about to become a first-grader, his parents, teachers, school administrators, and the community at large will mobilize themselves to make his entrance into the world of "real school" a most significant moment in his life. The preparation, the ceremony, and the carefully organized techniques for involving him in all the activity and its symbolism contribute to the importance of the day. When the day comes, administrators, teachers, staff, parents, and Kenichi himself will over and over again express commitment to the school, to his classmates, and to his own growth.

Once again Kenichi will become a blank slate, just as he was as he entered nursery school and kindergarten—a candidate for initiation into another group. The socialization at home and preschool give him only a limited kind of "credential" rather than a set of recognized skills that he can display as his personal property.

Preparations for Kenichi's adjustment to school begin early. Again, he and his mother are invited to attend an orientation day, and perhaps make another visit as the beginning of school approaches. While children who have had older siblings in the same school often have more confidence, all of them approach the first day with a certain degree of anxiety. Mother has fussed over her son, bought new clothes (most public elementary schools do not have uniforms), equipped him with backpack and handkerchiefs, lunchbox and pencil case. Most schools will serve lunch, but some private schools and junior high schools rely on mothers to provide a well-balanced, aesthetic, and appealing lunch daily. (Teachers are known to send notes home to a mother whose lunch doesn't meet class standards.)

The first day parents and children arrive together at the school, which is usually within walking distance of the child's home, unless the child attends a private school and must be taken by bus or train. Parents and children, dressed to the hilt, converge on the schoolyard. Mothers wear their very best dresses, grandmothers come in kimonos, and fathers wear the dark suits, white shirts, and polished black shoes which they may otherwise wear only to weddings and important company functions. The boys are in new dark suits with short pants and caps, the girls in new suits or party dresses and hats.

The ceremonies begin, with the whole school assembled to welcome the first-graders. The sixth-graders, the most senior in the school, act as big brothers and sisters to the first-graders, many of whom seem bewildered by all the novelty and attention. The older children pin name cards, with class assignments, on each first-grader. The principal of the school then welcomes everyone back, and offers some exhortatory and uplifting remarks to the students, parents, and teachers. Because his remarks are simple and not overdone, the audience takes his precepts to heart; parents and teachers will repeat some of his phrases to children in the days to come. The principal finishes with introductions of teachers and staff—including kitchen crew and maintenance people—and with a plea for caution while walking to school in traffic. Indeed, safety is one of the key responsibilities of the school, since it is school that has brought the children so far from their homes and through such perilous passage. Some words from sixth grade class leaders follow, as does introduction of the Parent-Teacher Association. The total effect of everything is a welcome into a new family, much vaster than the intimacy of the mother-child relationship but still caring and concerned. The school is always called "our" school.

Sixth-graders then accompany first-graders to their classrooms, and parents disperse or wait outside. The first day for first-graders is short, again only a taste of what is to come. The teacher gives them a brief welcome in the classroom and introduces them to its features and geography. She tells them that they will be working hard this year, but that they will also have fun. They are asked to respond to a roll call, by standing next to their desks and saying loudly and briskly "Present!" After a brief presentation of routines, materials, and plans, the teacher dismisses the class and the children wander back to their parents, who walk them home to change into play clothes and relax.

Detail and Process

When the year starts in earnest, the next day, the teacher does not wade directly into reading and computation or other academic subjects. She considers it far more important to socialize the children to the practices of group life and to the customs of this school.[1] She spends a very long time on such things as where one puts one's outdoor shoes, how one sits down and stands up, how one speaks in class, how one prepares one's desk for work (pencils at the top, notebook on the right, text on the left, etc.). As an American teacher knows, there are always some children for whom such things are difficult, and the girls tend to catch on early while some of the boys resist any routine.

One of the first lessons follows up on the first day's exhortation to speak up when roll is called. It is very important, children are told, to speak forthrightly and clearly in public, to project their voices and sound confident. The lesson here will stand them in good stead in school, work, and other situations to come.

This might seem paradoxical to a Westerner, who assumes that Japanese children are not encouraged to develop independent thought, speak their own minds, and project a strongly individualistic image to the world. Yet they are in fact, much more than our children, explicitly trained in public performance. This perhaps can be explained by separating *performance* as a skill, which anyone can learn, from responsibility for the content of one's own pronouncements. Once the distinction is made, the child is free to perform confidently since he is not usually displaying material of his own creation. So he isn't as vulnerable as a child who is asked to "state his mind." The quality of a Japanese child's performance is usually high but somewhat ritualized and predictable, thus perhaps minimizing risk to his ego. Later, of course, that same child does recite his own work, but by then he may well have justified confidence in his skill to perform.

Early on the similarly nonacademic lesson of self-reliance is also taught, which also may seem contrary to Western preconceptions of Japanese education. Self-reliance sounds to us like a big job for a first-grader, since it implies the prior development of a self with a set of independent motivations. We do of course push for independence among small children, but give them very little guidance about what this might mean and what they should do with it. So without clear domains for self-guided action, a Western child can find himself at sea, and later may lose the capacity for a truly independent, "creative" task. Meanwhile, the Japanese child is taught to master certain small, discrete, carefully delineated tasks, one at a time, and is given a long time to learn them. The teacher ensures that the approach has been learned well before the child is encouraged to go on. When he is, the child is then fully expected to be able to do *those tasks* self-reliantly. The goal of Japanese self-reliance is, finally, a capacity for self-motivated effort.

Japanese teachers are a very patient lot. Lessons are repeated as often as is necessary, and always in step-by-step fashion. The child is not expected to grasp a method or principle thoroughly at first, and doesn't feel any tension coming from high expectations. The teacher gives few overall explanations of the work at hand and many painstaking repetitions of small parts of the task or process. Moreover, verbal explanations are seen to get in the way of learning, though to an American teacher they may well come first. As a consequence of what is called "mastery learning," Japanese children often come up with the conceptual point underlying a lesson before the teacher has provided it.

By and large, American teachers are impatient with teaching minute details, and may feel that more value of "prestige" comes from imparting an understanding of abstractions and an ability to verbalize the relationship between an abstract principle and the concrete instance at hand. Furthermore, American teachers often see any kind of emphasis on the rote learning of "unexplained" detail as leading a pupil to become too dependent on the instructor. In general, Westerners feel that *principles* set the child's mind free, and want to release it for independent exploration as soon as possible. Japanese teachers, on the other hand, see pupil dependence as an important part of how one teaches, not in itself in any way infantilizing. And yet, as we shall soon see, "discovery learning" is also very significant in Japanese pedagogy.

Energy and Engagement

Because of our preconceptions of Japanese schooling, a walk into a typical fifth grade classroom in Japan may shock us. We might easily expect an environment suffused with rote learning and memorization, a structured and disciplined setting with an authoritarian teacher in control. This is far from the reality of most classrooms. Walking into a fifth grade math classroom, I was at first surprised: the mood was distinctly chaotic, with children calling out, moving spontaneously from their desks to huddled groups, chatting and gesticulating. An American teacher would wonder "Who's in charge here?" and would be surprised to see the teacher at the side of the room, calmly checking papers or talking with some students. When I came to understand what all this meant, I realized that the noise and seeming chaos was in fact devoted to the work of the class; children were shouting out ideas for possible answers, suggesting methods, exclaiming excitedly over a solution, and *not*, as we might suppose, gossiping, teasing each other, or planning something for recess or after school. The teacher was not at all upset as long as total engagement in the appointed set of tasks persisted; she actually felt that the noise level was a measure of her success in inspiring the children to focus and work.[2]

Later the teacher presented the children with a general statement about the concept of cubing. But before any formulas or drawings were displayed, the teacher asked the class to take out their math diaries and spend a few minutes writing down their feelings and sense of anticipation about the new idea. Now, it is hard to imagine an American teacher beginning a lesson with an exhortation to examine one's emotional predispositions about cubing.

After this, the teacher asked for any conjecture from the children about the process and for some ideas about how to proceed. The teacher then asked the class to form *han* (working groups) of four or five children each, and gave out materials to work on. One group decided to build a cardboard model of a cubic meter and took materials into the hall to do it. In a while they returned, groaning under the bulk of what they had wrought, and there were gasps and shrieks as their classmates reacted to the size of the model and some tried to guess how many of them might fit inside. The teacher then outlined for the whole class a very difficult cubing problem, well over their heads, and gave them the rest of the class time to work on it. The class ended without a solution, but the teacher made no particular effort to get or give an answer, although she exhorted them to be energetic. It was several days before they came up with the answer; there was no deadline, but the excitement did not flag.

Several characteristics of the class deserve highlighting. First, priority was given to feelings, predispositions, and opportunities for discovery rather than providing facts and getting to an answer fast. The teacher emphasized process, engagement, and commitment rather than discipline (in our sense) and outcome.

Second, assignments were made to groups. (This, of course, is true at the workplace as well.) Individual progress and achievement are closely monitored, but children are supported, praised, and allowed scope for trial and error within the group. A group is also competitively pitted against other groups; a group's success is each person's triumph, and vice versa. Groups are made up by the teacher and are designed to include a mix of skill levels. The teacher helps the *hancho* (leader of a *han*) to choreograph the group's work, to encourage the slower members, and to act as a reporter to the class as a whole. The *hancho* is thus trained as an apprentice teacher as well, a job that falls to each child in turn.

Teacher and Students: Motivation and Management in the Classroom

The pedagogies of a Japanese elementary school are based on the idea that all children are equal in potential, and that the excitement of learning can best be produced in a unity of equals. Teachers, especially those strongly influenced by the Teachers' Union, try to enforce this conviction and see themselves as stalwart defenders of the ethic of cooperation against the pressure exerted by a need to compete. For teachers, competition creates division and pulls a child toward a negative individualism. So the teacher uses group activity of various kinds to stem what he sees as a baleful threat, centrifugal and divisive, and resists singling out individual pupils except for short periods of time and in turn. To put it another way, the Japanese teacher wants to create and maintain a *kyoshitsu okoku,* or "classroom kingdom," of equals. His nurturant care surrounds the entire class, and can be graphically represented (see Figure 3.1).

The need and desire for unity and harmony sometimes produces extreme strategems. In a school musicale, the recorders of children who don't play well are sealed with tape so that while these youngsters appear to be playing, no discordant sounds emerge to disrupt the smooth sound of class performance.[3]

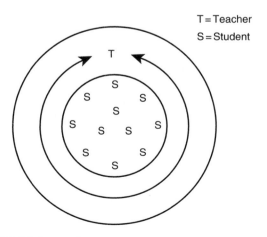

T = Teacher
S = Student

Figure 3.1

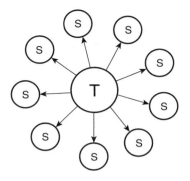

Figure 3.2

This sort of thing can be interpreted as unfortunate classroom public relations, but teachers feel that they are protecting the less able child from exposing inadequacy or "differentness." In general, a Japanese teacher will go to great lengths to protect a child from something he can't do very well.

A second model of classroom unity features a different view of the relationship of teacher to student. According to this model, the bonds which hold the group together are made up of the many dyadic relationships between the teacher and each student, as shown in Figure 3.2.

A more traditional model than the "classroom kingdom," this second model is the one employed by religious orders, artistic and craft schools, and other corporate organizations such as the prewar *zaibatsu* (holding companies) and academic departments in universities. The teacher here is presumed to skillfully manage all the individual relationships, knowing each student's strengths and weaknesses and attending to each individual's development. Most important, as the teacher relates to each student, he continues to stress the harmony of the whole, and he ardently tries to eliminate any sense of competition or alienation. This is the "vertical equality" model; and the other, an "equality of peers." Vertical equality is a way of teaching that demands much time and dedication. This means it is criticized by Teachers' Union supporters, who feel that the long hours of counseling and home visits required produce exploitation.

Japanese educators say that there is no evidence that one or another model produces greater academic success in the examinations. But many still believe that motivation for true learning can occur only in the second model, which they say has become hard to maintain in large classes.

Teachers often describe their work by telling the story of the cormorants, long-necked black birds that can be trained to dive for fish. Traditional cormorant fishermen owned flocks of such birds. Each bird was tied by a long cord held by the fisherman. If he had ten or fifteen birds, his handful of leashes would be hard to manage. While carefully keeping the leashes from tangling up, he had to handle each bird separately, even while minding the whole flock. This is the ideal classroom management mode: inducing harmony and paying close attention to the individual child.

The work team, or *han,* is used for both academic and nonacademic class purposes. It is, in fact, a part of pedagogical management, and its most common form is the *seikatsuhan,* or "daily life" *han.* For cleanup time, for lunch-serving time, for any other similar need, the unit of responsibility is the *han.* Teachers not only respect the didactic power of group learning, but also realize how appropriate it is for school activities of all kinds.

The *han* is also a teaching device used to engage children with diverse abilities in a single task. Though the group socializes children to see the value of cooperative teamwork, it also creates, teachers feel, an environment in which underachievers are stimulated to perform better, or at least feel fully included in what is going on. William Cummings talks about a socially backward boy put in a group with three "exceptionally tolerant" girls. They took him on as a "project," and "when he would not stand up for a class presentation, they would push him up, and when he struggled with an answer they would supply him with tips." Thus, Cummings says, "groups are conceived of as educational vehicles in the broadest sense rather than as mere instruments for rationalizing cognitive education."[4]

Unlike the teamwork of the *han,* American peer tutoring provides instruction devoted to individual rather than group needs. Not a way to make sure that everyone belongs, it is instead a way to reduce the problems some children have with the teacher-student authority relationship, permitting a more relaxed form of instruction. Learning is definitely not regarded as a group goal, and the usual form of peer tutoring is one-on-one. Since the teacher's authority carries no stigma and arouses no opposition in Japan, or rather, since authority per se engenders less anxiety than it does in the West, the Japanese seldom use it to motivate people. In the West, Esther Kohn says,[5] students need to feel control, or to feel that power can be shared, in order to feel self-esteem. In Japan, sharing power evinces the attainment of cooperation, which, I will say again, is itself a source of personal well-being.

Similarly, good human relationships are seen by Japanese teachers not only as means by which children can be taught various academic subjects but also as ends in themselves. So teachers try to watch friendships developing between children, and act as counselors to those who might be having trouble socially. Teachers know that children need to be appreciated and valued by other children, and that slow learners especially need peers to cheer them on. Friendships within the *han* are therefore regarded as developmentally important.

Most elementary school teachers say slow learners are few, especially in the early grades, but by the fourth grade there is more occasion to note problems. Here the "buddy system" of learning might be employed. Sometimes the parents of the faster learner will object, saying that to tutor another might slow down the learning of their own child. Teachers respond by asserting that not only is the role of the *oshiego*, or "teaching child," valuable for the learner, but the *oshiego* himself learns better through teaching. In any case, the faster learner usually finishes the classwork before the slower and has time on his hands, since Japanese schools have no accelerated program of any kind.

Besides the *han*, teachers use various physical arrangements of the classroom to facilitate learning. For some classes the desks, which are never fixed to the floor, are arranged facing front: when an experiment is to be conducted on the teacher's desk, slides are to be projected, or some other demonstration is to take place in the front of the room. At other times the desks may be arranged in groups of five or six, in the *hans* to which children have been assigned. For general class discussion, the teacher has the children move the desks into a U-shape, with the teacher's desk at the open end. The class may thus have as many as three different shapes during the same day, and preparing his or her study plan, a teacher indicates what the physical arrangement of the desks will be at what time.

Teachers also explicitly employ motivation techniques. One such is the concept of *donyu*, or "introduction," which means the initial moments of teaching a topic during which the children are "motivated to do the work actively." Consider the *seikatsu-tsuzurikata*, or "life composition," which has been around since well before World War II, especially in elementary schools. In a short essay, sometimes composed in a school diary, the child is encouraged to bring together what is learned in school with what is experienced in his life. The teacher often sets an example by relating a personal experience, and then gets the children to talk about it: "What would you have done if you had been me?"

A fourth grade art teacher once asked her class to paint a picture of "The Teacher's Treasure." She brought out her old, dirty, and much-used mountaineering boots and put them on her desk. At first the children couldn't believe that these were a "treasure." But the teacher told them stories of her college days when she would go to the mountains to hike, and regaled them with tales of her adventures with wild animals, of camping with friends, of the happiness she felt in the clean mountain air. The children were enraptured, and while their paintings may not have been technically skilled, they had color and feeling: the boots had become real and important to them.

Some teachers are not so successful. Another fourth grade teacher tried to get her class to sing a fall song about red maple leaves. She brought some leaves mounted on a large sheet of white paper and asked her class to "describe how wonderful they are." Dead silence followed, and then a few children, helping her out, tried to respond. Dead leaves, a dead exercise, and instead of motivation, only pity.

Fire and Air: A Science Class

A fifth-grader, of course, has to be motivated differently. Here a teacher may need only to be open to the children's response. As we see fifth grade science students finding their places at the laboratory tables, the teacher, a man in his late forties dressed in a white lab coat, asks for their attention and then puts a question: "What do you think will happen when you put a bottle over a burning candle?" All hands go up, and he calls on five or six children, noting their responses but approving or disapproving none. He writes down all of the speculations on a blackboard, after which he sends the children to get bottles, candles, matches, and some water to extinguish flames. He asks paired sets of children to light the candle, to place the bottle upside-down over it, and to observe what happens. They do, and note that the candle goes out.

Most of the children aren't content with that simple observation and introduce some variations, such as lifting the bottle a little, blowing under it, and so on. Others count the seconds it takes for the flame to die out. The teacher allows them to experiment, but keeps asking "Why did it go out?" The children all want him to visit their tables, to check the experiments they've devised, to answer questions. He answers no questions, except with more questions, or he asks that they try doing the exercise again. He insists that they all listen to each other's observations and queries, and finally asks for several of the teams to present their own trials, and their hypotheses about the results to the class. In turn, each team goes to the front desk, sets up the equipment, and demonstrates what it did—some holding the bottle at different heights, others lowering the bottle suddenly. The teacher now asks what there is about the bottle, its position, the flame, the candle, or anything else affecting the circumstances that makes the flame go out sooner rather than later. Some children raise their hands, he calls on them, and they respond with a variety of answers. He then draws a diagrammatic representation of the experiment on the board. Each team comes forward and provides explanations in firm, complete, and confident phrasing. The teacher also asks questions of those who haven't raised their hands, and some try to respond. But those who have nothing to say are in no way singled out and put on the spot.

The class then takes a ten-minute recess, since this is a double science session of two forty-minute periods. They then return noisily for the second session, which starts with a formal bow to the teacher. The ritual marks a clear break from the noise and a renewal of focus on the task of the day.

The children take up the question again, and this time the teacher asks if they know anything about oxygen, and the relationship between the flame and the air. The children answer somewhat tentatively, even though a few know a lot (most have only a sketchy acquaintance). The teacher surprises a daydreaming child by asking him a question in a rather peremptory tone. The child sits up suddenly, blushes, and has no answer. The teacher has been tough and sudden, and shocks everyone. He quickly resumes the friendly, Socratic tone established earlier.

For the last half-hour of the class, the children are asked to begin a report of the experiment. They take out paper, rulers, pencils, and start to draw the experiment and then to describe and explain it. After giving explicit instructions about how a proper laboratory report is prepared, the teacher moves around the room to advise and correct. The product is a lab report, half-finished today but to be completed at home. The children worked in pairs during most of the class, but the report is an individual assignment.

The teacher here demands a lot of his students but dictates very little. His lesson is the scientific method, and the experiment is a device by which method is taught rather than a conclusive demonstration of oxidation. Though this man is not one of the teachers in the school who "kid around" with the students, he is not known to intimidate. His method is exploration, but the limits are clear: children are not encouraged to go far beyond the constraints the materials themselves provide. And yet, the children are encouraged to push to the margin, to devise all the variations that their imaginations can bring to bear on the materials.

Thus, science in the Japanese elementary school is taught not through rote learning, but through direct experience, observation, and experiment. The curriculum is organized so that children's earliest experiences with science are gained through "friendly," everyday materials. In the first and second grades, children raise plants and observe the weather, and acquaint themselves with such basic principles as magnetism. They work through increasingly complex phenomena, principles, and contexts, so that by the sixth grade they are dealing with the basics of biology, physics, and chemistry.

The Value of Engaged Effort

Japanese elementary school pedagogy, like maternal socialization, is based on the belief that the teacher's job is to get all children to commit themselves wholeheartedly to hard work. In the United States, a teacher is expected to evaluate individual ability and to praise any level of accomplishment, even in the face of mistakes. In Japan, if the child gets 99 out of 100 right, the teacher will still say, "Not perfect, but it could be so if you *really* pay attention."

American educational rhetoric does invoke the idea of "the whole child," values "self-expression," and promotes emotional engagement in "discovery learning." But Japanese teaching style, at least in primary schools, employs all three in a mode that surpasses most American efforts. In the cubing class, I was struck by the spontaneity, excitement, and (to American eyes) unruly dedication of the children to the new idea. I was similarly impressed with the teacher's ability to create the mood. What's going on reflects cultural assumptions. American pedagogy usually separates cognition and emotional affect, and then devises artificial means for reintroducing "feeling" into abstract mastery. It is rather like the way canned fruit juices are produced—first denatured by the preserving process and then injected with vitamins to replace what was lost. The way Japanese culture works is more holistic.

As early as 1919, John Dewey also observed the absence of overt discipline in Japanese classrooms:

> They have a great deal of freedom there, and instead of the children imitating and showing no individuality—which seems to be the proper thing to say—I never saw so much variety and so little similarity in drawings and other handwork, to say nothing of its quality being much better than the average of ours. The children were under no visible discipline, but were good as well as happy; they paid no attention to visitors. . . . I expected to see them all rise and bow.[6]

The children in such a class *are* good as well as happy, since no one has taught them that any contradiction exists between the two. But it sometimes seems that American classrooms, and American parents as well, teach a different lesson: that goodness results from inhibition rather than joy, and that the demands on a child to be good cannot be consonant with whatever produces happiness. The kind of good-natured teasing and kidding, the uproarious noise that fills the Japanese classroom, the wrestling and hugging with the teacher after class, are clearly evidence of "happiness," but no one is "out of line." To be "in line" in an American classroom may mean no joy—the only source of which, sometimes, is behavior and forms of expression that are explicitly proscribed.

Social Lessons

The Japanese goals of the classroom engagement are early emotional maturity, compliance, and social courtesy, as well as engagement for its own sake. All this implies self-reliance, which seems to us inconsistent with compliant dependency. However, the "self" on which the child must learn to rely is in service to the social environment in which he must fit completely: thus, the child faces no real conflict.

For the Japanese child, social lessons are everywhere to be found, meaning that all activities during the school day are valued, not just those with explicit academic content. From the moment a child arrives until he leaves, every school-day performance and exchange is part of the learning experience. Earthquake drills are a good example.[7] Out of the PA system comes a sudden rumbling noise, the noise of a simulated earthquake. Children reach for their padded hoods, made by their mothers on a pattern provided by the school, or for their hard hats, provided by the school, and huddle under their desks. Later a whistle blows an all-clear signal and the children line up in pairs to file out into the schoolyard. There, after roll call is taken, parents sometimes come to collect smaller children; mothers have been alerted ahead of time, their availability for such events being all but mandatory. In short, the school and family have worked together to ensure the security of the children. In the well-coordinated action taken by all to prepare for the drill, as well as from the drill itself, everyone learns an important lesson: for a vulnerable nation, cooperation is a matter of life or death.

Imagine This Fish in the Sea

The Japanese teacher, like his charges, is given limits to how much he can invent within the curriculum. Yet Japanese teachers push themselves to present the material imaginatively and, most of all, to emphasize common sense and the relevance of whatever is taught to the everyday lives of the students.

A fourth grade social studies teacher, for example, devised a way to study something required on pisciculture and the Japanese fishing industry. He began class by dumping the contents of a shopping bag on the front desk. In the bag were fish of all kinds and supermarket packets of shrimp and other shellfish. The desk was covered with limp and smelly things. The teacher then turned on a projector to show a chart on the wall, which was a diagrammatic representation of the Japanese coastline with indications of sea depth. He pointed out to the children where each of the fish on his desk might have been caught, at what depth they lived, and by what means fish at different depths are caught. He showed them how far fishermen have to go to get different species, and what habits these fish have. As he talked, he constantly invited interruption and excitedly waved the fish in front of children's faces. This, of course, elicited cries of disgust, as some of the girls retreated under their desks.

The teacher was not told by the ministry of education's curriculum guidelines to provide examples of fish "in the flesh." Neither was he told to use the drama produced by a darkened room and projected images, nor to say anything about how fish are caught. By the end of the class, the children could recognize the fish and say something about their lives and habits, as well as the way fishermen go about making a living. And the smell of the fish would remain in the classroom for several hours, which could only remind the children of the lengths to which their teacher would go to help them understand.

This lesson in pisciculture is a good example of what Japanese teachers do to provide *sogo katsudo,* "integrated activities," for their classrooms. Elementary school teachers often put together interdisciplinary assaults on a theme. In the school where the abovementioned lesson took place, the social studies class considers the broad question of the importance of fish to Japanese life, the science class takes up the biology of fish, and the language class is devoted to writing stories about fish. For the third-grader in the same school, the theme is paper making. Children learn how paper is made, make their own, visit a paper factory, and in art class use paper in many ways as a medium. *Sogo katsudo* is an example of the freedom to innovate that can exist within a standardized Japanese curriculum.

Home and School

In home and school, learning reinforces human relationships and provides other emotional rewards. The lesson of supportive environments is that it is very important and entirely appropriate to be fully engaged in and excited by participation. Though Japanese children are thought to be obsessed by the prospect of exams that loom, in fact one finds little explicit stress on the distant future. Meanwhile, teachers spend time with the family of each of their charges, responsible for knowing the whole context of the child's life. While some teachers complain that mothers pressure children at home to study—"Don't play. Do your homework first!"—they genuinely feel that their own way of getting children involved works for any grade level or level of ability. Teachers suggest to mothers that they let the school handle the child's motivation.

Nevertheless, life at home mostly supports life at school constructively, except when it comes to handling examination anxiety. The examinations often involve parents in a child's education as early as elementary school. Parents can sometimes wield influence to get their offspring into the right middle schools, which are, of course, those with the best record of admission into the best high schools. And these are known by how many of their graduates enter the most prestigious colleges and universities.

But before exam anxieties begin in earnest, the mother as a member of the community comprising the school is very much caught up in her child's learning, and in most cases is as eager as the teacher to make the experience happy and relaxed, to engage rather than force or push the child. In that frame of mind, a mother will help her child with homework after school and in the evenings. This is usually regarded as positively integral to his education. The Japanese child needs maternal guidance and support, and the mother gets much satisfaction from helping him. But some teachers now say that they don't know who's being graded, the mother or the child.

Two Portraits

Two portraits, that of a third grade boy from a traditional shopkeeper's family and that of a sixth-grader already on a path to college, show us something about home and school during the elementary school years.

Jiro of the Bean Curd Shop. Jiro is an eight-year-old third-grader living in Osaka. He is the second son of a bean curd maker and his wife, who run a small shop in an older quarter of the city. Jiro's mother's father, a semi-invalid, lives with the family in their apartment behind the shop. The business consists of a front room facing the street—a room with cedar vats for soaking the soybeans, a motor-driven grinder, cauldrons to boil the beans, presses for making the tofu, and a small counter where customers are served. In a back room are sacks of beans and other supplies. The establishment is well known locally for its traditional bean curd; and even some suburban Osakans occasionally come here to buy. The shop has been in Jiro's family for four generations, ever since his great-great grandfather was adopted into the family as heir.

Jiro and his elder brother and younger sister have been raised among the sacks and in the steamy smells of tofu production. The older boy, now eleven years, will take over the shop upon his father's retirement and already works with him after school, waiting on customers during the late afternoon "housewives' rush hour." His mother keeps the books, cleans the shop morning and evening, takes care of her father's needs, and chats with customers. The tofu making itself is Jiro's father's job, at least to supervise, but the moment of curd formation is considered a sacred time which mobilizes the whole household.

Jiro's job is to do well in school, because his future depends on his wits, not on inheritance. His parents hope he'll get a job in a large company and become an admired "salaryman." But they train him at home in the skills of a shopkeeper, just in case, and because shopkeeping is what they know. Jiro is very much encouraged to develop the skills of human relationships, for it is by maintaining warm ties with customers and neighbors that his parents feel the shop prospers. He is taught, at least by example, to remember everyone's name and their regular order; he also observes how his mother prepares gifts for people who have just moved into the neighborhood, as well as ceremonial gifts for old customers at holiday times. She always has hot water for tea ready whenever someone stops in. At slow times, she will make the rounds of the other neighborhood shops of various kinds, to cement relationships with the owners. In times of crisis, she must count on them.

Jiro also learns from his mother how to keep the books. She herself learned on the *soroban* (abacus), but recently the family has purchased a small personal computer. Jiro loves to use it, but his mother discourages him, saying that he must learn to do the accounting in the old way, or at least with paper and pencil.

Jiro's school is nearby, and he walks there every day with his brother. Jiro is in Mrs. Okayama's third grade. His favorite subject is art, and he sketches nearly all day in the margins of his workbooks and on scraps of paper. In art class he is consistently commended for his work, but is also consistently reminded that he has a lot to learn. He is often chided for scribbling in his books. When the teacher assigned a project to the class in two-person teams, he and his friend composed and crafted a book of poems and sketches. The teacher was amazed at their skills and had the boys present it to the school. When Jiro and his friend took the project to the principal's office for the presentation, Jiro was nervous but proud. No one before in the class had ever been honored in this way. Jiro's mother and father were proud too, but quietly hoped the school would not encourage Jiro to become an artist: too risky a future.

Mrs. Okayama devotes the most class time to Japanese language, averaging one hour or more per day. The children are learning characters, and by the end of the third grade they will know about four hundred. But this is still not enough to read a newspaper, which requires about nineteen hundred. The books they read use characters plus *furigana,* or syllabic transliterations for characters they don't yet know.

Next to Japanese, the subject most emphasized is arithmetic, with four sessions per week and regular homework. Science and social studies follow, then music and art. (Physical education is given as much time as science and social studies.) The social studies curriculum covers a wide range of topics in an exploratory, interdisciplinary way. Children in the first grade usually start with an investigation of the local neighborhood and work out to their city, their prefecture, and their region. As the pupils grow older, social studies encompasses even larger geographical units, and moves back in time as well.

Neither Jiro nor his brother attend *juku*. They both get good grades in school, and for now their parents are satisfied, but there is talk of sending Jiro's brother to *juku* when he gets to junior high school. For even if he will eventually inherit the shop, the parents hope he can go to a good high school, which confers prestige on the family. It is Jiro whom they hope to send to college, so that he can enter a company, and he, too, will start *juku* in junior high school. His days, for now, are pleasant and unpressured, and he and his friends play after school before doing the evening's homework.

Tomoko at the Brink. Now let's look at a sixth grade girl, nearing the end of her elementary school career, as she looks forward to entering middle school. Five and a half years have passed since she was a timid first-grader, awed and excited by a new world. She is now a confident and accomplished student, seeing the school as a "family" that she is rather hesitant to leave.

To begin the second term of the sixth grade, Tomoko has returned to school after summer vacation. During that time, she, like nearly all her classmates, worked hard to maintain and advance her skills by taking classes in tutoring school and by reading and studying at home. Her class, along with all her teachers, also took a trip together to a hot-spring resort near the sea, and this was the high point of her summer. Her family took a one-week vacation to visit her uncle and his family on his tangerine farm in Shizuoka prefecture. Upon returning to school, she brought her summer notebooks, her summer science project (an insect collection), and an essay she wrote about the class trip.

Tomoko has been with her group of classmates for five and a half years—indeed with some since kindergarten. She knows them well, and although her friendships wax and wane in intensity and she seems to have a different "best friend" every year, they are still all her friends, and that sense of family was further enhanced during the class summer excursion.

Tomoko lives with her family, including her younger brother (a second-grader at the same school), in a condominium near the school. Her father, an executive in a general trading company, has spent much of the past eighteen months overseas, first in Oslo and then in Saudi Arabia. He was earlier asked by his company to help set up an office in Europe for two years, but he and his wife felt that the risks of taking their children out of Japanese schools outweighed the potential benefits (extra pay, for one). He declined (with some risk of losing promotional ground) and accepted instead a somewhat less prestigious "roving" position, which would allow him to return to Japan frequently. He says that if an overseas posting had been proposed when the children were very small he might have taken it, for he hopes that they can be more "international" in outlook. At this stage, however, he feels that Tomoko, especially, ought to stay in a Japanese school to ensure that she will be able to go to a good high school and university. Although he does not want to intensify prematurely the anxiety of the examinations to come, he feels that a long-range perspective on the children's future, which accounts for pressures on the horizon, is necessary. So, for the time being, Tomoko's mother is in sole charge of the household, and although the grandmother lives nearby and can help out occasionally, the children's educational lives are the mother's responsibility. Tomoko hopes that her father will be home for her sixth grade graduation in March.

The second term begins in the first week of September. The first day starts with a school assembly in the schoolyard, less formal than the opening of the year in April, but with a special message to sixth-graders from the principal. He reminds them that because this is their last term in the school, they must apply themselves to their work and to their friendships to make the year a meaningful and productive one.

Early in the morning, Tomoko and her friends choose to meet at a corner a few blocks from school, to enjoy a walk together. The younger children also meet at set locations in each neighborhood for the same purpose. Even getting to school is hence a lesson in community. Not to join *some* group on the way to school is a bit antisocial, or means that one arrives too early or too late, neither of which is good.

Tomoko's schedule is a busy one. She has classes in Japanese language (five classroom sessions per week), in social studies (three per week), in math, science, domestic science, sports, and music. She also works on the yearbook committee, and will have to help to prepare the copy for the book in only a few weeks. She has been chosen *toban* for about a month and feels both proud and nervous about the responsibility.

The *toban* is the leader of the class. The method of selection and the length of the term vary greatly from school to school. The children chosen to be *toban* and other class officers are often given preferment by virtue of their academic ranking, meaning that social responsibility and personal success are strongly connected. In some schools, the term is short and many children are given an opportunity to serve. Tomoko must meet with the teacher regularly to talk about matters that come up in class discussions, and issues perceived to be problems by students and the teacher. The *toban* also helps organize class outings, skits, and other events.

Last term there was a significant problem in a class that the *toban* had to help monitor. One boy had teased another child, whose mother is Korean, and the hazing had taken on a racial cast. The teacher had overheard remarks at recess in the schoolyard, and had brought the two children together to talk about it. It turned out, according to the weeping victim, that this was not the first time a child had "called him names"; accordingly, the teacher decided that a class discussion was needed.

Since there was then (and is now) in the press much coverage of *ijime,* or "bullying," the parents and teachers of the school were especially on the alert to any incident that might fall in the category. Their school had been free of such incidents up to then, and they wanted to nip this one in the bud.

There was an open-ended discussion in class, during which children presented their views of the situation and a heated debate developed about when children should solve their own problems and when they should be brought to adult attention. Some resolution was achieved. The children were asked to imagine how the victim felt, and to put themselves in his place, feeling his pain and his anger. They were asked to judge whether there had been any provocation, and whether the children who were teasing had any other reason to be acting out their feelings in this way. Only once were the perpetrators singled out, and they expressed sorrow at having teased the victim. Finally, the teacher asked the class to remember the importance of the sixth grade in the school; younger children look up to them for guidance and for examples of good behavior. The teacher and students together expressed a hope that such episodes would not blemish their own and the school's record again. Tomoko hopes that she will not have to help adjudicate such a crisis in her term as *toban.*

Tomoko's daily job at the start of the term is to help sweep the halls of the sixth grade's corridor. Children are responsible for cleaning the school. Not having maintenance crews, Japanese schools rely on the children to tend the rooms and halls; outside tradesmen arrive only for major cleaning and repairs. At some schools, the work is done in the early morning; at others, during the last period of the day. Children wear smocks and dust scarves over their hair; they sweep, dust the desks and other surfaces, and wet-mop the floors of halls and classrooms.

Children also serve lunch. Most schools do not have cafeterias, since space is at a premium, and lunch is eaten in the classroom. The hot lunch is picked up by a team of children, while the rest arrange the desks to form group "tables." The servers wear white smocks and usually caps and face masks. Lunch is usually not what we would consider "traditional Japanese" fare, but is usually bread, a main dish with some sort of meat, and a vegetable, along with milk. A typical meal at Tomoko's school: bread, margarine and marmalade; chop suey with pork and vegetables; a boiled egg and milk. Rice is almost never served, to the consternation of domestic rice growers; but since most of Japan's rice is now imported, it is no longer a local industry. Another group of chores gives children a sense of the importance of nature in their lives: children are responsible for caring for the school's animals and the garden that they have planted. Usually these tasks are taken care of in the early morning.

At recess, which is really an exercise break, children go out in all kinds of weather to perform calisthenics, led by teachers. Many teachers regularly wear exercise clothes and warm-up suits to school, so it is hard to tell who is the physical education teacher and who the science teacher.

Outside of school, Tomoko has several activities. Classes finish at 2:30, and on some days Tomoko stays later for extracurricular pursuits. On others she arrives home at 2:45, on Tuesdays and Thursdays leaving after a snack for her *juku* class—afternoon sessions at a small neighborhood tutoring school where she does extra work in math and has also begun to study English, a subject that she will formally begin in middle school next year. She is interested in having a job which will allow her to travel, and daydreams about being a stewardess or tour guide, or in grander reveries, about working for the United Nations.

Tomoko's *juku* class meets from 3:30 to 5:00, once a week in math and once in English. The tutoring school is not high-pressured like those attended by some of her classmates, especially the boys, but is aimed at "enhancing" the work she does in school. The English class, she says, is fun, and she enjoys using the language tapes. This year's "best friend" is taking the English class with her, and they take the bus home together, practicing their English noisily and falling into giggles as they imitate the accent of their instructor.

After the Saturday morning session at regular school, the weekend begins for Tomoko. She has gymnastics lessons during the afternoon, at a special gymnasium on the other side of the city, founded by a former Olympic gymnast, a Mrs. Ikeda. This class is very demanding, and the teachers have high expectations for the girls. Tomoko feels very anxious as the time for the spring gymnastics meet approaches, and she often cannot eat or sleep just before it. She once broke a toe in an event, but the tension before and embarrassment after the accident far exceeded the physical pain. The tone and feeling of the school is very similar to that of the fast-track *juku* that prepare children for the exams to the best high schools and universities, and the message is the same: doing your best is not enough, but with effort and the right attitude, one can exceed all standards.

Although Tomoko's evenings are spent studying, she watches an hour or so of television—usually one of the pop song shows featuring stars who are not much older than she. Her Sunday recreation time may be spent with her family, because it is her father's day off too, or she may go shopping with her friends, looking for records, clothes, and the latest "paraphernalia" for schoolgirls presented by the large department stores in a special section—keychains, school bag "mascots," handkerchiefs, decorated pencil cases, anything at all with a Snoopy motif or the latest cartoon character.[8]

Tomoko is not especially interested in boys. While her American counterparts might be dressing up, trying on some makeup, even in extreme cases participating in sexual encounters, Tomoko and her friends see boys as classmates, sometimes as pals, and sometimes as nuisances. In American terms we might say that Japanese children have a delayed adolescence, or—possibly—none at all. High schoolers, as Thomas Rohlen points out, are called "children" (kodomo), and although there are words in Japanese for "youths," people in their teens, if they are still in school, are not "dignified" by such a term, nor set apart as "teenagers."[9]

Tomoko's last term in elementary school will most likely be a positive and happy experience, full of real cheer. She is headed for a nearby middle school, not an elite or prestigious one, but one where her parents feel she will receive what she needs to get into a good high school, since she herself seems highly motivated in her studies. Tomoko has never discussed where she will go beyond middle school but assumes she'll attend a good high school and college.

Tomoko's parents have not pushed her. Her attendance at the juku, at least in the math class, was generated not out of anxiety that she might fall behind, but because her teacher at school said she might be understimulated in the sixth-grade curriculum. Anyway, her friends were all taking extra classes. There are examples in her class at school of children who are experiencing more school-related tension. Tetsuo, a boy who has strong interests in science, takes juku classes every afternoon, for his parents expect that he may have a chance at entering a national university, and think perhaps Tsukuba, a science-oriented university, would be appropriate. Tetsuo will attempt to enter a middle school out of the neighborhood, whose entrance rate into the best local high school is known to be high. It is fair to say that parents tend to focus more on boys' "talents" in school and to attempt to provide them with the best environment. While the educational future of girls is of course attended to, and admission into a good school is of great importance, the ladders are different, and ultimately, the investment in first-rate education not seen as important for girls.

Secondary school represents a major departure from the modes and content of learning experienced in elementary school. Tomoko and her friends are aware that they are about to leave a place and period in their lives where harmony and warmth are of primary significance and where cooperation is more highly valued than competition. The next three years in middle school, and the following three in high school, loom as periods of serious effort and testing, characterized at best as challenging, and at worst as a devastatingly harsh environment in which one's future becomes mapped.

Notes

1. Lois Taniuchi Peak, "The Psychological Transition from Home to School," unpublished paper, Harvard Graduate School of Education, 1982.

2. The similarity between this kind of classroom and a typical office is striking. Such an office is a large open room with many desks facing one another in rows, allowing everyone to be part of an active, usually fairly noisy environment. As in the classroom, productivity and "health" are measured by the visible and audible evidence of engagement.

3. Another example illustrates school, rather than class, uniformity. On the day when national achievement tests were given, a school requested that those children who were near failure stay home and not take the test, so that the school's record would not be blemished.

4. Cummings, *Education and Equality in Japan* (Princeton, NJ: Princeton Univ. Press, 1980), 127.

5. Esther Kohn, "Beyond the Self: Group Learning in Japan," unpublished manuscript, Harvard Graduate School of Education, spring 1985.

6. Letter from John Dewey, cited in Victor N. Kobayashi, *John Dewey in Japanese Educational Thought* (Ann Arbor: University of Michigan Press, 1964), 28.

7. Gary Swartz, "Wilf's School," *PHP* (Aug. 1984): 30–38.

8. It is interesting to consider the differences in audiences for these goods in Japan and the United States. Originating in Japan, under such labels as Hello Kitty, and Patty and Jimmy, these items were seen as excellent exports to the American market. In Japan they sell to girls from ten to twenty years of age, and in fact, to girls of almost any age before marriage. When performing a market analysis of the appropriate American audience for these "cute" things, the American researchers advised companies that the appropriate age group in America was girls aged four to seven. I am grateful to Liza Crihfield Dalby for this comment.

9. Rohlen, *Japan's High Schools* (Berkeley: Univ. of California Press, 1983), 196.

PART II

The Diversity
of Educational Life

4

Culturally Diverse
Families and Schools*

editor's introduction:

Mexican Immigrant Families and U.S. Education Systems. In this selection, the "case" is about the unfair perceptions regarding what appears to be Mexican parents' disinterest in their children's schooling in U.S. schools. Throughout the work, the author strives to propose alternative explanations for "behaviors that schools and school personnel interpret as indifference" (p. 65).

The author claims that first-generation Mexican working-class parents bring goals, life plans, and experiences that do not help them to make sense of what American schools expect of their children. Stereotypically, their children do not perform well in U.S. schools, but the parents and families tend to be nonparticipative in school affairs and appear to be indifferent about their children's experiences. The complete case study, covered by an entire book, endeavors to show how understanding these conditions might help to explain why U.S. school success for Mexican American children has been elusive.

The present selection summarizes the main arguments made in the case study, as well as some of the important methodological characteristics of the study. The parents typically want their children to "grow up right, to find ways of making an honest living, to marry someone who cares about them, and to find a way of settling somewhere close to the people they loved" (p. 66). Grandiose as these aspirations might sound, however, they fall short of the "job titles, prestige, or power" promoted

---

*Valdés, Guadalupe. (1996). *Con Respeto: Bridging the Distances Between Culturally Diverse Families and Schools* (pp. 1–8). New York: Teachers College Press.

by American systems and therefore appear "meaningless by the [American] society surrounding them" (p. 67).

Relevance of Case Studies: Working With the Specific and the General. This selection shows how case studies can represent both specific and general experiences—in this case, about a nonmainstream culture that is nevertheless becoming prominent in American schools.

The book is based on the everyday worlds of 10 Mexican immigrant families, newly arrived in an American community near the U.S.-Mexican border. Attention is given to 10 children attending American schools over a 3-year period. The case study becomes even more specific by focusing on individual children, such as Saúl, who is described in the selection for this anthology. Saúl was retained by his American school system at the end of the first grade—to the surprise and anger of his parents and family. Four of the other 10 children under study also were held back at either the first or second grade. The author's reconciliation of these events, with the apparent indifference of the children's parents, contributes immensely to our understanding of how U.S. school systems serve or do not serve well its diverse student bodies.

Saúl and His Family

Saúl Soto was a husky, brown-skinned child whose pudgy little belly usually peeked out from underneath his too-small T-shirt. He smiled often and laughed easily. During his kindergarten year and even during his first-grade year, winning was important to Saúl. Of all the cousins who played together, it was he who ran the fastest and pushed the hardest. "*Yo gané, yo gané*" (I won, I won), he would say enthusiastically after winning a race or beating the other children at a game they had been playing.

Saúl's mother, Velma, wished that he would win just a bit more quietly. She grew tired of Saúl's fights with other children, especially with his brother, Juan Pedro. "*No seas peleonero*" (don't be so quarrelsome), she would say. "*Es importante llevarse bien con todos*" (it's important to get along with everyone). For Velma, it was important that all her children get along. Any energy devoted to refereeing intensive family disputes meant less family energy available for surviving in the new world in which they found themselves.

Saúl's parents, Pedro and Velma Soto, were Mexican-origin immigrants. They had settled in a town close to the U.S.-Mexican border, and they were struggling with a multitude of problems. Work in construction was scarce for Pedro. Velma had injured her back in a work-related accident and needed surgery. Pedro's father, who was blind and crippled, lived with them; and Aydé, Velma's daughter from a previous relationship, was blooming into adolescence and creating problems within the household.

The year that Saúl entered first grade had been an especially hard one for the family. Pedro's son from his first marriage, who had lived with them for several years, returned to his mother's home in California and died there of leukemia. Velma's father also died. The entire family went back to Mexico for the funeral and was gone for almost three weeks.

Through all this, the three younger children, Juan Pedro (7), Saúl (6), and Melania (2), were watched over carefully by Velma. She worried about the seven-year-old, who often had seizures. She talked to Saúl about his fighting. She carefully monitored the children's comings and goings and agonized when they were late from school. Some days she could barely walk because she was in great pain, but she kept going. She looked after her father-in-law, got the children ready for school, and frequently drove two hours to the Mexican border to buy cheaper flour, cornmeal, and beans.

When we asked Velma and Pedro if education and schooling were important for their children, they both said yes immediately. They had had little schooling in Mexico, and they wanted their children to have more. They knew little about the American school system and how it worked, but they had taken the children to the neighborhood school, and had enrolled them in the programs the Spanish-speaking office worker had suggested. Every day when the children returned from school, Velma would ask them how they had behaved in school. She believed firmly that if they were going to learn anything at all, they had to learn to behave first.

Neither Velma nor Pedro, and least of all Saúl, were prepared for Saúl's retention at the end of first grade. "*No pasé*" (I didn't pass), Saúl said to us tearfully. His seven-year-old brother had ridiculed him for being dumb, and even his cousin Amapola, whom he always beat at everything, had laughed at him.

Velma was angry. She had spoken to the teacher only once that year through an interpreter. She had tried to explain that she had not gone to school before in response to her notes because she had a bad back and many family problems. But the teacher had not been sympathetic. In fact, in remembering that interaction, Velma recalled that the teacher had laughed at her. She wasn't sure whether the teacher had laughed *with* her or *at* her, but she had been both surprised and offended. In trying to make sense of why Saúl had been held back, Velma struggled with her own anger and confusion.

In many ways, we were also confused and upset by Saúl's retention. We first observed Saúl in school during his kindergarten year. He was enrolled in a "bilingual" kindergarten class that was taught by an English-dominant Mexican-American teacher and a Spanish-dominant aide.[1] All of the explanations about the activities to be carried out in class were conducted in English, and the teacher addressed the children only in this language. The aide provided Spanish explanations when needed by the few children who could not yet speak English. In general, however, English was the language of the classroom, and Spanish was used very little. Still, allowances were made for children who might not yet understand everything that was said. The aide could always be asked questions in Spanish, and even the teacher understood the children when they used this language.[2]

In the kindergarten classroom, Saúl appeared to do as well as the other children. He followed directions well, and when kept away from a particularly active classmate, he finished his work as expected. The end-of-the-year interview with his teacher and the aide did not reflect concern about his performance or about his ability in any way. At school, Saúl was neither troublesome nor unruly.

The following year Saúl entered the regular monolingual English-language program. In this program, children were assumed to be ready to learn exclusively in and through English. No special consideration was given to children who came from non-English-speaking backgrounds.

It is not clear to us why Saúl was placed in the regular or nonbilingual program, but apparently the school was under the impression that the parents had actively made this choice. In our conversations with the family, however, we learned that neither parent understood the difference between the bilingual program that, in theory, used Spanish for initial instruction, and the regular monolingual English program that used *only* English for all instruction. Velma did not remember having chosen one program over the other. (See selection 18 of this anthology for a related case.)

In terms of his English language development, Saúl seemed to us to be progressing well. By the middle of the kindergarten year, Saúl had begun to speak English at home both to his seven-year-old brother and to his half-brother, who was then living with them. Classroom observations during kindergarten and first grade also suggested that even though he was pulled out for ESL (English as a Second Language) help during the entire first-grade year, he was holding his own.

It became apparent at the end of that first-grade year, however, that all was not well. The teacher, Mrs. Lockley, recommended that Saúl be retained in grade. She felt that he was behind in reading and that he had not made enough progress.

Mrs. Lockley was neither unkind nor insensitive. She was a tiny, blonde, Anglo woman who at first glance appeared to be only a few years beyond her teens. Actually, she was in her mid-thirties, the mother of two school-age children, and a very experienced teacher. She had deliberately chosen to teach at Lincoln School, a school that primarily served Mexican-origin students, and she had high expectations for her students.

After Saúl was retained, Mrs. Lockley agreed to talk to us at the end of the school year. She was aware of our study and had allowed one of the members of the research team to visit her classroom during the entire year.

According to Mrs. Lockley, Saúl was "doing great in English." Overall, she viewed Saúl as having come a long way during his year in first grade. She commented that at the beginning he would hardly talk to her at all and that now, at the end of the year, he was even getting into little arguments with his peers. She saw this as great progress.

Mrs. Lockley did not consider Saúl to be a behavior problem and seemed surprised by our questions about Saúl's behavior that were based on information we had obtained from Velma. On the other hand, Mrs. Lockley admitted that she had had little contact with the family. She had seen Velma only twice, once when she had asked her to come in and sign the retention slip for Saúl and once in the middle of the year. She also had obtained little information about the family from Saúl. As opposed to the ESL aide who worked with Saúl and had been given many details about the family's comings and goings, Mrs. Lockley had not heard about the deaths in the family or about the reasons for Saúl's absence from school for a period of time.

She described her interaction with Velma at the time that she came in to sign the retention slip as unpleasant. She felt that Velma had been defensive. Through the interpreter (another teacher) that she had drafted for the job, Mrs. Lockley understood that Velma did not want to give her consent.

When questioned further and asked to describe Saúl's progress in the subject areas, for example in reading and math, Mrs. Lockley responded somewhat vaguely. She said that he was low average in math and very, very low in reading. According to Mrs. Lockley, Saúl was part of a group of three children that she believed had not made much progress. She described his limitations and lack of progress by describing those of the entire group.

She did recall, however, that when they were doing any writing at all, Saúl was very dependent on her. He would ask for assistance frequently. She had also noticed that he seldom participated in music or art activities and that story reading seemed to bore him. At first, she had suspected that he was not understanding the story because of language limitations, but later she decided that he simply wasn't paying attention.

For Mrs. Lockley, part of Saúl's problem was the "fact" that the parents were not "involved" in his education. She pointed to her lack of communication with Velma as evidence of both disinterest and lack of involvement. She had sent notes home with Saúl that were never responded to. Velma would simply not come to the school to talk to her. Still, Mrs. Lockley felt somewhat guilty about the situation, although she felt that she had given the family ample warning of the forthcoming retention.

As it turned out, Saúl did not repeat first grade. At our insistence and with the principal's blessing, he attended summer school the year after first grade and attempted second grade the next year. During the summer, as we worked with him on his reading, he was still angry. He had wanted to spend June and July at his grandparents' farm in Mexico, riding their old mare and wading in the creek. He was quite sure that working on his reading would make no difference. Since he was dumb, he told us, we all knew that it was useless for him to spend the summer reading.

The next year, the last year of our study, Saúl was a somewhat different little boy. He became best friends with a youngster who had been retained in second grade, he spoke a lot less English, and he wasn't quite as sure as he had been before that he could win all the games and all the races that he and his cousins played.

Velma talked to us a great deal about the retention. She tried to make sense of the papers the boys were bringing home, and she even enrolled the children in a mail-order book club in the mistaken belief that she was applying for a library card. She asked for help in making sense of the children's report cards, which were all in English, and she tried to understand why American teachers kept children after school. She did not, however, become more "involved" at school in ways in which the teacher could see or understand. It was thus easy for Mrs. Lockley and the other teachers to conclude that the Soto family, like so many Mexican families, simply did not "care" about their children's education.

Between Two Worlds

This selection is about Mexican families. It is about Mexican parents, and especially about Mexican mothers and their children. It is about values and beliefs, dreams and struggles, newly discovered expectations and serious misunderstandings. It is also about unfair perceptions and well-intentioned efforts to reform families so that their children can succeed in school.

It is my purpose here to examine what appears to be a disinterest in education by Mexican parents. By bringing to life the everyday worlds of

10 newly arrived Mexican immigrant families, I hope to propose alternative interpretations for behaviors that schools and school personnel interpret as indifference. . . .

In this selection, I argue that Mexican working-class parents bring to the United States goals, life plans, and experience that do not help them make sense of what schools expect of their children. At the same time, schools expect a "standard" family, a family whose "blueprints for living"[3] are based on particular notions of achievement. They have little understanding about other ways of looking at the world and about other definitions of success. I will further argue that in order to understand how school failure comes to be constructed in the United States for and by newly arrived groups, one must have an understanding of the worlds from which these individuals come.

For Mexican-origin children in the United States, the fact is that school success has been elusive. Indeed, to this day, Mexican-origin children continue to fail in American schools in large numbers. By most available measures (e.g., dropout rates, standardized test scores, college enrollment), it is still the case that educational institutions are not meeting the needs of Mexican-origin students. . . .

During the three years (1983–1986) in which we studied the children and the families, many things happened. First of all, I came to know the families well. I saw their strength, their pain, and their determination. I saw happiness, and I saw confusion. I saw sadness, and I saw hope. I also began to understand why it might be that these families and their children would not become models of immigrant achievement in a single generation. I began to see and to compare the differences between the values held by these new immigrants and those of the American mainstream society that surrounded them.

I also came to know the children. I saw them at home. I noted their enthusiasm at entering school, and I saw the sadness in Saúl's eyes when he was not promoted, when he began to believe that he really was slow and not at all like the other children in his classroom.

And yet, Saúl was learning English. The teacher had told us he was making good progress in English. I had recordings and analyses of his developing proficiency. We knew he interacted frequently with fluent-English-speaking cousins, that he watched television in this language, and that he even fought with his siblings in English. This was true of the other children in the study also. Yet, during the course of the study, four of these children were held back in either first or second grade. Teacher interviews clearly established that the children were not retained because of language.[4] What the interviews did not establish is why these little ones appeared to the teachers to be out of step and behind their peers.

In the light of what had been our assumptions, it was difficult to make sense of what happened to the children. For me, the project, as is often the case in ethnographic research, shifted gears. I began to reexamine the family and child data that we had gathered up to that point and to try to identify other factors that might be influencing the way children were being perceived by their teachers. This refocusing of the investigation, then, caused me to carefully analyze the ways in which children were being prepared by their parents to function within the family, in the outside community, and in the school setting. I invited the interpretation of the mothers, engaged them in long conversations, and, in essence, attempted to identify specific behaviors, attitudes, and characteristics that might account for the perception by teachers of these children as "not quite ready for the next grade."

As might be expected, the reexamination and reformulation of the central questions guiding the research project also changed its theoretical focus. While initially I had predicted that this research would contribute significantly to our understanding of the process of acquiring language and literacy in a bilingual environment, subsequently it became clear that I was seeking instead to understand and explain how multiple factors, including culture and class, contribute to the academic "failure" of Mexican-origin children.

In this chapter, I attempt to describe aspects of the domestic and work lives of these 10 newly arrived Mexican families. By presenting details about their everyday lives and by including their own perspectives about their experiences, I try to show the courage and the determination of these men and women and their children as they struggled to survive in a very alien world. In essence, the picture of the families that I present here is one of hardworking people who were dedicated to raising their children to become good human beings. Because of who they were and where they came from, their dreams and aspirations for their children were modest from an American perspective. Indeed, when talking about their dreams, most parents spoke of honest and hardworking sons, virtuous daughters, close families, and having *todo lo necesario* (the basic necessities of life). They did not think in terms of job titles, prestige, or power. What they wanted was for their children to grow up right, to find ways of making an honest living, to marry someone who cared about them, and to find a way of settling somewhere close to the people they loved. These were families where people worked hard, where both fathers and mothers often had several jobs, where children labored bent over in the fields next to their parents under a blindingly hot sun. These were people who hoped for a better life, but who believed that achieving that better life involved small things, perhaps getting paid a bit more than they had been paid in Mexico or having access to regular employment. They still wanted all the "good" things they had enjoyed in Mexico, like respect from their children, like the pleasure of growing old around them, like the happiness of spending free time around a large extended family. They were traditional people who were a product of the "third world" and who brought with them, in LeVine and White's terms (1986), their own models of the "good" life.

In coming to the United States, however, what these families discovered or would soon discover is that old codes of conduct and personal survival strategies often do not work. Goals that they believed in and hoped to achieve were often thought to be meaningless by the society surrounding them. They came face to face, instead, with the industrialized "first world" in which, as LeVine and White (1986) argue, educational development is conceived as "a universal form of progress consistent with all human aspirations regardless of ideology or culture" (p. 18). In the case of "working-class" Mexican immigrants, their beliefs about life and its meanings—useful as they might have been in a "developing" country like Mexico—placed their children in jeopardy in the eyes of American schools. . . .

Notes

1. Bilingual education programs are designed to provide mother-tongue support for children who do not speak English. For a complete discussion of the theory, practice, and history of bilingual education in this country, the reader is referred to Crawford (1989).

2. This particular classroom, although classified as "bilingual," did not actually provide instruction in Spanish. The teacher in this classroom was hired on a temporary basis and was not a credential bilingual teacher. She was, however, very much in favor of teaching in two languages and was actively working on her Spanish language skills in order to bring them up to par.

3. Blueprints for living, according to LeVine and White (1986, pp. 12–13), are models for living or "life plans" or "cognitive maps of the life course" that are "embedded in codes of conduct and local survival strategies that endow the life span with culture-specific potentials for personal development."

4. Some individuals concerned about the education of linguistic-minority children might argue that the problem was indeed linguistic. They would base this argument on Cummins's early work (1979, 1981). According to this work, the proficiencies that we observed were simply characteristic of BICS (Basic Interpersonal Communication Skills) in English. According to Cummins's early writings on this topic, children from non-English language backgrounds often experience academic difficulties because they have not yet developed English CALP (Cognitive Academic Language Proficiency), or the kind of academic language proficiency that is needed to make sense of reading and writing. Saúl, then, would have experienced problems because he had not developed this more academic English language proficiency.

While a discussion of this theory is beyond the scope of this book, in the particular setting in which the study was carried out, other children who had also *only* developed English BICS (and who had not developed CALP in their first language) did, in fact, succeed in school. Since these children shared Saúl's background, this suggests, as Cummins argues in his more recent work (1989, p. 34), that, "under achievement is not caused by lack of fluency in English. Under achievement is the result of particular kinds of interactions in school that lead minority students to mentally withdraw from academic effort." It is my intention in this book to examine the factors that contribute to these interactions.

References

Crawford, J. (1989). *Bilingual education: History, politics, theory and practice.* Trenton, NJ: Crane.

Cummins, J. (1979). Linguistic interdependence and the educational development of bilingual children. *Review of Educational Research, 49,* 222–251.

Cummins, J. (1981). The role of primary language development in promoting educational success for language minority students. In California State Department of Education, Office of Bilingual Bicultural Education, *Schooling and language minority students: A theoretical framework* (pp. 3–29). Los Angeles: California State University, Evaluation Dissemination and Assessment Center.

Cummins, J. (1989). *Empowering minority students.* Sacramento: California Association for Bilingual Education.

LeVine, R. A., & White, M. I. (1986). *Human conditions: The cultural basis of educational developments.* New York: Routledge.

5

Educating Students
With Disabilities*

editor's introduction:

Special Education Programs. U.S. school systems also are diverse in that they consist of a large number of special education programs. These programs serve students with disabilities and who cannot be served well by the "regular" curriculum. Sometimes, the programs are offered as an adjunct to the regular curriculum and in the same school building. Other times, they are administered by a totally different school, with its own administration and staff. The present case study is an example of the latter situation. The case study, again represented by an entire book, analyzes the teaching strategies of a single teacher ("Anne," a pseudonym) in a school for students with disabilities ("Brighton," also a pseudonym). The particular selection draws from two parts of the book.

The first part summarizes five specific features in the teacher's strategies. She focuses on students' strengths (not just their disabilities); the whole child (not just their academic performance); ways of making learning fun, to increase students' self-esteem; setting high expectations for her own performance; and maintaining a capacity to love her work in the face of constant challenges. The summary gives you an idea of what it might be like to teach special education students.

The second part gives the author's rationale for selecting this specific teacher and her class. The portion also goes into some detail regarding the author's data collection methods, which included the use of videotapes, direct observations, taped conversations with the teacher while watching the videotapes, interviews, and documentary evidence.

*Cambone, Joseph. (1994). *Teaching Troubled Children: A Case Study in Effective Classroom Practice* (pp. 37–43 and 191–196). New York: Teachers College Press.

Relevance of Case Studies: Building Case Studies From Career Experiences. Case studies can be written by people who have been involved in the case being studied, not just people who might be "external" to it (see also Selection 19 in this anthology, on "School Board Leadership"). Your own professional career may offer some life experience that appears worthy of being a subject of your own case study.

Under such circumstances, you should want to show how your case study nevertheless represents a fair and accurate rendition of the actual experience. The present selection, with its extensive use of various types of externally collected video as well as oral data, along with an explicit concern for minimizing any biases, gives you an example of how you might provide such a rendition.

An Explicit Mind Set

Anne engages with her work using a particular mind set. . . . Five recurring thoughts, or clusters of thought, orient and equilibrate her in the sometimes overwhelming flux of information that rushes toward her during any given classroom episode and amasses as the day progresses.

To begin, Anne focuses her energy and effort on the students' strengths. One cannot underestimate this ability, particularly when one considers how strongly the children present their aberrant behaviors. More important, though, one cannot overlook how this ability runs counter to common behaviorist practices in special education, where practitioners are exhorted to locate and remediate student behavioral and learning deficits, but where little encouragement is given to locate and exploit student strengths. . . . For instance, at one point in this study, when she was at the nadir of hope about finding a way to keep her class safe, and particularly Jason's ability to reduce his violent and sexualized behavior, she noticed him actively participating in a lesson. She immediately commented on his strengths. "I was just thinking," she said, "about how cute and polite and intelligent Jason is being in contrast to what I just said about feeling hopeless about him . . . he's starting to show some of his strengths again." And then, with a laugh and a sly glance toward me as if to reveal a secret, she said, "Maybe we can fix him after all!" Because she sees her students' strengths, she is always willing to re-engage, to push them to use those strengths, even at the risk of creating more short-term problems. She sees the boys as more than their problematic behaviors, and that vision propels her back into the work.

There are times when other workers at Brighton, usually therapists and child-care workers, think she pushes the boys in her class too hard to engage in school work. For instance, she related that during the first year of the study Paul's residence workers and therapists were concerned that her expectations were too high for him. No, she insisted, Paul has strengths that he needs to exercise if he is to begin to believe in himself: "I think that Paul is capable of a higher level of functioning than what they're expecting from him in the residence. And I'm pushing him harder, and he's having more behavioral problems, but in the long run, it's gonna be better for him 'cause he's going to learn that he can meet those expectations." There is a reason, a driving force to this decision to push them harder.

> In terms of high standards and pushing the kids . . . maybe [I'm] causing more behavioral problems cause I'm gonna push them to do things. It wouldn't be worth doing that if they were always going to be at a place like Brighton for their whole lives. Like *who cares,* you know, how much socially appropriate behavior they learn, and if they learn how to read and do math and those kinds of things. I think that there is always in the back of my head the thought and the hope that at some point down the road they're gonna go to some more normal setting. Whether they're gonna be adopted and stop living at Brighton, or they go back to a public school at some point. Or that they stay at a place like Brighton and are more successful there. You know or whatever. That there is a goal that each one of these kids is capable of more, [of] higher functioning.

Anne is of the mind that her students are more than their past, or their circumstances, predict. There is hope for students because they have strengths, and that's a good enough reason for her to do the necessary work.

The second component of Anne's mind set is her focus on teaching the whole child. She chose her career because within that discipline she could address more than just academics in her teaching.

> In choosing to work with these kinds of kids, clearly I'm not just interested in academic teaching. I'm interested in the social [and] emotional growth of kids. So I expect that some proportion of my time is gonna be spent dealing with social, emotional, [and] behavioral issues with kids and not just with teaching [academics].

Even though she believes that intellectual stimulation is crucial for troubled children, Anne makes choices in her classroom that reach beyond academic considerations. She puts substantial effort into planning "neat curriculum" ideas, but "the neat curriculum isn't as important to me as how the kids are doing altogether." Thus, for instance, when Brian had just heard that his social worker was coming for a visit to tell him some news about his mother, whom he had not seen in some time, he became increasingly impulsive and bizarre in his behavior. Anne went out of her way to keep him in class. She didn't want to "boot him off" to someone else so she could return to the academic task at hand. Seeing that the remainder of the group was in relatively good control, she kept him with her in an effort to both support and prepare him for the difficult meeting ahead, and she saw that emotional support and preparation as part of the job she loves to do.

While Anne is interested in the whole child, at the same time she is interested in academic production. She wants the children to have the experience of finishing their work, writing stories, doing science projects, and the like. She knows that the experience will enhance their sense of intelligence and power. She is oriented toward students producing products—she worries that she is too much so. Yet, it is her product orientation that provides the necessary balance to her process-oriented view of the whole child.

> You know, all my preschool education training says don't be product oriented, the experience is what is important . . . [and] the last thing I want to be is the traditional old-fashioned first-grade teacher. . . . That's not what I want. But at the same time, I . . . want them to have products. I know they would like the products and feel proud.

Without her product orientation, she knows she runs the risk of making excuses for the children to not finish their work, to not do normalizing activities. She has seen other teachers at other schools and institutions who, in their compassion for troubled children, mistakenly expect less from them. It is Anne's opinion that such lowered expectations foster the helplessness troubled children feel. On the other hand, she knows that being too product oriented might result in her being brittle, unable to understand why her "neat curriculum" needs to be pre-empted by the emotional baggage the children bring to school. She has seen teachers whose tolerance for anything but academic schoolwork is exceedingly low. Anne knows that it is in those classrooms that her students would inevitably fail.

One important benefit derived from her willingness to deal with the whole child, troubles and all, is that it predisposes her to accept and work with a wider field of explanations for their behavior. Hence, nothing really ever comes "out of the blue" for Anne. She is never thrown off her stride for long with the children if, for example, they present antisocial behaviors when they ought to be doing mathematics. Each is her concern, math as well as pro-social learning, and she is able to move fluidly from one to the other and back again. One would never hear Anne claim that it is not her job to deal with the troubles children bring from home, for instance. As far as she is concerned, that is her job exactly.

It is not uncommon today to hear many elementary teachers say that they are trying to teach the whole child. Anne is an elementary teacher who has made that phrase operational; it means very specific things that she can delineate in her mind and point to in her practice. Teaching the whole child requires a detailed understanding and tolerance for the behavioral, social-emotional, and academic aspects of student learning—and considerable skill at balancing the three.

The third component is closely related to the previous two: The best therapy for any of the children is to learn skills and competencies. A student's self-esteem can be founded only on an accurate self-assessment of his abilities. To help students reach that point, Anne insists that she must focus the largest share of her attention on her student's health and not on their pathology—and that she must find ways to make learning fun. This requires that she discover at what developmental level each boy functions in social, academic, and emotional domains. That knowledge helps her plan for each, as well as for the group as a whole; it gives her the ability to check when she has gone astray or expected too much or too little from an individual boy. . . .

A companion to her expectations of students, and the fourth component of her mind set, is her very high expectations for herself. She strives to be "perfect" as a teacher, is unflappable in the face of chaos and violence. She possesses knowledge of herself that allows her to be highly self-critical without being self-deprecating, and to laugh at herself and her faults without caving in under the weight of her controlling tendencies. Anne is emphatic that, although this group of boys is the hardest she has taught to date, she can and will make a difference, but only through considerable effort on her part.

> I guess I have incredibly high expectations for myself as well as for what is going to happen with the group. And so it's . . . not good enough for me to say that this is a hard group and that everyone says it's a hard group and it's just going to take some time. That helps because I know it's true. But at the same time I feel like there have got to be things I can be actively doing better to make it better. It's still gonna be a hard group; they're still gonna be crazy kids; it's still going to take a long time. But there have gotta be things I can be actively doing better to make it better.

To actively make things better means that she is continually critical of her lessons, of her approach, of her language. She picks lessons apart both when they are successful and when they fail, paying particular attention to the impact of her own actions and her own expectations on the lesson. If a lesson fails, or a period is disrupted, Anne rarely places responsibility anywhere but on herself: "I was some of the problem . . . my expectations were wrong," she told me after an early, disastrous lesson intended to teach about things being the same and different, using four different types of apples and the five senses as tools. She had done the lesson with students in former years and previous classes and it had always been a resounding success. But with this class, she concluded, she had misread their abilities, planned a lesson that was too advanced, "was a little stupid in saying, 'Well, this is a great lesson that I'd done before and I don't really need to think about it very much.'" She laughed at herself, as she often does when she is struck by the irony of being perfectionistic yet imperfect.

Anne believes that her work and her effort are important catalysts for growth. She smiles when she says, "I don't think I can 'fix' them." But her expression becomes earnest when she says, "I think I can be part of making them healthier people . . . I'd like to think that all the time and effort and energy that's going into everything that I'm doing and that others are doing with [them] is going to mean that 10 years from now [they] can lead some sort of productive, normal life." She believes that success or failure in help-ing the children is directly connected to her efforts. This aspect of her think-ing is important if we are to understand what and how she teaches. Her propensity for taking responsibility for what happens in her classroom is remarkable; she is not the kind of teacher who blames television for her students' lack of attention, for instance, or parents for students' lack of school readiness. Her nature is not self-deprecating; rather, she is like a strategist who replays every move she's made, searching for the false ones. Her attributions of success or failure are, in large measure, what propel her to use her considerable natural intelligence in increasingly flexible ways as she tries to cope with the whole child as he presents himself. . . .

Finally, Anne loves her work and she is satisfied with it, even though it is difficult, even discouraging. In the times when her energy is low and she feels defeated, she consciously reminds herself of that fact.

> I remind myself of the times when I feel hopeful or of the good things that can happen, and of my real belief that things will get better . . . I say to people "Well, it's a good thing that I love this kind of work, because it would be easier to forget this week!!"

This capacity to love her work in the face of intense and persistent chal-lenges binds her core values together and helps to shape her sense of voca-tion as a teacher. Throughout her working life with children, it is this set of attitudes and values to which she returns when she needs to re-calibrate her plans, her decisions, and her emotional responses. These values run deep, back through her life to her youth, her family, and the beliefs they first instilled in her. Anne knows herself well; her history, her present work, and her direction in life seem to her to be unified. To watch Anne teach is to witness a teacher who is confident, insightful, decisive, and, more often than not, effective. . . .

Methodology

Anne's is the youngest of six classes with the smallest number of students at Brighton. I selected Brighton and Anne's class for a number of reasons. First, for 14 years I had taught youngsters of junior high and high school age who were in some sort of separate setting as a result of behavioral or emotional difficulties, and I had, and continue to have, a strong interest in learning how troubled students can be successfully schooled. For the last 6 of those years, I worked at Brighton School. During the first 3, I was the teacher in the oldest classroom, teaching 12- and 13-year-old boys. For the next 3 years, I was a program director with primary responsibility for the older 3 of the 6 classes. Additionally, I was the coordinator of special education services and acted as liaison with the public schools. I have not worked at the school since 1988, except to consult with my successor during the first 2 years of transition. Thus, I had the benefit of knowing the institution—what it is like to teach at the school, to design and implement curricula, to be part of a treatment team, and to handle children's crises. I also had the benefit of knowing the institution from a management perspective, and have an understanding of the school's internal workings and its position in the larger community. As a researcher, I was able to be a fully acclimated participant-observer at Brighton.

My second reason for choosing Anne's class was that, for all my experience within the institution, I had had limited contact with her personally, except around certain administrative business, namely, the IEP conferences that I chaired. I approached her for this study, in part, because I observed the respect given her at IEP conferences by her students' parents as well as her professional colleagues. Additionally, the children in her class made academic progress, a fact that was my job to verify as coordinator of special education. Finally, her supervisor, who was my colleague, had high regard for her skill as a practitioner. Such universal regard, combined with her documented success in academics, suggested that she was a good candidate for my study.

My third reason was that I was a teacher of adolescents and preadolescents and had little expertise in the teaching of young children. Therefore, I believed I would not be encumbered by my own biases about pedagogy.

Although I knew little of what Anne did or how, I knew that both she and the children recognized me from the larger school community and that probably I would not be distracting as a participant-observer. Originally, I negotiated entry to Brighton and to Anne's class for a 1-year pilot study. When that fieldwork proved fruitful in shaping research questions, and because Anne was scheduled to teach the same group of boys, except for one, for a second academic year, I successfully negotiated the continuation of my fieldwork for a second year. I reasoned that this classroom provided a rare opportunity to conduct longitudinal research where the same teacher and students worked together for 2 academic years.

Fourth, the children who attend Brighton come from a wide geographical area and are considered by the professionals who have placed them there to be among the most challenging youngsters to teach. Fifty-four boys ages 5 through 12 attended the school in 1988, some staying for as short as 1 year and others as long as 5. At the time, the children came from 32 different towns in Massachusetts. There was a wide variability of family background, social status, and income. Boys come to Brighton through one of three routes: recommendation of a Special Education evaluation at the local school level because of pervasive emotional and learning problems; the Department of Social Services because they are in need of care and protection; or the recommendation of both agencies. At the beginning of the study, the five boys in Anne's class were diverse racially, socioeconomically, and in the troubling behaviors they presented. The class had one African-American and four white students. One boy was homeless, two were wards of the state, one was adopted at birth and, like the fifth boy, was living with his parents in an upper middle class, suburban home. In some important ways, the boys' characteristics represented a microcosm of those that many teachers of emotionally disturbed and so-called normal children have in their classes.

Fifth, and finally, because I was known to the school administration as well as students' parents, I was able to negotiate permission to access all data on the children in this class. These data included written reports from school, social work, and child-care personnel, as well as crisis reports. I was also given permission to attend meetings with parents, social service agency personnel, and school personnel.

I used four strategies to collect data for this inquiry: videotaped, ethnographic observations; taped conversations with Anne elicited from watching the videotape together; semistructured interviews conducted with Anne and other key informants; and document review.

I used a hand-held video camera as my primary means of collecting observational data in Anne's class, but I also used conventional fieldnote recording. I chose to emphasize videotaping over collecting fieldnotes because it enabled me to capture far more accurately the rapid talk of the boys and teacher, the quickly shifting goals of the teacher, and the frequent behavioral outbursts of the boys. After each session, I viewed the videotape and transcribed it into fieldnotes. This transcription enabled me to analyze and code the observational data very finely.

During the first year of study, I videotaped Anne's class once and sometimes twice every month throughout the school year in 30-minute sessions, usually, but not always, during writing class. Twice during that year, I conducted two 2-hour conventional field visits as well. During the second year, 1989–90, I videotaped Anne teaching in 2-hour segments once every month. These segments covered all reading and mathematics instruction, as well as oral language time. During the final months of the study (May and June 1990), I videotaped 2 full days in Anne's class. The object of full-day observations was to experience the classroom activity as an integrated day. During those observations, I gathered data particularly on the movement of students from activity to activity and Anne's transitions in curricular and pedagogical style as she moved between subjects. It gave me the opportunity to observe the boys doing such things as going to the library and at play, which I had not been able to do until then. Additional observations were conducted of Anne in supervision meetings with the school principal, while in a supervision meeting with her teaching intern, and while she was conducting individual year-end, academic testing with one boy.

After each videotaped class, Anne and I viewed the taped lessons together. During these sessions, I stopped the tape often to ask questions about what she was saying or doing in the lesson, if she recalled what she was thinking, and what she was thinking or feeling as we watched. Anne also would stop the tape when thoughts occurred to her. My goal was to locate the recurring themes in her thinking, the salient emotional and cognitive aspects of her as a practitioner. Those discussions of immediate, concrete feelings and thoughts invariably led to discussions of larger, more abstract philosophical and practical thoughts in teaching and learning with disturbed children. When an idea was spent, we returned to watching the tape. All of those conversations were audiotaped and subsequently transcribed.

During the first year, watching videotapes together elicited 10 hours of audiotaped conversation with Anne about the boys, the curriculum, and her pedagogy. In the 1989–90 year, the videotaped lessons elicited 5 more hours of taped conversation. These elicited conversations, combined with the videotaped lessons, constitute the largest portion of data to be collected for this study.

In addition to elicited conversations, I conducted three additional semi-structured, open-ended interviews to investigate Anne's personal history, her perceptions of her place in the Brighton institution as a whole, her professional relationships, and her philosophy of teaching.

Brighton is rich in written report data. I received permission to investigate three classes of documents written about the students over the 2 years of the study. The first class of documents included (1) the narrative reports, or what Brighton teachers call "Student Profiles," written by Anne and other educational personnel as the result of periodic academic testing; (2) narrative quarterly and yearly summation reports on academic and behavioral progress; (3) Anne's accumulated unit plans; and (4) the permanent products of students' work that Anne had saved. These longitudinal data assisted me in tracking Anne's thinking on paper about her students and then cross-checking it with her thinking gleaned from elicited conversations and my observations of her teaching.

The second class of documents included reports on behavioral crises that transpired during the academic day. These data were helpful insofar as they tracked the daily reasons and length of time students were out of class for behavioral problems. The third class of documents included the "Conference Reports" on Anne's students written by noneducational team members. These documents are not academic in nature; they are written by therapists, social workers, and child-care workers. But they assisted me in checking the validity of Anne's social and emotional assessments of particular boys.

I analyzed these data in four stages. In the first stage, I tested two hypotheses that I had drawn from sustained observation: first, that Anne was involved in three general types of instruction—behavioral, academic, and social/emotional; second, that over time her academic utterances increased, and her behavioral talk decreased. To conduct this analysis, I used the transcribed videotaped observations from the first 6 months of fieldwork. I coded every utterance of Anne's where she initiated some instructional move with the boys as *Behavior, Academic,* or *Social.* Analysis revealed that there were three areas of instructional talk, although behavioral and academic talk far exceeded social/emotional talk. Additionally, although the number of academic and behavioral utterances numbered approximately the same at the start, the number of behavioral utterances decreased while academic utterances remained relatively constant.

At the second stage of analysis, I reasoned that teacher utterances in a particular category of instruction might denote thought in that category. To test this hypothesis, I analyzed the conversations that were elicited from watching the videotapes. As I've mentioned, as Anne watched a tape she would comment on what she was thinking as she watched, and what she recalled thinking at the time of the episode on the tape. I, on the other hand, asked her to explain why she had said something to a boy, or what she was trying to accomplish with a given action. I coded all interviews for the first 6 months of the study using the three existing coding categories, and I matched the videotaped lessons of the first analysis with their corresponding conversations. This coding and matching strategy yielded evidence that corroborated my earlier findings, that is, that three areas of instruction/ thinking were salient for Anne. However, it also revealed that, although academic and behavioral teaching was evident in *what* she talked about with the children, social teaching was evident in *how* she talked with them and in how she structured the environment. In other words, in elicited conversation, Anne described how she was approaching social and emotional issues implicitly, something that was less obvious in her explicit talk with the students.

At the third stage of analysis, I conducted a cross-sectional analysis of the interview data, coding all of the interviews for the 2 years by category of instruction. Analysis of Anne's conversations revealed that, over time, there was a shift in her focus among the categories. That shift corresponded roughly to the shift in teacher utterances found in stage one of the analysis: Behavioral utterances during teaching episodes, and her preoccupation with talking about student behavior as we watched the tapes, both decreased in frequency, while academic teaching utterances and talk remained constant. Furthermore, coding and sorting of the interviews revealed that an increase in her comments about the social goals of the class coincided with the decrease in her behavioral comments. This longitudinal analysis led me to divide the data into three overlapping intervals corresponding with her periods of manifest preoccupation with behavioral concerns, social/emotional concerns, or academic concerns.

In a second pass through the interview data, I analyzed each of these three categories of instruction more specifically, coding each for curriculum as well as pedagogy. I then divided the academic category of instruction into its constituent subject areas (reading, math, and writing) and coded for curriculum and pedagogy in each subject area. This cross-sectional strategy enabled me to analyze the data in each instructional category more finely. Furthermore, I coded across interviews in other categories, including Anne's overall thinking, her background, and her stories about individual boys.

Finally, having determined (1) that there were three distinct, albeit overlapping, stages of teacher thinking and action in class; (2) that each stage had an instructional preoccupation (although all three areas of instruction were clearly evident at every stage); and (3) that each instructional category revealed substantial and salient content, I divided the data temporally into each of the three intervals and conducted the final analysis. In what was largely an inductive analysis, I used the videotaped data to create as objective a narrative of the class events as I could. I paid careful attention to verbatim transcription of the boys' and the adults' talk, as well as the movement in the class and the activities that were carried out. In parallel, I worked to capture Anne's subjective experience of those same class events. I did this by listening to her talk about the events, observing her physical responses to them, and using clinical interviewing techniques in our extended discussions to understand her understanding of the class phenomenon. I then placed one description next to the other—my attempt at objective description of observable phenomena and my transliteration of Anne's subjective experience of those same phenomena—and proceeded to analyze the relationship between the two, looking for recurring patterns, as well as obvious discontinuities, in Anne's thought and action. It is this final analytic stage that yielded the bulk of the information used in writing this book.

Because I am a special education teacher and a former staff member at Brighton, I was particularly careful to safeguard against bias throughout the study. I have been trained in the jargon and ways of thinking used in my field, as well as in the particular jargon and ideology of Brighton. As a result, I was concerned that I would overlook data that I simply took for granted, that I would under- or overinterpret particular events or discussions of significance, or that I would fail to notice and critique aspects of the school culture that I, as a former staff member, had once made my own. To address those validity threats, I engaged an independent researcher to conduct the data analysis described in stage one of my data analysis. Using the videotapes, she conducted tests of my coding system, and then together we refined the coding and analysis strategy. I also engaged a graduate student trained in videotape analysis, who was involved in research into the language development of autistic children, to view videotaped sessions that I transcribed and analyzed. She critiqued my analyses of Anne's use of language, looking particularly for unexamined data and assumptions.

A second threat to validity concerned my remaining objective about Anne and her teaching. After working together for 2 years collecting data on her practice, we had developed a friendly acquaintance. Although this acquaintance facilitated our deepening discourse, I took pains to remain objective and critical about her work with the children, using memos to explore my potential biases.

Finally, because I was the major instrument of data analysis and interpretation, I guarded against erroneously interpreting Anne. On two occasions after data collection had been completed, I shared written analyses with Anne in order that she might discuss them and correct or verify my interpretations. After the first completed draft of the book was prepared, she read the entire document and offered thoughtful critiques of my analyses of her thinking, made some minor corrections on such things as dates of events, authors of curriculum materials, and facts about the students.

It is important to underline the fact that in doing this project I had wide access to the private information of five children and families, as well as to Anne's classroom practice. I assured the boys, their parents or guardians, and the school's executive director that I would use only pseudonyms for the participants and the school. Thus, the name of the school as well as all the names of children and adults have been changed in this document.

6

School Inequality*

Federal Courts

editor's introduction:

Inequalities Among U.S. Schools. U.S. schools can be considered diverse in at least one other way: sharp differences in educational opportunities and financial resources, from school to school (and district to district, as well as state to state). The inequalities raised by this diversity have been the subject of heated controversy, with numerous court cases.

The present selection covers a landmark federal case (San Antonio Independent School District v. Rodriguez, March 21, 1973) brought before the U.S. Supreme Court. In this case, the Supreme Court overruled the earlier judgment of a federal district court in Texas. The earlier judgment had confirmed the inequalities in Texas's schools and had laid out a course of action to rectify them. However, the Supreme Court ruled that the entire matter dealing with inequality among U.S. schools fell outside of federal jurisdiction and in fact was a matter for state adjudication. As a result, equity advocates have had to take independent action in each state and state court system (see the next selection in this anthology, covering New Jersey).

In Texas, the pursuit of the issue in state courts finally led to favorable judgments, but only after 15 more years beyond the original Rodriguez case, with Texas's state supreme court ultimately calling for a more equitable distribution of resources.

---

*Kozol, Jonathan. (1991). "The Dream Deferred, Again, in San Antonio." In *Savage Inequalities: Children in America's Schools* (pp. 206–233). New York: Crown.

Similar rulings have been repeated in many states (e.g., Massachusetts and Connecticut in the mid-1990s). In some states, these rulings have in part accounted for subsequent and intensive statewide school reform efforts, continuing into the 2000s. How the rulings have affected actual local school systems is aptly captured by the present selection, authored by a highly recognized individual who has won many awards for his writings in the education field.

Relevance of Case Studies: Covering Complex, National Issues. The selection shows how case studies can cover more complex topics than single individuals, classrooms, or schools. This case study focuses on both a community and the legal case involving the equitable distribution of educational resources between wealthy and poor schools and school districts. The author combines an analysis of the case's documents with evidence from interviews and interactions held with educators and students affected by the court decisions.

More specifically, the complexity might be considered a case (a specific school district) within a case (the court decision)—a design paralleled by Selection 16 in this anthology, "An Urban Youth Program." The nested case (the specific district) provides a dose of real-life happenings, whereas the main case (the court decision) covers an otherwise rather abstract though nationally significant topic. The quality of the case study also is reflected by the author's endnotes, which provide extensive references to key citations in the literature, including references to numerous newspaper articles.

The case study appears as one of six chapters, each covering a specific school system in a specific historical and geographic setting. The entire book, a national bestseller and also written by an award-winning author, does not formally present itself as a series of multiple case studies but in fact eminently fits the definition used throughout this anthology.

According to our textbook rhetoric, Americans abhor the notion of a social order in which economic privilege and political power are determined by hereditary class. Officially, we have a more enlightened goal in sight: namely, a society in which a family's wealth has no relation to the probability of future educational attainment and the wealth and station it affords. By this standard, education offered to poor children should be at least as good as that which is provided to the children of the upper-middle class.

If Americans had to discriminate directly against other people's children, I believe most citizens would find this morally abhorrent. Denial, in an active sense, of other people's children is, however, rarely necessary in this nation. Inequality is mediated for us by a taxing system that most people do not fully understand and seldom scrutinize. How this system really works, and how it came into existence, may enable us to better understand the difficulties that will be confronted in attempting to revise it.

* * *

The basic formula in place today for education finance is described as a "foundation program." First introduced during the early 1920s, the formula attempts to reconcile the right of local districts to support and govern their own schools with the obligation of the state to lessen the extremes of educational provision between districts. The former concern derives from the respect for liberty—which is defined, in this case, as the freedom of the district to provide for its own youth—and from the belief that more efficiency is possible when the control of local schools is held by those who have the greatest stake in their success. The latter concern derives from the respect for equal opportunity for all schoolchildren regardless of their parents' poverty or wealth.

The foundation program, in its pure form, operates somewhat like this: (1) A local tax upon the value of the homes and businesses within a given district raises the initial funds required for the operations of the public schools. (2) In the wealthiest districts, this is frequently enough to operate an adequate school system. Less affluent districts levy a tax at the same rate as the richest district—which assures that the tax burden on all citizens is equally apportioned—but, because the property is worth less in a poor community, the revenues derived will be inadequate to operate a system on the level of the richest district. (3) The state will then provide sufficient funds to lift the poorer districts to a level ("the foundation") roughly equal to that of the richest district.

If this formula were strictly followed, something close to revenue equality would be achieved. It would still not satisfy the greater needs of certain districts, which for instance may have greater numbers of retarded, handicapped, or Spanish-speaking children. It would succeed in treating districts, but not children, equally. But even this degree of equal funding has not often been achieved.

The sticking point has been the third and final point listed above: what is described as the "foundation." Instead of setting the foundation at the level of the richest district, the states more frequently adopt what has been called "a low foundation." The low foundation is a level of subsistence that will raise a district to a point at which its schools are able to provide a "minimum" or "basic" education, but not an education on the level found in the rich districts. The notion of a "minimum" (rather than a "full") foundation represents a very special definition of the idea of equality. It guarantees that every child has "an equal minimum" but not that every child has the same. Stated in a slightly different way, it guarantees that every child has a building called "a school" but not that what is found within one school will bear much similarity, if any, to that which is found within another.

The decision as to what may represent a reasonable "minimum" (the term "sufficient" often is employed) is, of course, determined by the state officials. Because of the dynamics of state politics, this determination is in large part shaped by what the richer districts judge to be "sufficient" for the poorer; and this, in turn, leads to the all-important question: "sufficient" for what purpose? If the necessary outcome of the education of a child of low income is believed to be the capability to enter into equal competition with the children of the rich, then the foundation level has to be extremely high. If the necessary outcome is, however, only the capacity to hold some sort of job— perhaps a job as an employee of the person who was born in a rich district— then the foundation could be very "minimal" indeed. The latter, in effect, has been the resolution of this question.

This is not the only factor that has fostered inequality, however. In order to win backing from the wealthy districts for an equalizing plan of any kind, no matter how inadequate, legislatures offer the rich districts an incentive. The incentive is to grant some portion of state aid to *all* school districts, regardless of their poverty or wealth. While less state aid is naturally expected to be given to the wealthy than the poor, the notion of giving something to all districts is believed to be a "sweetener" that will assure a broad enough electoral appeal to raise the necessary funds through statewide taxes. As we have seen in several states, however, these "sweeteners" have been so sweet that they have sometimes ended up by deepening the preexisting inequalities.

All this leads us to the point, acknowledged often by school-finance specialists but largely unknown to the public, that the various "formulas" conceived—and reconceived each time there is a legal challenge—to achieve some equity in public education have been almost total failures. In speaking of the equalizing formula in Massachusetts, for example, the historian Joel Weinberg makes this candid observation: "The state could actually have done as well if it had made no attempt to relate its support system to local ability [i.e., local wealth] and distributed its 'largesse' in a completely random fashion"—as, for example, "by the State Treasurer throwing checks from an airplane and allowing the vagaries of the elements to distribute them among the different communities." But even this description of a "random" distribution may be generous. If the wind had been distributing state money in New Jersey, for example, it might have left most disparities unchanged, but it would not likely have increased disparities consistently for 20 years, which is what the state formula has done without exception.

* * *

The contest between liberty and equity in education has, in the past 30 years, translated into the competing claims of local control, on the one hand, and state (or federal) intervention on the other. Liberty, school conservatives have argued, is diminished when the local powers of school districts have been sacrificed to centralized control. The opposition to desegregation in the South, for instance, was portrayed as local (states') rights as a sacred principle infringed upon by federal court decisions. The opposition to the drive for equal funding in a given state is now portrayed as local (district) rights in opposition to the powers of the state. While local control may be defended and supported on a number of important grounds, it is unmistakable that it has been historically advanced to counter equity demands; this is no less the case today.

As we have seen, the recent drive for "schools of excellence" (or "schools of choice") within a given district carries this historic conflict one step further. The evolution of a dual or tripartite system in a single district, as we have observed in New York City and Chicago, has counterposed the "freedom" of some parents to create some enclaves of selective excellence for their own children against the claims of equity made on behalf of all the children who have been excluded from these favored schools. At every level of debate, whether it is states' rights versus federal intervention, local district versus state control, or local school versus the district school board, the argument is made that more efficiency accrues from local governance and that equity concerns enforced by centralized authority inevitably lead to waste and often to corruption. Thus, "efficiency" joins "liberty" as a rhetorical rebuttal to the claims of equal opportunity and equal funding. "Local control" is the sacred principle in all these arguments.

Ironically, however, as we saw in the New Jersey situation, "local control" is readily ignored when state officials are dissatisfied with local leadership. A standard reaction of state governors, when faced with what they judge to be ineptitude at local levels, is to call for less—and not more—local governance by asking for a state takeover of the failing district. The liberty of local districts, thus, is willingly infringed on grounds of inefficiency. It is only when equal funding is the issue that the sanctity of district borders becomes absolute.

But this is not the only way in which the states subvert local control. They do it also by prescription of state guidelines that establish uniform curricula for all school districts, by certifying teachers on a statewide basis, and—in certain states like Texas, for example—by adopting textbooks on a statewide basis. During the past decade, there have also been conservative demands for national controls—a national teachers' examination, for example, and a national examination for all students—and we have been told that the commanding reason for these national controls is an alleged decline in national competitiveness against Japan and other foreign nations: a matter that transcends the needs or wishes of a local state or district. The national report that launched the recent "excellence" agenda bore the title "A Nation at Risk." It did not speak of East St. Louis, New York City, or Winnetka. Testing of pupils is, in a sense, already national. Reading scores are measured "at," "above," or else "below" a national norm. Children, whether in Little Rock, Great Neck, or the Bronx, compete with all American children when they take the college-entrance tests. Teacher preparation is already standardized across the nation. Textbooks, even before the states began adoptions, were homogenized for national consumption. With the advent of TV instruction via satellite, national education will be even more consistent and, in large part, uncontested.

Then too, of course, the flag in every classroom is the same. Children do not pledge allegiance to the flag of Nashua, New Hampshire, or to that of Fargo, North Dakota. The words of the pledge are very clear: They pledge allegiance to "one nation indivisible" and, in view of what we've seen of the implacable divisions that exist and are so skillfully maintained, there is some irony in this. The nation is hardly "indivisible" where education is concerned. It is at least two nations, quite methodically divided, with a fair amount of liberty for some, no liberty that justifies the word for many others, and justice—in the sense of playing on a nearly even field—only for the kids whose parents can afford to purchase it.

We may ask again, therefore, what "local governance" in fact implies in public education. The local board does not control the manufacture of the textbooks that its students use. It does not govern teacher preparation or certification. It does not govern political allegiance. It does not govern the exams that measure math and reading. It does not govern the exams that will determine or prohibit university admissions. It does not even really govern architecture. With few exceptions, elementary schools constructed prior to ten years ago are uniform boxes parted by a corridor with six rooms to the left, six to the right, and maybe 12 or 24 more classrooms in the same configuration on the floor or floors above.

What the local school board *does* determine is how clean those floors will be; how well the principal and teachers will be paid; whether the classrooms will be adequately heated; whether a class of 18 children will have 18 textbooks or whether, as in some cities we have seen, a class of 30 children will be asked to share the use of 15 books; whether the library is stocked with up-to-date encyclopedias, computers, novels, poetry, and dictionaries or whether it's used instead for makeshift classrooms, as in New York City; whether the auditorium is well equipped for real theatrical productions or whether, as in Irvington, it must be used instead to house 11 classes; whether the gymnasium is suitable for indoor games or whether it is used for reading classes; whether the playground is equipped with jungle gyms and has green lawns for soccer games and baseball or whether it is a bleak expanse of asphalt studded with cracked glass.

If the school board has sufficient money, it can exercise some real control over these matters. If it has very little money, it has almost no control; or rather it has only negative control. Its freedom is to choose which of the children's needs should be denied. This negative authority is all that local governance in fact implies in places such as Camden and Detroit. It may be masked by the apparent power to advance one kind of "teaching style," one "approach," or one "philosophy" over another. But, where the long-standing problems are more basic (adequate space, sufficient teachers for all classrooms, heating fuel, repair of missing windowpanes and leaking roofs and toilet doors), none of the pretended power over tone and style has much meaning. Style, in the long run, is determined by the caliber and character of teachers, and this is an area in which the poorest schools have no real choice at all.

Stephen Lefelt, the judge who tried the legal challenge in New Jersey, concluded from the months of testimony he had heard, that "local control," as it is presently interpreted to justify financial inequality, denies poor districts *all* control over the things that matter most in education. So, in this respect, the age-old conflict between liberty and equity is largely nonexistent in this setting. The wealthy districts have the first and seldom think about the second, while the very poor have neither.

* * *

In surveying the continuing tensions that exist between the claims of local liberty and those of equity in public education, historians have noted three distinguishable trends within this century. From the turn of the century until the 1950s, equity concerns were muted and the courts did not intrude much upon local governance. From 1954 (the year in which *Brown* v. *Board of Education* was decided) up to the early 1970s, equity concerns were more pronounced, although the emphasis was less on economic than on racial factors. From the early 1970s to the present, local control and the efficiency agenda have once again prevailed. The decisive date that scholars generally pinpoint as the start of the most recent era is March 21 of 1973: the day on which the high court overruled the judgment of a district court in Texas that had found the local funding scheme unconstitutional—and in this way halted in its tracks the drive to equalize the public education system through the federal courts.

We have referred to the Texas case above. It is time now to examine it in detail.

A class-action suit had been filed in 1968 by a resident of San Antonio named Demetrio Rodriguez and by other parents on behalf of their own children, who were students in the city's Edgewood district, which was very poor and 96 percent nonwhite. Although Edgewood residents paid one of the highest tax rates in the area, the district could raise only $37 for each pupil. Even with the "minimum" provided by the state, Edgewood ended up with only $231 for each child. Alamo Heights, meanwhile, the richest section of the city but incorporated as a separate schooling district, was able to raise $412 for each student from a lower tax rate and, because it also got state aid (and federal aid), was able to spend $543 on each pupil. Alamo Heights, then as now, was a predominantly white district.[1]

The difference between spending levels in these districts was, moreover, not the widest differential to be found in Texas. A sample of 110 Texas districts at the time showed that the ten wealthiest districts spent an average of three times as much per pupil as the four poorest districts, even with the funds provided under the state's "equalizing" formula.

Late in 1971, a three-judge federal district court in San Antonio held that Texas was in violation of the equal protection clause of the U.S. Constitution. "Any mild equalizing effects" from state aid, said the court, "do not benefit the poorest districts."

It is this decision which was then appealed to the Supreme Court. The majority opinion of the high court, which reversed the lower court's decision, noted that, in order to bring to bear "strict scrutiny" upon the case, it must first establish that there had been "absolute deprivation" of a "fundamental interest" of the Edgewood children. Justice Lewis Powell wrote that education is not "a fundamental interest" inasmuch as education "is not among the rights afforded explicit protection under our Federal Constitution." Nor, he wrote, did he believe that "absolute deprivation" was at

---

[1]Per-pupil expenditures presented here are not adjusted for inflation.

stake. "The argument here," he said, "is not that the children in districts having relatively low assessable property values are receiving no public education; rather, it is that they are receiving a poorer quality education than that available to children in districts having more assessable wealth." In cases where wealth is involved, he said, "the Equal Protection Clause does not require absolute equality. . . ."

Attorneys for Rodriguez and the other plaintiffs, Powell wrote, argue "that education is itself a fundamental personal right because it is essential to the exercise of First Amendment freedoms and to intelligent use of the right to vote. [They argue also] that the right to speak is meaningless unless the speaker is capable of articulating his thoughts intelligently and persuasively. . . . [A] similar line of reasoning is pursued with respect to the right to vote.

"Yet we have never presumed to possess either the ability or the authority to guarantee . . . the most *effective* speech or the most *informed* electoral choice." Even if it were conceded, he wrote, that "some identifiable quantum of education" is a prerequisite to exercise of speech and voting rights, "we have no indication . . . that the [Texas funding] system fails to provide each child with an opportunity to acquire the basic minimal skills necessary" to enjoy a "full participation in the political process."

This passage raised, of course, some elemental questions. The crucial question centered on the two words "minimal" and "necessary." In the words of O. Z. White of Trinity University in San Antonio: "We would always want to know by what criteria these terms had been defined. For example, any poor Hispanic child who could spell three-letter words, add and subtract, and memorize the names and dates of several presidents would have been viewed as having been endowed with 'minimal' skills in much of Texas 50 years ago. How do we update those standards? This cannot be done without the introduction of subjective notions as to what is needed in the present age. Again, when Powell speaks of what is 'necessary' to enjoy what he calls 'full participation' in the nation's politics, we would want to know exactly what he has in mind by 'full' participation. A lot of wealthy folks in Texas think the schools are doing a sufficiently good job if the kids of poor folks learn enough to cast a vote—just not enough to cast it in their own self-interest. They might think if fine if kids could write and speak—just not enough to speak in ways that make a dent in public policy. In economic terms, a lot of folks in Alamo Heights would think that Edgewood kids were educated fine if they had all the necessary skills to do their kitchen work and tend their lawns. How does Justice Powell settle on the level of effectiveness he has in mind by 'full participation'? The definition of this term is at the essence of democracy. If pegged too low, it guarantees perpetuation of disparities of power while still presenting an illusion of fair play. Justice Powell is a human being and his decision here is bound to be subjective. When he tells us that the Edgewood kids are getting all that's 'full' or 'necessary,' he is looking at the world from Alamo Heights. This, I guess, is only natural. If he had a home here, that is where he'd likely live.

"To a real degree, what is considered 'adequate' or 'necessary' or 'sufficient' for the poor in Texas is determined by the rich or relatively rich; it is decided in accord with their opinion of what children of the poor are fitted to become, and what their social role should be. This role has always been equated with their usefulness to us; and this consideration seems to be at stake in almost all reflections on the matter of the 'minimal' foundation offered to schoolchildren, which, in a sense, is only a metaphor for 'minimal' existence. When Justice Powell speaks of 'minimal' skills, such as the capacity to speak, but argues that we have no obligation to assure that it will be the 'most effective' speech, he is saying something that may seem quite reasonable and even commonplace, but it is something that would make more sense to wealthy folks in Alamo than to the folks in Edgewood."

Powell, however, placed great emphasis on his distinction between "basic minimal" skills, permitting some participation, and no skills at all, which might deny a person all participation; and he seemed to acquiesce in the idea that some inequity would always be inevitable. "No scheme of taxation . . . ," he wrote, "has yet been devised which is free of all discriminatory impact."

In any case, said Justice Powell in a passage that anticipates much of the debate now taking place, "experts are divided" on the question of the role of money in determining the quality of education. Indeed, he said, "one of the hottest sources of controversy concerns the extent to which there is a demonstrable correlation between educational expenditures and the quality of education."

In an additional comment that would stir considerable reaction among Texas residents, Powell said the district court had been in error in deciding that the Texas funding system had created what is called "a suspect class"— that is to say, an identifiable class of unjustly treated people. There had been no proof, he said, that a poor district such as Edgewood was necessarily inhabited mainly or entirely by poor people and, for this reason, it could not be said that poverty was the real cause of deprivation, even if there *was* real deprivation. There is, said Powell, "no basis . . . for assuming that the poorest people . . . are concentrated in the poorest districts." Nor, he added, is there "more than a random chance that racial minorities are concentrated" in such districts.

Justice Thurgood Marshall, in his long dissent, challenged the notion that an interest, to be seen as "fundamental," had to be "explicitly or implicitly guaranteed" within the Constitution. Thus, he said, although the right to procreate, the right to vote, the right to criminal appeal are not guaranteed, "these interests have nonetheless been afforded special judicial consideration . . . because they are, to some extent, interrelated with constitutional guarantees." Education, Marshall said, was also such a "related interest" because it "directly affects the ability of a child to exercise his First Amendment interests both as a source and as a receiver of information and ideas. . . . [Of] particular importance is the relationship between education and the political process."

Marshall also addressed the argument of Justice Powell that there was no demonstrated "correlation between poor people and poor districts." In support of this conclusion, Marshall wrote, the majority "offers absolutely no data—which it cannot on this record. . . ." Even, however, if it were true, he added, that *all* individuals within poor districts are not poor, the injury to those who *are* poor would not be diminished. Nor, he went on, can we ignore the extent to which state policies contribute to wealth differences. Government zoning regulations, for example, "have undoubtedly encouraged and rigidified national trends" that raise the property values in some districts while debasing them in others.

Marshall also challenged the distinction, made by Justice Powell, between "absolute" and "relative" degrees of deprivation, as well as Powell's judgment that the Texas funding scheme, because it had increased the funds available to local districts, now provided children of low income with the "minimum" required. "The Equal Protection Clause is not addressed to . . . minimal sufficiency," said Marshall, but to equity; and he cited the words of *Brown* to the effect that education, "where the State has undertaken to provide it, is a right which must be made available to all on equal terms."

On Justice Powell's observation that some experts questioned the connection between spending and the quality of education, Marshall answered almost with derision: "Even an unadorned restatement of this contention is sufficient to reveal its absurdity." It is, he said, "an inescapable fact that if one district has more funds available per pupil than another district," it "will have greater choice" in what it offers to its children. If, he added, "financing variations are so insignificant" to quality, "it is difficult to understand why a number of our country's wealthiest school districts," which, he noted, had no obligation to support the Texas funding scheme, had "nevertheless zealously pursued its cause before this Court"—a reference to the *amicus* briefs that Bloomfield Hills, Grosse Pointe, and Beverly Hills had introduced in their support of the defendants.

On the matter of local control, Marshall said this: "I need not now decide how I might ultimately strike the balance were we confronted with a situation where the State's sincere concern for local control inevitably produced educational inequality. For, on this record, it is apparent that the State's purported concern with local control is offered primarily as an excuse rather than as a justification for interdistrict inequality. . . . [If] Texas had a system truly dedicated to local fiscal control one would expect the quality of the educational opportunity provided in each district to vary with the decision of the voters in that district as to the level of sacrifice they wish to make for public education. In fact, the Texas scheme produces precisely the opposite result." Local districts, he observed, *cannot* "choose to have the best education in the State" because the education offered by a district is determined by its wealth—"a factor over which local voters [have] no control."

If, for the sake of local control, he concluded, "this court is to sustain interdistrict discrimination in the educational opportunity afforded Texas schoolchildren, it should require that the State present something more than the mere sham now before us. . . ."

Nonetheless, the court's majority turned down the suit and in a single word—"reversed"—Justice Powell ended any expectations that the children of the Edgewood schools would now be given the same opportunities as children in the richer districts. In tandem with the *Milliken* decision two years later, which exempted white suburban districts from participating in desegregation programs with the cities, the five-to-four decision in *Rodriguez* ushered in the ending of an era of progressive change and set the tone for the subsequent two decades which have left us with the present-day reality of separate and unequal public schools.

* * *

Unlike the U.S. Constitution, almost all state constitutions are specific in their references to public education. Since the decision in the Texas case, therefore, the parents of poor children have been centering their legal efforts on the various state courts, and there have been several local victories of sorts. In the absence of a sense of national imperative, however, and lacking the unusual authority of the Supreme Court, or the Congress, or the president, local victories have tended to deliver little satisfaction to poor districts. Even favorable decisions have led frequently to lengthy exercises of obstruction in the legislative process, eventuating often in a rearrangement of the old state "formula" that merely reconstructs the old inequities. . . .

* * *

Let us return, then, for a final time to San Antonio—not to the city of 1968, when the *Rodriguez* case was filed, but to the city of today. It is 23 years now since Demetrio Rodriguez went to court. Things have not changed very much in the poor neighborhoods of Texas. After 23 years of court disputes and numerous state formula revisions, per-pupil spending ranges from $2,000 in the poorest districts to some $19,000 in the richest. The minimum foundation that the state allows the children in the poorest districts—that is to say, the funds that guarantee the minimal basic education—is $1,477. Texas, moreover, is one of the ten states that gives no financial aid for school construction to the local districts.

In San Antonio, where Demetrio Rodriguez brought his suit against the state in 1968, the children of the poor still go to separate and unequal schools.

"The poor live by the water ditches here," said O. Z. White as we were driving through the crowded streets on a hot day in 1989. "The water is stagnant in the ditches now but, when the rains come, it will rise quite fast—it flows south into the San Antonio River. . . .

"The rich live on the high ground to the north. The higher ground in San Antonio is Monte Vista. But the very rich—the families with old money—live in the section known as Alamo Heights."

Alamo Heights, he told me, is a part of San Antonio. "It's enclosed by San Antonio but operated as a separate system. Dallas has a similar white enclave known as Highland Park, enclosed on four sides by the Dallas schools but operated as a separate district. We call these places 'parasite districts' since they give no tax support to the low-income sections.

"Alamo Heights is like a different world. The air is fresher. The grass is greener. The homes are larger. And the schools are richer."

Seven minutes from Alamo Heights, at the corner of Hamilton and Guadalupe, is Cassiano—a low-income housing project. Across the street from Cassiano, tiny buildings resembling shacks, some of them painted pastel shades, house many of the children who attend the Cooper Middle School, where 96 percent of children qualify by poverty for subsidized hot lunches and where 99.3 percent are of Hispanic origin. At Cooper, $2,800 is devoted to each child's education and 72 percent of children read below grade level. Class size ranges from 28 to 30. Average teacher salary is $27,000.

In Alamo Heights, where teachers average $31,000, virtually all students graduate and 88 percent of graduates go on to college. Classes are small and $4,600 is expended yearly on each child.

Fully 10 percent of children at the Cooper Middle School drop out in seventh and eighth grades. Of the survivors, 51 percent drop out of high school.

In 1988, Alamo Heights spent an average of $46 per pupil for its "gifted" program. The San Antonio Independent District, which includes the Cooper

Middle School, spent only $2 for each child for its "gifted" program. In the Edgewood District, only $1 was spent per child for the "gifted" program.

Although the property tax in Alamo Heights yielded $3,600 for each pupil, compared to $924 per pupil in the San Antonio district and only $128 in Edgewood, Alamo Heights also received a share of state and federal funds—almost $8,000 yearly for a class of 20 children. Most of this extra money, quite remarkably, came to Alamo Heights under the "equalizing" formula.

Some hope of change was briefly awakened in the fall of 1989 when front-page headlines in the *New York Times* and other leading papers heralded the news that the school funding system in the state of Texas had been found unconstitutional under state law. In a nine-to-zero decision, the state supreme court, citing what it termed "glaring disparities" in spending between wealthy and poor districts, said that the funding system was in violation of the passage in the Texas constitution that required Texas to maintain an education system for "the general diffusion of knowledge" in the state. The court's decision summarized some of the most extreme inequities: District spending ranged from $2,112 to $19,333. The richest district drew on property wealth of $14 million for each student while the poorest district drew on property worth only $20,000 for each student. The 100 wealthiest districts taxed their local property, on the average, at 47 cents for each $100 of assessed worth but spent over $7,000 for each student. The 100 poorest districts had an average tax rate more than 50 percent higher but spent less than $3,000 for each student. Speaking of the "evident intention" of "the framers of our [Texas] Constitution to provide equal educational advantages for all," the court said, "let there be no misunderstanding. A remedy is long overdue." There was no reference this time to the U.S. Constitution.

Stories related to the finding dominated the front page and the inside pages of the *San Antonio Express-News*. "Students cheered and superintendents hugged lawyers in an emotional display of joy," the paper said. In the library of John F. Kennedy High School in the Edgewood district, Demetrio Rodriguez put his hand on his chest to fight back tears as students, teachers, and community leaders cheered his vindication and their victory. As the crowd rose to applaud the 64-year-old man, Rodriguez spoke in halting words: "I cried this morning because this is something that has been in my heart. . . . My children will not benefit from it. . . . Twenty-one years is a long time to wait." Rodriguez, a sheet-metal worker at a nearby U.S. Air Force base, had lived in San Antonio for 30 years. "My children got caught in this web. It wasn't fair . . . but there is nothing I can do about it now." The problem, he said to a reporter, should have been corrected 20 years before.

In an editorial that day, the paper said that what the court had found "should have been obvious to anyone" from the beginning.

The Edgewood superintendent, who had been the leader in the latest round of litigation, spoke of the attacks that he had weathered in the course of years. He had been a high school principal in 1974 when the original *Rodriguez* finding had been overruled by the U.S. Supreme Court. "It was like somebody had died . . . ," he said. In the years since, he had gone repeatedly to the state capitol in Austin, where he was met by promises from legislators that they would "take care of it," he said. "More and more task forces studied education," he recalled, while another generation of poor children entered and passed through the Edgewood schools. At length, in 1984, Edgewood joined with seven other poor school districts and brought suit against the state and 48 rich districts. The suit was seen by some as a class war, he said. He was accused of wanting to take away the "swimming pools," the "tennis courts" and "carpeted football fields" from wealthy districts. "They'd say I was being Robin Hood . . . ," he said. The district, he assured reporters, was not looking to be given swimming pools. All the district wanted was "to get us up to the average. . . ." Children in Edgewood, he said, had suffered most from being forced to lower their horizons. "Some of the students don't . . . know how to dream. . . . They have accepted [this]," he said, as if it were "the way [that] things should be."

The governor of Texas, who had opposed the suit and often stated he was confident the court would find against the claims of the poor districts, told the press of his relief that the Supreme Court hadn't mandated an immediate solution. "I am extremely pleased," he said, "that this is back in the hands of the legislature. . . ."

The chairman of the Texas Railroad Commission, who was running for governor as a Republican, voiced his concern that people might use this court decision to impose an income tax on Texas.

The U.S. Secretary of Education, Lauro Cavazos, came to Texas and provided fuel for those who sought to slow down implementation of the court's decision. "First," he said, "money is clearly not the answer. . . ." Furthermore, he said, "there is a wide body of research" to support that view and, he added, in apparent disregard of the conclusions of the court, "the evidence here in Texas corroborates those findings." He then went on to castigate Hispanic parents for not caring about education.

Meanwhile, the press observed that what it termed "the demagoguery" of "anti-tax vigilantes" posed another threat. "Legions of tax protestors" had been mobilized, a local columnist said. It was believed that they would do their best to slow down or obstruct the needed legislative action. Others focused on the likelihood that wealthy people would begin to look outside the public schools. There were already several famous private schools in Texas. Might there soon be several more?

Predictions were heard that, after legislative red tape and political delays, a revised state formula would be developed. The court would look it over, voice some doubts, but finally accept it as a reasonable effort. A few years later, O. Z. White surmised, "we'll discover that they didn't do the formula 'exactly' right. Edgewood probably will be okay. It's been in the news so it will have to be a showpiece of improvement. What of the children in those other districts where the poor Hispanic families have no leaders, where there isn't a Rodriguez? Those are the ones where children will continue to be cheated and ignored.

"There's lots of celebration now because of the decision. Wait a year. Watch and see the clever things that people will contrive. You can bet that lots of folks are thinking hard about this 'Robin Hood' idea. Up in Alamo Heights I would expect that folks have plenty on their minds tonight. I don't blame them. If I lived in Alamo Heights, I guess I'd be doing some hard thinking too. . . .

"We're not talking about some abstraction here. These things are serious. If all of these poor kids in Cassiano get to go to real good schools—I mean, so they're educated *well* and so they're smart enough to go to colleges and universities—you have got to ask who there will be to trim the lawns and scrub the kitchen floors in Alamo Heights. Look at the lights up there. The air is nice and clean when you're up high like that in Texas. It's a different world from Guadalupe. Let me tell you something. Folks can hope, and folks can try, and folks can dream. But those two worlds are never going to meet. Not in my life. Not in yours. Not while any of these little kids in Cassiano are alive. Maybe it will happen someday. I'm not going to be counting."

Around us in the streets, the voices of children filled the heavy air. Teenage girls stood in the doorways of the pastel houses along Guadalupe while the younger children played out in the street. Mexican music drifted from the houses and, as evening came to San Antonio, the heat subsided and there was a sense of order and serenity as people went about their evening tasks, the task of children being to play and of their older sisters to go in and help their mothers to make dinner.

"Everything is acceptance," said O. Z. "People get used to what they have. They figure it's the way it's supposed to be and they don't think it's going to change. All those court decisions are so far away. And Alamo Heights seems far away, so people don't compare. And that's important. If you don't know what you're missing, you're not going to get angry. How can you desire what you cannot dream of?" But this may not really be the case; for many of the women in this neighborhood do get to see the richer neighborhoods because they work in wealthy people's homes.

According to the principal of Cooper Middle School, crack addiction isn't a real problem yet for younger children. "Here it's mainly chemical inhalants. It can blind you, I've been told. They get it mainly out of spray-paint cans and liquid paper," he says wearily.

But a social worker tells me there's a crack house right on Guadalupe. "There is a lot of prostitution here as well," she says. "Many of these teen-age girls helping their mothers to make supper will be pregnant soon. They will have children and leave school. Many will then begin the daily trip to Alamo Heights. They'll do domestic work and bring up other people's kids. By the time they know what they were missing, it's too late."

It is now the spring of 1991. A year and a half has passed since these events took place. The Texas legislature has at last, and with much rhetoric about what many legislators call "a Robin Hood approach," enacted a new equalizing formula but left a number of loop-holes that perpetuate the fiscal edge enjoyed by very wealthy districts. Plaintiffs' attorneys are guarded in their expectations. If the experience of other states holds true in Texas, there will be a series of delays and challenges and, doubtless, further litigation. The implementation of the newest plan, in any case, will not be immediate. Twenty-three years after Demetrio Rodriguez went to court, the children of the poorest people in the state of Texas still are waiting for an equal chance at education. . . .

Notes

85 to 87 HISTORY AND WORKINGS OF SCHOOL FINANCE SYSTEM: Arthur E. Wise, *Rich Schools, Poor Schools* (Chicago: University of Chicago Press, 1967); Arthur E. Wise and Tamar Gendler in *The College Board Review*, Spring 1989; G. Alan Hickrod, Illinois State University, Normal, Illinois (conversations with author, 1991); James Gordon Ward, "An Inquiry Into the Normative Foundations of American Public School Finance," *Journal of Education Finance*, Spring 1987.

88, 89 A VIRTUALLY NATIONAL SCHOOL SYSTEM: "A National Curriculum," Quality Education for Minorities Network, Background, Issues, and Action Paper Note, vol. 1, no. 3 (March 7, 1991); *Boston Globe*, April 17, 1989.

90 CLASS ACTION SUIT IN TEXAS: Thomas J. Flygare, "School Finance a Decade After *Rodriguez*," *Phi Delta Kappan*, March 1983.

90 to 94 U.S. SUPREME COURT DECISION: *San Antonio Independent School District v. Rodriguez*, March 21, 1973, in "Cases Adjudged in the Supreme Court at October Term, 1972," United States Reports, vol. 411 (Washington, D.C.: U.S. Government Printing Office, 1974). The opinion of Justice Lewis Powell begins on page 4. The opinion of Justice Thurgood Marshall begins on page 70. Also see Richard Kluger, *Simple Justice* (New York: Vintage Books, 1977).

95 RANGE OF FUNDING IN TEXAS: *West's Education Law Reporter,* December 7, 1989.

STATE GUARANTEES AN AVERAGE MINIMUM OF $1,477: *San Antonio Express-News,* October 8, 1989.

95ff. O. Z. WHITE CITED: Author's interviews with Professor White, of Trinity University, 1989 and 1990.

VISIT TO COOPER MIDDLE SCHOOL: April 1989.

95, 96 DATA ON COOPER MIDDLE SCHOOL, SAN ANTONIO INDEPENDENT SCHOOL DISTRICT, EDGEWOOD DISTRICT, AND ALAMO HEIGHTS: Texas Education Agency, "1987–1988 PEIMS Fall Collection of Financial Budgeted Data" (Austin: 1988); additional data provided by principal of Cooper Middle School, school departments of Alamo Heights and San Antonio Independent School Districts, Terry Hitchcock of the Texas Education Agency, O. Z. White, and social workers in Cassiano neighborhood, author's interviews, 1989 and 1991.

96 RULING OF TEXAS SUPREME COURT: "*Edgewood* v. *Kirby,*" *West's Education Law Reporter,* December 7, 1989; *New York Times,* October 3, 1989.

96, 97 REACTION OF DEMETRIO RODRIGUEZ AND OTHERS IN SAN ANTONIO: *San Antonio Express-News,* October 3, 8, and 9, 1989.

97 REACTION OF TEXAS POLITICIANS AND COMMENTS OF U.S. EDUCATION SECRETARY: *New York Times,* October 3, 1989, and March 11, 1990; *San Antonio Express-News,* October 3, 1989.

99 NEW FORMULA, FURTHER DELAY: *San Antonio Express-News,* October 2, 1990, February 8 and 9 and March 1, 1991; *Dallas Morning News,* April 12, 1991.

7

School Inequality*

State Courts

editor's introduction:

How a Single State Has Dealt With School Inequalities. The case study in this selection follows logically from the preceding selection, which covered the landmark federal case (of San Antonio Independent School District v. Rodriguez, March 21, 1973), adjudicated by the U.S. Supreme Court.

The aftermath of the federal court case has been decades of court suits in many different states, ultimately adjudicated by state supreme courts. Whereas the federal (U.S.) Constitution says little about the role of government in providing education services, most state constitutions have explicit clauses proclaiming that a state shall provide public education and, furthermore, that such education be "efficient," "thorough," or "adequate" in some way. These words have been sufficient for plaintiffs to demonstrate that inequitable financial arrangements have led to disparities in educating students from low-income families and neighborhoods.

The case in the present selection covers events in the state of New Jersey, showing how favorable court rulings only slowly led to desired actions. The ultimate actions, however, in New Jersey as in other states, have assumed the form of broad educational reform, not just the redistribution of resources. In this manner, the original concern over inequality of financial resources can lead to systemwide improvements in the public schools throughout a state—aimed at producing local school systems that are "efficient," "thorough," or "adequate." The inequalities therefore

---

*Anyon, Jean. (1997). "Class, Race, Taxes, and State Educational Reform, 1970–1997." In *Ghetto Schooling: A Political Economy of Urban Educational Reform* (pp. 134–148). New York: Teachers College Press.

address educational opportunities, not just financial resources, the issue remaining highly salient to this very day.

Relevance of Case Studies: Tracing Events Over an Extended Period of Time. This selection shows how a single case study can cover the unfolding of events over a rather extended period of time (the 24 years from 1973 to 1997)—another distinctive feature of the case study method. The extended period is relevant because of the lengthy history of the case study—a single state's repeated (and directly related) court rulings on the equality of school finance.

The extended period of time shows that case studies need not be limited to the micro-study of highly focused, narrow, or time-limited topics. Some of the most important topics in education, such as school finance, may evolve only over a lengthy period of time in a particular setting. If you attempt such a case study, you are likely to rely heavily on the analysis of documents, but you also can incorporate interviews of key persons to give your case study a livelier flavor.

New Jersey School Finance and Related State Educational Reforms

In New Jersey as elsewhere, courts played a significant role in educational reform as school finance struggles unfolded in the majority of states. The first wave of cases grounded the argument for equal funding for all children in the equal protection clause of the U.S. Constitution. Thus, in 1971, the California state courts in *Serranno v. Priest* ruled that the unequal funding of school districts in California was unconstitutional because "the quality of education may not be a function of wealth other than the wealth of the state as a whole" (Tractenberg 1974, 312). Then in 1973 the U.S. Supreme Court in *San Antonio Independent School District v. Rodriguez* halted this avenue to school finance reform, ruling that education was not a "fundamental right" of the U.S. Constitution, and that school finance law relying on districts with disparate tax capacity was not unconstitutional (313).

Challenges to unequal funding in the years following *Rodriguez* were based on clauses that had been inserted in state constitutions during nineteenth-century constitutional conventions, when states were creating and consolidating their systems of public schools (Odden and Picus 1992, 29). Such clauses called for "efficient," "thorough and efficient," "thorough and uniform," "general and uniform," "complete and uniform," "free quality," "adequate," or "general, suitable and efficient," education throughout a state (Odden and Picus 1992, 38–45; Tractenberg 1974). As I mentioned earlier, the clause in the New Jersey Constitution, that the state must afford each child a "thorough and efficient education," was added in 1875 (New Jersey Constitution, article VIII, section 4, paragraph 1).

Robinson v. Cahill. There have been nine major court decisions related to school funding in New Jersey:

Robinson v. Cahill, 62 N.J. 473 (1973)

Robinson v. Cahill, 63 N.J. 196 (1973)

Robinson v. Cahill, 69 N.J. 133 (1975)

Robinson v. Cahill, 69 N.J. 449 (1976)

Robinson v. Cahill, 70 N.J. 155 (1976)

Abbott v. Burke, 100 N.J. 269 (1985)

Abbott v. Burke, 119 N.J. 287 (1990)

Abbott v. Burke, 135 N.J. 444 (1994)

Abbott v. Burke, M622, Slip Op., May 14, 1997

The first, in 1973, declared that New Jersey's system of financing public schools was unconstitutional because it violated the state constitutional mandate for a thorough and efficient education by basing school funding on local taxation (*Robinson v. Cahill* 1973). The court ruled that the system led to "great disparity in dollar input per pupil" between urban and suburban districts, yielding an inverse relation between property wealth and tax rates, and did not provide urban students an equal opportunity for a thorough and efficient education as required by the state constitution.

Emphasizing the importance of sufficient educational resources to urban districts, the supreme court required the state legislature to devise a "constitutionally sufficient" system of financing education (Tractenberg 1974, 329). Moreover, the court argued that the state constitution places ultimate financial responsibility on the state for a thorough and efficient education system. "If local government fails to provide [a thorough and efficient education] the state government must compel it to act, and if the local government cannot carry the burden, the State must itself meet its continuing obligation" (*Robinson v. Cahill* 1973, 513).

The New Jersey Supreme Court thus first defined unconstitutionality in dollar terms. Over the next 3 years, however, as further court decisions attempted to prod the New Jersey legislature to some action to meet the mandate, the court included in its purview not only funding disparity, but disparity in "substantive educational content." In a 1976 decision, the court required that "each pupil shall be offered an equal opportunity to receive an education of such excellence as will meet the constitutional standard" for a thorough and efficient education that would, as the constitution requires, equip students for their "role as a citizen and as a competitor in the labor market" (*Robinson v. Cahill* 1976, 459–460, in *Abbott v. Burke* 1990, 309).

In response to the court mandate, the state legislature passed the Public School Elementary and Secondary Education Act (PSEA) in 1975, but did not fund it. A year later the legislature still had not created a funding scheme, and to prod state action, the court closed the public schools to 100,000 summer school students on July 1. Legislators responded by passing the state's first income tax in several weeks. The proceeds would be dedicated to education, and would provide "equalization aid" to districts in carrying out the PSEA.

However, the act retained, with minor variations, the funding provisions from the system which the supreme court had found unconstitutional in 1973. Educational funding would still depend on local taxing and budgeting decisions and the abilities of districts to increase taxes, supplemented with a limited amount of equalization aid (*Abbott v. Burke* 1990, 288, 291). "Minimum aid" was provided to all districts, including the middle-class and the wealthy. The result was that districts containing more than three-fourths of New Jersey's students would receive education aid (Goertz 1991, 2).

In this legislative response to the supreme court mandate for a thorough and efficient education, equalization between districts would be attained not by an infusion of funds into poor urban districts, but by placing caps on local school district expenditures, for example, in the more affluent communities, by managerial efficiency, and, importantly, by requiring a minimum curriculum of basic skills for all students (*Abbott v. Burke* 1990; Centolanza 1986, 524). A basic skills curriculum focused instruction on rote, skill-drill exercises which typically emphasized cognitive skills of recognition and recall. Such a curriculum, utilizing primarily workbooks and worksheets, was relatively inexpensive, and would not require that the state invest in computers, science equipment, or other curriculum materials for urban schools. During the next two decades, the cities, which were closely monitored by the state, did offer a basic skills curriculum to students, while the suburbs continued to offer sophisticated curriculum programs and a range of courses (*Abbott v. Burke* 1990, 364; Centolanza 1986, 540–542; Firestone, Goertz, and Natriello 1997).

In 1976, state education commissioner Fred Burke expressed what seemed to be one factor in the reasoning behind the state's view that "pouring money" into the city districts was futile. He stated, "Urban children, even after years of remediation, will not be able to perform in school as well as their suburban counterparts. . . . We are just being honest" (*Star Ledger* April 2, 1976). (As everyone in New Jersey knew, "urban students" was a euphemism for "minority students.")

The state also argued to those—such as the New Jersey Education Association—who criticized its attempt to equalize education in terms of basic skills rather than an infusion of funds that

> the education [basic skills] currently offered in these poorer urban districts is tailored to the students' present need . . . these students simply cannot now benefit from the kind of vastly superior course offerings found in the richer districts. (*Abbott v. Burke* 1990, 364)

Basic skills instruction was also seen by the legislature as most amenable to statewide testing for the purpose of producing readily demonstrable results to the public (Centolanza 1986, 554). In line with a national trend toward minimum competency testing (there were such programs in 33 states by 1978), legislators' desire for standards would be satisfied by state minimum basic skills tests; districts in which students were not proficient would receive compensatory (remedial) funding. Until 1993, when a test requiring more complex cognitive skills was instituted, the state had in place a minimum competency, basic skills testing program (Firestone, Goertz, and Natriello 1997).

According to S. David Brandt, a member of the state board of education and former local school board member,

> Standards established under the basic skills compensatory ed program had nothing to do with educational quality. Instead these standards were set according to a reasonable estimate of how much state money would be available to provide remedial instruction to those students who failed the test, and not on educational assessment, theory or practice. Attaining a passing score on the test did not necessarily mean that the students had reached any reasonable level of educational achievement. The passing scores were based on the assumption that 25 percent would fail statewide and there would be adequate state money to back remedial efforts at the local level. (Centolanza 1986, 556–557)

An additional feature of the state remedial program was that it withdrew funds, and therefore, in cities, money for teaching jobs, if district standardized scores improved. This strategy, not lost on educators whose jobs depended on compensatory funds, penalized success and rewarded failure. On March 5, 1980, New Jersey became the first state to classify its schools according to their compliance with law and code and their students' success in mastering basic skills. State board president Paul Ricci declared, "Public education can regain its reputation and recapture public trust" (Centolanza 1986, 426).

The results of minimum basic skills testing in the late 1970s and early 1980s, however, revealed the failure of the 1975 act to provide a thorough and efficient education in the state's urban districts. In many cities, the majority of students failed the minimum basic skills tests. In Camden in 1978, for example, two-thirds failed reading in sixth and ninth grade and math in third. In Newark, more than 75% failed the sixth-grade reading test and 75% failed the sixth-grade math test. More than 70% of ninth-graders in Orange failed the ninth-grade reading test and about half of youngsters in Irvington could not pass the sixth-grade reading tests (554–555).

Moreover, financial disparities between districts had increased in the years of the PSEA. Prior to the 1975 act, in 1971–72, the spread between the lowest and the highest spending districts was $700 to $1,500 per pupil, a difference of $800. By 1984–85, districts at the 5th percentile spent $2,687, while districts at the 95th percentile spent $4,755, a disparity of $2,068 per pupil. When adjusted for inflation, in 1975 dollars the disparity grew from $898 per pupil in 1975–76 to $1,135 per pupil in 1984–85. The result was that a group of richer districts with 189,484 students spent 40% more per pupil than a group of poorer districts with 355,612 students (*Abbott v. Burke* 1990, 334). According to Goertz,

> More than $31 million *per pupil* in property wealth separated the poorest and wealthiest school districts in 1988. The 10:1 difference in per pupil property wealth between Trenton ($111,475) and Princeton ($1,128,051) was more typical of the disparities in property wealth across the state. (1992, 7)

The differences in property tax base were a major cause of education expenditure disparities, because of the heavy reliance on the local property tax to finance education across the state, despite the *Robinson v. Cahill* 1973 decision which ruled this method unconstitutional (*Abbott v. Burke* 1990, 477). Excluding federal aid and pension contributions, local revenues accounted for 60.4% of all educational expenditures in the state, while state aid accounted for 39.6% in fiscal year 1989 (Goertz 1992, 7). Despite the act's 1975 mandate that districts increase their school tax to make needed increased funds available, during the 10-year period of PSEA, "no substantially increased local funding through school tax increases" occurred (*Abbott v. Burke* 1990, 357). Moreover, the state legislature fully funded the education aid provisions of the PSEA in only 2 of the 10 years between 1975 and 1985 (1977–78 and 1978–79) (324).

Abbott v. Burke. In response to increasing inequalities, a second lawsuit was filed in 1981, by the Newark-based Education Law Center, on behalf of students in New Jersey's urban poor districts. The trial record was completed in 1987, and the state supreme court decision handed down in 1990 (*Abbott v. Burke* 1990).

During the trial, state documents were presented in defense of recent legislative approaches to school funding and educational reform. These documents argued that (as reported in the *Abbott v. Burke* 1990 decision):

1. Large infusions of state aid to the poorer urban districts were not necessary because "districts had unlimited power to raise funds to satisfy their constitutional obligation; and the state could take over the operation of any district that fails" (299).

2. There is not a strong relationship between property wealth and per pupil expenditures (297). The difference in education between poorer urban and affluent districts is not caused by amount of expenditures per pupil, but by district mismanagement (323). Funding should not be supplied to poorer urban districts, because it may be mismanaged and wasted (295). Beyond a minimum amount, "money is not a critical factor in the quality of education in the first place" (376). Further, the belief that greater funding was needed to assure a thorough and efficient education across the state "enthrones naiveté" (299).

3. Course offerings, experience and education of staff, and pupil per staff ratio cannot be considered reliable indicators of the quality of education (358). Rather, "thorough and efficient" should be measured against state education standards and mandates, which defined a thorough and efficient education in terms of minimum basic skills levels that all students in the state must meet (359).

The supreme court justices, however, disagreed. They compared education in the poorer urban districts with the educational finances, program offerings, and student achievement in affluent areas (*Abbott v. Burke* 1990, 289). They noted that the 1975 act "relies so heavily on a local property base that [in the cities] is already over-taxed to exhaustion" (357). They ruled the system of financing and achieving a thorough and efficient education unconstitutional as applied to poorer urban districts in New Jersey (288). The justices found that, as a result of the disparities in finances and educational programming, "students [in the poorer urban districts] simply cannot possibly enter the same market or the same society as their peers educated in wealthier districts" (368).

In this groundbreaking 1990 decision, the supreme court declared that the 1975 act had to be amended to ensure funding of education in poorer districts at the level of property-rich districts (i.e., financial parity had to be achieved); funding could not be allowed to depend on the ability of local school districts to tax, but had to be guaranteed by the state; and the level of funding of the poorer city districts by the state had to include sufficient additional funds to provide for the extraordinary educational needs of disadvantaged students (288). The state was required to assess what those needs were and provide programs to meet them. Other aid provisions of the 1975 act, "which had the sole function of enabling richer school districts to spend even more money, thereby increasing the disparity," were declared unconstitutional (291).

The supreme court made several additional points. Calling the cities social and economic "disaster areas," the court declared that "municipal overburden," the excessive tax levy that some municipalities had to impose to meet governmental needs other than education, effectively prevented districts from raising substantially more money for education despite statutory provisions increasing the districts' legal ability to raise taxes (289, 356).

Stating that the poorer urban districts were essentially "basic skills districts," while more affluent districts provided educational opportunities in areas such as exposure to computers, laboratory science, sophisticated math and science courses, foreign language programs, and art and music courses, the court declared that the constitutional requirement of a thorough and efficient education encompasses more than instruction in the basic communications and computational skills, but also requires that "students be given at least a modicum of variety and a chance to excel" (*Abbott v. Burke* 1990, 290). The court noted that it would not tell urban poor students that "they will get the minimum, because that is all they can benefit from" (375). Moreover, remarked the court,

> If . . . "basic skills" were sufficient to achieve [the mandate of a thorough and efficient education] there would be little short of a revolution in the suburban districts when parents learned that basic skills is what their children were entitled to, limited to, and no more. (364)

The court added that if as the state argued sophisticated curriculum courses are not integral to a thorough and efficient education, "why do the richer districts invariably offer them?" (364). The justices also stated that

> we have decided this case on the premise that the children of poorer urban districts are as capable as all others; that their deficiencies stem from their socioeconomic status; and that through effective education and changes in that socioeconomic status, they can perform as well as others. Our constitutional

mandate does not allow us to consign poorer children permanently to an inferior education on the theory that they cannot afford a better one or that they would not benefit from it. (340)

The court addressed the issue of district mismanagement. They said that the record supported the conclusion that although, as the state contended, there may have been "mismanagement, politics and worse" in urban districts, mismanagement was not a significant factor in the general failure to achieve a constitutionally required thorough and efficient education for students in poorer urban districts; and of great significance, the justices declared that "no amount of administrative skill" would redress the deficiency and disparity caused by insufficient funding (381; 290–291).

The material presented in historical chapters of this book suggests that there may have been incompetence, politics, "and worse" in urban districts—although one cannot conclude that this occurred only in urban districts. However, this history also provides a basis for understanding the politics and corruption as a reaction by local leaders to the lack of political access and economic resources experienced by urban governments in America for many decades. Just as poverty and lack of recourse make a fertile ground for youthful criminal activity in inner city neighborhoods, so do they in city and school governing circles. If and when adequate political and economic resources become available in cities—which to date they have not—the material need for money grabbing and power mongering will be weakened, and corruption may play a much smaller role.

The supreme court justices concluded their 1990 opinion by reminding citizens that New Jersey localities spend more dollars per student for education than those of almost any other state. They continued,

> The dilemma is that while we spend so much, there is absolutely no question that we are failing to provide the students in the poorer urban districts with the kind of an education that anyone could call thorough and efficient. . . . The need is great and the money is there. New Jersey is the second richest state in the nation. (394)

Events of the following few years proved that the financial capacity did indeed exist, but the state's overwhelmingly suburban voters did not want to spend money on the urban poor.

In anticipation of the 1990 *Abbott v. Burke* decision, which was widely expected to mandate significant increases in funding for urban education, the Democratic state assembly on June 18, 1990, approved a $2.8 billion tax package which doubled the highest income tax rate (for the top 20% of tax payers), raised the sales tax from 6 to 7%, and extended it to paper goods and luxury items (Goertz 1992, 12). This package came to be called the Quality Education Act (or QEA). The act increased state education aid by $1.15 billion. It guaranteed low-income districts a foundational level of spending for each child that approached parity with the wealthier districts.

In addition, 30 of the poorest urban "special needs" districts were identified by the legislature, and the foundation amount increased by 5% to these districts. The foundation level of support statewide was irrespective of local tax capacity, as long as each district raised its "fair share." The act also phased out general aid to wealthy districts and capped increases in district expenditures. To make more money available for education aid, the legislature made teacher pension and social security costs the responsibility of local districts, instead of the state (Goertz 1992, 12; Salmore and Salmore 1993, 275).

New Jersey homeowners had seen their property taxes almost double in the 1980s because of many state mandates that were either not funded by the legislature, such as recycling; or underfunded, such as the statute for school aid. The QEA would increase state taxes further. For example, in wealthier Bergen County, state income taxes could double to pay for the QEA. Three-fourths of the new school aid, disproportionally financed by Bergen residents, would go to the special needs districts, and to five cities in the south with lower than average incomes and property values. The Republican senate minority leader, John Dorsey of Morris County, another hard-hit wealthy northern county, enraged advocates of urban education but said aloud what many others were thinking when he declared that QEA and *Abbott* required "working-class people in middle-class communities who drive around in Fords to buy Mercedes for people in the poorest cities because they don't have cars." A Monmouth County Democratic assemblyman called the cuts to his wealthy district the act of "almost a socialist state," and proclaimed, "This is New Jersey, this is not Moscow in 1950" (Salmore and Salmore 1993, 252, 276).

Taxpayer opposition to the QEA tax increases was swift. A popular revolt swamped legislators before the act could go into effect, as taxpayers rallied at the state capitol in protest (Goertz 1992, 13). With the entire legislature up for reelection the next year, legislators revised the QEA (to QEA II) in March 1991, before it would take effect in September. As a result of the revision, in many districts—even the poorest—revised budget caps meant that new money covered little more than contractual salary increases and higher insurance costs. QEA II reduced the increase in state education aid from $1.15 billion to $800 million; cut funds to support the education of students from low-income households; guaranteed that no district would get less state aid than it had received the previous year; restricted the annual growth of state aid to education; and set more restrictive caps on districts' total budgets (Firestone, Goertz, and Natriello 1997).

No actual funding had taken place under QEA, because of the timing of the revisions. Out of the $800 million increase in total state aid for 1991–92 (the first year of funding under QEA II), the 30 poorest urban districts received a net increase of $44 million for their regular education programs; however, this amount represented only 3% of their aggregate 1990–91 regular education budgets (Firestone, Goertz, and Natriello 1994, 28).

Firestone, Goertz, and Natriello studied the use of QEA II money by 12 wealthy, middle-class, and poor urban districts. They report that all six urban poor districts that they assessed made good use of the increased funds from QEA II. The districts spent the money primarily for three purposes: "catch up expenditures" (new buildings, extra teachers, more supplies), social support programs for disadvantaged students, and expenditures to improve the quality of instruction, for example, staff development (1997; see also Firestone, Goertz, and Natriello 1994, 21).

However, the funding increases were relatively small. Indeed, in Camden, often cited as the state's educational worst case, the QEA II reduced new school aid from $50 million to $24.8 million. In Newark, when I asked how QEA II had affected the Newark school budget, a longtime executive at the Newark Board of Education told me that the additional funds were

> not really enough to do much with. . . . They [the state] made a big deal of it, but it was a game. Our costs went up two million, say, and we got two million from the QEA [II]. We used it for things we thought we were going to have to cut. We moved it around where we needed it. Some salary increases. We did go from several to over 100 all-day kindergartens, though, with QEA money. (Interview, July 10, 1996)

According to the director of school finance in the state education department, the net effect of the revisions of the original QEA was "an outflow of aid from the urban districts . . . to the middle- and upper-wealth districts," as compared with the QEA's original provisions (Salmore and Salmore 1993, 278).

Continuing Financial and Educational Disparity

The Quality Education Act II was found to be unconstitutional by the state supreme court in 1994, based on its failure to assure parity of regular education expenditures between the special needs districts and the more affluent districts for the regular education program, and its failure to provide for the additional, special needs of disadvantaged children. Reiterating the opinions of *Robinson v. Cahill* decisions and *Abbott v. Burke* in 1990, the court declared in 1994, "It is the state and only the state that is responsible for the present educational disparity, and only the state can correct it" (*Abbott v. Burke* 1994, 15).

A verdict on the results of almost two decades of school finance litigation and legislative educational reform aimed at the poorer urban districts was delivered by the state itself in 1989 and 1991 when it decertified schools in two large cities and installed state personnel to administer them. Newark became the third district "taken over," on July 12, 1995.

To determine whether or not to take over the Newark school system, the state in 1993–94 carried out a "comprehensive compliance investigation" (CCI) of the district. External consultants and state evaluators assessed finance, governance and management, education programs, and facilities. Teams of evaluators made unannounced site visits at 50 of the 82 Newark schools. The five-volume report was introduced by a summary, excerpted here.

> Children in the Newark public schools . . . endure degrading school environ-
> ments that virtually ensure academic failure. . . . [In many classrooms] there is
> nothing. . . . Science laboratories lack basic equipment.
>
> [Students] in the Newark public schools, with rare exceptions, sit dutifully
> in rows, filling in the blanks in workbooks with answers to items having to do
> with isolated skills, or listening to a teacher deliver facts or talk about skills,
> divorced from meaningful context. . . . In elementary classrooms the predomi-
> nant instructional activity observed was the filling in of blanks in workbooks,
> skill sheets or worksheets. . . . When direct instruction took place, it involved
> a teacher asking fact-type questions and students giving answers.
>
> Students in high school classes fared no better. For example, high school
> English classes, with few exceptions, focused on the learning of facts about lit-
> erature rather than participation in activities designed to enable students to
> experience literature. Seldom in any class observed, no matter what the grade
> level or subject, were students being taught how to write, how to read for
> understanding, how to solve problems, or how to think critically.
>
> Physical conditions in most of the schools observed by the comprehensive
> compliance team reveal . . . neglect and dereliction of duty. Holes in floors and
> walls; dirty classrooms with blackboards so worn as to be unusable; filthy
> lavatories without toilet paper, soap or paper towels; inoperable water foun-
> tains; . . . and foul-smelling effluent running from a school into the street,
> speak of disregard for the dignity, safety, basic comfort and sense of well-being
> of students and teachers.
>
> In many schools an air of unreality pervades. Attendance taking is erratic,
> often dependent on the whim of individual teachers. Clocks are wildly

inaccurate; classroom doors are unmarked or wrongly marked; the few lavatories equipped with appropriate supplies are barred to students and for teacher use only; fire exit doors are chained; fire doors marked "Keep Closed" are open, but closed is no better than open, because the glass panels are missing.

A virtual army of supervisors, administrators, and coordinators holds all this in place, passing various . . . forms from one layer of bureaucracy to the next, while schools go unpainted for as long as 14 years, and in classroom after classroom whole banks of lights are without fluorescent tubes or light shields.

These conditions tell of shocking neglect. Equally shocking, however, from the team's perspective, is the lack of indignation on the part of staff. One teacher interviewed explained it this way: "After a while," she said, looking around, "you lower your expectations." (New Jersey State Department of Education 1994, 43–44, 66)

Arguing that conditions such as these were a result of continued unconstitutional funding disparities, and in the absence of a state plan responding to the 1994 *Abbott v. Burke* reiteration of its 1990 mandate, the Education Law Center returned to court in April of 1996. Under the 1994 *Abbott* decision, the state had been given 3 school years (1995–98) to eliminate the 16.05% relative disparity in regular educational expenditures between the wealthiest districts and the poorest urban districts. This indicated an average annual reduction of 5.35%. Instead of bringing about steady progress, however, the state reduced the disparity by only 2.69% in 1995–96, and proposed a mere 0.76% reduction for 1996–97, leaving a projected 12.6% in disparity to be eliminated in the 3rd and final year (Education Law Center 1996, 2). This 12.6% figure places New Jersey at about the middle (27th of the 50 states) in the size of its spending disparity between the richest and the poorest districts (Education Trust 1996, 229). The Newark Education Law Center calculated that $341 million would be necessary to close the gap between the spending by rich and poor districts in 1997–98. However, in 1993 a gubernatorial candidate who had promised to cut New Jersey taxes by a huge 30% had been elected. Governor Christine Todd Whitman's resulting 30% tax cut in 1994 removed $1.2 billion in prospective taxes from the state's treasury—an amount that would have been more than sufficient to reach the mandate of the state supreme court.

The New Jersey state government has spent billions of dollars on education since 1975. While the number of dollars spent over the years has grown, the share of the state's contribution to education spending in New Jersey has not: In 1976–77, during the first year of increased funding from the 1975 PSEA, state aid was 38% of total school expenditures (Reock 1996, table 32). The percentage rose to 44% in 1985–86 and 1986–87 but fell in subsequent years. By 1996–97, state aid had fallen to the 1976–77 level of 38% of total school expenditures (McLaughlin 1996, 13). Although the state, under QEA II, in 1991–92 supported from 24 to 87% of the budgets of poorer urban districts (and 79% of Newark's, with an average support of these districts' budgets at 38.5%), state support of education in New Jersey is, at 38%, below the national average of 46.4% (Reock 1993, table 20; 1996, table 32; U.S. Department of Education 1994, table 155). Between 1993 and 1995, the New Jersey legislature actually decreased K–12 education funding by 3.1%, but *increased* the funding of prisons and other corrections budgets by 25.2% (Education Trust 1996, 143).

The New Jersey legislature's long-awaited plan to meet the Supreme Court's 1994 decision was passed December 19, 1996, and signed the next day by the governor. This law, the Comprehensive Educational Improvement and Financing Act (CEIFA), returns to a mandated minimum curriculum—comparable to the use of basic skills minimums of the seventies and eighties. Core curriculum standards, predetermined by the state and to be used as a basis for instruction, are required for all students, and are the means for providing "a thorough and efficient education." As with the previous basic skills mandates of the seventies and eighties, the required curriculum standards are the means by which educational parity is to be achieved (Sciarra 1997, 85).

Basing its figure on a hypothetical model school district, the legislature decided that $6,720 would be the cost of supplying each elementary school student in 1997–98 with a curriculum that meets these standards. They arrived at $7,526 for middle school and $8,064 for high school students. The state will provide foundation aid to each district according to the difference between its local fair share of property taxes, based on community wealth, and this amount. The figures have been widely criticized as inadequate. They are below the 1996–97 statewide average per pupil expenditure for the regular education budget, far below spending in more affluent districts, and even below that in many poor districts (Sciarra 1997). In efforts to meet the demands of this criticism, the law permits districts to go beyond this minimum by increasing local property taxes. Wealthier districts have the tax base to do so. Poorer urban districts, however, will not be able to raise more educational revenue from their depleted local resources, and therefore are dependent on the foundation aid as a maximum for their regular education budgets. Thus, increased disparities as a result of the act are inevitable. As the governor stated on December 2, 1996, "[In enacting this law], we very frankly said we are not looking for parity in spending" (*Trenton Times* December 2, 1996, in Sciarra 1997, 37). This act, one more example of purposeful noncompliance with the New Jersey Constitution, follows almost a quarter century of willful legislative defiance of constitutional requirements and the State Supreme Court.

On May 14, 1997, however, the Supreme Court delivered a decision that may have far-reaching consequences. The court determined that the regular education funding provisions of CEIFA are unconstitutional as applied to the special needs districts. Arguing that without adequate resources, content standards can have little actual impact on the quality of education, the judges ordered the legislature to ensure by the commencement of the 1997–98 school year that per-pupil expenditures in the poor urban districts are equivalent to the average per-pupil expenditure in the wealthy suburban districts. Of great significance, the court also held that because the documented needs of children attending school in the poor urban districts vastly exceed the needs of other school children, and because the state failed to meet the mandate of earlier Abbott decisions to provide supplemental programs over and above the regular education program that would meet these needs, the case is remanded to the New Jersey Superior Court (*Abbott v. Burke* 1997, 2–4).

This provides the courts an important form of leverage. The remand empowers the Superior Court to direct the Commissioner of Education to assess the needs of urban children, specify what programs will be provided, determine the cost, and plan for state-assisted implementation of these supplemental programs (*Abbott v. Burke* 1997, 4–5). The Superior Court also has the authority to determine whether legislative responses satisfy the requirements of the 1997 order. Moreover, the Supreme Court has retained jurisdiction: should the legislature refuse to appropriate the money the Superior Court finds necessary for the extra programs, the Supreme Court could order the suspension of current education spending in the state. Such an order would close schools and cause "administrative chaos and public outrage" (McLaughlin 1997, 34). Such anger would very likely be directed at political incumbents.

The history of school finance and related educational reform in New Jersey illuminates three dilemmas we as a nation face concerning funding for ghetto schooling: First, although nationally we spend a great deal of money on urban education, we are still failing to educate inner city youngsters. We spend far less on city schools than we do on suburban schools—and given the relatively large percentages of city school budgets that are removed from the regular education program for special needs purposes, the disparity is even greater. I believe, and will argue in chapter 8, that we ought to spend considerably more.

Second, on what should money be spent? By isolating city schools from their urban context, and then aiming funding at only the educational institutions, are we not "missing one whole side of the barn"? I will argue that we need to broaden our sights and focus, in addition, on the problems of what the New Jersey Supreme Court called the "economic and social disaster areas" that are our nation's cities.

Third, who should pay for educational reform? Should the consequences of 100 years of federal, corporate, and state policies that starved and isolated the nation's cities (as demonstrated in previous chapters) be placed on the shoulders of a state's suburban taxpayers? The history provided in part II of this book demonstrates that it is not the state alone that is responsible for the financial disparity between suburban and urban schools: Federal and corporate culpability suggests a large role for these entities in financial reparations, as well. . . .

References

Abbott v. Burke, 100 N.J. 269 (1985).

Abbott v. Burke, 119 N.J. 287 (1990).

Abbott v. Burke, 135 N.J. 444 (1994).

Abbott v. Burke, M622, Slip Op., May 14, 1997.

Centolanza, Louis R. 1986. The State and the Schools: Consequences of Curricular Intervention, 1972–1980. Ed.D. diss., Rutgers University.

Education Law Center. 1996. Plaintiffs' Brief in Support of Motion in Aid to Litigants' Rights. (April 18). Newark, NJ: Author. Typescript.

Education Trust. 1996. *Education Watch: The 1996 Education Trust State and National Data Book*. Washington, DC: Author.

Firestone, William, Margaret Goertz, and Gary Natriello. 1994. *The Myth of Bottomless Pits and Crumbling Lighthouses: Two Years of New Jersey's Quality Education Act*. New Brunswick, NJ: Center for Educational Policy Analysis at Rutgers University.

Firestone, William, Margaret Goertz, and Gary Natriello. 1997. *From Cashbox to Classroom: The Struggle for Fiscal Reform and Educational Change in New Jersey*. New York: Teachers College Press.

Goertz, Margaret E. 1991. *A Quest for Equal Educational Opportunity in NJ: Abbott v. Burke and the Quality Education Act of 1990*. Working paper no. 19, Woodrow Wilson School of Public and International Affairs, Princeton University.

Goertz, Margaret E. 1992. The Development and Implementation of the Quality Education Act of 1990. Consortium for Policy Research in Education, Eagleton Institute of Politics, Rutgers University. Unpublished paper.

McLaughlin, John. 1996. The Learning Curveball. Special section of *Star Ledger* (July).

McLaughlin, John. 1997. The Judging Will Put an End to the Fudging. *Star Ledger*, May 15, 1997, 34.

New Jersey State Department of Education. 1994. *Comprehensive Compliance Investigation of the Newark Public Schools*. Trenton: Author.

Odden, Allen, and Lawrence Picus. 1992. *School Finance: A Policy Perspective.* New York: McGraw-Hill.

Reock, Ernest C. Jr. 1993. *State Aid for Schools in New Jersey: 1976–1993. Part I: Report.* New Brunswick: Center for Government Services, Rutgers University.

Reock, Ernest C. Jr. 1996. *State Aid for Schools in New Jersey: 1976–1996.* New Brunswick: Center for Government Services, Rutgers University.

Robinson v. Cahill, 62 N.J. 473 (1973).

Robinson v. Cahill, 63 N.J. 196 (1973).

Robinson v. Cahill, 69 N.J. 133 (1975).

Robinson v. Cahill, 69 N.J. 449 (1976).

Robinson v. Cahill, 70 N.J. 155 (1976).

Salmore, Barbara G., and Stephen A. Salmore. 1993. *New Jersey Politics and Government: Suburban Politics Comes of Age.* Lincoln: University of Nebraska.

San Antonio Independent School District v. Rodriguez, 411 U.S. 1 (1973).

Sciarra, David. 1997. *Plaintiffs' brief in support of motion in aid to litigants' rights.* Newark, NJ: Educational Law Center.

Tractenberg, Paul. 1974. Robinson v. Cahill: The "Thorough and Efficient" Clause. *Law and Contemporary Problems* 38 (Winter–Spring): 311–332.

U.S. Department of Education, National Center for Educational Statistics. 1994. *Common Core of Data Survey, December, 1994.* Washington, DC: Author.

PART III

Schools

8

The Good High School*

editor's introduction:

Achieving Order and Decorum in an Urban High School. High schools represent
the culmination of K–12 public education. Unfortunately, this country's educational
efforts at the high school level have not been as successful as at the elementary level.
A common statistic is for urban public high schools to have dropout rates of nearly
50%, if comparing those enrolled in the freshman year with those graduating as
seniors. Whether the dropouts are for academic reasons or simply part of a broader
pattern of residential mobility, maintaining the continuity and cumulative benefits of
a four-year high school experience remains a daunting objective.

The present selection covers a high school located in the poorest area of a major
city and once considered "the 'dumping ground' of the Atlanta school system"
(p. 135). The case study tells you how the school attempted to regain its status and
achieved a mood on campus of "order and decorum" (p. 128). The case study cred-
its the principal for much of this accomplishment and explores his motives and
goals in considerable detail. At the same time, the case study shows how the school
still remains at the earliest stages of wrestling to attain higher academic standards
and to meet higher expectations—a scene not untypical of the entire education
enterprise.

Relevance of Case Studies: Combining Sweeping With Intimate Perspectives.
Sara Lawrence-Lightfoot has made significant contributions to a type of qualitative
research that also falls within the purview of doing case studies. Her "portraits"
(Lawrence-Lightfoot & Davis, 1997) freely admit the interaction between the observer

*Lawrence-Lightfoot, Sara. (1983). "George Washington Carver High School:
Charismatic Leadership—Building Bridges to a Wider World." In *The Good High
School: Portraits of Character and Culture* (pp. 29–55). New York: Basic Books.

(analyst) and the observed (subject of study), claiming to fit simultaneously within both the scientific and artistic worlds. The selected case comes from an early era in her professional work and is one of six case studies of specific high schools to appear in an award-winning book. The selection represents the entirety of the case study.

The portraiture process covers both sweeping and intimate scenes. For instance, the case study begins from a distant perspective—the Atlanta school district that includes the high school. The author then examines more closely the work of the school's principal, teachers, administrators, and students. Lengthy quotations are used to help reveal their lives at the school. The case study also discusses specific programs at the high school, in particular a work-study program. Such discussion is cast as part of another broader theme, the school's relationship to its broader community—especially its faith-based community. The case study's ability to shift perspectives, varying from far to near and near to far, provides another example of the way that case studies can represent real life.

Reference

Lawrence-Lightfoot, S., & Davis, J. H. (1997). *The art and science of portraiture.* San
Francisco: Jossey-Bass.

At the Top

When Dr. Hogans, the principal of Carver, speaks of "The Boss," he is refer-ring to Dr. Alonzo Crim, the superintendent of the Atlanta Public Schools. Hogans speaks of him with great respect and deference. He warns a belea-guered music teacher about a last-minute change of plans in the graduation ceremonies, an early morning "request" from Crim. "The Boss absolutely wants the band to play at the graduation on Sunday. So you know that means we'll have to change our plans and get instruments down to the Civic Center. . . . This is critical. . . . What can I do to make this happen?" The negotiations with the central office for more buses, extra rehearsals, and the program readjustments are made within ten minutes of Crim's call. Hogans is relieved to have quickly extinguished "another brush fire," and the young music teacher goes off looking dazed and overwhelmed. The system's hier-archies are clear, the chain of command vivid. Although not visibly present, Crim is a guiding force at George Washington Carver High School. His vision for Atlanta Public Schools is woven into the everyday life of Carver.

Alonzo Crim is a smooth, urbane, articulate man who is proud of the work he is doing in Atlanta. He exudes thoughtfulness, focus, and excitement when he talks about the challenges of urban education. Superintendent of Atlanta for seven years, Crim plans to stay for one more term of four years so that he will be able to see the culmination of many of his efforts. Before coming to Atlanta, he was a superintendent in Compton, California, a largely Black system of 45,000 students. When he enrolled in the Administrative Careers Program at Harvard's School of Education, Crim had not intended to become a superintendent. He had expected to return to being a principal at Wendell Phillips High, a big-city, all-Black school on the South Side of Chicago. But at Harvard, Crim's advisor, Harold Hunt, quickly recognized his student's potential and gently but persistently encouraged him to consider superintending positions. When Crim would return discouraged from job interviews that Hunt had engineered, his mentor would offer generous support and sound advice. With each venture out into the world, Crim became less awkward and more self-assured. His style ten years later is meticulously professional, practiced, and smooth. There are no traces of the early vulnerabilities and uncertainties. He seems to meet the inevitable crises with a clear head and a firm hand.

His experiences at Wendell Phillips still serve him well. They help him identify with the teachers and administrators who work on the front line. He fully recognizes the social and economic barriers that school people face as they try to motivate and teach poor and minority children. He vividly recalls his first year as principal in Chicago when he had to welcome 3,200 students, socialize 85 novice teachers, and structure the school day around five lunch periods in a cramped cafeteria. Fights and skirmishes would flare up like brush fires around the school. Crim worked to change the school from a violent atmosphere dominated by adolescents to a livable environment run by adults.

He brings this direct experience to his work as the superintendent of Atlanta. When he recounts the challenges ahead, he speaks with passion and precision in the same voice. He is both optimistic and piercingly realistic. "My intention," says Crim, "is to provide a good education for poor, urban Blacks . . . and for that I make no apologies." When Kenneth Clark and other old-time integrationists say he is misdirected in his efforts, Crim is filled with impatience and frustration. Why spend money and energy on an unrealistic goal? He sees his challenge as difficult, but clear: to provide quality education for the city's poor and minority children. There are 75,000 pupils in Atlanta's public schools; 54,000 are Title I students. Of the 121 schools in the system, only three are non–Title I schools. Ninety percent of the school system is Black. Crim reels off the statistics with ease.

His guarded optimism in the face of the harsh realities grows out of his childhood experiences. Born and reared on Chicago's West Side, Crim was a lonely survivor. Out of a class of about forty in which he began elementary school, only five finished high school, and only Crim went on to finish college. He cites the human casualties of his childhood as a way of giving perspective to the present. Today in Atlanta, 54 percent of the high school graduates go on to some form of higher education. Of the remaining 46 percent, 37 percent have secured jobs before they leave high school.

There are other signs of promise and success. In Atlanta, the schools' walls are not covered with graffiti, attendance is high, and there is minimal violence. Says Crim, "I think that the lack of violence is related to school size. Violence grows out of urban anonymity." Most of Atlanta's schools are comparatively small and there are explicit attempts to see faces in the crowd. In these signs of progress, Crim sees evidence of health and cause for hope. "We are now in the position to do something great. I get so tired of hearing folks say bad things about urban schools. . . . Next week I'll be asking the school board for the budget for a full day of kindergarten. I can expand here at a time when other systems are barely staying afloat." His job is part of a long mission, and a very serious one. It is almost as if Crim feels grateful for being "the chosen one," saved from the West Side of Chicago. He owes it to himself, his people, and future generations of city children to increase the survival rate, even to help a few thrive.

Three years ago, Crim was getting ready to close Carver High School. It was an ugly reminder of the deterioration, chaos, and unrest that plague many big-city schools. When the community got wind of Crim's intention to close the school, they rose up to defend it. "It's not much, but it is ours!" Hogans, an energetic, ambitious young principal of a nearby elementary school, was chosen to save Carver from total demise. Crim sensed that Hogans was capable of filling the void and thought he might take Carver on as a personal challenge. "He is a diamond in the rough, a jock who made good. . . . He's a man who learns and grows every day." In just a few years, Hogans has transformed Carver. He has used every ounce of his energy and spirit to turn the place around and Crim is proud of his efforts. "He has gotten the kids to listen. . . . He has disrupted the inertia."

The Other Side of the Tracks

George Washington Carver Comprehensive High School is in the southeastern section of Atlanta, the poorest area of the city. No matter what route you take from downtown Atlanta, you must cross the tracks in order to get to

Carver. On the fifteen-minute journey from downtown, the scenery changes dramatically. Downtown Atlanta, with its bold new high-rises and shiny edifices, symbolizes the hope and transformation of an emerging southern metropolis. In contrast, Southeast Atlanta looks gray and shabby. Fast-food joints, gas stations, small grocery stores, and low-cost housing line the main streets.

Carver High looks like a small college campus. An old gothic-looking structure bought from Clark College several years ago sits at the top of the hill and serves as the administration building. It is surrounded by several buildings—a modern concrete structure that houses the science and math departments; a building for gym, music, and the ROTC program; a long, two-story, brick building that houses the vocational education shops; a greenhouse; an auto-mechanics shop; other assorted small structures; and playing fields. In all, the campus has eight buildings on sixty-eight acres. A short distance away you can see the borders of the Carver Homes, the public housing projects where most of the Carver students live (75 percent of the students at Carver come from the Carver Homes, the remaining 25 percent are transfers from the twenty-two other high schools throughout the city). Built around World War II, row upon row of these simple, brick, two-level structures form an enclosed community. The low dwellings do not resemble the high-rise public housing of other major cities, but the sense of hopelessness and boundaries is just as apparent and the statistics are hauntingly similar. The median income for families in the Carver Homes is $3,700; 80 percent of the families are headed by single parents, and a higher percentage are on welfare.

The student enrollment at Carver High School has fluctuated, but seems to have stabilized at 890. As with all public high schools in Atlanta, Carver goes from eighth through twelfth grades. The five-year grade span is most vivid and visible with the boys. The young eighth-graders appear vulnerable and childlike in contrast to the tall, bearded senior boys who seem to have suddenly shot into manhood. Except for one White boy who had been bounced from several other schools and finally found a comfortable home at Carver, the students are all Black. The teaching staff is predominantly Black with a small sprinkling of White faces. The White teachers are so thoroughly interspersed into the faculty that everyone I ask finds it hard to say exactly how many there are. None of the seventy-five teachers on Carver's full-time staff live in the community. They travel several miles each morning from the more affluent middle-class sections of Atlanta and its suburbs. One teacher, who lives in a subdivision twelve miles away, is incredulous when I ask him whether he lives close by. "I can't imagine living close by . . . leaving the school, driving down the hill, and being home . . . my head couldn't take it."

A little uncertain about how his remarks might be taken, he counters, "But none of the teachers look down on the kids even though they live in much classier neighborhoods, because the kids are sensitive and they would pick it up." The head guidance counselor of the school feels very connected to the community even though she, too, lives miles away. "I really take my job as servant to the community very seriously. . . . That phone is one of the best things we have. Not only this one on my desk but that one at home. I let kids know because a lot of parents work during the day. A lot of them can't make parent meetings. They can't come up here during the day so I let them know that my phone at home is open to them at any time. Because they hold the key to these kids, and you have to let parents know that, too."

A Diamond in the Rough

Despite the grim statistics and relentless poverty that appears unchanged in the Carver community, the high school has undergone a major transformation in the last four years. Everyone speaks of the time before and after the arrival of Dr. Hogans. Norris Hogans, a dark-skinned Black man in his late forties, has been a catalyst of change. A former football player, Hogans is powerful in stature and character. He dominates the school. Hogans is a man of great energy. He walks about the campus in perpetual motion, looking severe and determined, always carrying his walkie-talkie. Hogans does not want to be out of touch with any corner of his sphere. Through the walkie-talkie he barks orders and makes inquiries. His requests sound like commands. There is an immediacy about him, an unwillingness to wait or be held back.

Everyone agrees Hogans is powerful. Some view his power as the positive charisma and dynamic force required to turn an institution around and move it in a new direction. These enthusiasts recognize his abrupt, sometimes offensive, style, but claim that his determined temperament is necessary to move things forward. They willingly submit to his autocratic decisions because they view his institutional goals as worthy and laudable. Hogans's detractors, on the other hand, tend to keep their complaints to themselves, forming a covert gossip ring and passively resisting his attempts to make changes by preserving their own inertia. Many of these resistant faculty have been at Carver for twenty-five or thirty years and are threatened by the changes that Hogans has forced on them. They were used to a more laissez-faire administrative policy that permitted more faculty autonomy. Some claim that these old-guard faculty were used to "sitting on their butts and not doing anything . . . and Hogans made them clean up their act." Although there must be a variety of responses to Hogans's leadership, he seems to be a person that people feel strongly about one way or the other. He is despised or revered. He is not a neutral figure but one who demands response and reaction from those around him.

Even those who applaud his great work speak of feeling threatened and submissive in his presence. His decisions are ultimate and non-negotiable, and his commands are sometimes delivered with a callous disregard for the feelings of the person to whom he is talking. Only a very few people seem to escape these assaults. They compose the "inner circle" that surrounds and supports Hogans, offering guidance and assistance, even private criticism. His closest colleague, friend, and confidant is Mr. James, the tall, slender, and impeccable vice-principal who Hogans brought with him to Carver. His visibility is high around campus as he maintains order and discipline, puts out "the brush fires," and serves as principal surrogate when Hogans is not around. He, too, carries a walkie-talkie and seems to be wired directly to Hogans. They are a pair, read each other's minds, and have a kind of intimacy that reflects a deep trust between them. Hogans is clearly the big boss, but James is his totally committed right-hand man. He takes care of the mundane, everyday, nitty-gritty details that elude Hogans, who is dealing with the larger picture. James's style is very similar to that of his boss. He is disciplined, autocratic, and uncompromising. Both men have an exuberant side and lively humor that appears privately and during after-school hours. Their laughter, storytelling, and ribbing behind the scenes seems to fuel them for the toughness that shapes their public image.

Joining in some of the backstage intimacy and fun is Ms. Powell, the registrar, and Mr. Thomas, a department head. Both are deeply committed to and protective of Hogans. They work very hard on his behalf and form a critical support system. Powell and Thomas see his weak and vulnerable side, and are privy to his mistakes and occasional poor judgment. Says Mr. Thomas, "I help 'Doc' out. Many times I've gotten him out of some tough jams." With great femininity and certainty, Ms. Powell provides a kind of disciplined attention to details. She is the recorder at important meetings, drafts letters for Hogans that require a subtle touch, and draws up the schedule of events for each day—all tasks that are not officially part of her job. She is valued by Hogans for her organizational talents, her hard work, and her candor. She lets him know gently and sweetly when he's off base and probably has more power than most realize. Underneath her soft exterior is a strong will, a keen intelligence, and a sturdy spirit.

Hogans's ultimate and uncompromising power is not without focus or reason. Certainly his temperamental tendencies appear to be authoritarian, and he has a large measure of personal ambition. But more important, he believes that he will only be able to realize his goals for Carver if he runs a tight ship. Discipline and authority have become the key to gaining control of a change process. His commitment is powerful and genuine. He believes that schools are transforming institutions that offer Black children the chance to participate meaningfully and productively in society. Schools must provide the discipline, the safety, and the resources that these students are not getting at home. And school must demand something from them. "I think we don't expect enough from our students. We seem to be content if they score two years below grade level." But before they can learn, Hogans believes they must be strictly disciplined and mannerly. A chaotic school setting and a permissive atmosphere can only lead to ruin and failure. So there is a preoccupation with rules and regulations at Carver. Radios and basketballs are confiscated by the vice-principal, boys can't wear caps or walk around with Afro-combs stuck in the back of their hair, and girls are not allowed to wear rollers in their hair. Visible conformity, obedience, and a dignified presence are critical concerns.

In fact, the mood on campus is one of order and decorum. There is not the edge of fear or the potential of violence that one often experiences going into large urban high schools. Bathrooms are free of graffiti, hallways are swept and kept clean, and students express pride in the restored campus. Students gathered in groups do not appear ominous and threatening, but well behaved and friendly. Throughout my visit students were mannerly and receptive. They were curious about my reasons for being there, and, when approached, were eager to tell their stories. The students' controlled demeanor is reinforced by their well-scrubbed appearance and their stylish and colorful dress. The external images seem to convey emerging feelings of self-esteem and hopes for moving up and out of poverty and ghetto life.

The discipline and control of students, however, does not appear to lead to a deeply engrained passivity. In response to questions about their lives at Carver, students are candid and critical. Some are even vociferous. They do not seem to fear the repercussions of being outspoken.

Terrence Tubman, a student leader, describes himself as a "fiery person." He is adamant about the overly oppressive rules at Carver which leave little room for exuberance and expression. For example, he complains about the callous abuse of authority Hogans showed when he abruptly disbanded the popular Friday afternoon student pep rallies:

> If it's on a Friday, nobody really wants to keep working Friday anyway. So, I couldn't see why we couldn't get a chance to release a little steam. But we had them cut to two and we just barely got four in during the whole year. I suggested, "Why don't we have one every other week?" "Uh, we'll see." No definite

answer. So it was just like at Hogans's whim. That's what it was. Whenever he felt like we should have a pep session, we'd have one. And he didn't see that this meant an awful lot to the students. This is something that they look forward to on Friday and I can see it because it's not every day they get a chance to release, you know, get down and holler. Even then we have restrictions on the pep sessions which I can't understand. When you come to a pep session, you come to act crazy and have a good time. Yet, we had to act a certain way at the pep session. I thought that was totally ridiculous and I've been to some fantastic pep sessions at other schools.

Although Terrence feels that students are disenfranchised and powerless, he thinks they are less silenced than teachers. He sees the grim passivity of teachers who are afraid to speak out:

Teachers are very uptight. I say this with freeness because I see the teachers and talk with them. I have been granted the opportunity to really get behind the scenes to see what's going on. They're kind of scared. They see things they don't like but they are scared to say them because they don't want to get transferred. I feel that maybe you don't want to buck the ways, but if something's not right you got to speak out about it. That's probably one of the reasons why I'm a thorn because I don't mind saying this isn't cool and that isn't cool. But the teachers, they get paid and Hogans is the boss and you can't rock the boat. They're really getting uptight because a lot of them are forced to do an extra amount of work and they can't really concentrate on the student. This is an uptight situation.

The timid behavior that Terrence sees in teachers' responses to superior authority are not mimicked in students' interactions with teachers. For the most part, the relationships between students and teachers do not seem to be shaped by threat and fear. Even when I saw teachers becoming frustrated and overwhelmed in class, I never saw them deal abusively with students. Some seemed to have the patience of Job as students made insistent and noisy demands. Some seemed to disregard the turmoil and turn off at points when students were overly aggressive and disruptive. Still others, in the face of impending chaos, became more demanding and insistent upon a good performance and obedience from students. But I saw no evidence of careless punishment or unleashed anger on the part of the teachers. Rather, I saw the opposite—a genuine concern for their charges, a dedication to their work, and a commitment to broad institutional ideals.

On a hot, steamy morning, the seniors are rehearsing for the graduation exercises in the school gym. The job of orchestrating this extravaganza belongs to Mr. Thomas, the head of the English Department, who is excited about the theme and format of the occasion. Rather than the traditional graduation speeches, Thomas has designed a complex series of skits that display Carver's commitment to work, careers, and employment. In small groups on the stage, students enact scenes from the different vocations they have learned at Carver—dry cleaning, tailoring, nursing, auto mechanics, and horticulture—while student commentators offer the accompanying descriptions. The speakers, who have all memorized their speeches, stand rigidly, voicing their well-practiced and flowery prose. Thomas insists upon perfection as he makes the seniors practice their parts over and over again. When the speakers' lines come out dull and over-rehearsed, Thomas bursts forth dramatically and harshly admonishes them, "You are not projecting and I feel no life in it. . . . I feel you are very jittery. . . . I'm totally dissatisfied. . . . When you walked up there you didn't have enough class. You need *class!*" Thomas's message is uncompromising. He wants and expects an excellent performance. But underneath his vigorous and grueling demands, there is a theme of respect and caring. "If I didn't love you like I do, I wouldn't do this. . . . I wouldn't come down so hard on you. I'm not going to lighten up until you get it right. It must be perfect. I won't stand for less. And I won't stand for any negative attitudes. There is no time for that."

A sense of order and structure and an atmosphere of caring and concern would seem to be prerequisites of a successful and productive education, but not the full and necessary ingredients. These prerequisites do not easily or inevitably lead to academic excellence or inspired teaching and learning. In many of the classrooms I visited, very little of substance was happening educationally. Teachers were caught up in procedural directives and students appeared disinterested, turned off, or mildly disruptive. The institution has begun to emerge as stable and secure, but attention to the intellectual development and growth of students will require a different kind of focus, new pedagogical skills, and a profound change in faculty views of student capabilities. This most difficult challenge is connected, I think, to the perceptions faculty hold of student futures and the place and station that students are expected to take as adults in the world beyond school.

Mr. Parrot, a slow-talking, slight man with a deep Southern accent, teaches a social science course to juniors and seniors. The late-afternoon class is depleted by the absence of the seniors, who have gone off to rehearse for graduation. Five students, who have all straggled in well after the bell, are scattered throughout the large, well-equipped classroom. One has her head on the desk and is nodding off to sleep; another girl is chewing gum vigorously and leafing through a magazine; a third student stares straight ahead with glazed eyes. These three never respond to the teacher's questions and remain glumly silent during the class discussion. Two boys, Lowry and Richard, sit right under the teacher's nose and spend most of the class period being noisy and disruptive. Mr. Parrot hopes for other students to arrive, but finally decides to begin the class about twenty minutes after the bell. His opening remarks sound formal. He seems to be addressing his comments to more than the few people present. Standing behind a podium at the front of the room, he says, "Young people, let me have your attention quickly." Lowry and Richard quiet down momentarily, but the others appear to ignore his announcement of the final exam. "The exam is something I give to help you, not hurt you. Say if Carolyn got a D or an F on the final, I would not hold that against her because she has gotten mostly Bs all year. . . . I tend to go on progression. If you start out bad and finish good, I take that into consideration." Another ten minutes are consumed as the two vociferous boys ask distracting questions about the examination. Now thirty minutes into the period, Mr. Parrot takes his place at the overhead projector and begins the topic for the day: "social distance." Out of left field, Lowry asks, "Has anyone ever broken the sound barrier?" The teacher tries to ignore the question and proceed with his explanation of social distance, saying that when people approach one another in Spanish culture, "two feet is far away . . . to us it is close." Richard, intrigued by Parrot's comments, offers his understanding of social distance. "I heard of a guy who killed a guy because he stepped on his feet." The teacher is pleased that someone is with him and rewards Richard's contribution. "Very good. That's what we mean by social distance." The rest of the class consists of disjointed and chaotic exchanges between the strongwilled teacher and two relentless students. In the fragmented conversation, sociological terminology is hurled around and terms like "propaganda," "mass communication," and "public opinion" are given dubious definitions. When I talk to Mr. Parrot after class, he is undiscouraged. Enthusiastically, he says, "This is the best school I've worked in. . . . The administration is great, the principal and vice-principal are as thick as thieves, and that helps. . . . And I think most people care about the children and work hard."

Although there are glimmers of more lively and skillful teaching going on at Carver and evidence of some sophisticated work done by a few students in biology, graphic arts, and literature, for example, the academic program seems to lag far behind the vocational training that is offered in the more than thirty shops at the school. Perhaps one reason that the shop training appears to be more successful and well focused is that teachers and students feel minimal ambivalence about what they are doing. Highly skilled technicians are clearly and systematically transmitting their knowledge to the next generation of workers. Mr. Ward, the instructor of the dry-cleaning shop, has been at Carver for over thirty years. He teaches what he knows best to over eighty students majoring in dry-cleaning. The appreciative and responsive learners can see the connections between the skills they are learning and jobs in the real world. And Mr. Ward is teaching something he feels proud of and values. His heart soars when students learn to do the job with exactness, thoroughness, and punctuality. These skills, translated to values concerning work and life, fit with Mr. Ward's notion of where his students will find themselves in the future. There is, then, an economy of effort, a promise of some return for one's work, and a lack of ambivalence in the minds of shop teachers.

This clarity of vision and purpose is reinforced by a strong history. For the one thing that seems continuous about this rapidly changing environment is the training for vocations. In times past, perhaps the shops were less well equipped and more run-down, but the educational efforts led toward the same explicit goals—to teach poor, outcast Black students to become responsible workers, to move children from lives of poverty and chaos to futures of disciplined, steady, hard work. Historically, if these goals were met, teachers felt successful and rewarded.

But Hogans's vision for the school is far more ambitious and much less clearly focused. It is not that he looks down upon or devalues technical training, but that he wants a more comprehensive and sophisticated education for Carver students. As a matter of fact, he is intolerant of people who emphasize academics to the exclusion of shop training, and feels that realists and pragmatists must recognize the value of technicians. "After all, most plumbers get paid a lot more than teachers," he says. But in redesigning the school's curriculum, Hogans wants to create more options and more choices for expanded futures. He wants to open more doors in business, industry, and academia. Hogans's vision of a "comprehensive" high school (which includes the three realms of general, vocational, and academic training) is shaped by his wish to change and broaden the institutional processes and goals. But almost inevitably the broader horizons are not clearly defined; there are dispersion of effort, less clearly focused goals, and ambivalence in the hearts of many. The academic side of life seems undeveloped and embryonic at the same time the vocational training feels rooted in history and clearly drawn.

Shaping a New Image

Part of the struggle for a broader, more lofty definition reflects Carver's attempt to regain status. Its image as the city's dumping ground lingers on and casts a dark shadow on the new and enlightened attempts at change. Sometimes one gets a feeling that more efforts are going toward redefining the image than facing the reality. In fact, teachers in the other city high schools still continue to use Carver as a threat: "If you don't act right, we'll send you to Carver." Carver teachers are sometimes asked by their upwardly striving, middle-class friends why they have chosen to work with "those dumb kids over there," and other schools continue to dump their "bad kids" onto Carver's rolls. (This year, when it was discovered that many of the students from outside the district had been transferred to Carver because other schools could no longer handle them, Hogans transferred them out and the school size dropped from 1200 to 850.) Carver will no longer willingly accept outcasts from other schools and knows that their presence will prolong the negative images.

Despite his attempts to shape a new image, Hogans still seems to enjoy Carver's location "on the other side of the tracks." But his own continuous allusions to Carver's low status are heard as humorous self-deprecatory gestures—a way to get the upper hand on visitors who may feel uncomfortable venturing from one side of the tracks to the other, and a way to express his commitment to working in this community. At the same time he makes reference to Carver's poverty and lowly image, he fights to change it. With all his energy, he battles to turn the school around. I think he would be extremely satisfied if he managed to do the unthinkable—make the dumping ground into a place of excellence and productivity, a place that could be selective, a place where students would clamor to be admitted.

The promotional material on Carver begins to convey the new image. The first thing I am shown when I come to Carver is a slide tape that was originally prepared for a presentation on educational innovation given by Hogans at the National Academy of Science. It is a slick effort at public relations. In the slides, Carver looks like a snazzy college campus buzzing with activities, students are pictured as well scrubbed and ambitious, and explicit connections are made between the world of business and profit and the curriculum and culture of the school. The language is flowery, even pretentious. As with most promotional attempts it expresses the optimistic ideal, not the reality. It conveys a sense that life at Carver is intense and productive, when it sometimes appears as unfocused and wasteful. Most pointedly, the vision and energy of Hogans shines through this slide tape—his orchestration of the myriad realms that constitute Carver, his imagination and ingenuity in building partnerships between business and education, and his ability to convince others of the worth of it all. Hogans is a very sophisticated entrepreneur, a packager of ideas, and this slide tape is one of his public expressions of image making.

There are many who complain that Hogans devotes far too much time creating images and expanding his empire and feel that his efforts are mostly designed to gain public attention and applause. In fact, he is already beginning to become something of a national figure, traveling around the country hoping to sell his ideas and spread his "model" of a comprehensive education. Recently, he appeared with Crim before a Congressional subcommittee and told the audience that he "did not come to ask for money but for a commitment to the challenges ahead." And he is planning a trip to Portland, then maybe to parts of Texas, to consult with school administrators on their educational plans.

Hogans clearly enjoys the exposure and the attention. It appeals to the extrovert that dominates his character. But he also seems to think of his role at Carver as largely external. He has an ambitious vision and he expects that the resources for executing his plan will be found in the connections he creates with sources of power and influence far beyond the poor Black community. So much of his energy and intellect is spent making and sustaining these connections, moving outward and away from Carver.

As they watch Hogans go off to wheel and deal, some Carver people feel neglected, left behind, and deeply envious. Students complain of his invisibility and his seeming disregard for their need for attention. For weeks they try to see him for an appointment, only to have their meeting cancelled for more important priorities. A senior angrily spoke of Hogans's disregard for students:

> I had to run him down to the office to get him and even then he's so busy I can barely get a word in edgewise to him, and if it's not that, there's somebody in his office at all times when I can't get in there. And I say, well, let me schedule an appointment so maybe I can come. And every time I come in, he's hopping to Washington or another place. Half the students on this campus can't even relate to him. It's not like he goes in with the students and tries to talk with each one. You get the feeling he's kind of way back, distant. I mean, he's just in the office and that's it. That's the way I feel about the administration. I feel that they have set themselves apart. If a student don't like it, they got to leave.

Occasionally, Hogans is abruptly reminded of his inattention to the internal life of Carver.

> In a faculty meeting of department heads and program administrators, Hogans interrupts the largely bureaucratic proceedings by saying, "I want to share a personal problem with you." His tone immediately becomes softer and his face shows more concern. The day before, Hogans had been visited by Sylvia Brown, a seventeen year-old student at Carver. Sylvia's mother died several years before. Her eighty-two year-old father became disgusted with her adolescent ways and threw her out of the house eight months ago. In the meeting, the normally fast-moving Hogans pauses to contemplate Sylvia's story. "Sylvia kind

of slipped through our fingers while all of this was going on. . . . Sylvia's a basically good girl. This is not a discipline problem. This is a counseling problem. . . . We spend far too much time on administrative and staff problems and too little on the well-being of individual students." Hogans concludes by expressing his own feelings of guilt. "The worst part about it was she said she had tried to see me for a week. I really caved in when I heard that."

A few faculty express these same feelings of neglect. They regard Hogans's promotional activities as efforts at self-promotion and self-aggrandizement. But most recognize the inevitable trade-offs of having a principal who is willing to track down resources and broaden horizons. They accept his neglect of the daily operations of school in exchange for the benefits of his external activities. Without his strong political acumen and his energetic search for finances, they know that Carver would have fewer resources with which to work and that school life would be less abundant.

One of the potential casualties of model building and the packaging of ideas is that more attention is paid to selling than producing; that before the ideas have been adequately formed, tested, and refined, there are attempts to disseminate them abroad. (One of the tensions that must plague Hogans is his realization of the discrepancies between image and reality at Carver, and the unfinished state of his operations there. He is eager, even impatient, to "close the gap" and move toward a smoother stability.) Carver is certainly not alone in its imperfections. Any social institution, particularly if it is growing and evolving, copes with weaknesses and rough edges. But Carver's imperfections are made more visible by contrast with the projected, idealized images being portrayed to the wider public. It seems to fall short only in relation to the public relations picture, not if one views its tortuous history or the difficult realities that shape its present. One is, in fact, exceedingly impressed with what has been accomplished at Carver if one looks back a few years.

When Hogans was assigned to Carver and told to report there the next day, he sat up all night and drank a whole case of beer. Hogans had been principal of the elementary school right down the hill from Carver and was well aware of the chaos and deterioration that existed there. And for years, he had heard Carver identified as the "dumping ground" of the Atlanta school system. So it was with dread that Hogans approached his new assignment. His trepidation was also mixed with a sense of challenge and promise. This seemed a good place to test his imagination, his energy, and his commitment to poor Black children. He also recognized that if he were successful, he would be recognized as a great educator, as one who had the magic key to the complex problems facing urban education.

On his first day at Carver, Hogans faced a curious and skeptical faculty. It was also a depleted and discouraged faculty that needed renewal, energy, and direction from their new leader. For several years, they had existed under a laissez-faire, weary administration; a principal who was chronically ill and who let things erode and deteriorate around him. Teachers were used to a great deal of autonomy, little interdependence, and almost no sense of cohesion in the staff. Hogans's first response to the aimlessness and laziness that he perceived was "to show them who was in charge." He started the first faculty meeting with fighting words: "You are either part of the team or you are not." Tough standards of behavior and decorum were stressed with his new faculty; rules and regulations were consistently and rigorously enforced. Hogans began with a heavy hand and an autocratic style—an orientation that matched his temperament, but also one that he believed would re-establish order and control in an environment that had lost all sense of direction and stability.

The physical environment matched the deteriorating human spirit. "Roaches were running around like cats. . . . There was dirt and filth everywhere. . . . The band instruments were all broken up. . . . Athletic trophies were falling out of the broken glass cabinets!" Hogans says incredulously, "I can't believe no one stood up and screamed about it!" Climbing out of the rubbish took optimism, perseverance, and hard work, all qualities that Hogans seems to possess in good measure. But in order to get people to conform to the imposed structure, Hogans also used limits and threats. No deviations or improvisations were tolerated by the new principal. Some almost suffocated in this claustrophobic atmosphere that allowed little room for self-expression and professional autonomy. Others welcomed the imposed order, the new sense of collectivity, and the big-daddy, paternalistic image of a take-charge principal.

Hogans believes that faculty found the transition more difficult than the students did. Four years later, some faculty are "dragging their feet" and resisting his direction. He recognizes that in general adults are more set in their ways and less malleable than adolescents, but he uses similar strategies for molding their behavior. Strict obedience and absolute conformity are required of both groups. Privileges and rewards are withheld when teachers or students do not follow orders. A teacher who has not followed the standard procedures for signing out for off campus is given no chance to defend himself. Hogans responds immediately and angrily: "That person is going to be docked. Hit them in the pocketbook. . . . When teachers are irresponsible, the kids always get the short end of the stick."

Hogans recognizes that a preoccupation with discipline will not shape good teachers or inspire faculty commitment, although he does feel that order is a precondition for educational progress. He knows that faculty need to be energized and shored up. They grow stale after years of teaching and need periodic in-service training that offers new approaches and ideas. Hogans sees a need for this kind of external stimulation of experienced staff as well as the need for some "new blood" on the faculty. He wants to rid the faculty of the lingering lethargy that he perceives as inhibiting to student success in school. But behind his call for increased energy and commitment seems to be the budding realization that inspired teaching cannot be enforced—that the creativity and productivity of teachers must be generated from within, and requires the complex and subtle mixture of inputs from students and teachers. It is that elusive combination of psychic and intellectual forces that continues to be beyond the reach of Hogans.

He does make meaningful attempts to provide sustenance and nourishment for needy teachers. How can teachers give to students when they themselves feel hungry? Hogans speaks proudly of the daily expression of nourishment. "I feed the faculty a hot breakfast every morning . . . grits, eggs, bacon . . . the whole thing." Additionally, the faculty are not required to patrol the halls or stay for afternoon meetings. All faculty meetings take place between 8:00 and 8:30 in the morning, and there is only one full faculty meeting per month. Hogans insists that these meetings be organized and efficient. "We don't have busy-work meetings. We can't waste our time on nothing." Although he recognizes the difficult challenges they face, Hogans sees his faculty as a privileged and respected group that gets its fair share of benefits. He wonders out loud why some continue to be complaining and recalcitrant and has no sympathy for those who do not make an energetic contribution.

The Spiral, the Hub of All Activity

The promotional slide tape on Carver describes the school as "the spiral, the hub of all activity." The forces at Carver are centrifugal. As it spins around in energetic activity, it tends to move away from center. The school's orientation is outwards and into the wider community. As a matter of fact, a description of the internal organism of Carver would offer a very narrow view of the nature of this complex, far-reaching institution. It is the multiple networks that are attached to Carver that account for its unique character.

The dominant connection seems to be with the world of work and industry. Many programs establish the alliance between work and schooling, making them often inseparable. The vast majority of students say they have come to Carver in order to learn salable skills and gain an entree into the work world. Education is viewed as pragmatic and oriented towards the economic "slots" in industry, business, and the service occupations.

A primary program that establishes the direct connections between work and schooling is the Work-Study Program. Approximately 150 juniors and seniors are involved in this program that places them in skilled jobs throughout the city of Atlanta. Half of their day is spent at Carver and half in positions at banks, hospitals, offices, service stations, and fast-food establishments. Students are paid from $3.15 to $4.85 an hour and allowed to pocket all the money they make. This is a highly selective program whose status and image have been primarily generated by Ms. Gertrude Taylor, an energetic woman committed to shaping her students into dedicated, disciplined careerists.

Before coming to Carver four years ago, Ms. Taylor had worked as an executive secretary, office manager, accountant, and proposal writer. One afternoon while taking shorthand and typing for Dr. Benjamin Mays, the president of the Atlanta Board of Education, he presented her with a challenge that she could not resist. "Would you be interested in training young people for jobs?" Dr. Mays asked in a soft but persuasive tone. Admiration and respect for Dr. Mays as well as her wish to "make a contribution to the lives of young Black students" made her hesitate for only a moment before saying she would do it. Within three days, she had a teaching position at Carver.

Her love for her work and her belief in what she does is immediately obvious. With enthusiasm and pride, she recounts her many successes with students, her shaping of their skills over several years, and her rigorous selection process. Ms. Taylor's approach to students is respectful and demanding. A student coming in late to school is reprimanded for his casual laziness, warned that his behavior will never earn him a position in the Work-Study Program, and firmly prodded to shape up. Her manner is strong, imposing, and uncompromising, but the message is one of deep care and understanding. Part of her caring comes from knowing her students very well. Beginning with their eighth-grade entrance into the school, she watches them carefully and tests their potential as responsible workers.

> I try to learn about my students . . . the total student—the make-up, the attitudes, the way the student thinks, the ability, et cetera. But there are other characteristics that I must learn . . . the habits, the temperament of the student.

Along with observing students herself, Ms. Taylor consults with others who know them well.

> I work closely with homeroom teachers, classroom teachers, and especially with the registrar and counselors. . . . Along with the information I pick up there, I call the homes and go into the neighborhood. . . . This is my perspective. I'm

looking into the future. I tell the parent the advantage of putting the student out in the world of work early. . . . They can use this as a reference. This is experience. It looks good on the résumé. It helps when the student goes to college. . . . I keep close contact with the parents.

Once Ms. Taylor has gathered all of the information on "the whole child," she begins the subtle process of matching students with the work settings. She must be concerned with responding to the needs of the employers, the skills and temperament of the students, and establishing a "track record" that will ensure the stability of "work slots." For a slot in the "Coin and Currency" department at the Federal Reserve Bank, Ms. Taylor searched for a student who was "very pleasant and highly honest." For a job at General Motors that required balancing the skills of accounting, data processing, computer programming, and record keeping, Ms. Taylor found a young woman with a "calm temperament who would not get flustered" by all the demands being made of her. Occasionally, a match between student and job does not work out.

> Now I have had to take students out of jobs and move them from slot to slot because the student was unhappy. I just did that the other day. A young lady was very unhappy. Mr. Jordan at the Federal Labor Department is a lovely person. But Mr. Jordan has been there twenty-five years and this young lady is one of those hyperactive types. She's a good worker but she has some attitudes that just didn't work. And she detected that. And she came to me and expressed some sort of dissatisfaction.

Clearly, Ms. Taylor thinks of herself as part entrepreneur ("I sell my program"), part psychologist ("I have to find out what deeply motivates these students"), and part technical trainer ("They must feel confident in these basic office skills before we send them out into the world of work"). She actively seeks to combine the environments of work, school, and family as she guides and shapes students for career positions. In the process of molding students, Ms. Taylor becomes deeply involved with them, convinced and determined that they can be successful, and links her ambitions for the program with their best efforts.

The Work-Study Program culminates in an extravagant ritualistic event called Free Enterprise Day. Students who have successfully completed the program receive generous acclaim as they parade on stage and tell the audience about their work accomplishments and future career objectives. It is a carefully staged and dramatic presentation of the value of discipline, perseverance, punctuality, and civility for rising in the world of work. It is a public event that symbolizes Carver's new image. Vocational education no longer has to be linked with tough and menial work for people of low status, but can be seen as training for jobs of choice, skill, and honor. On the cover of the program for Free Enterprise Day there is a workman's hand "laying the foundation to success." The bricks of the pyramid being constructed are labeled "business," "community," and "education," and the major inscription reads: "What a youngster becomes later in life is a direct result of what that youngster is exposed to early in life."

The architects of the new Carver believe in the principles of democracy, free enterprise, and capitalism. Their images are classically mainstream. They communicate to students their belief in the fairness and rationality of "the system"—a system that they believe will respond to the hard work, determination, and calculated risks of individual will. At Carver, however, there is a slight variation in the traditional view of capitalist enterprise. It is a common minority perspective. There is the realistic perception that Blacks, particularly poor Blacks, have for generations been disenfranchised, powerless, and excluded from society's resources and bounty. The experience of exclusion and oppression has led some to fight for their meager share of the American pie, but has led many more to withdraw from the race, to assume it is rigged and refuse to run. The new ideology of Carver conveys a double message and conflicting imagery. It says that Blacks have been treated unfairly, but that the system is basically fair. In order to overcome the profound injustices, Carver students need to learn how to successfully negotiate the system, must refuse to become discouraged by the barriers that they will face, and must become exemplary models of discipline and civility. Carver opens the first window to this wider world of entrepreneuring and profit. It offers a taste of what lies beyond the ghetto walls. School people hope that these frequent trips to the other side of the tracks will inspire a belief in the system and a commitment to the fight for inclusion in the mainstream.

These trips across ghetto boundaries are institutionalized as part of the Explorers Program begun by Hogans three years ago. Every tenth-grader at Carver becomes a member of the Explorers Program, an adaptation of the Explorer Scouts, "designed to provide an initial linkage to the world of work." Each month, students are bused downtown amidst the shiny glass high-rises to visit the major businesses and agencies of Atlanta, to explore how they function, and to receive orientations to the careers they offer. The public relations material on the program claims that students gain "an awareness of vocation, accurate images of work life, awareness of the full range of job settings and opportunities available, motivation for learning, increased access to job opportunities, and a broad base for vocational and career decisionmaking." It is unlikely that any single program could accomplish all of these lofty goals. But many point to the Explorers Program as critical to the new purposes and direction of Carver. Tenth-graders all receive clean, white Explorer jackets, and it becomes an important collective experience for them. Perhaps the immersion into the work world is made less threatening because students "explore" the new environments as a group, and do not have to worry about being individually inadequate or awkward. The hope is that this initial exposure to business and industry in the tenth grade will not only lift the sights of Carver students, but also help them make more informed curricular and vocational decisions in the eleventh and twelfth grades. The 1980 graduating class was the first group to experience the Explorers Program at Carver, and Hogans claims that compared to their predecessors he sees striking differences in the graduates' understanding of the work world, their career choices, their determination, and their dedication to achievement.

The Explorers Program was Hogans's brainchild. In characteristic fashion he raised money, made connections, and convinced the Boy Scouts of America that an entire class of students—both boys and girls—could, by virtue of their student status, join the program. But Carver Explorers do not leave the city for hikes and camping in the woods. Their explorations carry them to the urban, industrial turf of business and banking. They are not learning survival skills for outdoor jungles but the calculating skills of entry and industry. But a central theme prevails that is rooted in the Boy Scout tradition: scouting is supposed to make strong men out of undisciplined boys. Likewise, the Explorers Program stresses honor, honesty, and rigor—all critical pieces of the new school image.

Most of the doors to the business world could not be opened without David Tanner, the man Superintendent Crim describes as "the second most important person" to Carver's turnaround and a man whom Hogans describes as a father figure. A more apt description might be one of a godfather, because the father image implies a kind of judgment and generational competition which is not evident in Tanner's relationship to Hogans. Rather, their fifteen-year relationship is marked by enormous generosity, trust, and intimacy. They are an odd couple. Tanner is the privileged, smooth, cosmopolitan banker with broad connections and a humanitarian spirit. Hogans is the rough-edged, ambitious, and resourceful Black man with big plans for himself and his people. Tanner admires Hogans's unleashed energy and aggressiveness. Hogans is appreciative of the prosperous and genteel style of Tanner. It is out of their mutual admiration and trust that Carver has been conceived and shaped. They are the architects, the visionaries, the builders playing interdependent roles.

David Tanner is the vice-president for community affairs for a major trust company in Atlanta. His office sits on the eleventh floor of a tall glass and metal structure that rises twenty-five stories into the Atlanta skyline. The floors are plushly carpeted, and the atmosphere is one of efficiency and polish. There is a sprinkling of Black faces among the secretarial staff, but the bank seems strikingly White after spending some time at Carver. Tanner's office is comfortable, not opulent.

Contemplative and slow to speak, Tanner talks about his mission in a way that is almost religious. But he speaks with humility, minimizing his part in the building of Carver, and giving Hogans most of the credit. "I am a behind-the-scenes person. . . . I coordinate the relationship with the business community." His commitment to Carver grew out of his long, personal attachment to Hogans, but also his increasing concern for the deterioration of urban communities. "We seem to have forgotten to tell the young people of today that with opportunity comes responsibility." Tanner fears the lack of commitment and industry in today's youth, and worries that their irresponsibility will lead to societal chaos and violence. The repercussions will fall hardest on poor and minority communities. Tanner assesses the task of restructuring society as an integration of efforts from the political, economic, social, and spiritual realms. But he is clear about the boundaries of his own involvement. "I am fortunate," says Tanner, "that the bank allows me to do the work which I most want to do. . . . I have been in foundation work for over twenty years, and I continue to believe in the philosophy of my mentor, who is now ninety-three years old—search out and identify strong, indigenous people and support them in their work . . . and that is what I'm doing with Norris."

Tanner's philosophy sounds very general and full of platitudes, but actions are highly specific, focused, and calculated. Behind that generous and smooth veneer of a southern gentleman, one senses a tough-minded and savvy operator. Most of his backstage activity has been focused on establishing ties between the business community and Carver. The monthly visits for tenth-graders in the Explorers Program are largely arranged by Tanner. For years he has been a prominent member of the Inter-Agency Council, a coalition of public schools, private enterprise, higher education, and social agencies that comes together each month for collective learning, problem solving, and action. Recently, he has been involved in beginning the Carver Corporation, a group whose efforts are designed to respond to the economic, social, and health needs of young, unwed mothers living in the Carver Homes.

Tanner's most visible moment came recently when he was master of ceremonies at this year's Free Enterprise Day. Yet even on this occasion, he was reluctant to take center stage. He feels ineffective working directly with the Carver students and thinks he must be perceived as distant and irrelevant by them. He points to the persuasive powers of the Black woman newscaster, who was the keynote speaker on the same program. "She was absolutely magnificent. . . . She told them things they would never hear if they came from me."

Although they move in different spheres, Hogans and Tanner share the same view of the complex interdependence of social institutions in our society. They are constantly seeking connections to new sources of influence and building networks that will draw in more resources to Carver. Hogans claims that more revenue flows from these independent connections than comes from the school system's budgetary allocations.

Carver's relationships to business and industry seem most prominent, but connections to other institutions are being slowly shaped and clarified. One such connection is to four prosperous churches that form the Ecumenical Council. The council was Tanner's inspiration. It grew out of his concern for the increasing separation between the sacred and the secular in this society, and his sense that churches were not taking a responsible social role in community life. Tanner worried about the complacency and introversion of the affluent parishes in Atlanta that were content to worship on Sundays, but never move beyond Christian rhetoric. A member of an upper-class, predominantly White Presbyterian church, Tanner began conversations with three other prominent parishes in an attempt to combine forces to participate on social action. After much persuasion and groundwork, another Presbyterian, an Episcopal, and a Lutheran church (all affluent, three White and one Black) joined together to create the Ecumenical Council. Guided by Tanner's determination and strategy, they decided to focus their resources on the Carver Homes and offer support in the form of an active ministry in that community. Collectively, the churches raised money to send Black divinity students into the Carver community to live and work. Says Tanner realistically, "They are not there to save souls. . . . Just to help in any way they can."

The divinity students are joined by a "circuit rider," a minister who also works in the Carver Homes and travels among the four churches on Sundays, bringing the messages of urban distress to the congregations. Tanner calls him an "urban translator" and clearly recognizes the mutual ignorance and threat that prevail between rich and poor, Black and White. The parishioners need to hear the word and be reminded of the separations, just as the Carver folks need their support and resources. As Tanner talks about organizing these churches for action, he speaks with the same calculated purpose that characterizes his business acumen. Clearly, his spiritual life is inseparable from his business interests. Many of the same people who inhabit Atlanta's corporate offices are found in these church pews. With this in mind, Tanner persuaded Hogans to join his all-White Presbyterian parish. He knew that Hogans's presence at church would be a visible reminder of the church's commitment to Carver. Perhaps more importantly, he wanted to further encourage Hogans's ascent into the circles of influence and power in Atlanta.

The beautiful, gleaming edifices in which Tanner and Hogans worship every Sunday are far away from the modest Black churches that surround the Carver Homes. Dotting the landscape, these small buildings are closed all week long. Their ministers can only afford to open the churches on Sunday. The other six days of the week, they are off making a living in real estate, teaching, dry-cleaning—jobs that will subsidize their almost voluntary status as ministers of poor churches. The closed church doors don't only symbolize their other commitments, but also what some identify as a negligent, condescending attitude of the churches towards people in the Carver Homes. Over the past few decades, distance and hostility have grown between the closed churches and the needy community. It is with this legacy of skepticism and distrust that the urban ministers, sponsored by the rich White churches, entered the Carver community almost four years ago.

They came to live and work in the poorest community in Atlanta. The Carver Homes crowd 5,400 people into 990 apartments. The two-story, brick buildings lined up along nine streets were built twenty-five years ago as public housing. They do not appear as ominous and isolating as the high-rise public housing of Chicago or New York. There is something more humane about the scale of these buildings. There are stoops and porches to sit on and more possibility for neighborly contact. Yet the people here are just as poor and just as imprisoned by poverty and discrimination. What might have once been planted lawns and greenery has long since turned to gray, beaten-down dirt, and there are no sidewalks for people to walk on from house to house. Through the eyes of a Northeasterner, the Carver Homes look semi-rural, even though they are part of a big-city problem.

Velma King, an articulate, forceful young woman, and one of the three original divinity students to come and live in the Carver Homes, told of their long struggles for community acceptance, their battles with bureaucrats, and their ambivalent relationships with the sponsoring churches. King is direct and uncompromising as she tells her story: "Even in attempting to be good, I have to be me." Her certainty, strength, and wisdom make her seem older than her twenty-eight years. When she decided to take on the urban ministry assignment, her father encouraged the new venture. "You send off special rays that will help people . . . and you need to experience the pain of poverty," he said.

Round, brown-skinned, and simply dressed, there is no visible evidence that King is a minister. She says, "It is so easy to hide behind a clerical uniform. Let what I am come from what you see me doing." Her "community ministry" in the Carver Homes has been related to her struggle to become "one of the people," not separate from or above them in status. She has purposely not become an ordained minister because she is suspicious of organized religion and "very critical of the people who work with social systems." Her inclinations to work outside the system have only been reinforced and strengthened by her increasing identification with community folk.

King arrived at the Carver Homes with two male colleagues, both Black. Of West African origin, Cyrus Lungu brought his wife and children with him and maintained close contact with St. Bede's, the prosperous Black Episcopal church that joined in sponsoring their ministry. On Sunday mornings people in the Carver Homes could turn on their televisions and see Lungu administering the sacraments to his wealthy, well-heeled, St. Bede's parishioners. This bourgeois connection stirred suspicion in the Carver people, who tested his commitment by slashing his tires and robbing his home. They sensed in him an arrogance derived from his upper middle-class life in West Africa and the cultural misunderstandings that grew out of their different origins. It was also difficult for Lungu to balance the needs of his family with the heavy demands of his ministry. Leroy Green, a young, dapper, single man, was tested in another way. Rumors grew up around him as people interpreted his smooth style as the behavior of a police plant. One day when he came home, he found his apartment broken into, all of his furniture and clothes taken, and his ordination certificate torn up in a neat pile on the floor. Velma King faced a more subtle kind of community exclusion and skepticism. Most of the dominant forces in the community were women, and they worried that this new woman minister would draw some of the power and influence away from them. King's womanly presence was not muted by ministerial garb or manners. She came on like a neighbor ("I wanted to be recognized as their friend"), and this more modest approach increased their wariness of her.

For all three ministers, their first year was a difficult and trying time. During this period of great suspicion, they chose to begin their ministry by offering a visible, pragmatic, and much-needed service—emergency medical transportation from the Carver Homes to nearby hospitals during the times of the day when it was virtually impossible to get hospitals to respond to their cries for help. It was a year of slowly growing trust as the ministers tried to stay visible and responsive to people's needs and began to shape a different image of a religious presence. They began to erode the once severe separations that had existed between church and community.

Even though Tanner and Hogans had been central in developing and sponsoring the urban ministry at Carver, during the first year there was no attempt to build alliances with Carver High School. As a matter of fact, the ministers learned to be generally suspect of all the established institutions that served the community. For example, they soon recognized the importance of confidentiality and the dangers of providing any information to the social service agencies that probed for their secrets. "We are successful because we don't have a tattletale system." Their identification with the community and their persistent advocacy stance often put them in positions of conflict with other "care givers," but they knew that a breach of friendship and trust would destroy years of labor and commitment. Alliances with the community have also been shaped by the passage of time. Over the three years of the urban ministry, the management of the Carver Homes has changed at least six times and the staffs of the other social agencies serving the community are in constant flux. In the midst of this shifting scene, the most stable force has been the community ministry.

In its second year, the ministers established a central office in one of the Carver Homes apartments, and each one took responsibility for developing a new program direction. King carved out the services for senior citizens and children, Lungu worked with alcoholics, and Green formed liaisons between the community and the schools. Because of Hogans's membership in one of the sponsoring churches and his genuine support of the urban ministry, the connections to Carver were easily made. The other surrounding schools were not receptive to Green's initiations. Says King, "There seems to be lots of rivalry and territorial jealousies among these schools." Green was given an office at Carver, and he spent much of his time counseling students with problems, working with their families, and providing support to teachers. The crises and problems that he confronted were severe and often unrelated to schoolwork—issues of sexual assault and harassment of teenage girls, child abuse and neglect, murder, homosexual promiscuity. In the third year of the ministry, many services have been expanded and strengthened. Green and Lungu have left the Carver Homes to pursue more traditional pastoral roles, and Velma King has been joined by another young, Black woman divinity student. The work within Carver High School is less visible, but the ministry is more embedded in community life, and the urban pastors continue to be a source of solace and support for Carver students and their families.

The school is merely the hub of Carver's fast-spinning wheel. The spokes that whirl around the center are attached to businesses, universities, churches, health facilities, and community agencies. Hogans and Tanner work to coordinate the complex relationships among the myriad supporting enterprises. The impact of the business connections are most clearly visible at Carver. The Work-Study Program, the Explorers Program, and the other student apprenticeships are vital, well established, and meaningful to students' lives at Carver. Less clearly drawn are the connections to academia. For instance, the contributions of university resources are not evident in Carver's academic program, which appears to need revitalization, new ideas, and clearer goals. The urban ministry suffers the same invisibility and disconnection. No one is currently responsible for maintaining close connections and negotiating the realms of families, community, and school. Although the effects of these weaker linkages may be indirect and less visible, it is not clear that they should be imitative of the sturdier networks to business and industry. One of the many challenges facing Carver will be in finding the balance between its centripetal and centrifugal forces.

9

Low- and High-Performing Schools Serving Native American Students*

editor's introduction:

Differences in School Performance. Why some schools perform well and others do not has been an ongoing concern of educators, parents, students, and policy-makers alike. This selection compares a low- and a high-performing school with regard to: a day in the life of a child; teachers' teaching styles; the influence of parents; and a variety of administrative conditions. Both schools are Canadian schools, and both have large numbers of Native American (First Nations) students, although one school is urban and the other rural. The comparisons reveal no partic-ular pattern that might account for the difference in student achievement, at least in the education of the First Nations students, for whom "things were not as simple as they seemed" (p. 153).

The selection highlights the heterogeneous nature of the students within the same school, especially among the First Nations students, calling it an example of "differ-ential school effectiveness" (p. 160). A possible lesson from this case study is the potentially misleading nature of asking aggregate, school-level questions in the first place. Such a possibility then poses an even more difficult task—how to formulate

---

*Epp, Walter, & Epp, Juanita Ross. (2002). "North America—Canada." In David Reynolds, Bert Creemers, Sam Stringfield, Charles Teddlie, & Gene Schaffer (Eds.), *World Class Schools: International Perspectives on School Effectiveness* (pp. 85–95). London: Taylor & Francis.

education policies and to design schooling and school assessments that acknowledge education as a matter of individual student performance, not the aggregate performance of an entire school or even the disaggregated performance of particular subgroups of students.

Relevance of Case Studies: Presenting Two Contrasting Cases as Part of the Same Case Study. This selection shows how the same case study can in fact present two "cases," different from the preceding selections in this anthology (but similar to Selection 14 of this anthology, "State Departments of Education"). The two cases were deliberately chosen to be contrasting ones, the authors' objective being to compare a "more" effective with a "less" effective school. A "word table" at the end of the selection summarizes their differences.

The two schools were initially defined as contrasting cases because of large differences in their student achievement scores. The bulk of the investigation was then devoted to determining whether other features of the schools could consistently account for the contrast. For instance, you might have expected certain instructional practices to have been present in one school but absent in the other.

A key to this "extreme cases" design is that you must confirm the existence of the contrast based on data collected prior to doing the case study. Once you have established the contrast, you then proceed to do the complete data collection, analysis, and case study. A potential problem arises when the initial contrast requires extensive data collection to be established. You then risk having to invest much time and effort just to select your cases, without yet having started to study them.

Introduction/Context

The eclectic nature of Canadian education makes diversity a hallmark of the Canadian system. There is no "typical" schooling in Canada. Education is the responsibility of the provinces and territories, and each has its own set of regulations and its own peculiarities. In British Columbia and Ontario, school principals are not included in the teachers' unions. In the other provinces, teachers and principals belong to the same union. Most provinces have one public school system, but in three of them (Alberta, Ontario and Saskatchewan) there are publicly funded, separate schools for Roman Catholic students. In Quebec, there are four publicly funded school systems based on language and religion (English Catholic, French Protestant, English Protestant and French Catholic). The geographic and political diversity of the country is recreated in its school system.

The Low-SES Schools: General Characteristics

Inner-City: The More Effective School. The Inner-City School was situated on the corner of two main intersections in a residential/business area in a city of 113,000. Approximately one-half of the students were of Caucasian extraction. Several students were of First Nations ancestry or came from mixed ethnic backgrounds. Many students at the school came from single-parent families. About half of the students arrived on buses from other parts of the city. Extra-curricular activities usually occurred at lunchtime, so as not to interfere with busing schedules.

The two-storey building was one of the first schools constructed in the city. It was very old and was starting to show its age. The schoolyard was fenced in to keep children from running into traffic. The hallways inside were decorated with student artwork.

The First Nations people who had left the reserve sent their children to inner-city schools such as the one in our study. The Inner-City School was attended by about 300 students between the ages of four and twelve. There were two classes of each of grades 1 through 6, with an average pupil-teacher ratio of 23:1. There was a staff of sixteen including the principal and vice-principal. One-third of the teachers had been on the staff for more than five years.

Fly-In: The Less Effective School. The remote Fly-In reserve in Northern Ontario was accessible only by air, for the majority of the year. For three months (January to March) the community could only be reached on a winter road built over the ice. Vehicles were brought up to the community on the winter road and were used for local transportation along with snowmobiles and all-terrain vehicles. There was a nursing station, a Northern Store (the contemporary Hudson Bay post), a modern school, a community centre, and a scattering of houses. Sixteen hundred people lived in this community, 90 per cent were unemployed. The school was the main employer and others worked at the Band administration office, the nursing station and the store.

The word "Band" is used here to describe a group of people, the First Nations population of the community as well as the administrative unit, consisting of a chief and a group of elected councillors charged with running the reserve. Until recently, the community was under the control of the federal government and the affairs of the community were taken care of by a White "First Nations Agent." In more recent years, the running of the community had become the responsibility of the "Band Council"—the chief and the councillors.

The loss of traditional lifestyle and decades of intervention—learned dependency, residential schools and loss of opportunity for economic self-sufficiency—had resulted in a lifestyle characterised by *ennui,* lack of hope and a proliferation of social problems. The reserve had been "dry" for approximately ten years, which meant that alcohol was forbidden and, therefore, only available on the black market. Even so, half of the residents suffered from severe alcohol problems and other drug-related problems, and diseases were rampant. Officials were particularly concerned about the number of violent deaths on reserves, especially the incidence of accidents and suicides.

In spite of these problems, the local people had made great strides in taking control of the issues and seeking improvement. Education had become the vehicle for change. The school had been controlled by the Band since 1988, and the Band Council received money from the federal government on a yearly basis based on the number of students enrolled. The Band Council, after receiving a budget from the Education Director of the local education authority, gave the money to the school through its financial officer. This increased autonomy and encouraged site-based decisionmaking.

The school was a modern building with a gymnasium and a library, and looked very like any other school except for the First Nations artwork, some by local artists and some by the children themselves, that was displayed in the halls and classrooms. There were about 500 students enrolled and the education authority employed eighty-two people—administrators, teachers, teacher aides, bus drivers, support personnel, janitors, etc. There were twenty-eight teachers, which translated into a pupil-teacher ratio of about 18:1. Nearly half of the teachers were First Nation, mostly local people who had been able to get their teaching certificates through a university program which allowed them to study in the community. It was not uncommon to find local people who lacked official qualifications, but who had gained the confidence of the education authority, in charge of classrooms. The non–First Nations teachers were mostly from Newfoundland.

The "Newfoundlanders" were a potential source of information on the clash between the two cultures. They seemed to stay in the community for extended periods of time, perhaps because Newfoundland is quite similar to the region in harshness of climate, size of population and feeling of community. These "outsider" teachers stayed long enough to grasp some of the difficulties and differences between First Nations and non–First Nations cultures. They felt, for example, that the standards at the school were different from those in other communities and were especially concerned about attitudes toward attendance.

Students attended this school from pre-kindergarten to grade 11. There were two classes of each grade and most classrooms had a teacher as well as a teacher aide. Students wishing to finish their senior matriculation had to leave the community to attend school at a First Nations–run residential school or in the nearest city, both of which were at least 400 kilometers away.

These two schools both had large numbers of First Nations students. The statistics comparing these two schools would suggest that the Inner-City School was more effective. The average grade score for the CTBS test scores in mathematics, for example, showed the Inner-City School to be more effective by an entire grade. But, as we examined the two schools using more qualitative processes, we found that, at least for the education of First Nations students, things were not as simple as they seemed.

A Day in the Life of a Child

At both schools, children started to arrive by bus and on foot at about 8:40 a.m. The Fly-In students played outside until the bell rang to indicate the beginning of classes at 9:00. In Inner-City, there was a bell to permit entry to the school at 8:40, although if it was really cold students could wait in the entry. Another bell rang at 8:55 and the students lined up at the outside doors to proceed in an orderly fashion to their classrooms. A third bell rang to indicate the beginning of classes at 9:00. These bells were indicative of the differences in philosophy which marked these two schools. At Fly-In, time and order were of lesser importance than was encouraging attendance. Children often came late and there was some coming and going throughout the school day since students did not require permission to visit the bathroom. Inner-City was more regimented and student behavior was monitored more carefully.

In both schools there were morning exercises. At Inner-City the exercises were broadcasted over the intercom. The principal's message was followed by the national anthem and a minute of silence. Prayer was no longer allowed in Ontario schools because it might infringe on the rights of non-Christian students. At Fly-In, the exercises took place in each individual room under the direction of the teacher.

It was perhaps ironic that there was prayer here. There were seven missionary churches in this community, and although Christianity had caused deep divisions among the local people, overall it was a strong presence. Technically, education at this school was the responsibility of the Canadian federal government, which made this school immune to the province's regulations forbidding the use of prayer. Expressions of First Nations' spirituality were evident in the artwork on the walls but not in the daily observance of Christian ritual.

Inner-City: The More Effective School. There was a formal schoolwide discipline plan, based on both rewards and punishments. For example, if a teacher saw a student behaving in a positive manner, the student received a "ticket." This ticket was placed in a drum and at the end of each month, the principal drew several tickets and winning students were rewarded with small prizes. Baseball caps, books, tickets to local sporting events and other treasured items were among the prizes. When students were seen behaving in an unacceptable manner, they lost tickets. This reduced their chances of winning a prize. At the end of each month, the principal announced the winners to the rest of the school. A student who behaved well and was rewarded many times in a month had a greater chance of winning.

Fly-In: The Less Effective School. There were general school rules and expectations, but discipline in the school had been left to individual teachers. The principal placed less emphasis on instructional or disciplinary leadership than did her counterpart at Inner-City. She focused mainly on liaison work with government-funding agencies and educational consultants.

Teachers' Teaching Style

Inner-City: The More Effective School. The grade 2 teacher was anxious to succeed and believed in firm discipline. He was kind and careful with the children, but was given to sudden explosions in which he raised his voice to students who had broken the rules or had failed to grasp his meaning. His lessons were well planned, although they were generally continuations of textbook materials—twenty minutes of instruction, followed by seatwork. The day was divided equally between mathematics and language arts, which were taught every day, and other courses such as art, music, physical education, and social skills.

Cooperative learning methods were expected by the local board, so he did, therefore, use group work on occasion. However, the processes were often variations on teacher-led instruction. Students were given worksheets and instructions and were asked to sit together in groups to do the work. This allowed for some interaction among the students, but they could as easily have done the work alone at their seats. The teacher was not pleased when groups communicated too much and engaged in off-task behaviors. He spent the time admonishing groups who were getting too loud and explained the work to groups who did not understand the assignment. He felt that these students were not good at cooperative learning because they could not remain focused.

Fly-In: The Less Effective School. The teacher at Fly-In was a First Nations woman who loved to teach. She was well organized, firm, and confident. She was well planned and, although her techniques were similar, in that she taught the lesson and used seatwork to follow it up, there was a sense that she was exceedingly interested in the subject at hand and eager to help the children to understand it. She used both lecture and small-group methods. The students did get loud, especially when they were working in a group but she appeared to control the students by her "presence"—she did not yell, and displayed a confident and consistent approach.

The Curriculum

Inner-City: The More Effective School. At Inner-City, the curriculum was a standard provincial curriculum of language arts, mathematics, sciences, etc. However, they too had implemented an additional course which was intended to teach students social skills. Its delivery was divided among the teachers at the various grade levels and everyone felt that it had improved relationships among everyone at the school and had had a positive effect on safety both in class and on the playground.

Fly-In: The Less Effective School. At Fly-In the provincial curriculum had been modified somewhat to make it more relevant to the needs of the students. The stated goals for the school at Fly-In were excellence in education, openness to new and innovative ideas, and maintenance of some of the traditions of the people.

The school had a mandatory First Nations languages program for all grades from kindergarten through grade 11 and there were two full-time First Nations language teachers on staff. Most of the students who came to the school for the first time were bilingual in English and Ojicree. The language program was one way to ensure that the young people maintained their Ojicree language skills and maintained communication between generations.

A recently introduced program, "The Journey Within," emphasized self-awareness and self-esteem for First Nations children. The program was an attempt "to enhance the child's sense of physical, mental, emotional, and spiritual well-being." The course included units on personal awareness, family, community, culture and environment. This program had been credited with helping the community to maintain a much lower rate of teen suicides than some other reserves. Another program was the "Artists in the School" program. Local artists and crafts people came into the classrooms to give children instruction, guidance, and inspiration in art, as there was a healthy and vibrant artistic community.

Ontario law forbids the teaching of religion in public schools, but, as mentioned earlier, this school was not bound by Ontario law. It had a Bible studies program which was taught weekly to all grades in the school—a non-denominational program with its main focus on the Bible. This was a contentious issue as there were several different denominations of Christians on the reserve and some of the local people would have preferred an emphasis on traditional First Nations spirituality.

The Influence of Parents

Inner-City: The More Effective School. There was an active parent-teacher association and parent volunteers were common. They helped out on field trips and one volunteer came into this particular class for one afternoon per week. School newsletters were sent out to parents at least once a month to inform the parents of special events or student successes. Parents were notified of their child's progress seven to ten times per year. This included the use of "meet the teacher" evenings, private phone calls or in-class meetings at the end of the day.

Fly-In: The Less Effective School. Parents were less often seen at Fly-In. These parents had a healthy respect for professionals as they were regularly attended to by social workers and health officials. They trusted the teachers to do a good job and saw no need for input into daily life at the school. Distances precluded many trips out of the community, although there were some wilderness field trips which parents participated in. School newsletters were sent out to parents occasionally, and parent-teacher interviews were held three times a year.

The Headteacher/Principal

Inner-City: The More Effective School. The principal described his management style as interactive. He included teachers in many decision-making processes, especially since this style of management was mandated by the local school board. The principal was available if students wished to talk to him. Many students stopped at the office to let the principal know of their successes or concerns. The vice-principal dealt with discipline problems. It was not uncommon for both the principal and the vice-principal to be working over the lunch hour.

The principal said that although he set the goals for the school, he attempted to be flexible; to change the goals to meet the changing needs of the school. The emphasis at the time of this study was on developing a curriculum to promote cooperative learning and provide a safe environment for all students. A school-growth team, composed of the principal, vice-principal, support teacher and teacher representatives, met regularly to discuss issues arising at this particular school. This team was examining issues pertaining to school improvement.

Fly-In: The Less Effective School. The principal and vice-principal were both local people. This served both to enhance and undermine their status. The administrators allowed teachers full autonomy in the day-to-day running of their classrooms and concerned themselves more with liaisons with the Band Council and negotiating funding. They tried to be available during breaks in the staffroom in order to keep in touch with what was going on in the school.

The principal carried out teacher evaluations twice a year, based on a classroom visit. These evaluations were extremely important for teachers, as those in Band-controlled schools had no job security. They were working from yearly contracts and a bad evaluation could mean not being rehired the following year. The goals for the school were set by the education authority and staff were expected to carry them out.

Inter-Staff Relations

Inner-City: The More Effective School. Staff relations may have been a bit strained due to outside issues which had in the mid-1990s affected all schools in Ontario. As a part of budget constraints, the provincial government imposed legislation which negated standing board/teacher contracts. Each school board was forced to cut costs and, in some places, this was done by scheduling unpaid days off for teachers and cutting school programs. In this city, the cuts forced teachers to forgo the nine days of teacher development that they would have received during an ordinary school year. Salary freezes and hiring limitations were also put in place. This "social contract" had a negative effect on teacher development, morale and job security.

The teachers had little to do with each other as each teacher usually did his or her work at a desk in the homeroom. Even though each teacher received a certain amount of planning time per week, the teachers' schedules were not conducive to group planning. They met at staff meetings approximately once a month.

Fly-In: The Less Effective School. There was much more inter-staff visiting because staff members were all a part of an isolated community. However, there appeared to be two separate staffs—the First Nations and the non–First Nations—and each group was critical of the other. The non–First Nations teachers felt that First Nations teachers were allowed to "get away with" too much—that they took too much time off, that they set a poor example by a higher level of absenteeism and by allowing students to "run wild." The First Nations teachers felt that the non–First Nations were too controlling and interventionist and were lacking in understanding of First Nations culture.

Resources

Inner-City: The More Effective School. At Inner-City, the budget was decentralized, in that some decisions on spending were made at the school level. However, the cost of teachers and the selection of new personnel was taken care of by the board. Schools were encouraged to order their supplies through the school board office because of the economies of scale.

Teachers at Inner-City had access to resources at the Instructional Material Center located at the board office. Audio-visual material, curriculum textbooks and supplementary material were available there, along with resource kits for a variety of subjects. Teachers from all over the city had access to this material at no charge, but they must have reserved the material they wished to use approximately two weeks in advance.

Teaching material could also be obtained from other school boards at a cost. Teachers also had access to materials through the local university and local public libraries.

Fly-In: The Less Effective School. Fly-In was funded by the federal government but the budget was locally controlled. Budget decisions were made by the local education authority in consultation with the administration. The school was very well equipped and there were no shortages in supplies and personnel. However, there were no supporting community resources and there were complications of time and travel in order to bring in resources from outside.

Relationship With Local Authorities

Inner-City: The More Effective School. Inner-City was a local entity which was generally free from political interference, although it was very susceptible to funding issues. There was ongoing contact with police because the police were automatically summoned if there was violence, and any issues pertaining to the illegal use of drugs had to be reported to the local authorities. The local police force employed officers responsible for delivering educational programs to a variety of city organizations. Once a year, officers came into the classroom to teach bicycle and street safety or drug and alcohol awareness.

Local health nurses administered fluoride treatments to the children on a regular basis. Hearing and vision checks were conducted in most grades. Students in each class were regularly checked for head lice (once or twice yearly) by parent volunteers and school personnel. This check usually coincided with a visit from the local health nurse.

Fly-In: The Less Effective School. At Fly-In, the relationship with the local authorities was very much an aspect of tribal politics. There were allegations that jobs and job security were based on nepotism. A Band Council resolution could bar anyone from the reserve, so teachers had to be careful not to offend. For example, teachers caught with alcohol could expect to be dismissed. This made teachers, especially the non–First Nations teachers, nervous about job security and their futures. The local teachers would always be local whether they taught in the community or not. The non–First Nations teachers were there only to teach and as such were never regarded as permanent members of the community.

School Image

Inner-City: The More Effective School. For Inner-City, their reputation and image was of little concern. The schools in this city were not in competition with each other for students. Students were assigned by the residence of their parents. The only other option was to switch to the separate school system, which some parents could do, but this was not a major concern. The school did keep in touch with parents, through parent organizations but there was little effort to be high profile with the community in general.

Fly-In: The Less Effective School. Fly-In had a positive image in the community and was considered to be innovative and provided leadership for other Band-controlled schools. Parents appeared to be quite confident that the school was providing quality education for their students and were pleased with the growing number of First Nations teachers in the school and the school's stated eventual goal of educating for a self-governing future for aboriginal people.

Conclusions

A walk through Inner-City showed the orderliness and control which allowed this school to function effectively. Teachers treated the students with respect, especially if they were complying with the school rules and guidelines. It was perhaps this adherence to routine and personal interaction which made this school work for most students. The consequences of misbehavior were known, the expectations were made clear, and the teachers and principals were committed to their work. Traditional attributes of standard school practice allowed this school to produce quiet hallways and positive academic outcomes.

The central problem of examining for effectiveness lies in the criteria to be used to indicate effectiveness. The First Nations students in these two schools served as representative evidence of this difficulty. At Inner-City, students were learning the useful skills of listening, understanding expectations, and carrying out orders. The people who did well in this school would be prepared for the job market in the traditional sense. However, there were students at this school who did not respond well to the strong structure, routine, and control. Among those students were many children of aboriginal ancestry. Insistence on control and routine could cause these students to withdraw from school as soon as possible, in order to avoid it. There were, in other words, issues of differential school effectiveness (see Teddlie and Reynolds 2000).

At Fly-In, on the other hand, there was a very different approach to student performance. The entire community was plagued with the problems of violence, abuse, and poverty, and the school attempted to make allowance for these difficulties. Individuals, both students and staff, were recognized, and special circumstances were understood and accepted. In spite of the community problems and organizational challenges, the educational initiatives at this school had been remarkable. The First Nations artist program—the self-esteem initiatives and the community-based teacher education programs—all spoke of a hope for a more positive future that included these students. The community-based teacher education program, for example, was intended to integrate local people into the school system. They studied on the reserve, then were employed by the local school authority, team teaching with existing teachers or taking over classrooms which were previously staffed by non–First Nations teachers. The process symbolized a community hoping to take charge of its own future, which means that the social outcomes of this school may have been substantial in ways that the academic outcomes were not. Differences between the two schools are summarized in Table 9.1. . . .

Table 9.1   Summary of Differences Between the Two Low-SES Schools Across Twelve Dimensions

Dimension of Contrast	More Effective Low SES (Inner-City)	Less Effective Low SES (Fly-In)
General characteristics of the school	CTBS scores ahead of low effectiveness Low-SES school Situated in inner city Good reputation built up over time 50 per cent white, 50 per cent ethnic minority 300 students Pupil/teacher ratio 23/1 Old building	Low CTBS scores Geographically isolated, on a reserve Building a reputation First Nations population 500 students Pupil/teacher ratio 18/1 New building, good facilities
A day in the life of a child	Time well managed	Low attendance rate (60 per cent) Tolerance of lateness
Teachers' teaching style	Firm discipline, some shaming of troublesome students Mostly whole-class interactive instruction	Well organized Use of small-group methods as well as whole-class instruction
The curriculum	Commitment to basic skills Standard provincial curriculum	Emphasis upon First Nations culture in art work, etc. First Nations language programme Modified provincial curriculum Native language programmes
The influence of parents	Active involvement in PTA Use of newsletters to parents Regular meeting of parents with their child's teacher	No PTA—teachers left alone Infrequent newsletters Rare parent/teacher interaction

(Continued)

Table 9.1 (Continued)

Dimension of Contrast	More Effective Low SES (Inner-City)	Less Effective Low SES (Fly-In)
The principal	Committed to 'order', instruction leader Involving teachers in decision-making; Available to all students Strong sense of 'mission' inculcated to all	Entangled in outside commitments Involvement in staff social relationships Emphasis on teacher autonomy
School expectations of pupils	Firm discipline, generated by reward system with schoolwide orientation	Discipline left to individual teachers
School goals	Strong social control Importance of routine Respect for students	Building strong, distinctive social identity Social outcomes emphasized because of community disintegration
Inter-staff relations	Business-like; slightly strained because of budget constraints	Cliques, with a split between 'non-First Nations' and 'First Nations' teachers
School resources	Good quality of audio-visual material; curriculum textbooks and learning material	Good quality of audio-visual material; curriculum textbooks and learning material
Relationship with local authorities	Conventional relationship with educational district; close links with health, welfare and police agencies	Complex relationship with local authorities
School image	Little concern with image because of an absence of competition between schools	Positive image in the community

162

[Editor's Note: The text then continues by examining three middle schools.]

Reference

Teddlie, C., and Reynolds, D. (2000). *The International Handbook of School Effectiveness Research*. London: Falmer Press.

10

Schools on Probation*

editor's introduction:

School Accountability. One of the most important federal initiatives during the early part of the 21st century took place in the form of the passage of comprehensive education legislation—the No Child Left Behind Act (NCLB) of 2001. The main thrust of this legislation was to assess school performance and to make school administrators accountable for student performance, especially student achievement.

If schools did not perform up to standards, they were deemed "low performing," with specified sanctions. If a school remained "low performing" for over a pre-identified number of years, it then risked being disbanded or "reconstructed"—or "reconstitution eligible," in the current selection.

You can imagine being the principal of such a school or teaching in it under those conditions. The present selection describes such conditions as part of a study of school accountability in two states, Maryland and Kentucky. The selection focuses on a school ("School B") that was subjected to state policies mimicking but also predating the NCLB. The authors chose the school, a middle school, because it had been designated as "low performing" (the original work also includes case studies of four other schools besides School B). The School B case demonstrates the stresses placed on a school's staff when accountability for student performance is at issue. You should not be surprised at the intense focus on students' test-taking skills and behavior.

Relevance of Case Studies: Revealing Dissidence and Disagreement. The case of School B is presented anonymously, a tactic frequently used in case studies. Such anonymity helps authors to gain the cooperation of officials and interviewees—in

---

*Mintrop, Heinrich (with Curtis, Kim, & Plut-Pregeli, Lea). (2004). "Schools Moving Toward Improvement." In *Schools on Probation: How Accountability Works (and Doesn't Work)* (pp. 76–86). New York: Teachers College Press.

this selection, the staff of a middle school—and to protect them from possible repercussions stemming from their participation in the study. However, the assurance of anonymity also opens the possibility of your case study being able to examine some delicate issues, especially those involving dissidence or disagreement on the part of the participants being interviewed.

At the same time, the result is a text where neither the school nor the individual interviewees are identified. You can see for yourself that the text loses a degree of reality, compared to the other selections in this anthology. As an alternative tactic, you can consider using pseudonyms, for both the school and individual staff members. You need to judge whether such a tactic might have made any difference in the present selection or with your own case study.

D espite its low-performance label, School B was in a more fortunate situation than many other Maryland schools on probation. Of the middle schools in the sample, it scored highest on the MSPAP [Maryland State Performance Assessment Program] from the inception of the account-ability system. With a student mobility rate of approximately 30% and just 40% of the school population qualifying for free or reduced-price lunches, the school was less impacted by poverty. Its surroundings, a fairly solid neighborhood, bolstered its image. It was located in a district that had rela-tively few schools on probation, so the school was supported with an addi-tional $150,000 to its regular budget. The school had a magnet program, and even though a recent state auditing team could not detect a curricular differentiation between the magnet and the regular programs, teachers in the school thought the program was useful in attracting better students.

The school was identified as reconstitution-eligible in January of 1998, when its 1996–1997 MSPAP composite index plummeted by more than 9 points. Hence, at the time of data collection, the low-performance label was fresh. Prior to this drop, the school had been making relatively steady progress on both its MSPAP and MFT [Maryland Function Test] test results. According to those at School B, the severity of the decline, as opposed to a persistent pattern of low performance, was the reason the school was added to the state's probationary list. As dramatic as the 1997 test score decline was for School B, its rebound the following year proved to be even more dra-matic, though in subsequent years test scores either stagnated or even dipped a little. Staff members were at a loss to explain these fluctuations. Given consistency in improvement strategies, teachers mentioned the mindset of student cohorts from year to year and teacher turnover.

Although turnover was high, School B had been able to maintain a level of stability that was higher compared to other schools on probation. Exemplifying this stability is the fact that the principal had been at the school for 18 years, an increasingly rare situation in a school district that had experienced a principal turnover rate of over 40% in the study period. 1997 marked a turning point for School B, when it lost half of its eighth-grade teaching staff, a key testing grade for the state test.

Approximately 50% of the core teaching staff working at School B during the 1999–2000 school year had arrived in the years since it was placed on probation in 1998. Hence, they were not around when the school declined. In particular, the math and science departments were especially hard hit, with 8 of the 10 teachers in each of these departments either in their first or second year of teaching at School B. During interviews, members of both the administration and teaching staff commented on an unusually large turnover after the 1998–1999 school year, School B's first full year as a probation school. While the majority of teachers interviewed said they enjoyed working with the faculty and staff at School B and noted that they would not leave for a school with similar characteristics, many remarked that they had either seriously considered or would consider taking opportunities elsewhere.

Leadership and Interactions

Relating to School B's faculty and staff in a paternalistic way, the principal possessed a quiet, steady demeanor. He was generally described by teachers as easily approachable, willing to listen, and responsive to their needs. According to teachers, while he tried to use a consensual approach when making decisions, he always had the last say. Reflecting findings from interviews, 72% of surveyed teachers viewed the principal as "supportive and encouraging" and 69% characterized him as being responsible for setting priorities, making plans, and seeing that they were carried out. His leadership style was generally top-down, but also caring.

Although he was low-key by nature, many teachers who had been at the school for a number of years noted a striking change in the principal's intensity level once the school had been identified as low-performing. The principal himself noted that he took the news very personally and felt as though he had "failed" as an educator. Pressure from the state department to have him removed made it clear to him that his future as principal of School B hinged on MSPAP improvement. Thus, he made it his overriding concern to raise test scores at the school. From the very beginning, he tried to keep his staff informed about "what was coming down the road" and sought to reinforce the "advantages" of the school's new status—namely, that the school would receive additional funds and assistance. He communicated to teachers and parents that he saw no sense in "fighting" the situation. At the same time, he asked for their assistance in moving forward to implement the school improvement procedures that had been laid out by the state.

Teachers reported that probation made the principal much more interested in what was going on inside their classrooms. In fact, a full 89% of teachers surveyed found that, as a result of reconstitution eligibility, they received more attention from the administration. The principal made weekly visits to classrooms to observe lessons and ensure compliance with school reform measures. During these visits he evaluated teachers' performance using a checklist system. Those found to be not in compliance received memos in their boxes the next day. Having previously enjoyed a relatively high level of autonomy within the classroom, teachers found the new intrusive policies to be stressful. A feeling prevailed that "it's like everything is MSPAP. We're being watched" (B-4).[1]

At the same time, the principal also authorized his administrative support staff, including the instructional coordinator, the master teacher, and the school improvement resource teacher (SIRT), to be a very visible presence in teachers' classrooms. In response to the pressures of probation and with the help of new probation-related funds, the principal had recruited some of his most capable teachers into these new positions. Highly skilled and generally well regarded, these teachers were responsible for the majority of the day-to-day teacher-administrator interactions that occurred at School B. They were frequently found observing classrooms, meeting with teachers, and providing in-service training opportunities. But they also oversaw the day-to-day implementation of improvement measures enumerated in the school improvement plan (SIP). For example, they co-chaired weekly team meetings with the principal and reviewed faculty lesson plans for alignment with the SIP. While the instructional coordinator bemoaned this "negative way to operate" (B-20), she believed that without the administration's follow-up, the SIP's school improvement measures would languish.

But this new oversight role was delicate, and it brought with it the disadvantage that, in the words of one of them, she "had been a teacher the year before and here [she] comes back in August and suddenly can come in and say: 'So what's going on in here.'" (B-20). The teachers understood that the principal backed up his new leadership team, but tact, a nonthreatening

---

[1]Code numbers used throughout the text refer to specific interviewees without identifying them.

demeanor, cheerful disposition, and visible skill on the part of the instructional specialists eased their transition into a supervisory role.

Not all teachers were open to heightened scrutiny at the hands of their former peers. For example, one science teacher specifically said that she was initially upset when she found out that "someone from the English department" was "grading" her lesson plan and making suggestions about her content. Indeed, many teachers privately grumbled about their need to comply with numerous administrative mandates. However, although this grumbling was at times loud, compliance appeared to be relatively high. One teacher of unusually long standing attributed the high level of teacher conformity to School B's large number of new teachers so that there was "nobody to oppose [the principal]" (B-4). She believed that if the building had been filled with more experienced teachers, he wouldn't have been able to push through so many changes so quickly. Indeed, the open conflict between the administration and faculty members that led to the departure of many highly experienced teachers during the school's first post-probationary year serves to confirm this sentiment.

Interestingly, while several of School B's teachers expressed disdain for many of the new measures implemented by the principal and his administrative team, most did not express dislike for the principal himself. In fact, a striking number of teachers commented that the principal had played a large role in their decision to stay on at School B despite their various grievances, most notably the high level of stress brought on by heightened teacher accountability. The principal proved adept at deflecting responsibility for the numerous interventions and teacher accountability measures instituted at the school since it had been named reconstitution-eligible. He succeeded in diffusing teacher ire by playing the role of the reluctant enforcer. As one teacher noted, the state "is putting a huge amount of pressure on him and he in turn puts huge amounts of pressure on the teachers" (B-4).

Once on probation, the principal began to conduct weekly meetings with the various grade-level teams that divided into magnet and nonmagnet subdivisions. These weekly team meetings, conducted in the principal's rather cramped office, were the only faculty meetings that regularly took place at School B. Assemblies of the whole faculty were discontinued. While the leadership team viewed these meetings as mini in-service opportunities where teachers were given tips and strategies for improving student performance on MSPAP-related tasks, teachers perceived their function at least in part as a means to "check up" on their performance:

> During weekly team meetings, if you haven't . . . if you've dropped the ball, he will let you know. He doesn't call you out individually, but within the group he will emphasize more. . . . Lets you know specifically, you dropped the ball. (B-12)

That the meetings were conducted in the principal's office only reinforced their accountability bent to the teachers. In almost all of the observed team meetings, either the principal or a member of the leadership team presented the tasks for the week, leaving it to the teachers to ask questions of clarification or make suggestions for implementation.

Outside of these team meetings, collegial interaction occurred in informal channels, though many teachers perceived their faculty as unified and supportive. The team structure impeded significant cross-team interactions in the building, and opportunities to come together in formal meetings without control of the leadership team were few. Many teachers commented that they were generally unfamiliar with the methods and practices of other teams. Some teachers reported feeling isolated by School B's team emphasis, and others expressed a desire for more regular content-area interactions. However, most seemed to accept their limited peer interactions as unproblematic. Undoubtedly, teachers' willingness to forgo additional faculty exchanges stemmed from their fervent desire to keep meetings to an absolute minimum, lest they impinge on scarce planning time that was already taken up in large part by meetings with the principal and student and parent conferences.

According to teachers, discussions concerning curricular issues or instructional strategies were not common occurrences outside the weekly team meetings. Apart from instructions received from administrators, instructional specialists, and external consultants, teachers made no mention of instances in which they were asked to share their expertise with their colleagues in any systematic manner. Nor were there any discussions about the goals and wisdom of the accountability system. Some teachers bemoaned this lack of meaningful opportunity for formal collegial interactions:

> Something that I would like to see implemented would be more collaboration among the teachers, in a, in sort of a cross-curriculum way, sharing of ideas mainly to observe one another. I mean, I think if we could have more interaction, other than casual passing through, that that could possibly help to build us . . . because there are some very strong, experienced teachers and a lot of times teachers just don't get an opportunity to talk to their colleagues about what they're doing and see, and actually see, how they do it. (B-13)

Strategies for Improvement

Once being named reconstitution-eligible, School B implemented several wide-ranging strategies aimed specifically at improving MSPAP performance. An in-depth analysis of MSPAP data conducted by the school's instructional coordinator served to focus the selection of these school improvement strategies. Her careful study of School B's MSPAP data allowed her to recognize some recurrent student testing weaknesses, which she then translated into a set of generic instructional strategies that were tailored to the test and applicable across the curriculum. The school's intensive focus on MSPAP was affirmed by the instructional coordinator when she noted: "I could very confidently say that MSPAP is driving every single action and thought in this building" (B-20).

Teacher in-service training and weekly team meetings provided the settings for instruction in generic test-taking strategies that virtually all teachers incorporated into their daily lessons. These strategies were designed to promote student acquisition of skills needed to do well on the MSPAP test, such as writing persuasive arguments and answering reading comprehension questions in paragraph form. Using these "tricks" to crack the performance-based format of the MSPAP (B-20), teachers instructed students in how to structure responses so that they met MSPAP grading standards. One teacher explained:

> Now I am just trying to teach some strategies here for the MSPAP. I know that when they grade the MSPAP, it is an assembly-line process. And I am thinking, I am just personally thinking then if they see a good topic sentence on these sentences, that would help squeeze some points for us. (B-19)

Several teachers conveyed their sentiment that the school had become much more "test focused" (B-3, B-6, B-20) at the expense of subject content. In fact, the school's tremendous emphasis on generic test preparation strategies was made evident in the thick instructional handbook developed by the instructional coordinator. This handbook, filled with a veritable alphabet soup of tips and pointers designed to orient instruction toward building MSPAP skills, was distributed to every teacher in the building at the beginning of the 1999–2000 school year. Concerning the handbook's purpose, the instructional coordinator commented: "The kind of work that is happening here is naming skills, very specific skills, that can be applied to each content. Content-specific skills? No" (B-20). Most teachers reported that they believed the strategies to be helpful in the classroom, and their use was widely observed during classroom observations. In fact, 92% of School B teachers surveyed reported using new instructional methods in their classrooms as a result of the school's reconstitution-eligible status.

While teachers reported their satisfaction with many of the new strategies brought to the school after being placed on probation, several expressed concern that the constant focus on MSPAP reduced their ability to teach the basic competency skills they believed their students needed. Concerning this issue, one sixth-grade teacher commented that the state "is trying to get higher-order thinking when the kids are having a hard enough time with the basic skills. They're making kids jump levels, and they're missing a lot in the middle . . . missing the foundation" (B-14). When asked about this issue, 70% of those teachers surveyed believed that teaching to the MSPAP required them to neglect skills that were needed by their students. Indeed, the inherent conflict in the state's requirement that students must be equally well prepared for both the MSPAP and the MFTs did not go unnoticed by teachers. As one seventh-grade teacher noted: "We have the Functionals through the state, which are all multiple-choice and basic. And then [the students] have MSPAP next year. So what do you want me to prepare for? You can't teach kids one way, and give them a different format" (B-9).

In addition to test-taking skills for the performance-based test, the school focused on reading remediation for the vast majority of its students reading below grade level with the help of a reading lab and an additional period of reading for all seventh-graders. This scheduling change meant that approximately 10 minutes was shaved off the class time of other subjects. Teachers of other subjects expressed frustration with this schedule change because, despite the shorter class periods, they were still expected to cover the same curriculum. In addition, the capacity of the reading lab was insufficient. Because it accommodated only 15 students at a time, teachers of all subjects were required to teach reading to those who could not be in the lab. Some of those teachers, while supporting students' use of the lab, felt ill equipped to teach reading and concluded that the classroom portion of the reading period tended to be of little use for the students:

> What happens is I'm actually a babysitter for reading. Because half of my class goes to the reading lab for 15 or 20 minutes, so they leave, they go there, they come back. The other half goes down, and there is no way that I'm teaching reading . . . there's a true interruption in my lesson (if I had one), but I don't bother to do one because it's just not good. (B-11)

After the school was identified as low-performing, School B's administration worked hard to create what it considered a consistent learning environment for its students. This consistency was built around the establishment of uniform practices for classroom teachers governing lesson planning, pedagogy, and classroom appearance. Examples of these standardized practices included the following: that lesson plans promoting the acquisition of MSPAP skills be written daily and collected weekly for administrative review; that course objectives, warm-up, and closure activities be written daily on the chalkboard; that timers be used to time student classroom activities; and that student materials and MSPAP words/rubrics be hung on classroom walls and changed regularly.

As noted earlier, this standardization was met with mixed reviews. Some teachers believed that consistency was helpful because it allowed students to become familiar with a uniform set of expectations. As one teacher noted: "This administration is trying to get things together, they are trying to have all teachers on one accord and not be on 'I'm doing my thing, you do your thing.'. . . And we are working on that; trying to get a cohesiveness" (B-2). However, other teachers resisted these measures, with one teacher even going so far as to consider the uniformity as potentially damaging to students: "I think that seeing it done more than one way fosters creativity in a kid. I mean, if you're saying this is the way to do it, this is the way . . . then you don't have those kids with powered perspectives" (B-10). Others considered increased control of instruction as superfluous and not very substantive:

A lot of times we feel we're being watched all the time. Which is kind of insulting, especially with people who have been teaching for 20 years. . . . Now all of a sudden they have to write up these picayune little lesson plans, and they have to have certain things on the walls. Not that the kids read them or anything, but, you know, it's just another thing that we're required to do, another thing that's going to take up our time. (B-16)

Teachers worried about the fact that they were expected to have a different lesson plan each day, complete with new objectives and activities, despite their personal belief that their students might need to focus on the same work for more than one day. However, whether or not they were in agreement, they tried to exhibit the structures and activities that the principal would check. Several teachers said they felt stressed about the fact that they might be "caught with [their] pants down" during these inspections (B-11). As one teacher noted:

You never know when the principal is going to come and check the [lesson plan]. He checks to make sure it's completed. Makes sure that the correct date is on there. He's making sure that it's different basically every day. He wants papers up . . . graded papers, corrected class work, corrected homework on the board and on the walls. And he's checking for different posters we should have up to enrich the kids. I think he's checking for timers, making sure we're using the timers and making sure that we're closing the lesson. (B-6)

As a result of its probationary status, School B was the recipient of approximately $150,000 in school improvement funds. The money bought additional library books and financed after-school activities, but it was primarily used to finance additional instructional specialist positions, technology, a reading lab, and a comprehensive school reform model. Virtually all teachers were aware that the school had been the recipient of a large amount of funding, and they responded positively to the variety of new resources and assistance. However, as mentioned previously, they expressed regret that the school needed to be labeled low-performing in order to obtain them.

When the district in year 2 of probation mandated the adoption of a comprehensive reform design for all middle schools on probation, the school selected a technology-based model that was expensive and required the purchase of new hardware. Although anticipated to be the centerpiece of school improvement for the 1999–2000 school year, the required computers were not purchased and installed until the end of the year. The delay was initially caused by the county's incoming school superintendent, who refused to release school funds until she had conducted a detailed review of the school system's 1999–2000 budget. The computers were further delayed when the vendor with whom the school had placed its order suddenly stopped doing business with the district because its account had fallen into arrears. Nevertheless, the administration moved forward with all scheduled in-service activities for teachers. This proved to be a controversial action among School B's faculty. While most teachers noted their interest in being able to incorporate technology into the classroom, they found it difficult to incorporate the model without Internet access. As a result, the training was viewed by many teachers as simply a waste of their time: "Without the computers in the classroom, we don't understand why we're meeting with [the model consultants]. What they expect us to do is not realistic" (B-14). Interestingly, while the model actually encompassed a variety of activities in addition to the use of classroom computers—such as project-based instruction and portfolio assessment—teachers focused almost exclusively on its technological aspects. The model managed to help a few teachers implement group projects focusing on high-interest topics such as the portrayal of teens in the media. However, it was telling that these teachers were directed to implement these creative group projects designed to promote higher-order thinking skills only after the completion of that year's MSPAP preparation and examinations.

In addition to test preparation and model-specific in-services, the school also provided staff development aimed at the upgrading of teacher skills particularly for its large group of young and inexperienced teachers who fluctuated from year to year. Each Wednesday afternoon the master teacher offered teacher-training sessions covering such diverse topics as how to write a lesson plan, classroom management, and active learning strategies. Many of the more experienced teachers noted the decidedly "new teacher" bent to these in-services. As one experienced teacher noted: "The professional development that we have . . . I believe is working tremendously, especially with the younger teachers" (B-10). More experienced teachers, however, did not find these in-services particularly relevant to their needs. Some of these teachers expressed frustration with the lack of focus on content:

> We have several workshops here, and they're mainly on lesson planning, long-range planning, but it is for all of the content and doesn't really focus on that one subject, like social studies, for example. It doesn't focus on one particular subject matter as far as things that you can take to your class. (B-6)

Summary

In summary, probation increased administrative control at School B, but control came with a smiling face. The principal was warm and paternal but had made it clear that they—he with the rest of the school—had their backs against the wall. The demands of accountability were a given, and conversations in meetings revolved around how to implement the principal's directions. The instructional specialists were accommodating and always full of ideas, but the teachers knew that their proposals were what the principal wanted to get done. Teachers at School B felt controlled and supported. Many of our interviewees empathized with the principal's difficult position, they "understood" that accountability dictated stronger measures, and they appreciated the sense of direction that was provided for them, but at the same time many wished to escape the pettiness and pressure and work somewhere else. After the first year of probation, and despite the school's success in raising test scores, 70% of the surveyed teachers were contemplating leaving the school.

In designing its improvement strategies, School B closely followed the demands of the accountability system and fulfilled district mandates. Test preparation strategies, reading remediation, a mandated comprehensive school reform project, and the basic support of inexperienced teachers were the strategic foci. The caliber of support received from the instructional specialists backed up by the principal's regular classroom visits opened classroom doors and made teachers' instruction subject to external intervention. It is noteworthy, however, that these interventions were restricted to elements of instruction that could easily be monitored by the principal or covered by the specialists' areas of expertise. Strategies resulted in add-ons to the regular instructional programs, which remained largely untouched. The strategies, however, ran into implementation problems and trade-offs that hampered the school's forceful response. The school benefited from additional resources. Without them probation would have been met with much more teacher dissatisfaction, which remained high despite the fact that the school was moving.

11

Public School Choice*

editor's introduction:

Having the Ability to Choose Your Specific Public School. School systems usually assign students to schools on the basis of local residence, producing the traditional "neighborhood" school. Public school choice gives students and their families the opportunity to attend public schools other than their closest (or neighborhood) school (note that the choice is different from the traditional one between attending a private versus a public school).

In many school districts, such choices already have existed at the secondary school level, with students able to choose to attend various magnet school programs across an entire city. Charter schools also represent alternatives. However, in addition to magnet and charter schools, the ability to attend virtually any school in a public school system (e.g., by having open enrollment procedures) has been espoused as a potential way of improving contemporary school systems.

District 4 in New York City has been among a small number of systems that has provided public school options for a long period of time. The district's schools are encouraged to develop distinctive programs that might be attractive to different kinds of students. The desired effect is not simply to provide increased choice but to improve the whole system of schools. For this reason, expanding school choice options has become increasingly popular. And for this reason, the overall objective of the case study is to determine whether sufficient evidence supports the conclusion that the fastest growth in mathematics and reading scores in District 4 happened

*Teske, Paul, Schneider, Mark, Roch, Christine, & Marschall, Melissa. (2000). "Public School Choice: A Status Report." In Diane Ravitch & Joseph P. Viteritti (Eds.), *Lessons From New York City Schools* (pp. 313–338). Baltimore: Johns Hopkins University Press.

"during the greatest expansion of choice programs" (p. 192) and that "choice be recognized as a catalyst" (p. 200) in improving test scores.

Relevance of Case Studies: Using Quantitative Evidence. Contrary to some stereotypes, case studies also can be the occasion for extensive analyses of quantitative data. You may choose not to do such a case study yourself. However, if you are unable to read or interpret others' quantitative research, you would be neglecting an important form of case study. The present selection gives you an idea of the level of skill needed, showing you the care with which the relevant data were collected (and the special problem of amassing comparable annual data to cover a lengthy time period), as well as the statistical models that permitted the analysis to incorporate relevant control variables (these variables all represent rival hypotheses that needed to be ruled out).

Despite its quantitative bent, the selection may be considered a case study for several reasons. First, the authors are reporting about a "case" (the expansion of school choice options) within its real-life context (a district in New York City). Second, the research question was retrospective (whether changes that already had taken place in the schools could be associated with improved student achievement). Third, the authors relied on different sources of evidence (the archival achievement data and the interviewing of district officials). Classifying the selection as a case study is incidental, however, to the fact that the research was extremely well conceived and well executed.

In 1992, the New York City Board of Education approved a system of *inter*district public school choice, making it possible for parents to choose a school for their children outside of the community school district in which they live. This choice plan eliminated the need for parents to get a waiver from their zoned district (an "exit visa") in order to apply to a school in another district. This effectively allowed the thirty-two community school districts that operate the elementary and middle schools in New York City the opportunity to promote choice for students within their areas, which some have done more actively than others.

Choice is not a new concept in New York City. At the high school level the city has long had a tradition of a large number of public schools of choice. These range from elite schools for academically talented students, such as Stuyvesant and Bronx Science, to schools for students with particular talents, such as Performing Arts, and career-oriented magnet schools.[1] In addition to this formal choice mechanism, many parents, as is well known, have "scammed" the system by using false addresses to get their children into schools or districts they prefer. Also, the alternative schools sponsored by New York Networks and the Annenberg program in the 1990s,[2] which now serve nearly 5 percent of the more than one million students in New York, are mainly schools that parents choose for their children. Finally, rounding out the list of choice programs found in the city's school system, a few of the thirty-two districts adopted *intra*district choice plans before 1992. Thus, although New York State is one of about twenty states that did not have a charter school law until 1998, there were several forms of public school choice technically available to a considerable number of parents and students prior to then.

Despite these mechanisms, the city Board of Education has mostly paid lip service to interdistrict choice since 1992. As a result, even though interdistrict choice is stated policy, parents trying to select a school usually find it extremely difficult to exercise choice. Most of the desirable schools are already oversubscribed with students from within the district, and procedures for entry from outside the "home" district vary widely across the city. According to Hill et al., open enrollment in New York City is "rendered virtually meaningless by the fact that the nonselective magnet schools to which all students may apply get 10 to 30 applicants for every seat. The majority of students who try to choose a school other than the one in their neighborhood end up back in the school they tried to flee."[3]

Just getting accurate information about the schools and about how to exercise choice is difficult. Clara Hemphill, who recently wrote an advice book about choosing New York schools, notes that getting information from districts and schools "can be like nailing Jell-O to the wall."[4] In theory, schools cannot discriminate based on race, gender, or special needs, and are supposed to utilize random lotteries when applicants exceed seats. However, bureaucratic obstacles and lack of information can make it extremely difficult for parents, unless they are extremely energetic, to find a spot in a school outside their district.

We were unable to locate anyone or any office at the Board of Education that tracks interdistrict choice programs and no one could supply us with comprehensive figures on the number of students or the number of schools involved in interdistrict choice. This alone suggests that the Board of Education is not strongly committed to that form of choice. Instead, each community school district can keep track of its own student figures, but they do not do so in a consistent format. Willen found that District 2 in Manhattan, a district with considerable intradistrict choice, had 1,422 students apply from outside the district in 1997, with 1,027 accepted for admission.[5] One of the top-rated districts, District 26 in Bayside, Queens, had 767 students seek entry in 1997, and accepted less than half. District 4 historically has had more than one thousand students come into the district from outside. These three districts represent some of the most desirable districts. If we assume, liberally (as the true number is probably smaller), that another five hundred students have been accepted into schools outside of their home districts in thirteen more districts, then about nine thousand students from grades K–8 are now utilizing interdistrict choice. While this number may put some pressure on unattractive schools and districts to improve their performance, it represents a mere 1 percent of the 1.1 million students across the city. (Including the choices made at the high school level would, of course, increase this percentage.) In contrast, the Annenberg-sponsored alternative schools now represent a far larger number of students, at nearly 5 percent.

Thus *inter*district choice in New York City does exist, but we do not believe it is yet a major factor in stimulating much educational change. We now turn our attention to choice at the *intra*district level.

As noted above, intradistrict choice is allowed throughout New York City. However, some districts had adopted such choice plans on their own prior to the 1992 citywide legislation. Indeed, District 4 has a history of choice tracing back nearly twenty-five years. Most of this chapter is devoted to analyzing performance issues associated with choice in District 4. Existing studies of school choice are limited by the simple fact that reforms such as vouchers and charter schools have been in place for relatively short periods of time, making the assessment of the effects of choice difficult. In contrast, we believe that looking at the effects of choice in District 4 over the more than two decades it has been in place can give us analytic insight on how broader programs of choice in New York might affect school performance.

If imitation is the sincerest form of flattery, District 4 should consider itself highly flattered. In recent years, partly in direct imitation of District 4's successes, a few other districts have developed and/or expanded choice within their boundaries. District 2 has gone the furthest in this effort. These changes took place in the eleven years in which Anthony Alvarado, who not coincidentally led the efforts to implement choice in District 4, was District 2 superintendent (1988–98). District 1 in Manhattan established five alternative schools of choice in the 1990s, and some other districts have made similar but limited forays into choice programs.[6] After we explore the relationship of choice to performance in District 4, we will present a more limited examination of District 2's experience with choice. This provides a useful contrast, as District 4 has a student body that is of lower than average income for the city, while District 2 has a student body with higher than average levels of income.

Our goal is to try to identify the effects of choice on performance. While our data and analysis focus on intradistrict choice, we believe that some of the lessons we draw from this study can apply to other forms of choice that are being implemented in New York.

Choice in District 4

There is considerable anecdotal evidence that choice in District 4 has increased the performance of the schools in the district. However, the argument that choice in District 4 has been a success has been based on relatively little quantitative evidence. In turn, some scholars have argued that the data used to show District 4's successes are flawed. Beyond the question of whether or not District 4 has been successful, others have argued that any successes may be attributable to such factors as administrative leadership and innovation, small school size, and "extra" resources generated from external federal magnet programs and from District 4's overspending its budget. If these points are accurate, then we might not expect any improvements from choice in District 4 to be replicable in other districts. To the extent possible with the existing data, we try to isolate the effects of choice from the effects of other factors on changing performance in District 4 schools.

In presenting our results, we address two critical dimensions of this question: (1) Has student performance in District 4 really improved since the implementation of choice, and if so, has choice contributed to this improvement? (2) Has choice expanded the range of educational opportunities for all parents and students in District 4, or only for a select group?

Student Performance in District 4

Supporters of choice point to considerable evidence that academic performance improved after the implementation of choice in District 4. A few studies illustrated an improvement in raw reading and math test scores in District 4 over time.[7] These studies also showed that more District 4 students were accepted into prestigious selective high schools than in the past.[8] For example, in 1973, only ten District 4 students were accepted into Bronx Science, Stuyvesant, Brooklyn Tech, or the LaGuardia School of Music, but by the mid-1980s, District 4 was placing three hundred students annually in these schools.[9] The rate of acceptance gradually but steadily increased throughout the 1970s and 1980s, and by 1987 the rate of acceptance from District 4 was twice that of the rest of the city.

Several schools in District 4 are truly excellent. For example, today over 90 percent of graduates from Central Park East Elementary School go on to earn high school diplomas, and 90 percent of Central Park East Secondary School students go on to college (a rate that is nearly double that for the city as a whole).[10] In 1996, the New York City Board of Education reported that the elementary school with the highest reading scores of the city's 670 schools was District 4's TAG school. The schools have so dramatically improved that many parents from outside the district have tried to send their children to District 4 schools. This demand is in marked contrast to a past pattern of flight from the district and a continuing pattern of flight from most other New York City districts with similar demographic characteristics. However, some analysts have questioned whether District 4's purported successes are "real" and whether choice was the actual cause of any such improvements. They often note that, at a minimum, the existing analysis of District 4 performance is incomplete. As Boyer notes more generally, "In states and districts where choice has been adopted, little effort has been made to record the process carefully or to document results."[11]

The arguments questioning the success of school choice in District 4 are based on several interrelated issues. One major set of concerns is based on the instability of test scores over time. The New York City Board of Education has changed its test several times over the past twenty-two years. Kirp argues that the largest improvement in test scores (a gain of 13 percentage points) occurred in 1973 when choice was first getting started, and in 1986 (10 percentage points) when New York City switched to a different test.[12] He notes that in both years reading levels improved dramatically for the city as a whole, and thus he questions whether District 4's gains were independent of citywide gains. Furthermore, he reports that after new norms were established in 1989, the proportion of District 4 students doing grade-level work dropped to 42 percent (vs. 48 percent citywide). Cookson argues that the more detailed study prepared by Domanico just recycled Fliegel's data and "does not attempt to expand upon these data somewhat by comparing District 4 reading scores to citywide reading scores."[13] Given these problems, in this chapter we control the extent to which test instruments affect performance by standardizing District 4's test results relative to the citywide average for the tests administered by the city in that year, creating a common baseline for a reliable over-time analysis.

Some scholars argue that while District 4 test scores may have improved over time, the improvement was the result of bringing in better prepared students from other districts.[14] They argue that these students came from higher socioeconomic status backgrounds and were more motivated than students living in the district. According to Henig, several different articles reported that between eight hundred and two thousand students came into District 4 from outside the district.[15] Kirp states: "It is largely because of this hidden selection process—which screens for both levels of skills and traits of character—that some very good schools have been created in East Harlem."[16]

Fliegel argues that staff in District 4 analyzed these data and found that the profile of incoming students was virtually the same as the District 4 resident students in terms of test score performances.[17] In our analysis in this chapter, to address this issue, we control for the demographic characteristics of students enrolled in the district schools, including race and poverty levels.

Some scholars have also argued that any improvements in District 4 were driven more by extra money from federal magnet programs and from the district's running over budget during the 1980s.[18] Indeed, at one point District 4 received more per capita federal aid than any other district in the United States.[19] Thus we model the effects of resources using proxies for expenditures (such as pupil/teacher ratios, since expenditure data are not available over the years by district). We note at this point that this criticism also reflects a belief in an extraordinary sensitivity of test score performance to enhanced resources, a belief that has not been documented in the literature (see below).

Some of those who are skeptical of District 4's success argue that, rather than choice, the key factor in District 4's success has been the creation of smaller schools. (Note that this concern involves not the creation of smaller *classes,* which requires greater resources, but the creation of smaller *schools* through the establishment of many minischools). Harrington and Cookson argue that "probably the most important ingredient was school size. Every one of the alternative schools was small. . . . Size alone made these alternative schools nontraditional in New York City, where public schools are about as large and impersonal as you can get, even at the elementary level."[20] In our analysis we control for the possible effects of school size on student test score performance.

Another perspective on District 4's choice program is that any increase in test scores was driven by a small number of elite alternative schools of choice. Many scholars are concerned about stratification and its effect on those "left behind" in an education system in which there are already significant educational inequities.[21] According to Young and Clinchy, "East Harlem's practice of allowing individual schools to set admissions criteria and select students aggravates, rather than reduces, such inequities."[22] Thus we examine the performance of students in the non-choice elementary schools, to see if they were indeed "left behind."

Some scholars believe that the attention focused on District 4 created a "Hawthorne effect" in which teachers, administrators, students, and parents responded to an experimental setting by changing their behavior in the short run, and that such an effect is unsustainable over time.[23] Cookson argues: "Clearly there is something of a Hawthorne effect going on in District 4. . . . It is little wonder that this positive feeling is reflected in student's attitudes. . . . Change preceded choice in East Harlem, not the other way around."[24] To address this concern, we examine school performance in

District 4 today, when any Hawthorne effect would now be nearly twenty-five years old.

A final concern often expressed is that leadership was more important than choice.[25] Some argue that District 4 benefited from outstanding leadership, from Alvarado, Fliegel, Meier, and others, who have become symbols and practitioners of successful education, and that their leadership produced more positive benefits than did choice. It is very difficult to separate the emergence of strong leaders from the opening up of opportunities that choice allowed. It is also reasonable to ask why outstanding leaders have not emerged in such numbers in districts without choice. By examining performance today, when none of the above leaders has been active in District 4 for many years, we can partially distinguish the two causes.

Thus those who are critical of the simple arguments about success in District 4 suggest that choice did not drive improvements, but instead that any actual improvements were driven by leadership, innovation, stratification, Hawthorne effects, and/or extra resources. Cookson argues: "In fact, one could say that there is almost no convincing evidence that there is a relationship between school choice policies and student achievement."[26] Fortunately, many of these issues now can be addressed with data we gathered and with data reported by the New York City Board of Education. Before we present these analyses, we examine briefly the large and often very contentious literature on whether any school reforms have been shown to improve student performance.

Can Schools Do Anything to Improve Student Performance?

In recent years, scholars in economics, political science, and education policy have developed a large and often contentious literature exploring whether and how school resources or institutional arrangements affect student performance. We review briefly the empirical research focusing on student performance on standardized tests. We do this to help establish reasonable expectations for the size of the effects we might expect of any reform, including the intradistrict choice programs we study.

Coleman et al. initiated much of this research by examining student test score performance as a function of three sets of variables: (1) those related to the family background of students, (2) those related to peer groups, and (3) those related to school resources.[27] The "Coleman Report" and other studies found little evidence that school resource policy variables had any significant impact on test scores, and instead found that family background had the strongest effects. In perhaps the most widely cited study on school effects after Coleman's work, Hanushek examined 187 different equations of educational "production functions" from thirty-eight publications and found inconclusive evidence that school resources, such as pupil/teacher ratio, teacher education, teacher salary, total expenditure per pupil, administrative expenditures, and quality of facilities, affect test score performance.[28]

Recently, a few researchers have challenged Hanushek's findings. Hedges et al. argue that in contrast to Hanushek's simple "vote count" methodology, a more sophisticated meta-analysis that combines different results shows that resources do affect test scores.[29] Card and Krueger argue that test scores are not necessarily the best measure of school performance, and instead analyze future earnings of individuals as a function of the educational resources devoted to them, controlling for a range of other factors.[30] They find evidence of the effects of school resources, such as teachers' salaries, on future earnings, as well as on higher educational attainment.[31] Sander finds that in Illinois, high school graduation rates by school district, controlling for average family background, are significantly higher for districts with lower pupil/teacher ratios.[32] Other recent studies find that school resources affect test scores.[33] Ferguson and Ladd studied both student- and district-level data in Alabama and found that teacher education and class size affect student learning.[34] They also argue that test scores are a reasonable proxy for future success and earnings. Perhaps most convincing, Mosteller illustrates how experimental data from Indiana and Tennessee show that smaller class sizes produce better test scores and other outcomes.[35]

The random experiments with different class sizes might seem to be enough to establish definitive results. But Hanushek points out that the effect takes place only in kindergarten and perhaps first grade, and there is no evidence that reduced class sizes in later grades further improve test scores.[36] Not convinced by this recent research showing that smaller classes and better trained teachers can lead to higher performance, Hanushek summarizes nicely: "The existing work does not suggest that resources never matter, nor does it suggest that resources could not matter. It only indicates that the current organization and incentives of schools do little to ensure that any added resources will be used effectively."[37]

The literature on school choice has been directly aimed at those questions of organization, incentives, and effectiveness. Chubb and Moe argue that school choice provides more autonomy for school-level decision making, which they find to be associated with better performance.[38] They suggest that marketlike settings, rather than local politics, are more likely to create the incentives for effective schools. Only a few studies have addressed the question of whether choice actually leads to improved outcomes. A heated debate has emerged in the study of Milwaukee's limited experiment with private school vouchers for some low-income children. Witte found no significant improvements in test scores over time for the children utilizing vouchers, compared to others, but Peterson et al., using a different comparison and methodology, have found positive effects on test scores after three years.[39] By the fourth year, Peterson finds significant math score increases of eleven points and reading score increases of five points. A recent reanalysis by Rouse finds a result in between Witte and Peterson, in which math scores are shown to have improved for voucher students in Milwaukee (though not to the extent that Peterson reports), but not reading scores.[40]

Without entering this debate directly, we surmise, for our purposes here, that these studies suggest that any test score improvements from resource or institutional changes should be expected to be moderate, rather than overwhelming, in scale. They also clearly indicate that analyses must try to control for student backgrounds as much as possible, while testing school or district-level effects.

Analyzing District 4 Performance Over Time

To study the effects of choice, it is imperative to look at performance indicators in District 4 over time. To do this, we gathered historical data on the reading and math scores in the district and in the city as a whole. We quickly discovered why no one else has taken on this task—it was extremely difficult to gather these data going back to the late 1960s, when decentralization first created community school districts. By combining data from the Board of Education archives at Teachers College of Columbia with more recent data held at the Board of Education's headquarters, we were able to put together this time-series, which includes the years 1974–96.

Using the data from tests administered by the New York City Board of Education, we examine the percentage of district students reading (or performing math) at or above grade level in each year, averaged for all grades 3–8.[41] One concern noted by critics is that the actual test administered has changed over time. For example, for reading tests, from 1974–77 the test used was the 1970 version of the Comprehensive Test of Basic Skills; from 1978–85 it was the 1977 version of the California Achievement Test; from 1986–88 it was the 1982 version of the Degrees of Reading Power Test; from 1989–92 the 1988 version of the Degrees of Reading Power Test. Thus students in District 4 might have performed differently over time simply because of taking different tests, with different nationally normed baselines.

To address concerns that the baseline of tests administered in New York City has changed over time, we divided the average District 4 performance by the citywide average figure for grades 3–8. Thus we have a "standardized" measure of performance, reflecting how well District 4 is doing relative to other districts in the city. This is a consistent measure over time that can be used to evaluate changes in District 4.

The over-time patterns are presented graphically in Figure 11.1. The graph shows a significant increase over time in both reading and math scores in District 4 relative to the city average. While we were not able to get data tracing all the way back to 1969, Figure 11.1 shows that when choice started in District 4 in 1974, the district was one of the worst in the city, performing only about half as well as districts in the city as a whole. After the implementation of choice, the relative scores in District 4 climbed, and by the early-to mid-1980s, District 4's performance nearly reached the city average for reading. Note that there has been a recent decline, but that today District 4 schools are still working at a level higher than 80 percent of the citywide average—almost twice as high as in 1974. District 4 math scores also climbed, though not as high, and they also showed a leveling off after the late 1980s.[42]

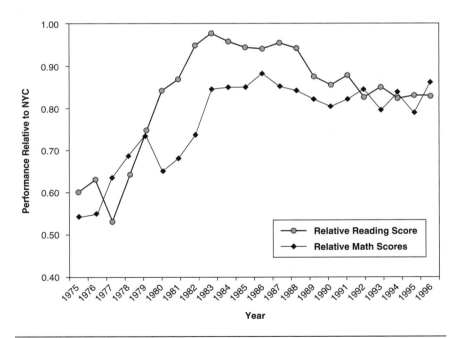

Figure 11.1

To see if the overall positive trend remained after controlling for other factors that might affect performance, we created a pooled data set, combining data from all thirty-two New York districts over the years 1974–96. While this does not cover the entire period since choice was instituted, these were the only years for which data are available—and even then, not all the data we wanted were available for every year. Fortunately, our major indicator, test scores, was available over the full range of years. For those variables that were missing for certain years, we interpolated values to fill in the observations in our time-series. In the case of demographics, which change very slowly over time, these interpolations are quite reliable. However, we also interpolated values for the teacher variables, which do change more rapidly. This greater fluctuation leaves us less confident in the reliability of the estimates for those independent variables.

We examined time trends employing the following control variables: the percentage of students in the district eligible for free lunches (a poverty measure); the percentage of Black and Hispanic students in the district; the average pupil/teacher ratio in the district; and the percentage of teachers in the district with more than five years' teaching experience.

The most important independent variable in our model is the measure of the expansion of choice in District 4 over time. We measure the prevalence of school choice as the percentage of choice schools out of the total number of operating schools in the district each year. In District 4, this measure increases from 0 percent in 1973 to 55 percent by 1996, and is set to zero for all other districts in all other years.[43] With these controls in the model, we can assess the extent to which basic underlying factors are responsible for the improvement in scores. We rely on Ordinary Least Squares to estimate our model and report panel-corrected standard errors.[44]

The results in Table 11.1 show a statistically significant relationship between the expansion of choice in District 4 and both reading and math test score performance. As we estimated a linear model, the coefficient on the percentage of choice schools is easy to interpret: on average, each ten-percentage-point increase in the proportion of choice schools in District 4 increased the reading scores six percentage points and the math scores four percentage points, relative to the citywide average. For example, if the percentage of District 4 students reading at grade level, relative to the city average, was 60 percent, and during the time period we studied four new choice schools were opened, out of forty currently operating schools, District 4 reading scores would rise to 66 percent of the city average.[45] These are not trivial improvements. For example, recall that studies have found mixed results for the use of vouchers to send low-income children to private schools; the most positive such findings show gains of about five points for math scores and eleven points for reading scores after four years.[46]

Table 11.1   District 4 Test Score Performance over Time Compared to Other Districts in New York City, 1974–1996[a]

Independent Variable	Reading Scores Coefficient[b]	Math Scores Coefficient[b]
% of schools in District 4 that are choice schools	0.59** (0.11)	0.36** (0.13)
Pupil/teacher ratio	0.07 (0.16)	−0.02 (0.20)
% of teachers with more than 5 years of experience	−0.04 (0.04)	−0.09 (0.05)
% of students eligible for free lunches	−.70** (0.28)	−0.69 (0.10)
% of Black students	−.71** (0.10)	−0.86** (0.12)
% of Hispanic students	−0.64 (0.08)	−0.79** (0.10)
Constant	203.26** (8.06)	222.28** (19.04)
	N = 715; Adjusted R² = 0.91 Significance $p < .000$	N = 683; Adjust R² = .087 Significance $p < .000$

a. Pooled district-level fixed effects model of relative test scores as a function of district characteristics and District 4 location. We also included, but do not report, dummy variables for 31 of the 32 districts and 22 of the 23 time points.

b. Panel-corrected standard errors.

**Significant at 99% level of confidence.

Our findings also show that districts with higher percentages of students in poverty (for reading only) and districts with higher percentages of Black and Hispanic students are likely to have lower test scores.[47] Our results also address some of the concerns of critics by identifying the effects of resources (teacher/pupil ratio) and teacher quality (percentage of teachers with more than five years of experience) on student performance. Neither of these variables has a statistically significant effect on relative performance. Partly, this lack of effect may result from a measurement problem—recall that because of missing data we had to interpolate some of the data. But note, too, that in New York City budgets are allocated such that low-income and low-performance districts receive more resources—thus reducing the possible effects of resources on performance. Despite these issues, our analysis shows that a higher proportion of higher SES students, possibly coming into the district from other locations, does not explain District 4's improved performance, since demographic characteristics are controlled in our model.

Performance in District 4 Schools Today. From the time of the decentralization decision in 1969, which created the thirty-two local school districts now responsible for K–8 education in their areas, the New York City Board of Education has been required to prepare a district-by-district ranking of reading scores. For 1996, the board prepared a more detailed study of reading scores, by school, and also conducted its own study of school performance.[48] Because this study adjusted for the characteristics of schools that may affect performance, it allows for a meaningful comparison of student performance across individual schools. In particular, this analysis controlled for: (1) the percentage of students eligible for free lunches in the school, a measure of poverty; (2) the percentage of students with limited English proficiency, a measure of academic disadvantage; and (3) the percentage of the students who were in that school for the full year, a measure of population stability.

Controlling for these factors, the board generated "predicted" average performance scores for each school. The board then developed an "honor roll" of high-achieving schools, which included those schools in which students scored at least fifteen points above the predicted value. With seven such high-performing schools, District 4 currently has more such schools than any other district in the city. However, with its emphasis on many small schools of choice, District 4 has more individual schools than most other districts. To address this difference, we examine the percentage of schools in a district that the Board of Education finds to have high-performing schools. In this calculation District 4 ranks fourth of the thirty-two districts, with 15 percent of its schools noted on this honor roll. Taking this calculation to its logical conclusion, since school sizes vary, we examine how many of the students who took the reading tests in each district are enrolled at schools on this honor roll. Here District 4 regains its top position in New York City, with 20 percent of tested students in high-performing schools. Thus, by whatever measure of high-performing schools, District 4 is the top, or nearly the top, district in New York City.

In analyzing the current performance of District 4, we are able to go one step further, thanks to the availability of more complete data. Having obtained data on school performance for the last three years for each school in the city, we are able to analyze how schools in District 4 today are performing compared to schools across the rest of the city. And, because this analysis is done at the school level, we are able to create more refined models than was possible for the district-level analysis over time. As we are analyzing data at the school level, we utilize the New York State performance tests.

The results of our analysis for grade six test scores are presented in Table 11.2. Our data show that, for both math and reading scores in 1996, on average schools in District 4 performed significantly better than schools in the rest of the city. This analysis is more refined because it controls for

Table 11.2   Test Score Performance (1996) at the School Level[a]

Independent Variable	Reading Scores Coefficient[b]	Math Scores Coefficient[b]
District 4	8.00**	4.64**
	(3.03)	(2.39)
Size of school population	0.001	0.0009
	(.002)	(0.0001)
Limited English %	−0.54**	−0.28**
	(0.10)	(0.08)
Free lunch %	−0.009	0.004
	(0.01)	(0.01)
Less than 3 years in US %	−0.11	0.08
	(0.16)	(0.13)
% in school all year	0.55**	0.26*
	(0.18)	(0.14)
% Black	−0.38**	−0.19**
	(0.04)	(0.03)
% Hispanic	−.032**	−0.12**
	(0.05)	(0.04)
% Asian	0.09	0.08
	(0.07)	(0.06)
Constant	45.2**	75.1**
	(17.43)	(14.53)
	N = 467;	N = 453;
	Adjusted R^2 = 0.49	Adjusted R^2 = 0.26
	Significance $p < .001$	Significance $p < .001$

a. Sixth grade test scores as a function of school factors and District 4 location.

b. Standard errors.

**Significant at 99% level of confidence.

*Significant at 95% level.

many variables, including race (percent Black, percent Hispanic, and percent Asian students in each school), school size, poverty (percent eligible for free lunch), turnover of students (percent in the same school all year), immigration status (percent in the United States less than three years), and percent of students with limited English proficiency. This is a robust test of today's performance, and our analysis shows a strong District 4 performance.

The coefficient on the District 4 variable shows that, with other variables held equal, schools in District 4 score nearly eight points higher on sixth grade reading tests than other schools: increasing from a base rate of 45 percent of students performing at or above grade level to 53 percent at or above grade level. Schools in District 4 again show significantly better performance, with an increase of over four points in math scores, compared to equivalent schools in other districts.

These results also address some of the concerns expressed by scholars skeptical about the independent effect of District 4; our results show that it is not smaller schools that drive District 4 test performance nor is it higher SES students "imported" into the district. Moreover, any "Hawthorne effect" must be incredibly powerful to still be in place in 1996, after twenty-two years of experience with choice.

We also ran these same models using test scores from 1995 and 1994, to test whether 1996 was a year of exceptional performance in District 4. Except for math scores in 1994, the District 4 effect is significant and positive in all of these cases. New York City students are also given New York State performance tests in the third and eighth grades. We ran these same models, and for third grade scores, the District 4 variable is significant and positive in half of the six cases (reading and math, over 1994, 1995, and 1996). Students are only tested for reading in eighth grade and here we do not find a District 4 effect. We believe that studies that show that minority adolescent students are less likely to be influenced by any school-related activities at this age may explain this finding for eighth grade test scores.[49]

Thus we have documented significant district-level improvements in math and reading scores, with the fastest growth happening during the greatest expansion of choice programs. Using more detailed, school-level data, we have shown a large and significant district-level effect for sixth grade reading and math scores, in a model with strong controls for student and school characteristics. The size of these improvements in test scores is not trivial. For example, in the literature we reviewed on other school reforms and their effects on test scores, even when researchers can document positive effects, and this happens in less than half of the studies, the percentage improvements are rarely larger than those documented here.

We note that, even with these improvements, District 4 is far from the top district in New York City. For example, in 1996 on average 35 percent of District 4 children in grades 3–8 read at or above their grade level, while the percentage performing math at or above grade level was 51 percent (citywide averages in 1996 were 42 percent and 59 percent, respectively). It would be impressive indeed if we could argue that a reform-like choice, or any reform, could break the relationship between test scores and parent socioeconomic status. There is still room for schools and students in District 4 to do better, and 80 percent of the district's students are enrolled in schools that did not make the "honor roll." But it is impossible to dispute that test scores have improved and that they are better today than in schools in New York City districts with comparable levels of poverty and disadvantage.

How Has Choice in District 4 Improved School Performance? Many analysts who are skeptical of school choice programs wonder how choice alone can lead to better schools. For schools to improve, there must be pressure from the "demand" side of the market-like setting that choice encourages, as well as improvements on the "supply" side by the schools themselves. District 4 encouraged both types of responses. By providing choice and information to parents, District 4 encouraged important changes on the "demand" side.[50] Here we address briefly the supply side of choice in District 4.

Starting in 1974, District 4 encouraged smaller schools that would experiment with new teaching ideas and approaches. Administrators hoped that parents would discover the schools that were improving and "vote with their feet," enrolling their children in these schools. District officials also hoped that competition would stimulate improvements in the non-choice schools as well, a point we address in the next section.

But the creation of alternative schools responsive to parent interest and scrutinized for quality inevitably raises the problem of what to do about schools that are not successful. Many advocates of choice argue that, for choice to work, unsuccessful schools must be closed or face some other negative consequences. While everyone recognizes that closing a school is painful, and nearly impossible during the school year, advocates of choice argue that the occasional closing of schools should not be viewed as a failure but instead as a necessary step for improving schools. Choice advocates also point out that few unsuccessful schools are actually ever closed in non-choice districts.

We interviewed current officials in District 4 to identify the conditions they view as indicators of problems. Among the most important is declining enrollment, a concrete form of "exit" through which parents are clearly signaling unhappiness with a school. The use of "voice" or complaints from parents also can help draw attention to a problem school, but parents who have children who attend poorly performing schools do not complain as often as other parents.

While parental actions are the most important indicators of school problems, other signs of a school's decline monitored by District 4 officials include significant decreases in test scores and problems with the staff—high turnover, low morale, and weak leadership. None of this requires outstanding leadership: all these indicators—"consumer" dissatisfaction through exit and voice, declining performance, and poor staff morale—are typically used by private sector organizations to monitor performance. What is important is that choice has expanded the incentives and the opportunities for district administrators to monitor the quality of school performance.

If a school is performing poorly, administrators can attempt to change the school's approach or close it down. Closure, while not simple, is often more successful for a basic reason: Once a school has a negative reputation, it is very difficult to change. However, not all schools with low test scores, low enrollment, and staff problems are closed—only the worst schools have actually been shut down. District 4 schools that have been closed in the past include the School of Communications and Health Services, which was closed because of difficulties with student discipline, structure, and leadership. The Sports School was also closed, because its students were not meeting academic standards.[51] After its closure, the Sports School was remade into New York Prep, which is still open today. The School of Communications and Health Services was remade into Creative Learning Community, which has also recently been closed. Other recent closures include the Key School, Bridge School, East Harlem Maritime School, and the East Harlem Performing Arts School.

As the earlier examples illustrate, when District 4 closes schools they are often replaced by schools with new themes and new leadership. This provides some dynamism to the supply side of choice in District 4. As choice has matured and as the role of parents in the district has solidified, the source of inspiration for new schools has changed. Whereas in the 1970s and 1980s ideas for schools were mainly provided by individual teachers, ideas today are often provided by community-based organizations. Three new schools have been created in District 4 in the last five years. One of these new schools, the Young Woman's Leadership School, has attracted considerable attention in the national media because of its status as a publicly funded single-sex institution.

Has Choice in District 4 Affected the Distribution of Educational Opportunity? Our second, and related, research question focuses on whether or not choice has left students in non-choice neighborhood schools worse off than they otherwise would have been had the schools of choice not been created. This is important because the majority of K–6 students in District 4 are still in neighborhood schools. We address this issue by investigating how neighborhood elementary schools have performed over time. By gauging the performance of these schools, we can assess the degree to which District 4 test score performance has been driven only by a top tier of elite schools.

We analyzed performance on the city-administered tests in the ten neighborhood elementary schools (of sixteen) in District 4 that had the lowest reading scores in 1996.[52] Earlier we analyzed the performance of these schools relative to the citywide average twenty years ago and today. If choice in District 4 has led to skimming and stratification, then, as better students choose to enroll in alternative schools of choice, these neighborhood schools should be particularly hard hit.

The evidence suggests that the neighborhood schools have *not* been adversely affected by the creation of alternative schools. We examined reading scores at grades three and six and math scores at grades three and five (there are no time trends for grade six math). Again, we compared the actual scores to citywide averages to address the problem of changing tests over time. For all ten schools taken as a whole, reading and math scores were actually *higher* relative to citywide averages in the period 1994–96 than they were in 1974–76. Third grade reading scores improved from 57 percent to 69 percent of the citywide average over this period, while sixth grade reading scores improved from 59 percent to 84 percent. For these ten schools, math scores improved even more; third grade scores went from 55 percent to 87 percent of the citywide average, while fifth grade math scores improved from 49 percent to 95 percent.

One possibility is that by combining all ten schools, we might be overlooking the fact that a few may have fallen substantially over the past two decades. But this is not the case. Combining four separate sets of scores (two different grades for reading and two for math) across the ten schools, we have forty comparisons. Of these forty comparisons, thirty show improvements over time, six show no change, but only four show decline over time.[53]

Thus there is no evidence that neighborhood schools have been left behind; indeed, the data show quite clearly that choice in District 4 has not produced any "loser" school. To the contrary: our data show most of these schools have improved over time, relative to the citywide averages, suggesting that choice has put competitive pressure on all schools to improve. Even if neighborhood elementary schools are not "choice" schools, parents can still opt out of them for alternative school programs, giving them the "exit" option. In turn, neighborhood schools are competing to retain, if not to attract, students and this has put pressure on them to maintain, if not improve, their academic performance. These patterns suggest that choice in District 4 has expanded the range of educational alternatives for parents and students of various types.

We believe that our results present strong evidence that intradistrict choice "works"—that at least in District 4, it has unleashed strong forces in the community and in the local school system that have led to significant improvements in academic performance. However, if we can "replicate" these results in another district that has implemented choice, then our confidence in these results should increase.

Choice in District 2

Community School District 2 covers much of midtown Manhattan, including a wide range of neighborhoods. Geographically, it is a large district, in part because it includes many office buildings without residences. With 22,000 students, it is nearly twice as large as District 4. Many of the residents in more affluent neighborhoods in District 2 had sent their children to private schools, as only a few of the district public schools were considered to be high quality. In contrast to District 4, which has higher percentages of low-income and Hispanic students than the citywide averages, students in District 2 are above city averages for income and are more likely to be White.

In 1988, Anthony Alvarado became superintendent of District 2, after he briefly had been chancellor of the New York City Board of Education, but lost that position due to a financial scandal. He quickly began to do in District 2 much of what he had done in District 4 some fifteen years earlier. Especially at the middle school level, he encouraged the creation of new, smaller schools of choice. As in District 4, this idea expanded, until the number of middle school programs reached twenty-five in 1998. In addition, there are four option schools at the elementary school level, and parents are allowed and encouraged to send their children to zoned, neighborhood schools other than their own, if they find the approach of that school more appropriate.

Associated with this expansion of choice, in recent years there has been considerable anecdotal evidence of test score improvements and exciting school environments, resulting in parents' clamoring to get their children into District 2 schools. For example, one author wrote that District 2 "has been a powerful magnet for many of the middle-class parents who have quietly been returning to public schools in droves."[54] This improvement was apparent to many observers and parents. Hemphill writes: "Anthony Alvarado . . . over the course of a decade, transformed the schools of midtown, downtown and the East Side of Manhattan from old-fashioned, lack-luster institutions, avoided by anyone who had a choice, into exciting, creative places much in demand. . . . So popular are the schools in District 2 . . . that several students have been caught sneaking into them from the suburbs."[55]

While this analysis risks providing fuel for those who would argue that it isn't choice that improves performance but rather the magic leadership of Alvarado, again we suggest that the two factors are related, and that choice can continue to work without a particular leader. To see the effects of choice in District 2, we replicated the over-time analysis we performed for District 4. Here, we utilized a measure of the expansion of District 2 schools of choice, starting in 1988 and building through 1996. This variable equals zero for the period 1974–88, before District 2 began choice, and increases from zero in 1988 to forty by 1996 to capture the percentage of District 2 schools that are now choice schools.

The results, reported in Table 11.3, show that District 2 reading scores, again relative to the citywide average, went up over this period, associated with the increase in the district choice variable. Math scores, however, do not show any statistically significant change. Thus, while we can be very confident that District 2 reading scores have improved over this period relative to the citywide averages on these tests, we cannot say that for math scores. The other variables in the empirical model are mostly significant, all in the expected direction and all quite comparable to the results in Table 11.1.

The coefficient for the District 2 choice variable means that, on average, reading scores improved by three percentage points, relative to the city average, for every ten-percentage-point increase in choice schools provided from 1988 to 1996. This is about half the size of the same increase in District 4 reported above, but the improvement took place in less than half the time. This supports the statement by Goldstein that "in eight years under Alvarado's tutelage, District 2 has moved from eleventh to second out of 32 districts in student test scores."[56]

We also ran a parallel cross-sectional analysis for 1996 test scores at the school level, comparable to the analysis reported in Table 13.2 for District 4. Here, we did not find a significant effect for District 2 schools, although the coefficient is positive. This suggests that, contrary to the case for District 4, we cannot say that reading and math test score performance in District 2 today is significantly better than the demographics of the student body would "predict" that it should be.

Together, these results suggest that prior to the implementation of choice by Alvarado, students in District 2 were performing below expectations, given their socioeconomic status. Anecdotal evidence confirms this pattern. Choice has helped to raise performance, in eight years, to the "predicted"

Table 11.3   District 2 Test Score Performance over Time Compared to Other NYC Districts[a]

Independent Variable	Reading Scores Coefficient[b]	Math Scores Coefficient[b]
% of schools in District 2 that are choice schools	.25* (.13)	−.14 (.15)
Pupil/teacher ratio	.04 (.16)	−.05 (.20)
% of teachers with more than five years' experience	−.06 (.04)	−.10* (.05)
% of students eligible for free lunches	−.69** (.09)	−.74** (.10)
% of Black students	−.73** (.10)	−.84** (.13)
% of Hispanic students	−.68** (.09)	−.78 (.11)
Constant	208.04	227.66**
	$N = 746$; $Chi^2(59) = 8898$ Significance $p < .000$	$N = 730$; $Chi^2(59) = 6178$ Significance $p < .000$

a. Pooled district-level fixed effects model of relative test scores as a function of district characteristics and District 2 location, 1974–96. We also included, but do not report, dummy variables for 31 of the 32 districts and 22 of the 23 time points.

b. Panel-corrected standards errors.

**Significant at 99% level of confidence.

*Significant at 95% level.

level for such a group of students. In contrast, District 4 was performing only a little below its "predicted" level twenty-five years ago, when choice was started, and it has now improved to be above "predicted" levels.

Conclusions

Since 1992, parents of New York City public school children have theoretically had the opportunity to send their children to any school in the city system. In reality, the opportunities for interdistrict choice are extremely limited by space constraints and by procedural hurdles. While the central board keeps no comprehensive figures, perhaps 1 percent of public school K–8 students are now enrolled in districts outside of their own. A larger number of students are involved in the Annenberg alternative schools. And a larger number are participating in choice within their own community school districts. The district with the longest history of choice in New York is District 4, and District 2 has the second longest experience. We studied the effects of choice in these districts.

Previous studies have provided some evidence that choice in District 4 was successful in improving performance. Scholars have attacked this evidence as insufficient and open to multiple interpretations. In this chapter we provide stronger evidence about the success of District 4 students. Where possible, we have shown how these successes are linked to the expansion of school choice in District 4. Moving to a more detailed, school-level analysis, we have shown that reading and math scores in District 4 are significantly higher today than in comparable schools in other districts.

By incorporating relevant control variables into our statistical models, we are able to address directly some of the concerns that thoughtful skeptics have expressed about the analysis of District 4 as a choice experiment. We find that smaller schools alone do not predict higher test score performance. We find that, to the extent that the pupil/teacher ratio is a reasonable measure of resources, these ratios do not influence academic performance in schools in New York City, and they do not explain the rising academic performance of schools in District 4 in the 1970s and 1980s. By controlling for student demographics, we show that the rise in District 4 test scores is not a function of bringing in more well-prepared students from outside the district. By showing that District 4's scores remain significantly higher today than in comparable schools, we show that if District 4 benefited from the "Hawthorne effect" of getting considerable attention and resources showered upon it in the 1980s, it has been a very long-lasting effect. Given that the original District 4 leaders have left the system, the continued higher performance of District 4 schools suggests that leadership is not the only factor in their improvement.

On the "supply side" of choice, we discuss several ways in which District 4 officials have responded to failing and under-enrolled schools—for example, by closing them or by reorienting their approach. We also address the concern that District 4 has stratified its students into "winners and losers," by illustrating that students in the non-choice schools also have shown improvements in their test scores over time.

We supplement the evidence from District 4 with an analysis of test scores in District 2, which implemented choice fifteen years after District 4. We show that a similar expansion of choice schools in the more affluent District 2 also led to improvements in test scores. This evidence of District 2 test score improvement is important because it shows that the District 4 experience was not a "fluke" related to some unmeasured conditions within that district. It also shows that the District 4 improvement was not a function of the specific time period or the specific tests administered at certain times.

While the data do not allow us to establish absolutely that choice itself caused all of these improvements, we have partially ruled out several alternative explanations. We believe that a complete explanation requires that choice be recognized as a catalyst of these improvements.

Performance in District 4 and in District 2 today is still not at the level that educators and parents want. But performance has improved markedly over time in both districts, and it is significantly better in District 4 than performance in comparable urban districts. District 4 used choice to achieve positive results without causing a higher level of stratification than we see in other American school districts.

The broader literature on educational policy changes, including increasing school resources and altering institutional structures, does not provide clear evidence of improved performance. Given that students with perfect attendance are only in school about 15 percent of the time from age 5–18, this should not be completely surprising. As Coleman found more than thirty years ago, student performance is heavily affected by family, home, and neighborhood characteristics. In this context, the finding that choice policies in District 4 are associated with significantly higher levels of performance is impressive.

Not all policy changes are easy to replicate, and the concept of "scaling up" success stories to a larger context is a major concern in educational policy circles. In part because of the success of District 4, the New York City Board of Education implemented choice across districts. But without adequate space in desirable schools and districts, without a centralized mechanism to make the choice process more accessible for all parents, and without even a "tracking system" to determine where students are going to and leaving from, the board's commitment can hardly be described as "strong." Given the now documented successes of New York districts that have embraced choice as part of a reform philosophy, this is unfortunate.

Notes

1. Robert Crain, "New York City's Career Magnet High Schools," in *School Choice: Examining the Evidence,* ed. Edith Rasell and Richard Rothstein (Washington, D.C.: Economic Policy Institute, 1993).

2. See chapter 3, Ravitch & Viteritti (2000), from which the present selection of this anthology is also taken.

3. Paul Hill, Lawrence Pierce, and James Guthrie, *Reinventing Public Education: How Contracting Can Transform America's Schools* (Chicago: University of Chicago Press, 1997), p. 97.

4. Liz Willen, "School Choice: Parents' Primer," *Newsday*, June 7, 1998, p. A7.

5. Ibid.

6. William Ubinas, "Introducing Choice in an Urban District," in *Privatizing Education and Educational Choice,* ed. Simon Hakim, Paul Seidenstat, and Gary Bowman (Westport, Conn.: Praeger, 1994).

7. Seymour Fliegel, with James McGuire, *Miracle in East Harlem* (New York: Times Books, 1993); Raymond Domanico, *Model for Choice: A Report on Manhattan's District 4,* Center for Educational Innovation, Education Policy Paper No. 1 (New York: Manhattan Institute for Policy Research, 1989).

8. Fliegel, with McGuire, *Miracle in East Harlem;* Domanico, *Model for Choice;* David Kirp, "What School Choice Really Means," *Atlantic Monthly,* November 1992, p. 127.

9. Seymour Fliegel, "Creative Non-Compliance," in *Choice and Control in American Education,* vol. 2: *The Practice of Choice, Decentralization, and School Restructuring,* ed. William Clune and John Witte (New York: Falmer, 1990).

10. Deborah Meier, *The Power of Their Ideas: Lessons for America from a Small School in Harlem* (Boston: Beacon Press, 1995).

11. Ernest Boyer, *School Choice* (Princeton, N.J.: Carnegie Foundation, 1992), p. 9.

12. Kirp, "What School Choice Really Means."

13. Peter W. Cookson Jr., *School Choice: The Struggle for the Soul of American Education* (New Haven: Yale University Press, 1994), p. 78.

14. This argument has been made by several authors, including Howard Hurwitz, *The Last Angry Principal* (Portland, Oreg.: Halcyon House, 1988); Peter W. Cookson Jr., *The Choice Controversy* (Newbury Park, Calif.: Corwin Press, 1992); Jeffrey Henig, "The Local Dynamics of Choice: Ethnic Preferences and Institutional Responses," in *Who Chooses? Who Loses?: Culture, Institutions, and the Unequal Effects of School Choice,* ed. Bruce Fuller, Richard F. Elmore, and Gary Orfield (New York: Teachers College Press, 1996); and Kirp, "What School Choice Really Means."

15. Henig, "The Local Dynamics of Choice," p. 131.

16. Kirp, "What School Choice Really Means."

17. Fliegel, *Miracle in East Harlem.*

18. Kirp, "What School Choice Really Means"; Diane Harrington and Peter W. Cookson Jr., "School Reform in East Harlem: Alternative Schools versus Schools of Choice," in *Empowering Teachers and Parents,* ed. G. Alfred Hess (Westport, Conn.: Bergin and Garvey, 1992).

19. See also Amy Stuart Wells, *Time to Choose: America at the Crossroads of School Choice Policy* (New York: Hill and Wang, 1993), p. 56.

20. Harrington and Cookson, "School Reform in East Harlem," p. 181.

21. Jeffrey Henig, *Rethinking School Choice: Limits of the Market Metaphor* (Princeton, N.J.: Princeton University Press, 1994); Valerie Lee, "Educational Choice: The Stratifying Effects of Selecting Schools and Courses," *Educational Policy* 7, no. 2 (1993).

22. Timothy Young and Evans Clinchy, *Choice in Public Education* (New York: Teachers College Press, 1992), p. 25.

23. Henig, "Local Dynamics of Choice"; Myron Lieberman, *Privatization and Educational Choice* (New York: St. Martins, 1989).

24. Cookson, *School Choice,* p. 55.

25. See, for example, Kevin Smith and Kenneth Meier, *The Case Against School Choice: Politics, Markets, and Fools* (Armonk, N.Y.: M. E. Sharpe, 1995).

26. Cookson, *The Choice Controversy,* p. 91; see also Richard Elmore, "Public School Choice as a Policy Issue," in *Privatization and Its Alternatives,* ed. William Gormley (Madison: University of Wisconsin Press, 1991).

27. James Coleman et al., *Equality of Educational Opportunity* (Washington, D.C.: U.S. Government Printing Office, 1966).

28. Eric Hanushek, "The Economics of Schooling: Production and Efficiency in Public Schools," *Journal of Economic Literature* 24 (1986).

29. Larry Hedges, R. Lane, and R. Greenwald, "Does Money Matter? A Meta-Analysis of Studies of the Effects of Differential School Inputs on Student Outcomes," *Educational Researcher* (April 1994).

30. David Card and Alan Krueger, "Does School Quality Matter? Returns to Education and the Characteristics of Public Schools in the United States," *Journal of Political Economy* 100, no. 1 (1992).

31. But see Robert Speakman and Finis Welsh, "Does School Quality Matter? A Reassessment," Texas A&M University, Department of Economics paper, 1995; Jeff Grogger, "Does School Quality Explain the Recent Black/White Wage Trend?" *Journal of Labor Economics* 14, no. 2 (1996).

32. William Sander, "Expenditures and Student Achievement in Illinois," *Journal of Public Economics* 52 (1993).

33. Ronald Ferguson, "Paying for Public Education: New Evidence on How and Why Money Matters," *Harvard Journal on Legislation* 28, no. 2 (1991); J. Folger, "Project STAR and Class Size Policy," *Peabody Journal of Education* 67, no. 1 (1992).

34. Ronald Ferguson, "How and Why Money Matters: An Analysis of Alabama Schools," in *Holding Schools Accountable,* ed. Helen Ladd (Washington, D.C.: Brookings Institution, 1996).

35. Frederick Mosteller, "How Does Class Size Relate to Achievement in Schools?" in *Earning and Learning,* ed. Paul Peterson and Susan Mayer (Washington, D.C.: Brookings Institution, 1999).

36. Eric Hanushek, "The Evidence on Class Size," in ibid.

37. Eric Hanushek, "School Resources and Outcomes," *Journal of Educational Research and Analysis,* 1997.

38. John Chubb and Terry Moe, *Politics, Markets, and America's Schools* (Washington, D.C.: Brookings Institution, 1990).

39. John Witte, "Evaluation of Choice in Milwaukee," in *Who Chooses? Who Loses?: Culture, Institutions, and the Unequal Effects of School Choice,* ed. Bruce Fuller, Richard F. Elmore, and Gary Orfield (New York: Teachers College Press, 1996); Paul Peterson, Jay Greene, and Chad Noyes, "School Choice in Milwaukee," *The Public Interest* 125 (1996).

40. Cecilia Rouse, "Private School Vouchers and Student Achievement: An Evaluation of the Milwaukee Parental Choice Program," *Quarterly Journal of Economics* 113 (1998).

41. Because of limited data, we could average only grades three, six, and eight in the years 1974–81. However, this three-grade average is highly correlated with the full 3–8 grade average in years when both averages can be computed.

42. Note that sometimes when the tests were changed the variance of the thirty-two community school districts around the city average also changed. Without detailed figures on the national variances of these tests, it is not clear how to handle this issue. It is clear that in the 1980s the variance of the thirty-two districts for math got much smaller, meaning that lower-performing districts generally moved closer to the mean, as did higher-performing districts. This may imply that the improvement in District 4 math scores relative to the city average overstates the "real" improvement, or it may have to do with the variance of the tests generally. In general, "regression to the mean" is a phenomenon in which districts tend to converge over time toward an average level—that is, over time, the worst districts should do better, while the best districts are expected to do worse. We tested for this problem by examining District 4's performance in the early days of choice in the mid-1970s. We found that, controlling for race and poverty, District 4 was performing about as "predicted" at that time.

43. We believe that this percentage is a reasonable measure of the extent of competition involved in District 4 choice. A better measure would be the percentage of students enrolled in choice schools, but we were unable to get the information going back twenty years. Note that we could also create a simple model with a "counter" that grows by one each year. Since math and reading scores in District 4 increase over time, any variable that reflects the temporal expansion of choice will correlate with this increase in scores. But we have theoretical reasons to expect that choice was associated with improved performance, as well as empirical data.

44. When estimating a pooled model, researchers must address a complex set of problems that includes those normally arising in a cross-sectional analysis, as well as additional problems due to the spatial and temporal nature of the data. In this chapter, we follow Beck and Katz in relying on OLS when estimating our models (Nathaniel Beck and Jonathon Katz, "Nuisance vs. Substance: Specifying and Estimating Time-Series-Cross-Section Models," *Political Analysis* 6 [1995]). Since different districts are likely to perform at different levels, we follow a fixed-effects approach and correct for different levels of the dependent variable across districts by including a dummy variable for each district in both models. We also include a dummy variable for each year but one, to deal with time effects. And finally, in both models, we report the panel-corrected standard errors.

45. Of course, as with any linear regression model, one must be careful about projecting these results beyond the range for which they were estimated. That is, there is clearly some limit to the payoffs that can be expected to be achieved by creating additional choice schools, and we should not expect improvements to be unbounded.

46. Peterson et al., "School Choice in Milwaukee."

47. Note that we include the racial variables as statistical controls for different student body characteristics across districts and schools. That Black and Hispanic students score lower on these tests is a function of the data reported by the Board of Education. We do not in any way suggest that school officials or parents do or should have lower expectations for minority student performance. But if we do not include racial variables in these equations, we will not be comparing properly different student bodies and may mistakenly attribute or not attribute changes to choice or other policy variables.

48. This is the Board of Education's "Ranking of Schools by Reading Achievement: Overall Comparison of Reading Achievement in Similar Schools," prepared by the board's Division of Assessment and Accountability.

49. See, for example, Ronald Ferguson, "How Professionals in Community-based Programs Perceive and Respond to the Needs of Black Male Youth," in *Nurturing Young Black Males,* ed. Ronald Miney (Washington, D.C.: Urban Institute Press, 1991).

50. See, for example, Mark Schneider, Paul Teske, Melissa Marschall, and Christine Roch, "Shopping for Schools: In the Land of the Blind, the One-Eyed Parent May Be Enough," *American Journal of Political Science* 92 (1998).

51. Fliegel, *Miracle in East Harlem,* pp. 120–26.

52. These schools are PS 7, 50, 52, 72, 96, 101, 102, 108, 121, and 155.

53. Of these four negative trends, two are from PS 155, where reading scores in grades three and six declined; however, over the same time period, math scores in the school improved. Scores for grade three reading in PS 57 declined, but performance in two other tests remained steady and the school improved on one test. The final decline occurred in PS 96, where performance on grade five math dropped, but the three other comparisons showed improvement over time.

54. Michael Goldstein, "The Trials of Anthony Alvarado," *New York Magazine,* October 13, 1997, p. 82.

55. Clara Hemphill, *The Parents' Guide to New York City's Best Public Elementary Schools* (New York: Soho Press, 1997), p. 39.

56. Goldstein, "The Trials of Anthony Alvarado."

PART IV

Districts and States

12

The Superintendency*

editor's introduction:

Superintendents With "Nontraditional" Qualifications. School administrators are as essential as teaching staff to the well-being of schools. Among the most important but least understood administrators in the U.S. public school system are superintendents—people who must lead entire school districts and not just single school buildings.[1] As examples of the kinds of practices at the school district level, the present case study highlights various initiatives undertaken by the superintendent (see "Key Features of the Educational Reforms," pp. 217–223).

Contemporary superintendents have unbelievably challenging jobs. Candidates for the superintendency usually rise through the ranks of a school system, many having served previously as principals, teachers, or in other positions in the system. The present selection, representing the entirety of a case study, describes the work of two "nontraditional" superintendents who succeeded each other in the same system— the Seattle Public Schools. They came to the position from other professions (one military and the other business). Neither had prior experience in the education system. Such incumbents are still uncommon, but the possibility that superintendencies might benefit from experiences in other professions has made the "nontraditional" superintendent an intriguing topic of study and a potentially promising prospect for school districts.

---

*Yee, Gary, & McCloud, Barbara. (2003). "A Vision of Hope: A Case Study of Seattle's Two Nontraditional Superintendents." In Larry Cuban & Michael Usdan (Eds.), *Powerful Reforms With Shallow Roots: Improving America's Urban Schools* (pp. 54–76). New York: Teachers College Press.

[1]In a small minority of places, single districts may, however, only consist of a single school building.

Relevance of Case Studies: Studying People in the Public Eye. This selection shows you how case studies of individuals also can cover people who are in the public eye, not individuals (like the teachers in the earlier selections in Part I of this reader) operating within limited confines (e.g., a classroom). Such case studies can involve a broader scope of inquiry and also call upon a wider range of evidence available about the case. Note how archival documents, numerous interviews with related individuals, and citations to news and other media sources all can become relevant, in addition to observations and discussions with the individuals who are the subjects of the case study.

The present selection provides you with ample description of the community conditions and educational policies within which the two superintendents had to operate. The case study profiles the "whole person," including behavior, decisions, thinking, and managerial and personal style. The combination of context and phenomenon helps you to understand the "person, place, and circumstances" for creating positive changes in the school district. As an added note, the present selection is one of six case studies that appeared in a single book and is therefore part of a "multiple-case" study (see the next selection).

Introduction

In recent times, the urban superintendent's job has been described as one requiring a "miracle worker"[1] or the "Lone Ranger."[2] These mixed images create only a slightly exaggerated composite of the modern-day school leader—a highly principled man or woman with unusual courage, who is unafraid to do battle (usually with the teachers' union, or the bureaucracy, or special interest groups), and who is willing and able to pass swift, often ruthless judgment. In district after troubled district, the quality of superintendents' leadership is often measured by their willingness and ability to act quickly to fire incompetent principals and central district bureaucrats, to rally teachers and administrators around a common educational vision, to present a balanced budget, and in the process to raise student achievement.

Within a few short years, urban districts seem to quickly lose momentum, and school boards and their superintendents become mired in intractable policy debates at interminable board meetings. Tumultuous tenures and tenuous public support, with little recognition, seem to be the common working conditions experienced by superintendents in each large city school system. In district after district, that same leader who seemed to be everywhere at once in the beginning is castigated for failing to produce significant change. With diminishing political support, the superintendent's tenure frequently ends in a rancorous dismissal or resignation, to be followed by recrimination and blame and a search for a replacement. The public no longer sees the superintendent as the "messiah," but instead the superintendent becomes the "scapegoat."[3] Where their arrival brought a fresh breath of hope, each departure leaves teachers and the public at large with a sense of hopelessness.

If one assumes that every superintendent requires a reasonable length of time in order to develop and implement a districtwide school improvement agenda, different questions arise about leading an urban district. Does it require a knowledgeable insider, who comes up through the ranks of teacher, principal, and central office administrator, or a seasoned administrator with a proven track record of success as a superintendent in another, usually smaller district? Could someone from another sector succeed? Could a CEO from industry lead a school district? Could an investment banker? Could a general?

While the urban superintendency has for many decades represented the pinnacle of a long, successful career for public school educators, more recently urban school boards have selected candidates with little formal training in education, and little if any professional experience teaching in, let alone managing, a school or a school district. In the 1990s, the Seattle Public Schools' board of education did exactly that, by selecting not one, but two, nontraditionally prepared superintendents. In 1995, the school board selected General John Stanford, its first noneducator superintendent and its first African American. After his 3-year tenure was tragically shortened by a terminal illness, the board promoted the man Stanford had selected to be his chief financial officer, Joseph Olchefske, to be his successor. Unlike other urban superintendencies, Stanford's ended with an affirmation of the public's strong belief in schools, and Olchefske's appointment confirmed the optimism that the "dream" of educational excellence could be fulfilled.[4]

In this chapter we examine the actions of Stanford and Olchefske as case studies of the leadership behavior of two nontraditionally prepared superintendents—what they have accomplished and achieved, and under what conditions. We begin by reviewing the context of Seattle's schools within its city and its cultural identity. We document some of the major initiatives begun under these two superintendents. We report on the general sentiment that surrounds their work, as reported by Seattle educators, policy makers, community leaders, and other stakeholders. And we consider whether or not there are distinctive characteristics of nontraditional superintendents that make them particularly appealing, or perhaps uniquely suited, for leading urban school districts across the country, as opposed to candidates who have climbed the long traditional educational ladder, from teacher, principal, central office staff, to superintendent of a small "starter" district, to the urban superintendency. Finally, we ask whether their leadership will produce better schools and better outcomes for children.

For our data sources, we relied extensively on published newspaper reports and articles, several research studies that have been conducted on various aspects of Seattle's schools, reports produced by the Seattle Public Schools, and interviews with Seattle Public Schools administrators, teachers, and school board members, former Seattle Education Association leaders, and community and business activists and leaders.[5]

The Context of the Seattle Public Schools

Seattle itself does not fit the stereotype of a decaying urban center with a majority population of largely poor and minority residents, served by a troubled school system that fails most of its students, and epic board-superintendent-teacher union battles played out in the press and in political campaigns. Compared to the other cities in this study (see the next selection in this anthology), Seattle is the smallest, and it has the lowest unemployment rate, the lowest poverty rate, the smallest proportion of African American and Latino residents, the fewest high school dropouts, and the lowest percentage of children who live in distressed neighborhoods.[6]

The largest city in the Pacific Northwest, Seattle's population consists of about 500,000 residents; Whites continue to be in the majority, with Asian Americans the second largest population group, followed by African Americans and Latinos. Seattle continues to grow slowly in population, possessing both quaint, tree-lined neighborhoods, and a city center booming with high-rises, redevelopment, and new, luxurious housing that takes advantage of the sweeping views of bays and lakes and mountains. The city has a reputation among its residents as a prosperous, cultured, liberal city of and for the middle class, a place where people from the surrounding countryside come, if they can afford it, not the other way around. Seattle politics are described by residents as generally civil.[7]

Historically, Seattle's citizens were proud of their public schools.[8] While Seattle's total population continues to grow slowly, its student population has remained fairly steady over the past decade at about 45,000 students, a significant decrease from its high water mark of 100,000 students in 1962. Approximately 40% of all students receive free or reduced-price lunch support; about 15% of White students and 64% of Black students qualify. About 13% of the students are considered limited English proficient. Best estimates are that 35% of children in the more affluent north-end Seattle neighborhoods attend private schools, while only 10% in the poorer south end do.

Over the past decade, Seattle's students have consistently performed at or above the national average on the California Achievement Test (CAT), a nationally norm-referenced, standardized test administered and scored by the district. In 1990 through 1995, scores were consistently above the national average in reading, language, and mathematics for each year, at the elementary, middle, and high school levels.[9] In 1996, the district replaced the CAT with the Iowa Test of Basic Skills (ITBS). Students performed at about the same level as indicated on the CAT—at or above the national average—and in the elementary grades, students showed significant gains in 1998 and 1999, with average performance at about the 60th percentile.

Despite establishing a generally favorable climate of fiscal and political support for its schools, Seattle residents have also struggled to address three pressing issues that have surfaced time and again throughout the last 50 years with respect to their public school system: the significant disparities in student achievement levels across the city's schools; the negative effects in schools of racial isolation based on housing patterns and neighborhood characteristics; and the development of prudent and coherent strategies to close underutilized schools and upgrade aging and overcrowded ones.

Seattle's schools have historically been relatively successful for most of the city's children. High school graduates have been able to find work in the air-craft and shipping industries, and more recently in the large telecommunications and computer companies and related support infrastructure that has emerged in the nearby suburbs. Using the nationally normed, standardized tests as an achievement indicator, over the last 5 years, from 1996 to 2001, Seattle's students have scored at or above the 50th percentile at most grade levels in the core content areas. The national percentile ranking of the "average" Seattle third-grader has increased by about 10 percentile points over the past 4 years (47th percentile to 57th percentile in reading; 48th percentile to 65th percentile in math).[10] In a television interview, businessman-turned-school-board-member Don Nielson said, "We have a city that's not broken, we have a system that's not broke; we're not as we used to be, but it's not broken, but it needs to be better."[11]

However, when performance is disaggregated by ethnic groups, there has been a persistent, 20 percentile points difference between the overall achievement level of White students and the achievement level of African American and Latino students. While all ethnic groups have shown academic improvements over the past 5 years, the achievement gap has stubbornly persisted. In 1999, while White and Asian American students, who make up about 65% of the student population, perform well above the national average, Native American, African American, and Latino students lag behind. White students perform as a group at the 70th percentile level; African American students perform at about the 30th percentile level overall.

The efforts of the Seattle school district to address issues of racial segregation in schools generated significant tension and debate during the 1960s, as it did for urban school districts across the country. During that time in Seattle, there were numerous demonstrations and even a student boycott. In contrast to many other urban centers, however, Seattle chose to voluntarily adopt a mandatory busing strategy to desegregate schools and provide more balanced enrollments from overcrowded south-end schools to underutilized north-end schools.[12] This policy resulted in sporadic recall efforts of board members that failed, and other challenges, but busing essentially remained in place until the late 1980s, when it was replaced with a "controlled choice plan." In 1995, after seeing that for every north-end student who rode a bus to a south-end school, 10 south-end students were bused to north-end schools, Superintendent Stanford decided that he needed to end busing, declaring, "I don't have to sit next to someone of another color to learn."[13]

The need to modernize some schools but close others due to shifts and declines in enrollment also created many acrimonious debates centered on schools as sources of pride and identity for many neighborhoods and severe drains on limited district resources. Influential and highly vocal neighborhood activists were able to keep schools open, despite very small enrollments and very expensive-to-maintain facilities. Others questioned why the district would spend money on rebuilding schools in neighborhoods where children were being bused in to maintain enrollment, while schools in the "less desirable" inner-city core were left to decay. Despite elaborate planning rubrics designed by district staff, politically mobilized neighborhood groups put great pressure on the school board, creating divisions based on narrow neighborhood issues and delaying all school closure decisions for a decade. As one researcher put it: "School communities were extremely upset when their schools were named for closure and argued that those schools belonged to them and the citizens of their neighborhoods."[14]

Desegregation and school closure policies were inextricably intertwined; underutilized schools in the north end were kept open by busing students from the south end, and while this served to help desegregate those schools, north-end students rarely accepted busing to the minority-majority schools in the south end. The local school helped to define each neighborhood community, so when the district adopted the mandatory school busing strategy to desegregate its schools, not only did this exacerbate fears of ethnic conflict and misunderstanding, but fears arose that it would sever friendships among neighbors and separate neighborhood children from each other.

Ironically, most of the excess classroom space was available in mostly White neighborhoods, so mostly minority children rode the buses to schools outside their district and White children stayed in their neighborhoods. By some accounts, 10 Black children attended schools in White neighborhoods for every White child who was bused to a school in a Black neighborhood.

Schools in White neighborhoods with enrollments of under 200 children were recommended for closure, but those recommendations were fiercely resisted by neighborhood residents who feared that their children would then have to be bused into other, "less desirable" neighborhoods.

These tensions were ever-present through the 1970s and 1980s, and the school levy system, which required the district to go before voters for reauthorization every 2 or 3 years, served as a referendum that reflected public support for, or irritation with, the school district administration, especially with respect to school desegregation efforts and/or school closures. Levies required a super-majority of 60% of the numbers of voters in the previous election, so votes taken after a national election required widespread support across the city, from traditionally active neighborhoods in the north end to the less active south end. Unsuccessful campaigns were often followed by the dismissal or departure of the superintendent during that period.

The Present Era: John Stanford (1995–1998) and Joseph Olchefske (1998–Present)

By most accounts, William Kendricks's 10-year tenure as Seattle's superintendent ended with a soft thud in 1994. With a student assignment plan in place that included busing, with school closures completed, and with the student population stabilized at about 45,000 students, informants barely remember anything about his tenure, except that the schools were bureaucratic black holes, where ideas and resources and reforms never really took hold. Kendricks was remembered as a "nice" superintendent, but hardly one to lead a world-class school system. His last years were remembered as "without energy," but even worse, Seattle's school board meetings were remembered as sessions of bickering, name-calling, and promotion of narrow interests. In 1994, another tax levy failed to pass, and after that defeat, Kendricks chose to retire, a decision, many suggest, welcomed by his board.[15]

Those we interviewed unanimously recall the charisma and charm that General John Stanford brought to his interview for the superintendency in 1995. A member of the interview committee remembered that General Stanford stood formally beside the table that was provided for each candidate and never sat down or referred to notes. There was some concern about his lack of educational experience and his military background, but in the end, he impressed the entire committee as a person who could unite and mobilize the entire community. In a televised interview conducted shortly after his death, teachers and city leaders reported that every Seattle child knew who John Stanford was, and they loved him because they knew he was sincere.

A parent and city official remarked: "He convinced us as a community that schools were getting better and that they could be great. We don't know if that's true, but we believed him, and that was just as good."[16]

Perhaps most significant, the business community felt very comfortable and familiar with Stanford, and he felt comfortable with them. In his former roles as head of logistics for the U.S. Army and chief executive of Fulton County, Georgia, Stanford had been accustomed to working with business executives. The Alliance for Education, a business group that consolidated most other business groups in Seattle, was able to mobilize important and credible political backing for Stanford's superintendency and financial support for his initiatives.

Historically, the business community had always viewed support for schools as a civic duty, but business leaders usually sponsored only one school or project at a time through small, one-time grants to schools and corporate sponsorship for various ad hoc projects. Some businesses participated in Adopt-a-School programs, and there was a formal monthly meeting that brought the chief executive officers of major Seattle corporations together with city and district leaders. But in the 1990s, the private sector and civic leaders grew increasingly concerned that the district's graduates were not being adequately prepared for the increasingly technical jobs being created in the technology-rich environment of the new economy. During this time, there was a collective sense that the district as a whole had begun to lose momentum, no matter who was superintendent.

Business leaders sought changes in the governance and the leadership of the school district. They decided that schools would never improve unless a different type of board member were chosen. They increasingly believed that ineffective school board members were micromanaging district efforts. Forming a political action committee, Step Forward, they identified civic leaders interested in running for the school board and actively campaigned for their election. Subsequently, in 1993, two new board members were elected, both with strong business connections.

Unlike other cities where mayoral selection committees chose a nontraditionally prepared superintendent, Seattle's mayor did not play a significant role in the selection process in Seattle. Instead, much of the impetus came from school board members themselves, who wanted to widen the pool of candidates to be considered. Stanford was chosen over one other finalist, also an African American, a superintendent from a midwestern city school district, who by most accounts would have been an excellent choice, if Stanford had not been available. Some city leaders questioned whether Stanford's lack of education experience would limit his effectiveness, and whether his military background would fit into Seattle's liberal, "process-driven" political process. Seattle, after all, was a city that had declined to host a Gulf War parade.[17] Nevertheless, having just experienced a long-term, traditionally prepared superintendent and a micromanaging school board, the community as a whole seemed ready for a strong, take-charge, highly visible superintendent like John Stanford. As superintendent, Stanford's first senior appointment was Joseph Olchefske, an investment banker whose work experience and professional training was also not in education, but in finance. They had met in an elevator and struck up a friendship, just as Stanford was beginning his superintendency. Stanford believed not only that Olchefske's fiscal and business acumen was necessary to solve a serious budgetary shortfall, but that his intelligence and commitment to developing a systemic strategy for improving Seattle's schools would lead to districtwide gains in students' academic performance.

Stanford himself acknowledged that the district's goals as developed under Kendricks were fine; what was missing, Stanford argued, was an implementation strategy to achieve those goals and a community-wide campaign to engage and find support for those goals.[18] He agreed with Kendricks on two basic academic priorities—to raise student achievement for all and to close the achievement gap between White and minority students throughout the district. As reported in his own published book, Stanford freely drew on his military experience in developing his management style as superintendent, but that style was far different from the stereotypical one of the autocratic military leader whose commands are followed without question. Stanford's leadership style was to empower everyone to follow his lead.

Stanford outlined his strategic plan as follows:

Increase academic achievement for all students.

Close student achievement gaps.

Attract, develop, and retain an excellent multicultural workforce to provide students with successful role models.

Provide students with a healthy, safe, and secure learning environment.

Provide stable and adequate funding to ensure that students will receive a high quality and consistent education.

Meet diverse student and parent needs to attract and retain students.

At the very beginning of their tenure, Stanford and his chief financial officer, Joseph Olchefske, immediately confronted a looming budget deficit that would have derailed any curriculum and instructional reform effort.

According to their analysis, the district would need to cut $35 million from the budget over a 3-year period, and they would need to mount another levy campaign not only for operational enhancements but needed facilities modernization. Stanford believed that he needed to create a business plan focused on student outcomes, retool the district's infrastructure to overcome system lethargy, and reengage the community and the district's rank and file. Those plans will be discussed in greater detail in the next section.

Two years into his tenure, Stanford announced that he was being treated for leukemia. He vigorously fought the illness, and because he was convinced that he would recover, he continued to stay at the helm of the district. While the board and most staff continued to operate, key central office administrative positions began to turn over, especially in the leadership of the critically important academic areas. This was particularly significant because of Stanford's own inexperience with the specifics of curriculum and instruction. Arlene Ackerman, his chief academic officer, became superintendent in Washington, D.C., and the directors of academic achievement and curriculum and educational reform also left. While board members urged him to fill those vacancies, they did not press him to replenish his leadership team, and Stanford left the positions unfilled.

Stanford's untimely death in November 1998 left the board members with the significant problem of executive succession. They considered three choices: They could appoint Olchefske, who had assumed most of Stanford's executive responsibilities during his illness; they could conduct a national search for a replacement; or they could reconfigure the position of the superintendent. The third option would allow the board to create a dual superintendency, with a chief academic officer and a chief operations officer who would both be chosen by the board and report to it. This strategy was seriously considered in order to take advantage of Olchefske's knowledge of the budget and the organizational changes undertaken under Stanford, while supplementing them with the educational experience of a senior educator. According to press reports, principals, the teachers' union, and other veteran staff were in favor of the second option, a national search, not because they disliked Olchefske, but because they wanted to underscore the need for more academic leadership.[19]

In February 1999, the board chose the first option and decided to appoint Olchefske. They were impressed with the leadership he had shown during the interim term, and they did not want to lose the positive momentum that had been created under Stanford. Olchefske declared, "I own this—I've been part of shaping the path we're on. Clearly, we have to move beyond into the next phase; we like the path we're on, but the work is far from done."[20]

Satisfaction with Olchefske's appointment was confirmed in four influential sectors. First, the Bill and Melinda Gates Foundation pledged $26 million to Seattle schools to further school reform efforts, and the members of the business-driven Alliance for Education pledged to raise additional resources from a broad spectrum of the community as a sign of its commitment to Stanford's legacy. Second, an annual survey of Seattle's parents and residents reported their belief that the schools were improving and indicated their continued support for and satisfaction with the new superintendent. Third, the school board praised Olchefske's performance in his second annual review, and in October 2000 raised his salary, commending him for strengthening his senior staff with the hiring of June Rimmer, a veteran of the Indianapolis School District. They also noted that he had acted to remove ineffective principals.[21] Finally, in February 2001, the city's voters passed two levies that raised additional funds for the Seattle schools, an indication of the community's willingness to tax itself to support the schools and, by association, the new superintendent.

Two campaign messages vividly illustrate the linked focus and work of these two nontraditional superintendents. The first, which describes Stanford's commitment to systemic reform, is taken from the district's 1997–1998 annual report: "The vision: to build a world-class, student-focused learning system."[22] More recent district documents articulate an operational goal, established during Olchefske's tenure: "Delivering on the Dream: academic achievement for every student in every school."[23]

Key Features of the Educational Reforms

New Academic Content Standards for Every Grade. Stanford and Olchefske had outlined their vision for the Seattle school system in the following way:[24] "to create the highest possible standards for students, teachers and principals—and then hold our people to them . . . to focus our entire operation on our children . . . to get the community involved in making our district successful."[25]

With the state adoption of the Washington Essential Academic Learning Requirements in 1993 as a guide, Stanford's and Olchefske's notion of a systemic transformation began with a focus on student learning, not on the practice of teaching and instruction. The Washington Requirements outlined the performance standards expected of students, not teachers. By 1999, the Office of Standards and Assessment, working with administrators and teachers, converted those state standards into academic standards for each grade level, in each of four content areas. In future years, professional development, and the adoption of new curriculum materials and assessments will be driven by these standards. Olchefske hoped that those standards would be highly visible at every school, in every classroom; in visits to three schools, large posters highlighting the key content standards were evident in classrooms, bulletin boards displaying children's work had elements of the standards connected to them. Work has begun to connect those standards in explicit ways to teachers' lesson plans, and it is viewed as a priority area by Rimmer, the chief academic officer.

A New Student Assignment Plan and a Subsequent End to Mandatory Busing. In order to restore widespread public support for schools, Stanford and others believed that Seattle had to eliminate mandatory busing, a process they believed drove many White families from the public school system and frustrated African American parents whose children required long and wasteful bus rides across town, with little proven academic benefit. Stanford's staff created a neighborhood school assignment policy which offered students a preference for attending a school in their own geographic region but options to attend other schools if their parent so chose. An economist by training, Olchefske believed that continuing to offer school placement choices to parents used market forces to stimulate school competition for students.

Only by increasing the visible quality of all schools could they avoid accusations that the neighborhood school policy would result in unequal education based on housing patterns. Olchefske wanted schools to adopt appealing programs, create visible marketing strategies, and publicize results, all of which he believed would attract students and families to their neighborhood schools. If any school had more students applying than it had capacity for, students would be chosen based on a complex series of "tiebreakers" that included preference for students who were from an ethnic group that was underrepresented at the school. By staff estimate, over 80% of all students have been offered their top selection.

The shift to neighborhood schools may result in a resegregation of schools, reflecting the historic geographic concentration of minority families in certain neighborhoods across the city, and the choice of parents to keep their children close to home. One-third of the elementary schools now have 80% or more minority students.[26] Nevertheless, the great majority of parents, when given a choice of schools, have been consistently choosing schools near their homes, an indication of general approval of the neighborhood schools of choice strategy. To ensure that the neighborhood schools policy worked for all and provided adequate resources for schools where students had greater needs, Olchefske's strategy used fiscal incentives that assigned a value, through a weighted student formula, that apportioned dollars based on the needs and programs that a student was entitled to.

Weighted Student Formula. Olchefske believed that creating meaningful competition for students among schools could encourage districtwide improvement, but there was concern that schools would try to recruit only the most academically gifted students. There needed to be incentives to recruit all children, even those with special needs or from lower income communities in the vicinity of some of the schools. In order to address fears that the new student assignment plan would create a world-class system for the affluent north end and a second-class system for the poorer south end, Stanford and Olchefske sought a strategy to redistribute limited school resources to schools that would see an influx of new students returning to their schools in the south end. The resource allocation system they developed, the Weighted Student Formula, was drawn from a similar program that they had observed in Alberta, Canada.[27] Olchefske assigned more resources to needy students, and tied those resources to the school that the students attended, making them relatively more financially "valuable" to the receiving school.

Schools that gained enrollment as a result of the Weighted Student Formula (see below) have added extra services, including full-day kindergartens or smaller class sizes, and that has meant that the schools needed more classrooms. Thus the initial benefits from the Weighted Student Formula are sometimes compromised because schools are forced to erect portable buildings to handle the additional classrooms, as students return to their neighborhood schools or select highly attractive schools.

In addition, while it is true that additional funds followed students to their new schools, those funds came from compensatory sources, such as Title 1 and Special Education, and reflected the additional needs that these students already had. The basic general-purpose support that students carried with them remained the same, and so in most cases, movement of a student from one school to another simply meant a gain in funding to the school based on increased enrollment, plus a smaller "weight" gain if the student qualified for special funding based on need. For a school, most of the increased funding translated into additional teaching staff to accommodate the increased enrollment, so there was little "value-added" impact that accompanied these student transfers.

More recently, researchers at the Center for Reinventing Government at the University of Washington identified significant, unintended imbalances in funding that continued to favor some schools serving wealthier communities, despite the weighted student formula.[28] According to them, if one calculates the total budget for a school, including the actual salaries of staff, then many in fact cost more to operate, per student, than do schools serving lower income communities. This is because the teaching and administrative staffs at schools in wealthier communities were in general more highly experienced and therefore were more highly paid. A teacher with 11 years' experience was paid about 50% more than a new teacher; their experience level placed them higher on the salary scale. The Center's analysts support the concept of the Weighted Student Formula, but argue that it should be fully implemented to reflect the actual cost of teacher and administrative salaries. While there is ongoing discussion about this apparent issue, the Weighted Student Formula remains as a district policy.

Higher Professional Standards for Principals. Stanford and Olchefske believed that principals needed to be treated as chief executive officers of their schools. That meant principals should have more discretion over their budgets, selection of new teachers, and school-site professional development programs. Stanford established a principal's leadership institute in his first year, which was funded by the Alliance for Education, and every principal participated. He suggested that principals knew how to educate, but that they needed additional skills "in inspiring, motivating, and guiding their diverse communities of students, teachers, and parents."[29] While all principals who were serving at the time participated in the yearlong training, there has been a great deal of turnover in the administrative ranks, and it is a priority to provide ongoing professional development opportunities for each new group of principals, as well as for principals serving in new schools.

According to press reports, a departing personnel director had suggested that 25% of the principals were ineffective. Stanford immediately defended the principals and resisted calls for more drastic transfers and demotions.[30] The reporter suggested that Stanford, like the superintendents before him, seemed reticent to remove or fire principals; according to the reporter, Stanford had not begun to formally evaluate his principals until December 1998, more than 2 years after he had assumed the superintendency. In response, Stanford noted, "Because I am a general, people wanted me to come in here and fire people. That's not my style. My style is to love 'em and lead 'em."[31] In the same interview, Olchefske pointed out that the pool of principals was so thin that it constituted a "people crisis." During his tenure, Stanford had personally assigned nearly 70 principals, but most were veterans from within the system who had been transferred from one school to another or promoted from within. While his transfer policy had benefited some schools when he replaced a weak principal with a more successful one from another school, the school that lost its successful principal sometimes experienced a drop in test scores.

Olchefske's tenure has already been shaped by his willingness to demote and transfer ineffective principals. Within his first year as permanent superintendent, he demoted four principals and hired five principals from outside the district, indications, he said, of his determination to have "a high-quality principal as a leader for every school."[32] It was later announced that a longtime principal of a high school had been forced to resign that spring, but was allowed to receive a large severance package. "I [Olchefske] wanted to move and move aggressively. If it cost some money to move that way, I was willing to pay something."[33] In the case of the high school principal, parents and teachers had campaigned for over a year to have the principal removed. More recently, Olchefske removed a controversial director of special education but allowed him also to receive a severance package.[34]

Appointment and replacement decisions have been restricted to the superintendent, and those actions are highly visible symbols of a superintendent's willingness and ability to exercise authority. But they are also among the most desired decisions that school-site staff and parents want to make. This reflects the tension inherent in efforts to increase responsibility and autonomy at the school site, without jeopardizing working rights of administrators, the independence of their managerial authority, or the oversight responsibility of the superintendent for each school site.

Site-Based Management and a New Trust Agreement With Teachers. A key feature of Stanford's efforts to stimulate change systemwide, but especially at the grassroots school-site level, was treating principals as CEOs and shifting more decision-making authority to the school site. Part of that shift entailed a new, more positive working arrangement between the district and the Seattle Education Association (SEA). The SEA had already initiated, in negotiations with then Superintendent Kendricks, a peer review evaluation program called the STAR (Staff Training Assistance and Review) program, which matched new teachers with experienced teachers who act as mentors.[35]

The standard collective bargaining contract between the teachers association and the district expired, and, following the model of the labor-management trust agreement that had been signed by General Motors and the United Auto Workers for their Saturn division, the SEA and the district agreed to sign their own trust agreement. Stanford acknowledged the SEA's leadership in urging this form of labor agreement, and union leaders of that movement underscore Kendricks's important foundational work.[36] The underlying principle of the agreement was that at the site level, staff and administration would create a common vision, with an "authentic" decision-making role for teachers. The trust agreement that went into effect during the 1996–97 school year reflected the positive operational relationship between Stanford and Olchefske and the SEA. The final collective bargaining arrangement was driven by "interest-based bargaining," a process that emphasizes problem solving rather than position-based negotiations, spearheaded by the city's chief labor negotiator. The contract is now in place, and includes:

> A shared, decision-making role for teachers in their schools with respect to budget, strategic planning, curriculum, and professional development, through the establishment of a leadership team selected by the site as a whole.

> More hiring flexibility and teacher input on hiring decisions: revisions in the teacher transfer policy, through site-hiring teams, with seniority retained as a factor but not the decisive factor in hiring, transfers, and layoffs.

> A new teacher evaluation policy, tied in part to student achievement, with measures of achievement jointly determined by administration and staff.

Development of a New Student Accountability System Based on a Value-Added Measure of Success. Seattle recently hired William Sanders, a Tennessee statistician who had developed a "value-added" technique that tracks student performance from one year to the next for students, and then compares that growth with students from similar background characteristics, and against other children in a class.[37] The important contribution this can make is that it focuses on student progress over a school year, not simply a single snapshot of student performance. Sanders's system has been used in Tennessee to calculate the average improvement that can be attributed to a teacher's effort, and could provide the beginning of a system for Seattle that uses student performance as a measure of teacher effectiveness, although that has not yet taken place.

Teachers and their organizational representatives have usually objected to using student achievement as part of teacher evaluation because students begin with different academic skills and have access to different sets of community and family assets. To compare one teacher to another, or even to a standard expected level of student achievement or student growth, requires a capacity to control for those variables. Tying teacher evaluations to student achievement requires a capacity to assess the effect of the teacher's classroom performance on student achievement, irrespective of the impact of demographic factors, and even irrespective of the quality of instruction in preceding years. If the student progress of an entire class can be measured as Sanders suggests, then it is possible to compare the "teacher effect" in one class to that of another.

Some objections to this effort have arisen. First, the focus on standardized test score performance, on a test not tied to the standards, might detract from more important efforts to develop assessments tied directly to the content standards. Second, the cost and complexity of the assessment system is an expense that could be better spent elsewhere, and in different ways. More important, some critics question whether the quality of teaching is best evaluated by this kind of measurement of student outcomes. According to a Seattle principal, principal evaluations now include a component that focuses on schoolwide improvements in student outcomes.[38]

Analysis

It is clear from the review of Stanford's 3-year tenure within the context of what Seattle wanted and needed, that there was a combination of person, place, and circumstances that created strong incentives for positive change. While people complained about "an educational malaise" that existed in Seattle prior to his arrival, and despaired of the low quality of some of the schools, in fact, there was no significant labor unrest, test scores were higher than in most cities of its size, and through elections the district was governed by a corporate-style board of directors. Executives of the SEA reported an amicable, positive, and productive relationship with Kendricks that focused on teaching and learning, including 10 years of management-labor cooperation.[39] The city's political and business leadership, while unhappy with school performance, was nevertheless not interested in taking over the schools, something that has occurred in other cities. Nevertheless, the struggle to pass the levy signaled that Seattle's voters were not satisfied with the school system as it was performing.

What everyone wanted was a superintendent who could restore the community's confidence in its school system, and who would reinvigorate the schools. There was no mandate to choose a nontraditionally prepared superintendent, but the community wanted new and different leadership, and there was little resistance when a superintendent candidate was found who had no professional school experience.

Stanford created a powerful media campaign on behalf of children that challenged everyone to work together to create better schools. His personal high visibility in the schools during his 3-year tenure produced much positive public enthusiasm for the schools and substantial concrete support for the school district as a whole by the business community and residents who personally invested in the Alliance for Education. While most attributed the dramatic turnaround to Stanford, others pointed out that many of the pieces were in place before he arrived: an orderly succession process; strong and visionary teachers' association leadership; a vibrant and growing local economic base; organized support from the business community; and a solid school board. These are the very factors that have often subverted and undermined new superintendents from the day they arrived.

Stanford emphasized the importance of a fundamental shift from a system focused on adult issues to one focused on children's achievement, and he repeatedly articulated this as his system reform strategy. He personally led the campaign with his high visibility in interacting with children. Yet most of the significant changes that characterize his tenure focused on adult issues—school funding, school assignment choices for parents, a new labor contract for teachers, new site-based decision-making structures, and the principal as the school's CEO. These changes were all shaped and directed toward the goal of improving student achievement. They certainly set the stage for improved use of teaching and learning resources. However, they had yet to address the technical core of education—teaching and learning—in a particularly strategic way. In fact, there seems to have been little in the way of actual definition and change in terms of what was actually being taught and how, at the end of Stanford's tenure, it was clear that the district needed academic leadership, and that appointment became Olchefske's top priority when he succeeded Stanford.

Olchefske's appointment was in large measure an endorsement by the board of the direction of Stanford's superintendency and an unwillingness to take chances with another search. In 2002, Olchefske enters the fourth year of his tenure as permanent superintendent. One can view his tenure as an extension of many of the initiatives begun under Stanford's tenure, while at the same time it is clear that Olchefske has firmly planted his own imprimatur and is the district's CEO. The work that remains involves extending the curriculum changes into the classroom, or as Olchefske would say, into every classroom.

As research has repeatedly shown, uniform classroom implementation of district-level policy changes is a very complex enterprise.[40] It includes several aspects: seeing that teachers adopt and accept the new standards as applying to every child; developing and utilizing classroom practices that support the academic standards; providing adequate support to meet the needs of under-performing students; ensuring that resources, especially qualified and committed teachers, are adequately deployed in the schools with the neediest students; and maintaining public support for the entire school system, even as parental attention is now refocused primarily on the local neighborhood schools where their children attend.

Two areas in which Stanford received some criticism—that his instructional program was unfocused and that he failed to remove ineffective principals—were among the first actions on Olchefske's agenda. Within 6 months, Olchefske hired an academic officer, and the board had adopted a set of learning outcome standards as well as broad exit criteria for high schoolers. Less than a year after his appointment, the press announced that Olchefske had demoted 4 principals.[41] But recent difficulties with filling several key high school principalships have also created some public questions about both the selection process and the final appointments.[42] He also continues to refine the Weighted Student Formula as a way to provide differential support to schools. But as he noted in our interview, the curriculum has not yet changed as much as he desires.

Stanford and Olchefske have developed tremendous community support for their leadership and avoided organized challenges to the directions they undertook. The support of the business community will in all likelihood be sustained. It remains to be seen whether the deliberate implementation of standards-based instructional strategies and accountability systems will succeed in raising student achievement and closing achievement gaps. The purpose of returning to neighborhood school assignment was to improve opportunities for minority children and to reconnect parents to their neighborhood schools. Most parents seem to be pleased with the new assignment policy, but there are persistent challenges from parent groups to the race-based assignment priorities.[43]

The educational reforms initiated in the past 6 years by Superintendents Stanford and Olchefske are significant for the Seattle Public Schools, but they are not significantly different from others that have been proposed and implemented in other cities by more traditionally trained superintendents. The systemic approach of aligning standards, assessments, curriculum and instruction, and professional development has been advocated for more than 10 years.[44] As increased attention is given to formal teacher and administrator evaluations tied to student performance—high-stakes evaluations—there may be significantly more tension that emerges. In contrast to Stanford, Olchefske has increased his central office staff's responsibility for the evaluation of principals and has tied student performance to that evaluation. He has shown a willingness to reassign, demote, and dismiss school principals. Whether and how staff will respond to, or resist, efforts to increase overall accountability at the classroom level, and whether Olchefske will be able to identify and place highly skilled leadership at school sites is also a challenge that superintendents across the country face.[45]

With the current high level of community and professional support in place, there is reason to believe that Olchefske and his leadership team will continue to make steady progress in implementing a standards-based educational reform agenda, in partnership with the SEA, although the teachers' association itself has undergone a significant leadership changeover.[46]

The standard that Olchefske has set for himself, to significantly reduce the achievement gap between ethnic groups, will be the greatest challenge, since the district is now concentrating on teaching and learning in the classroom, and the gap still has persisted (although every ethnic group has made steady gains). The test results to date suggest that closing the gap will continue to be a difficult enterprise and more resources will be needed, especially an expanded pool of talented, well-trained, and committed teachers and administrators. The board and superintendent will need to monitor the achievement of African American students, especially with respect to the achievement gap, to ensure that both the neighborhood school assignment plans and the educational reforms have had the anticipated effect. Disparities not only in achievement, but in district application of suspension and discipline policies, may also lead to increased scrutiny of the effect of the system reform policies implemented over the past 6 years. As these complex problem areas emerge, Olchefske and his team will be judged by their willingness and ability to effectively manage these policy dilemmas.[47]

Conclusion

The charismatic persona that Stanford publicly communicated, that captured that imagination of the community and moved it to action, seems to have been at least as important as the management skills that he actually brought, the initiatives that he proposed and supported, and the authority that many associate with a military leader. Stanford was fondly remembered as an "idea-a-minute" manager, meaning that he floated many ideas and left it to staff to figure out how to implement them. Some interviewees suggested that he failed to address low-performing administrators, either through a more deliberate evaluation process or through the outright removal of ineffective principals. It must be remembered that Seattle schools were performing at a level that would be the envy of many other urban districts. It is also difficult to identify the specific teaching and learning strategies that were implemented during his brief 3-year tenure.[48]

Still, the notion of restoring hope and confidence, convincing parents and the business community that the Seattle schools could be "world-class," and re-focusing attention on academic achievement for all children, were valuable outcomes of his tenure and in all likelihood will be his most important legacy. Other superintendents have declared such goals, but most have simply not been able to convince their communities that it was really possible and mobilize residents and business and political leaders toward positive action. The benefits to the district cannot be simply measured in gains in efficiency or academic achievement; they are gains in goodwill, in a sense of community participation in the education of the next generation, in the possibilities and expectations of high-quality education for all children.

If raising community optimism about its schools and its neighborhoods is one of the most important roles of the superintendent, then boards of education responsible for the selection process may well want to include candidates from outside education who have been similarly inspiring in their work settings, for example, writers, religious leaders, community and labor organizers, and politicians. At the same time, we should not exclude educators who may possess the same charisma, simply because they have chosen to develop their leadership skills in the schools. There is a danger in believing or assuming that only generals, or noneducators, can ignite such optimism within a community. Thirty years ago in Oakland, California, an African American from Philadelphia arrived on the scene as superintendent of schools, and generated similar energy and hope; his name was Marcus Foster, and he was a longtime veteran public school educator.[49] And educators who were interviewed, who remembered the tension and suspicion that occurred when Seattle's teachers went on strike in 1985, recall with admiration the healing that occurred and the optimism that was generated by then newly hired superintendent William Kendricks.

The lesson here is that the ability to work with the external environment in which schools are embedded is an essential ingredient to a successful superintendency.[50] That environment includes political activists who speak for disadvantaged and disempowered communities, neighborhood activists and parents who choose to live in certain communities and desire to maintain the quality of life for themselves and their children, and a business community whose support provides significant additional resources and political legitimacy to the district's efforts. Stanford seemed to have been at ease, well respected, and successful in all of these areas, even if all sectors did not always agree with him. This is an important quality that superintendents, whether they are traditionally prepared or come from another sector, need to possess and convey, and as Kendricks's 10-year tenure suggests, it is an ability that is affected by time and circumstance.[51]

Joseph Olchefske possesses the kinds of fiscal and administrative expertise and entrée to the business community that most educators lack. Those talents, and the fortuitous meeting with Stanford as he began his tenure, gave him the initial position as CFO for a major school district without any professional school experience or exposure. Stanford's extended illness and untimely death subsequently gave him the opportunity to lead the district on an interim basis. But Olchefske's own skills are the product of significant and demanding academic preparation as well as real-life experience. His technical skill in identifying the looming budget crisis and controlling the budget process helped to drive creative solutions to differential funding in schools. Olchefske gained large-system management experience in the interim period when he was able to assume operational authority for the entire district. When the board's search committee decided on Stanford's successor, Olchefske was chosen in part because he was now the "insider." This confluence of opportunity and expertise are uncommon, but it also took a strong sense of self-confidence, adventure, and civic duty to take on such complex challenges when they were presented.

To his credit, Olchefske was willing to serve in a highly political position paying considerably less than he was making as an investment banker. He was also wise enough to realize the professional limitations of his background, and he quickly hired two highly qualified educators—one a local superintendent, and the other a strong instructional leader—to serve as a leadership team. Focusing on student achievement as measured by standardized tests has many detractors, but one thing is certain: When a superintendent is a noneducator, such measures provide a straightforward and logical way to measure district performance and are clearly understood by business, political, and community leaders. This is a lesson that is applicable to traditionally trained superintendents as well.

In the end, Seattle's residents and educators seem to be well satisfied with their choice of John Stanford and Joseph Olchefske. However, sustaining systemic change requires an understanding of how teachers and school staffs work to make the school improvements that are necessary conditions for high achievement for every child in every school. Even with standards and accountability instruments in place, there are many questions about whether instructional classroom practice will change sufficiently for comprehensive school improvement, and whether fiscal and human resources are sufficient to provide opportunities to learn for every student in every school, no matter where those schools are located. For that to occur, experienced professional educators in the district office and in schools, who possess deep personal knowledge of instructional practice in real school settings, must offer instructional leadership. More than any other actions, Olchefske's selection, support, and evaluation of principals for school sites and central office administrators will establish his instructional reputation, and his managing of competing neighborhood interests with respect to student assignment strategies will demonstrate his political skills.[52]

There will be some who will invoke Stanford's legacy to support narrow, parochial interests, or as justification for challenging difficult decisions that the superintendent must make. To some extent, the community's recollections of Stanford suggest that he was the Lone Ranger and the Miracle Worker, and at this time, neither he nor Olchefske has yet been made a martyr or scapegoat. Yet it must be remembered that the success of these nontraditionally prepared superintendents builds on the tenure of their predecessor, William Kendricks;

the support of enlightened teacher leadership; the generous financial support of the community in an era of significant economic expansion; the general achievement level of Seattle's students; and the professional expertise of senior, traditionally prepared educators. Their tenure brings hope not only that Seattle schools can improve but that urban school improvement is possible and that it can occur within the context of cooperative and ethical political, managerial, and instructional leadership that draws together all of the strengths of educators and the community. That hope is remarkable because it was expressed eloquently throughout the entire city in words and action.[53] What remains to be seen is whether or not it can be sustained and mobilized through community action long enough without fracture so as to fulfill the dream—academic achievement for every child in every school.

Notes

1. Mark Starr, "Miracle Workers Wanted," *Newsweek*, 14 January 1991, 40–44.

2. *Seattle Post-Intelligencer*, 5 May 1975, quoted in Stephen Rowley, *School Closure in Seattle: A Case Study of Educational Decision Making* (Ph.D. diss., Stanford University, 1984).

3. Hugh Scott, *The Black Superintendent, Messiah or Scapegoat?* (Washington, DC: Howard University Press, 1980).

4. "We can call Stanford HOPE." A quotation from seventh-graders Jackie Lopez and Mutanda Kwesele, a *Seattle Times Special Section*, 3 December 1998, p. C2.

5. Initial interviews were conducted over a 2-day period in Seattle, 24–26 January 2001, using a semistructured interview protocol. Interviewees included Seattle Public Schools superintendent Joseph Olchefske, veteran and newly hired central office administrators, Seattle public policy researchers, and Seattle civic and political leaders. Subsequent interviews were also conducted with school principals and teachers on 17 April 2001 in a visit to three Seattle schools, and on 28 April 2001 with a former Seattle Education Association leader.

6. For a detailed comparison of the social context of schools, see the Annie Casey Foundation's *City Kids Report, http://www.aecf.org*.

7. This is a consistent response from our interviews.

8. Rowley, *School Closure*.

9. Student Information Services Office, *Data Profile: District Summary, 1996*, Report 95-1 (Seattle: Seattle Public Schools, 1997).

10. Seattle Public Schools, *Data Profile: District Summary, November 1999*, Report 99-1 (Seattle: Seattle Public Schools, 2000).

11. John Merrow, *The Tale of Three Cities: The Mayor, the Minister, and the General* (New York: The Merrow Report, 1998 [*http://www.pbs.org/merrow*]), for the Don Nielson quote.

12. Rowley, *School Closure.*

13. Ruth Teichroeb, "End to Forced Busing Creates New Problems for Seattle's Schools," *Seattle Post-Intelligencer,* 3 June 1999 (*http://seattlep-i.nwsource.com/local/race03.shtml*).

14. Rowley, *School Closure,* p. 171.

15. Interviews with school administrators, 24–26 January 2001.

16. Merrow, *Tale of Three Cities.*

17. Interviews with civic and political leaders, 25 January 2001.

18. John Stanford, *Victory in Our Schools* (New York: Bantam Books, 1999).

19. Ruth Teichroeb, "Olchefske's First Priority: Find Academic Officer for City Schools," *Seattle Post-Intelligencer,* 11 February 1999 (*http://seattlep-i.nwsoruce.com/local/skull11.shtml*).

20. Ibid.

21. Keith Ervin, "Superintendent Earns Good Marks from Board," *Seattle Times,* 19 October 2000 (*http://archives.seattletimes.nwsource.com*).

22. Stanford, *Victory in Our Schools.*

23. Seattle Public Schools, *Good News: A Quarterly Publication of the Seattle Public Schools Community Relations Office,* no. 2 (fall 2000).

24. See Paul Hill, Christine Campbell, and James Harvey, *It Takes a City: Getting Serious about Urban School Reform* (Washington, DC: Brookings Institution, 2000).

25. Stanford, *Victory in Our Schools,* p. 15.

26. Ruth Teichroeb, "Two Schools Illustrate North-South Divide," *Seattle Post-Intelligencer,* 3 June 1999 (*http://seattlep-i.nwsource.com/local/skul03.shtml*).

27. Stanford, *Victory in Our Schools,* p. 186.

28. Marguerite Roza, "Policy Inadvertently Robs Poor Schools to Benefit the Rich," *Seattle Post-Intelligencer,* 24 September 2000 (*http://seatlep-i.nwsource.com/opinion/focus24.shtml*).

29. Stanford, *Victory in Our Schools,* p. 65.

30. Ruth Teichroeb, "Weak Leaders Threaten John Stanford's Goal of 'World Class' Schools in Seattle, Critics Say," *Seattle Post-Intelligencer,* 13 July 1998 (*http://seattlep-i.nwsource.com/awards/principal/princl.shtml*).

31. Ibid.

32. Debera Harrell, "Demotions of Principals Send Message to Improve," *Seattle Post-Intelligencer,* 17 May 2000 (*http://seatlep-i.nwsource.com/local/prin17.shtml*).

33. Keith Ervin, "Rainier Beach Principal Paid $173,500 by District to Resign," *Seattle Post-Intelligencer,* 18 September 2000 (*http://archives.seattletimes.nwsource.com*).

34. Rebekah Denn, "Special Education Chief Quits," *Seattle Post-Intelligencer,* 3 March 2001 (*http://seattlep-i.nwsource.com/local/resign03.shtml*).

35. Seattle Education Association, *Seattle Education Association and Seattle Public Schools Launch Mentor Program,* undated flyer to SEA membership.

36. Interview with former Seattle Education Association leader, 28 April 2001.

37. William Sanders and Sandra Horn, "The Tennessee Value-Added Assessment System: Mixed-Model Methodology in Educational Assessment," *Journal of Personnel Evaluation in Education,* 8(3): 299–311 (October 1994).

38. Interview with principal, 17 April 2001.

39. Interviews with principals, teacher, and former union leader, 17 April 2001, and 28 April 2001.

40. Michael Fullan, *The New Meaning of Educational Change* (New York: Teachers College Press, 1991).

41. Harrell, "Demotions of Principals."

42. Rebekah Denn, "Garfield High Again Seeks Principal after Day Reconsiders," *Seattle Post-Intelligencer,* 26 May 2001 (*http://seattlep-i.nwsource.com/local/24816_garfield26.shtml*).

43. Rebekah Denn, "Parents Challenge Seattle Schools' Race Rule," *Seattle Post-Intelligencer,* 29 March 2001 (*http://seattlep-i.nwsource.com/local/parents29.shtml*).

44. Marshall Smith and Jennifer O'Day, "Systemic School Reform," *Politics of Education Association Yearbook, 1990* (1991): 233–267.

45. Institute for Educational Leadership, *Leadership for Student Learning: Reinventing the Principalship,* Report of the Task Force on the Principalship (Washington, DC: Institute for Educational Leadership, October 2000 [*http://www.iel.org*]). Rebekah Denn, "Seattle Schools See Need to Hire 2,000 New Teachers," *Seattle Post-Intelligencer,* 9 March, 2001 (*http://seattlep-i.nwsource.com/local/staffing09.shtml*).

46. Interviews with teachers and principals, 17 April 2001.

47. Larry Cuban, *How Can I Fix It? An Educator's Road Map* (New York: Teachers College Press, 2001).

48. Interviews with teachers and principals, 17 April 2001.

49. Gary Yee, *Miracle Workers Wanted: Executive Succession and Organizational Change in an Urban School District* (Ph.D. diss., Stanford University, 1995). See also Marcus Foster, *Making Schools Work* (Philadelphia: Westminster Press, 1974).

50. Barbara McCloud and Floretta McKenzie, "School Boards and Superintendents in Urban Districts," *Phi Delta Kappan, 75* (January 1994): 384–385.

51. Other cases include Waldemar Rojas (San Francisco and Dallas); Ramon Cortines (San Francisco and New York City); and Laval Wilson (Berkeley and Boston).

52. Larry Cuban, *The Managerial Imperative and the Practice of Leadership in Schools* (Albany: State University of New York Press, 1988).

53. Marc Ramirez, "Keeping His Vision Alive," *Seattle Times,* 3 December 1998, p. C3.

13

Reforming Urban Districts*

editor's introduction:

Strengthening Whole Districts, Not Just Single Schools. As illustrated by the preceding selection, most geographic areas are served by a single school system—a school district. The single system provides the governance and management for all of the public schools in the area, whether urban, suburban, or rural. Although most of these systems have individual schools that have excelled for long periods of time and have established strong academic reputations, a continuing challenge for school districts is to optimize the performance of the entire system (i.e., all of its schools).

The present selection summarizes the experiences of six urban districts (located in Baltimore, Boston, Chicago, Philadelphia, San Diego, and Seattle) in attempting to strengthen their systems. The efforts were supported by the business and political leaders of the community, in addition to educators. The breadth of the efforts covered all facets of the system, thereby invoking the authors' use of the term reform. The resulting enormity of the efforts gives you an idea of the difficulties confronting civic leaders, and the entire book focuses on the districts' reform efforts and accomplishments. A major contribution of this case study is to demonstrate how urban school districts have gone about their work and how they have engaged the support and collaboration of the business and political sectors.

Relevance of Case Studies: Drawing From Multiple Cases. An increasingly common use of case studies is to design a case study that involves multiple cases. You would then draw your conclusions on the basis of the entire set of cases. The present selection is from the final chapter of a book in which each of six individual cases

*Cuban, Larry, & Usdan, Michael. (2003). "What Happened in the Six Cities?" In Larry Cuban & Michael Usdan (Eds.), *Powerful Reforms With Shallow Roots: Improving America's Urban Schools* (pp. 147–170). New York: Teachers College Press.

was previously covered by a single chapter (see the previous selection of this anthology for one of the individual cases).

The selection gives you a good example of a qualitative, cross-case analysis. The outset of the piece systematically presents evidence from all six cases, in the form of "word tables." They cover key topics of interest: demographic profiles, political and governance reforms, managerial and instructional strategies, and outcomes. These are the data used in the cross-case analysis. The data cover each of the six cases equally, avoiding a selectivity or imbalance among them. Furthermore, the data are presented apart from the subsequent interpretations made by the authors in the remainder of the analysis, permitting you and other readers to inspect the data apart from their interpretations—another procedure not always followed by other case studies.

The data are varied: Some are numeric scores and dates, and others are "judgment calls" or ratings made by the authors. Although the basis for the ratings is not amplified by the authors, the data do support the overall interpretation of "mixed outcomes" from the six cases. The authors also use the findings from the six cases as a platform for their explanation of the mixed outcomes—"powerful reforms" but "shallow roots."

"There is no better constructive publicity for a city than to be known over the entire country as a city of good schools," said a member of the Portland Board of Education in 1915. Connecting strong schools to a growing, family-friendly, culturally rich, and economically healthy city binds Progressive reformers from almost a century ago to their twenty-first-century counterparts who see better schools as a vehicle for creating better cities. Bumper stickers then and now could well read: Good schools = a vital city.[1]

In the early to mid-1990s, business, political, and educational leaders in the six cities profiled in this book sought to fix the problems crippling students' academic performance. They defined the problem as quarrelsome school boards; inept management that couldn't clean buildings, deliver supplies, or help teachers do their jobs; and little accountability for producing satisfactory academic outcomes among administrators and teachers. The problem was not located in society, the local neighborhood, or in insufficient funds; the problem was in the governance and management of schools. In city after city, these business and civic leaders urged district officials to restructure their control of schools and apply sound business principles in order to improve students' academic performance. They believed that higher achievement would produce smarter, independent, and reliable high school graduates who would function as suitable employees and dutiful citizens. How would this happen?

Business and civic leaders counted on governance reforms—that is, changes in political authority and supervision in tax-supported institutions—wedded to more effective district management and individual school accountability to prod teachers to teach better and students to learn more. These reforms, in turn, would lead to improved student scores on standardized achievement tests and, ultimately, yield graduates with marketable skills and attitudes to perform satisfactorily in an information-based economy.[2]

Better urban schooling, then, would mean that mayors could attract companies (and increased tax revenues) to the city. Employers saw better schools in the city as an incentive to offer potential employees and their families. More companies locating in the city provide a deeper and broader tax base to fund a rich array of cultural, recreational, and social services that would reinvigorate urban economic and social health. Fix the schools' political problems of inept command-and-control authority and little accountability first, then educational performance will improve and cities will reap the benefits. Good schools = a vital city!

These beliefs, repeated to us again and again in an amazingly common refrain with can-do enthusiasm, became the dominant theory of action put into practice by mayors, business and civic leaders, school boards, and superintendents in these six cities during the 1990s. Less agreement, however, occurred over which political tools—mayoral control of education or appointing nontraditional educators, or both—were the best strategies. In Chicago, Philadelphia, San Diego, and Seattle, nontraditional educators became CEOs. In Chicago, Boston, and Baltimore (until 1997), mayors directly appointed school boards and superintendents and controlled the school budgets.[3]

The snapshots we took in 2000–2002 of the governance reforms—managerial strategies to improve instruction and achieve desired outcomes in the six cities—capture nearly a decade of reform and make it difficult to generalize for all cities across time and to extract lessons for others to heed. Later in this chapter, we offer some reflections, informed by our knowledge of the past, which put these snapshots in a larger context. Before we analyze the governance and leadership changes that occurred in these cities, we summarize some basic facts about our six cities.

Table 13.1 shows the demographic profiles of the six cities. Given the historical connections between poverty and low academic achievement, Baltimore, Boston, Chicago, and Philadelphia had three-quarters or more of their students eligible for free or reduced-price lunch, a primary indicator of poverty. San Diego and Seattle had far lower percentages of impoverished

Table 13.1   Demographic Profiles

	Baltimore	Boston	Chicago	Philadelphia	San Diego	Seattle
Total population[1]	651,154	589,141	2,896,016	1,517,550	1,223,400	563,374
School district population[2]	108,759	63,588	421,334	212,150	133,687	47,883
Dollar expenditure per pupil[3]	6,370	9,545	7,827	7,669	5,328	6,723
Percent Black and Latino	86	76	86	78	55	32
Percent poor	75	74	86	80	47	40
High school dropout rate[4]	10.4	8.3	15.5	11.8	14.4	13.4

1. www.demographia.com/db-uscity98.htm

2. Baltimore figures are for 1996–1997 in Gary Orfield and John Yun, *Resegregation in American Schools* (Cambridge, MA: Civil Rights Project, Harvard University, 1999), p. 9. Other figures come from each district's website for 2001.

3. Figures for school district population, expenditures per pupil, and percent black and Latino come from National Center of Education Statistics, "Characteristics of the 100 Largest Elementary and Secondary School Districts in the United States: 1997–1998," Tables 9 and 10, July 1999. Other figures come from each district's website for 2001.

4. Dropout rates come from websites for each district, 2000–2001.

children attending school. With these demographic figures in mind, we turn to the changes that civic and business leaders implemented in the six cities.

Table 13.2 lists seven aspects of political and governance reforms and their roles in each city. Business and civic leaders in five of the cities, strongly influenced by state legislation, designed and implemented districtwide changes from the top, that is, without much teacher or parent involvement. Also, school leaders who stayed 5 or more years—either having no experience in education or products of the traditional career path in schools—drew from the same sources in constructing their reform strategies.

Historically, superintendents performed three leadership roles simultaneously: managerial, instructional, and political. Often, a superintendent who was strong, say, in managing the district and dealing politically with community groups, would appoint a deputy strong in instruction. In the 1990s, David Hornbeck, John Stanford, Joseph Olchefske, and Alan Bersin [superintendents in Philadelphia, Seattle, Seattle, and San Diego, respectively]

Table 13.2 Political and Governance Reforms

Action	Baltimore	Boston	Chicago	Philadelphia	San Diego	Seattle
Mayoral control of schools	Before 1997; state/district control since	1991	1995	1999; state/mayoral control since 2001	None	None
Noneducator superintendent	None	None	1995, 2001	1994, 2001	1998	1995, 1998
Superintendent tenure during reforms	Hunter 1987–1991 Amphrey 1991–1997 Booker 1997–2000 Russo 2000–	Payzant 1995–	Vallas 1995–2001 Duncan 2001–	Hornbeck 1994–2000 Goldsmith 2001–	Bersin 1998–	Stanford 1995–1998 Olchefske 1998–
Role of state in funding, setting standards, testing, and so on	Heavy	Moderate to heavy	Minor except for laws that authorize changes	Heavy	Moderate to heavy	Moderate
Union role in school reform	Episodically supports or opposes	Supports mayor	Supports mayor	Opposes	Opposes	Supports
Business elites' role in school reform	Episodic	Strong	Strong	Episodic and lessening	Strong	Strong
Parental involvement initiatives	Few	Few	Some	Some	Few	Few

performed roles that played to their respective strengths while delegating to key subordinates those roles in which they needed help. Tom Payzant, Paul Vallas [superintendents in Boston and Chicago] and a succession of Baltimore school chiefs focused on both the managerial and instructional while dealing politically with groups inside the system and letting their respective mayors handle overall negotiations and political responsibility for the district's performance.[4]

Table 13.3 shows which managerial and instructional strategies were implemented by the six cities. In almost every city, top school officials reorganized district staff; concentrated managerial and instructional authority in the superintendent's office; constantly searched for grants to fund reforms; aligned state and local standards, texts, and professional development; and installed rewards and sanctions for students, principals, and schools. Seeking to restructure a school system, corporate and civic leaders pressed school officials to use successful business practices in overhauling the district, including creating clear goals and tying those goals to high academic standards, frequent testing, and a brace of incentives and penalties to hold students, principals, and schools accountable for results.[5]

In the mid- to late 1990s, then, a national civic coalition of business leaders, public officials, and educators endorsed systemic reform, a phrase drawn from an academic article written by Marshall Smith and Jennifer O'Day. Since then, "systemic reform" has merged with the early to mid-1990s movement for creating curriculum, standards, performance standards for students and schools, expanded testing, and an array of accountability indicators aimed at prodding both students and adults to work harder in raising academic achievement as measured by tests. Part of this movement included state and district interventions into low-performing schools from reconstitution through state and district takeovers. Centralizing authority on school matters into the hands of district superintendents and aligning the different elements of school operations became a familiar recipe for improving district management and students' academic performance.[6]

What also became familiar in these districts were the difficulties in creating an instructional infrastructure and culture that supported principals and teachers to improve teaching and learning. Whether to centralize or decentralize instructional operations within a district was a question that the six districts answered throughout the 1980s and 1990s by switching from one to the other without much certainty over which was better and why. No research findings or expert advice could point with confidence to the most effective form of district organization.[7]

Uncertainty over district organization seldom spilled over to educators—e.g., to determine what to do about the role of principals or professional

Table 13.3   Implemented Managerial and Instructional Strategies

Strategy	Baltimore	Boston	Chicago	Philadelphia	San Diego	Seattle
Sought more funds from state, business, foundations	Yes	Yes	Yes	Yes	Yes	Yes
Consolidated district offices and administrative posts	Yes	Yes	Yes	Yes	Yes	No
Centralized/ Decentralized control of reform	Decentralized (1988–1997) Centralized (1997–)	Centralized (1995–)	Decentralized (1988–1995) Centralized (1995–)	Decentralized (1955–) Centralized (2001)	Decentralized (1980s–1998) Centralized (1998–)	Decentralized (1995–)
Aligned instructional support with higher academic achievement *principal role *teacher professional development	Yes Moderate to high	Yes Moderate to high	No Low	No Moderate	Yes High	Yes Moderate
Aligned curriculum, texts, tests, professional development	Yes	Yes	Yes	Yes	Yes	No

development for teachers. In aligning district standards, curriculum, textbooks, and tests to make instruction both coherent and directed toward raising students' academic performance, at least three of the cities (Boston, San Diego, and Seattle) focused on converting principals from their historical role as managers to becoming instructional leaders. All of the cities reconceptualized (but implemented differentially) teacher professional development to concentrate on expanding practitioners' knowledge and skills in reading, math, and other subjects while building trust among teachers and principals and between them and their superintendents.[8]

Table 13.3 reveals that such efforts were spotty. Whether as union members or as individuals, teachers played a minor role in designing reforms aimed at improving students' academic performance. Moreover, school board and superintendent efforts to amend teacher union contracts on issues of seniority and accountability in four of the six cities—an item placed on school officials' agenda by civic and business leaders in these cities—implicitly targeted unions as part of the problem of low-performing students. School leaders' undisguised hostility toward unions in Philadelphia and San Diego, for whatever reasons, strongly tainted relationships between those superintendents and their teachers. Whether establishing such a coherent instructional guidance system, supported by new roles for principals, and a capacity-building infrastructure for both teachers and administrators actually produce improved students' outcomes is much too soon to judge. A few researchers, however, have claimed that governance reforms, particularly mayoral takeover of school districts have resulted in improved standardized achievement test scores in the lowest-performing elementary schools but have little to no effect on secondary schools.[9]

And what about outcomes in the six districts? Since states and districts have so often reduced students' academic performance to the results of standardized achievement tests, referring to "outcomes" has meant test scores. We want to include, however, other outcomes that civic coalitions in these cities sought from governance and leadership changes.

The implicit theory behind changing how urban school districts are governed and managed requires certain conditions to be in place either prior to or simultaneous with test score improvements. So, for example, tightly coupling district goals, curriculum, professional development, and tests in addition to accountability measures represents an important condition consistent with the internal logic of this reform. We determined whether the tight coupling materialized. Or to cite another example, in those districts where mayors have exerted control over schools, and business elites have actively endorsed the direction (e.g., Chicago, Boston), we would expect two outcomes to have occurred: first, increased coordination of city and school services since schools in those cities have largely become departments of the mayor's cabinet, and second, heightened political support for schools from mayors, business leaders, and major media outlets. We found only partial evidence of increased city and school coordination and, except in Baltimore and Philadelphia, moderate to strong political and media support.

We also know from the history of school reform in the United States that often there are unintended outcomes. For example, a stable corps of teachers and principals is critical for full implementation of desired changes in classroom practices to occur. Increased teacher and principal turnover in the six cities, then, would be unanticipated outcomes and might well threaten the long-term viability of the reform. Table 13.4 includes both intended and unintended outcomes.[10]

Table 13.4 shows a mixed bag of outcomes. By 2002, Boston, Seattle, and San Diego had moved ahead albeit unevenly toward aligning the various elements geared to supporting principals and teachers in helping their students improve academic performance. The other three cities were floundering or were just inching into the early phases of alignment. Although improved coordination of recreation, the arts, and medical and social services had seldom been a top item on the political agenda of civic coalitions stumping for mayorally controlled school districts, it is a reasonable expectation derived from superintendents becoming part of mayors' teams. In Baltimore (until 1997), there was no perceptible increase in coordinated services. Only in Boston were modest efforts made to tie city and school services together; in Chicago and Philadelphia efforts occurred but they could be only characterized as gestures.

Even with edgy criticism from parents and community groups over topdown decision reducing their participation and hardly any service coordination between cities and schools, political support from business elites and city leaders remained strong in Chicago, Boston, San Diego, and Seattle. In those cities, school boards had extended their superintendents' contracts, and newspaper and television editorials praised the direction school leaders were taking. Paul Vallas worked hard for 5 years restoring the confidence of business and civic leaders. Although Mayor Daley in Chicago did remove Vallas, the CEO's earlier shoring up of political support paid dividends for his successor.[11]

And what about test scores? Table 13.4 displays our judgments about elementary and secondary school test scores and the stubborn discrepancy between White and minority scores. Except for slight to moderate improvements in elementary school students' test scores across the cities, little improvement emerges for secondary school students, and the gap in achievement test scores remains largely as it was prior to initiatives undertaken by the urban school leaders since the mid-1990s.

Table 13.4 Outcomes

Outcome	Baltimore	Boston	Chicago	Philadelphia	San Diego	Seattle
Aligned curriculum, professional development, tests, and rewards/penalties	Low	Moderate	Low	Low to moderate	High	Moderate
Political support of district reforms	Low	High	High	Low	High	High
Improved coordination of city and school services	None	Moderate	Low to moderate	Low	None	None
Increased turnover among:						
Teachers	Not available	Moderate	Moderate	High	Not available	Not available
Principals	Not available	High	High	High	Not available	Not available
Improved test scores:						
Elementary	Yes	Yes	Yes	Yes	Yes	Yes
Secondary	No	No	No	No	No	No
Reduced gap between White and minority scores	No	No	No	No	No	No

Such test scores are neither a victorious trumpet call nor an epitaph for urban school governance reform. The theory of action behind changes in governance and leadership called for installing effective managers, aligning closely the key elements of a school system, and establishing individual school accountability. Systemic reform, advocates believed, would press principals, teachers, and students to work harder and produce better scores on standardized achievement tests. As the data from these six cities reveal— as do data from states that have engaged in standards-based systemic reform—the theory is shot through with ifs, ands, and buts. In a few cities, the theory is slowly and fully being implemented, but in other districts, much less so, or even abandoned.[12]

Moreover, in the early years of systemic reform both in cities and states, test scores are primitive measures and offer little proof of success or failure. Few noneducators, parents, and voters have come to realize or even appreciate the following points about standardized test scores about which informed policymakers, researchers, and seasoned practitioners are well aware:[13]

- *Different students get tested each year.* Because most urban districts administer their standardized achievement tests to a different group of students once a year, it is unclear whether the test score gains (or losses) seen in a year will be sustained or reversed in the subsequent year. Following a cohort of students year after year offers stronger evidence for the impact of changed instructional approaches. Few urban districts conduct such analyses, and when they do, few make them available to the public. Thus, attributing test score improvements in elementary schools to district governance reforms and new managerial and instructional strategies after 1 or 2 years is at best premature and at worst misleading.

- *Test preparation raises scores.* Gains in elementary schools across the six cities can come from determined (and ethically appropriate) efforts from teachers and principals to prepare all (not just selected) students for the test, tailoring of the curriculum to the test, extensive coaching of those students who can make the largest gains, and combinations of the foregoing. Thus, determining clearly why in a particular year elementary students score higher than previous groups is dicey without careful, detailed analysis of in-school and across-school practices.[14]

- *Test scores are poor predictors of future performance.* Few experts are willing to say with confidence that test score improvements in reading and math skills translate into students' applying those skills outside of school, displaying a greater desire to learn, or continuing their education.

- *Urban high school students do poorly on standardized tests.* Test scores for urban high schools enrolling high percentages of poor and minority students have been historically low and resistant to improvement. Accumulated reading and math deficits, repeated failure in earlier grades, substantial numbers of noncredentialed and inexperienced teachers, the large size of most high schools and the structure and organization of secondary schools—as compared to elementary schools—have worked against individual and group interventions to improve teaching and learning in these settings. Beyond calls for reconstituting failing schools, breaking high schools into smaller units, creating charter schools, and personalizing instruction, there is little research that points to credible formulas to improve academic achievement in secondary schools.[15]

- *Closing the test score gap has been elusive.* Reformers have proposed many solutions for reducing the test score gap between White and minority students. Proposals include increased racial integration of students, teaching that is responsive to cultural and ethnic differences, and extensive preschool and elementary school interventions. Research findings have yet to endorse these varied solutions.[16]

The previous points on testing argue for restraint in rushing to judgments about the linkages between test scores and reforms. Patience harnessed to a deeper understanding of how school districts work, the limits of applying business principles to schools and tests, especially how scores are evaluated, we believe, is sensible before leaping to conclusions about the success or failure of urban school governance reform. At least 5 to 7 years of full implementation of the theory of action and test scores will reveal clearly trends and patterns, especially if the performance of particular groups of students in and across schools are aggressively pursued for that period of time. The lust for quick results and the inexorable media rush to crank out a new story distorts what occurs in urban schools and prevents figuring out cause and effect.

What does all of this add up to? We conclude that civic coalitions in the 1990s seeking governance and organizational reforms—mayoral control or appointing noneducators as superintendents—may have established certain conditions for improved academic achievement, but have not yet led directly to improved classroom teaching and learning. The chain of command flowing from district decisions to classroom teaching and learning has many links; weak or nonexistent links can interrupt what occurs and break the chain. Even with shared views of what caused students' unacceptably low academic performance (e.g., poor district management, unresponsive bureaucracy) and common solutions (e.g., systemic school reform), one needs to look no further than Baltimore and Chicago to see that political effectiveness in launching governance changes and organizational success in implementing corporate-style management in the 1980s and 1990s have yet to reach the goal of sustained and widespread overall growth in educational effectiveness.

Another assumption driving the political logic of governance and managerial reforms leading to better teaching and learning is that in drawing leaders from noneducational organizations, more efficient and effective management practices anchored in business principles would be put into place. Bureaucratic obstacles would be reduced and students' academic performance would improve. San Diego becomes an attractive advertisement for the managerial part of this assumption in the 4 years that Bersin has been superintendent. Yet, even here, test score gains plateaued in 2000 and varied greatly between elementary and secondary schools. Attributing gains to effective management and systemic reform, for the reasons offered above, still remains premature. Although Chicago offers an instance of a CEO decisively acting in determining budgets, waiving rules, and slicing through bureaucratic layers, the accumulated evidence for the city counters civic and business leaders' deep wish to connect governance changes and better management to improved student outcomes.[17]

Finally, reformers believed that school leaders who were wired into existing city political and economic structures (including business elites) would increase chances of improving and sustaining students' academic achievement. While promoters of these reforms could nicely point to Boston in support of this assumption, skeptics could just as easily point to counter examples of Baltimore, where two-term mayor Karl Schmoke had his appointees running the schools with paltry results, and Chicago, where the mayor dumped the superintendent and school board president when elementary school test scores leveled off.[18]

Explaining Mixed Outcomes

Why have the highly motivated reformers' political, organizational, and educational theory of action and assumptions shown such mixed results in these six cities? One reason may stem from how we did this study.

Basically, we collected documents covering events over the past decade in each city and interviewed key players in the reforms. Thus, we have a snapshot of large school districts undergoing change, taken at one point in time. Snapshots are very helpful in describing events but less helpful in figuring out patterns. It may well be that the picture we have laid out for readers is part of an evolving process of change within a school district that would yield very different conclusions had we had an album of photos, much like an in-depth history of the district. Had we taken the longer view, we could see more clearly whether the events we recorded and the outcomes we documented were singular or patterned. Perhaps in time the reforms would have matured and the desired results would have emerged. So much (but not all) of the recent literature on urban school districts consists of snapshots rather than albums, resulting in a curious set of pictures frozen in time. Thus the mixed bag of outcomes may be a result of our methodology.[19]

Variation in outcomes may also result from a history of decentralized decisionmaking within a federal system of divided powers. In 2001 there are 50 state school systems with nearly 15,000 school districts housing almost 90,000 public schools. Such a decentralized system of school governance means that variation in districts—urban, rural, and suburban—is a constant. Thus, the mix of outcomes may have occurred because of different urban contexts.

Although reformers in the six cities held common political conceptions of what caused the problem of low academic performance in schools (e.g., too much district bureaucracy, poor management, and so on) and what political solutions should be applied (e.g., mayoral control, standards-based curriculum, testing, and accountability), each district's demography, history, and past leadership inside and outside the schools influenced what occurred.

To understand Boston, for example, one must know the ethnic and racial school politics that colored the district since World War II, the explosive growth of largely White suburbs prior to, and accelerated by, the conflict-filled court-ordered desegregation battles of the mid-1970s, the growth of the parochial school population, the concentration of poor minorities in the city schools, and the elected school committee's loss of political respectability. The struggle to eliminate the elected school committee took many years and is a unique story unlike Seattle, San Diego, or Baltimore. Thus mixed outcomes may well result from the simple fact of historical and demographic differences among these districts.[20]

If context matters in shaping the direction and texture of reform in a city, as we believe it does, so does concerted city, business, and district political leadership. Seattle's business community joining with the teachers' union to endorse and support John Stanford, a former U.S. Army general, and then his trusted lieutenant, Joseph Olchefske, after Stanford's death speaks to the importance of not only initiating political changes but a continuity in civic and business leadership that extends beyond one term of a superintendent. Similarly, stability in political leadership has led to Tom Payzant's contract being extended to 2005, as have contracts for Alan Bersin and Anthony Alvarado in San Diego.

Hard as it is to find leaders to initiate reforms aimed at improving teaching and learning, it is doubly hard to keep leaders (or replace them with like-minded successors) who sustain the reforms over time. Consider that the decentralized organization and major reform initiatives that Philadelphia's David Hornbeck promoted in "Children Achieving" for 5 years were thoroughly dismantled a few months after he left.[21]

Reforms tailored to unique city contexts and political coalitions supporting school leaders are far from a recipe for improving urban districts. The fevered search among reformers for just the right formula of urban school improvement to apply to each and every city—what policymakers call "going to scale"—given the experiences of these six cities in the 1980s and 1990s, is a fool's errand. That has been the sorry record of urban school reform for the past quarter-century and represents the major challenge to these six cities. Establishing the right conditions for district reform matched to the unique features of a city is painstakingly crafted work that often puts off impatient advocates but is necessary, based on the evidence of these six cities. And that is why we have entitled this book *Powerful Reforms with Shallow Roots*.

Of the six cities, three stand out now as examples of powerful reforms uniquely fitted to their settings: Boston, San Diego, and Seattle. We also believe that the roots that these cities have thus far sent down into their soil are shallow. Why powerful? And why shallow?

Why Powerful? Boston and San Diego are very different districts in size, history, cultural diversity, and socioeconomic composition. For example, Boston has 74% of its children receiving free and reduced-price lunches while San Diego has 47%; Boston has 76% minority school enrollment, mostly Black and Latino students, compared to 55% for San Diego, mostly Latino and Black. Even with these demographic differences the business-driven civic coalitions that placed Payzant and Bersin into the superintendencies are still active, have continued to give full support to their school leaders, and ensured that their contracts are extended. . . .

Bersin has had no experience as an educator, although he did appoint a veteran school administrator from New York City as second-in-command. Bersin has had few contacts with the mayor, city manager, and council in San Diego and remains at loggerheads with the school board and teachers' union. Payzant—former school chief in San Diego—sits in Mayor Tom Menino's cabinet and has congenial relations with the teachers' union. Both superintendents, with very different personal styles and working at very different paces, have leveraged private funds and state legislation to design and put into action an instructional infrastructure sharply focused on teaching and learning. Budgets are built around the mission of improved academic achievement in literacy and math so that teacher-coaches assigned to schools, professional development, and principals acting as instructional leaders are increasingly aligned to both performance benchmarks and state and local tests. Both school chiefs are trying to implement the theory of action by creating district and school cultures that support teaching and learning. In effect, a powerful machine fueled by top-down decision making and geared to helping teachers teach better and students achieve has been built piece by piece, amid errors and fumbling, in each city.

Why Shallow Roots? Shallow roots is a metaphor for unstable political support among civic and business leaders for school reform, and intense, unrelenting conflict between and among the school board, administration, and teachers over the direction and logistics of the reform agenda. The phrase suggests the overall fragility of top-down, centralized reform.

Based on our study of the six cities, the reforms are "shallow" in three senses. First, these reforms are heavily dependent on the visible presence and continuity of school leaders. The history of urban school leadership since the 1960s has seen civic coalitions championing a reform and losing interest in it after a few years. No surprise then that some of our city coalitions lost steam and abbreviated school board and superintendent tenures resulted.[22]

Second, constructing an inviting instructional infrastructure for principals and teachers is tough organizational work. Sustained and rich professional development accompanied by accountability measures that translate into a district and school culture leading to improved classroom teaching and learning is logistically demanding and requires school-based professionals to remain in their jobs. Building this infrastructure and creating a culture that concentrates on classroom teaching and learning requires school leaders' strong commitment, extensive time, access to specialists, and much money.

Third, because the aim of top-down systemic reform is to impact classroom teaching and learning, securing teachers' endorsement and parents' support for changes are essential. Evidence of substantial parent and teacher approval and shifts in classroom practice has yet to emerge. Based on the history of classroom innovations, without parent endorsement and active teacher cooperation in putting the changes into practice, urban school reformers again will be disappointed.[23]

In 2002, for Philadelphia, Chicago, and Baltimore, "shallow roots" in the three senses that we have used applies all too clearly. Deep changes have occurred in the three cities' reform coalitions. There have been leadership mishaps, intense conflicts between powerful constituencies, tortuous difficulties in establishing instructional infrastructures and cultures, and the absence of teacher enthusiasm for converting reforms into classrooms practices.

For San Diego, Boston, and Seattle where the conditions for sustained powerful reform have been put in place, "shallow roots" also applies. Their civic coalitions, demography, leadership, and determined actions, however, offer more promise for sinking deeper into soil than the other three cities.

In San Diego, *shallow roots* refers to the ongoing struggle between the teachers' union and Bersin and the slim 3-2 majority the superintendent carries into each school board meeting. Subsequent school board and union elections may change the school board configuration and union leadership. The possibility of continued hostility of the teachers union leadership may seep into the rank and file to the point of teachers' ignoring and undermining school and classroom reforms. Few urban district leaders have altered classroom practices without the cooperation of teachers and, ultimately, the endorsement of their union.

Moreover, although the superintendent has pointed out 2 years of gains in test scores—always acknowledging that more has to be done—the gap in minority and White test scores remains substantial and unchanged thus far. San Diego reformers have tackled the bottom tier of lowest-performing schools where cultures of failure have persisted for years and whose students are largely poor, minority, often nonnative language speakers, and disproportionately assigned to special education. In such schools, small victories come at great cost to both adults and children and take much time.

Finally, both Bersin and Alvarado, even with extended contracts and continued support from business elites, may still throw in the towel and say "enough." Reform fatigue from armor-piercing criticism takes its toll; it is a common ailment among school leaders.

For Boston, *shallow roots* refers to the slow improvement in test scores in elementary and secondary schools, the low level of those improvements (e.g., going from the 15th to 20th percentiles), and the high percentages of secondary students failing the state test. Impatient reformers deeply concerned over the undiminished gaps in test scores between White, Latino, and Black students combined with flagging support from business leaders and community activists deprived of access to an elected school board may take its toll on Mayor Menino by increasing political pressure on him to find a more aggressive superintendent who will produce the desired results faster.

Seattle is a different story. Powerful changes have been underway since 1995, and while questions remain about how deep the reforms' roots are, chances of sustaining the reforms appear to be the strongest of the districts we studied.

Of the six cities, Seattle has the smallest enrollment (under 50,000 students) and has the lowest number of children in poverty (40%). Demographically, then, the scale of the city and its population is seemingly more manageable than, say, Baltimore, which is double the size of Seattle and far poorer.

In addition, with higher test scores than the other cities, a decade-long friendly union-board relationship, and a business-led civic coalition wanting improvements but hardly a takeover of the district, as in Chicago, San Diego, Boston, and Baltimore, conditions in the Seattle schools were favorable for any superintendent seeking to increase public confidence in the schools. What deeply troubled business and civic leaders were the differences in Black and White achievement on standardized tests and the seeming inability of the school staffs to aggressively attack these discrepancies.[24]

General John Stanford in his brief tenure focused on academic achievement through new funding formulas for schools; site-based decision making; school assignment choices for parents, a new labor contract; and reshaping the principal into a school-site CEO. He convinced key constituencies that these strategies would yield higher academic achievement and that teachers and principals would be focused on teaching and learning. He connected the community to the schools in his persistent trumpeting of a can-do attitude in raising students' achievement. He worked smoothly with the business and civic elites, community activists, parents, and students. Even when disagreements arose, Stanford listened and responded openly to critics, often enlisting their help in improving schools.

In effect, Stanford helped restore confidence of key political constituencies that schools can succeed in crafting better teaching and learning. This is a major achievement in itself when one considers the open hostility of groups critical of school district leaders in Baltimore, Philadelphia, and San Diego.

After Stanford's death in 1998, the school board appointed Olchefske as permanent superintendent. Since then, he has basically forged ahead with initiatives begun under Stanford, particularly translating a standards-based curriculum into every Seattle classroom. The school board's decision to appoint Olchefske and his actions since taking on the superintendency reflect public confidence in the public schools and a basic continuity in district direction. Whether the civic coalition and union support will continue, and whether sufficient funds will be available in the years to come to sustain the building of the instructional infrastructure and create school-based cultures that, indeed, will alter classroom practices and reduce the gap in achievement between White and minority students is too early to say.

Of the cities with powerful reforms and shallow roots, Seattle's history, demography, district leadership, and broad civic coalition that has provided continuous political support offers the most promise of sustaining changes begun in 1995 through the first decade of the twenty-first century.

Reflections on Urban District Reform

For readers who appreciate irony, contrast the actions of school reformers a century apart. At the beginning of the twentieth century, Progressive coalitions fought to eliminate political influence from schools. Progressive reformers transformed big city school districts with unwieldy school boards, often appointed by mayors and political bosses who dispensed school jobs and contracts, into smaller corporate-looking copies composed of elected business and professional men and women who hired university-prepared superintendents to run districts in an efficient business-like manner.

In these decades, reform-minded superintendents, working closely with their boards, expanded the role of the school to take in the health, social, recreational, and economic needs of the child. Administrators used scientific management to develop policies and procedures and new specialized positions. They expanded layers of district bureaucracy to implement policies in schools and classrooms aimed at achieving broader social and economic goals. In divorcing education from partisan politics and hiring professionally trained superintendents to manage their schools efficiently, boards of education reaffirmed beliefs that good schools alone could make children into fine citizens and workers.[25]

That was then. Reform slogans of getting politics out of schools and having professionally trained managers run schools have been forgotten and since the 1970s have been replaced by charges that big city schools had become bloated, mismanaged, and unresponsive bureaucracies.

Late-twentieth-century reformers have latched onto solutions for dysfunctional urban schools by making them more political, business-like, and responsive to market competition. For current civic and business leaders, urban districts should become another department in a mayor's city government, or noneducators should be appointed to reverse the district's failures. With educators and noneducators using managerial practices based on business principles, bureaucracies would become responsive and monies would be found to fund an instructionally coherent system that helps principals and teachers do a better job of teaching. Moreover, establishing clear lines of responsibility and holding students, teachers, and principals accountable for results would breathe vigor into a lethargic organization. Solutions such as these, reformers believe, will make districts into lean, efficient machines that will increase academic achievement, reduce the differences in test scores between White and minority students, and prepare good citizens and workers.

A combined corporate/political model of urban district governance has— in 2002—become the prevailing wisdom among political reformers, media pundits, and educational experts. Even with increasing mayoral influence, centralized control in urban districts, and obvious losses in public participation in education, few voices call for a return to the older reform model of separating politics from schools, sticking with superintendents who rise through the ranks, or establishing closer ties between communities and their schools.

Common to reformers in the late nineteenth and late twentieth centuries, then, is an unalloyed enthusiasm for corporate language, organization, managerial principles, and the deep-seated belief that a district system's application of effective business practices will improve both teaching and learning and the futures of poor minority children.

The irony we describe, of course, gets compounded when Progressive governance reforms of the past century had become by the 1970s the very problems a later generation of reformers claimed had blocked urban school improvements, locking poor minority students into lifetimes of despair. Current solutions for these problems are to import political authority (a mayor, a governor, a president) back into school governance.

By the early twenty-first century, reformers had embraced a political solution of tying urban districts directly or indirectly to city governance and concentrating on improving classroom teaching and learning. Then and now, both Progressives and current reformers look solely to the school in overcoming poverty and social inequities while largely ignoring issues of race and class. This "schools-alone" strategy shows promise in a few cities but hardly constitutes a recipe for sustaining urban school reform over a decade given the obvious variation among cities and their resources, much less the critical institutional conditions that need to be in place prior to and during the changes.

In making the schools-alone assumption, reformers then and now excluded other explanations (and thereby, other solutions) for students' unsatisfactory academic performance. The core assumption is that once largely poor urban schools have new principals and hardworking teachers, they can overcome by themselves the grim effects of poverty, racism, and community neglect.

Certainly there is some basis for the strategy. Much has been written about urban principals and teachers holding low expectations for poor and minority students' academic performance. Studies have shown again and again how children in large schools easily get lost in the impersonal throng and overlooked by overworked, underpaid staffs. Other studies reveal that low-performing schools suffer few consequences. This research gives credibility to the belief that hard work, high standards, and accountability will translate into improved student academic achievement.[26]

What weakens the assumption, however, is other evidence that civic and business leaders neglect. When the economy is expanding and jobs are plentiful, employers plead for more and better-trained workers. But when an economic downturn occurs and unemployment rises, the unforgiving spotlight on high school and college graduates' skills dims because of labor surpluses. "Stay in school" becomes the mantra civic and business leaders repeat. Employers and policymakers care less about what students know and can do than that they are occupied; more schooling is a better alternative than unemployability no matter the skills learned.[27]

Other evidence is also unnoted. Anyone who has visited an urban school for at least one week (not a drive-by visit) to sit in classes, listen to teachers and students, observe lunchrooms, playgrounds, corridors, and offices would begin to appreciate a simple but inescapable truth: An urban school is deeply influenced by the neighborhood and families from which it draws its students.

Also of importance is that tax-supported public schools in a democracy are more than training grounds for future employees. Schools are expected to instill in students civic and social attitudes and skills that shape how graduates lead their adult lives in communities. Schools are expected to build respect for differences in ideas and cultures. These are historic civic aims of public schools that have been largely neglected in the rush to direct urban schools to be engines for the local and global economy.

Yet the present agenda for urban school reform, narrowly concentrating on all students taking the same academic curriculum, raising test scores, going to college or getting jobs, largely ignores the pervasive influence upon the school of the community's particular racial, ethnic, and social-class strengths and limitations. In middle-class and wealthy neighborhoods, focusing only on what the school can do is reasonable since these families have the money and networks to provide help for their children should there be academic, health, economic, and emotional problems.

That is not the case in poor, often racially or ethnically isolated, communities. Families lack the personal and institutional resources middle-class communities take for granted. They put their hopes on their children's shoulders and depend upon the local school and other public agencies. In short, in cities with impoverished neighborhoods, schools can't do it alone.

Thus, the theories of action at the heart of urban reform then and now flip-flopped over the relationship between politics and schools, yet both rested upon the same assumption: Schools alone can solve severe social inequities while producing fine citizens and workers. Note that of the six cities we studied, only one—Boston—had made some effort at building closer ties between the city's medical and social services, recreation and arts, and daily activities in schools. The assumption still casts a long shadow.

Treating schools as isolated institutions is unwise in the post–World War II social geography of the city that finds urban neighborhoods divided by class, race, and ethnicity. Extensive walking in most big cities establishes this basic social fact of residentially segregated neighborhoods. In the contemporary passion for governance-driven reforms few elected public officials care to tackle elite and popular commitments to maintaining homogenously separate communities that characterize so many American cities today.[28]

Depending upon changes in governance anchored in an assumption that schools can do it alone is both rational and politically strategic to federal, state, and local policymakers. It is rational because past and contemporary reforms assume a command-and-control connection between superintendents, principals, teachers, and students. Yet what appears rational has not been what occurs daily in school systems, past or present.

The reforms are politically strategic to policymakers at all levels in restricting the reform agenda to governance, organization, curriculum, and instruction. Avoided are mentions of race and poverty in dealing with issues of housing and access to jobs as they relate to schooling. To include families, neighborhoods, and city agencies in the reform agenda would entail major expenditures by officials such as reconceptualizing schools as youth-serving agencies rather than places where the single most important job is to produce higher test scores. It would mean reorganizing existing city cultural, civic, medical, housing, employment, and social services. Contemporary urban school reformers stammer when faced with the scale of such changes.

Of course, broadening the urban agenda to encompass a community-based strategy to school improvement does not mean that students, teachers, and principals should be held less responsible for working hard to achieve their goals. Nor does this recognition of a racially, ethnically, or class-segregated school being nested in the larger community suggest that there should be different standards for those who are well off and those who are poor. The obvious fact that schools are entangled in their communities and in the larger economy only sharpens the tasks that face urban school reformers. They need to mobilize civic and corporate elites and educate these opinion setters to the plain fact that raising academic achievement in big city schools involves far more than designing merit pay plans, paying cash bonuses to schools that raise test scores, threatening teachers and principals, or withholding diplomas from students who failed a graduation test.

Nowhere is this fundamental fact more evident than in the inability of the leaders in six cities to improve academic performance in urban high schools with high percentages of low-income minorities. High school size, departmental organization, curricular choices, teachers' subject matter specialization, and the societal demand that graduates be prepared for the workforce, military, or continued education is too often mismatched to urban youth. Many have either experienced failure in earlier grades, found school next to useless in improving their daily lives, or want to do well in school but face unqualified teachers, dumbed-down programs, and inhospitable surroundings. High school becomes a salvage operation skimming off the highly motivated students whose resilience has carried them through the ninth grade and trying to keep the rest from being harmed.

Punitive measures to fire a school's staff and start anew or create a charter school out of the ruins of a failing high school comprise one strategy. Another approach is to develop community-based high schools, establish youth-serving agencies that work closely with small groups of teachers and students, cultivate small high schools and personalized instruction, and enlist employers to hire high school students as interns while attending school to connect neighborhoods, work, and going to college. These initiatives show at least as much promise as threatening to fire staff of underperforming schools or maintaining the prevailing approach of focusing on all students taking the same curriculum and taking out large chunks of instructional time to prepare students for tests that determine whether diplomas are awarded.[29]

Our reflections, if anything, suggest that schools in our six cities require more than a one-size-fits-all strategy, particularly one that rests on century-old theories of school reform that assume governance and managerial changes will produce higher student achievement. District leaders need to reframe the problem of urban school reform to take into account the varying contexts of their cities and schools, the multiple goals of tax-supported public education, and the social geography that sustains segregated neighborhoods.

If schools are as vital to the future of cities as reformers say—and we concur—then a broad vision, not a politically clever strategy, fortitude not impatience, and courage not caution become virtues in the struggle for fairness, equity, and better schools.

Notes

1.   *Portland Oregonian*, 1 January 1917, cited in David Gamson, "District by Design: Progressive Educational Reform in Four Western Cities, 1900–1940" (Ph.D. diss., Stanford University, 2001), p. 2.

2. Dorothy Shipps, "Regime Change: Mayoral Takeover of the Chicago Public Schools" in *Reforming Urban School Governance: Responses to the Crisis of Performance,* ed. J. Cibulka and W. Boyd (Westport CT: Greenwood Press, in press).

3. The phrase "mayoral control" applies to those places where mayors have, indeed, taken over school operations in Boston, Chicago, Cleveland, Baltimore (until 1997), and New York City. But there are cities where mayors are involved but have not taken over full control of the schools, such as Philadelphia, Los Angeles, and Oakland. In addition, there are cities where hybrids of influence and control exist. We thank Mike Kirst for helping us see this continuum of mayoral control to mayoral influence. These tables represent snapshots at one point in time and our interpretations of the evidence we gathered in the six cities. Our judgments of level of effort and success, of course, are limited by the time period in which we collected our data, what our informants told us, and the familiar human frailties that researchers bring to bear on the data they collected.

4. Larry Cuban, *The Managerial Imperative* (Albany: State University of New York Press, 1988).

5. Ibid. See also Susan Moore Johnson, *Leading to Change: The Challenge of the New Superintendency* (San Francisco: Jossey-Bass, 1996); Arthur Blumberg, *The School Superintendent: Living with Conflict* (New York: Teachers College Press, 1985).

6. Marshall Smith and Jennifer O'Day, "Systemic School Reform," *Politics of Education Association Yearbook, 1990* (1991): 233–267. See also M. Knapp, "Between Systemic Reforms and the Mathematics and Science Classrooms: The Dynamics of Innovation, Implementation, and Professional Learning," *Review of Educational Research,* 67 (2): 227–266 (1997). Also Ken Wong and Francis Shen, "Does School District Takeover Work? Assessing the Effectiveness of City and State Takeover as a School Reform Strategy" (paper presented at the annual meeting of the American Political Science Association, San Francisco, 2001).

7. Allan Ornstein, "Centralization and Decentralization of Large Public School Districts," *Urban Education,* 24 (1989): 233–245. See also David Tyack, "Restructuring in Historical Perspective: Tinkering toward Utopia," *Teachers College Record,* 92 (2): 170–191 (1990).

8. Tying policy changes to pedagogy, that is, policymakers guiding classroom teaching and learning, was a direction administrative Progressives in the early decades of the twentieth century pursued with great confidence. See David Tyack, *One Best System* (Cambridge, MA: Harvard University Press, 1974). In the past 2 decades, the work of David Cohen, Richard Elmore, and others have inspired policymakers and school administrators committed to systemic reform to tightly connect policy to classroom instruction. See David Cohen and James Spillane, "Policy and Practice: The Relations between Governance and Instruction," *Review of Research in Education,* 18 (1992): 3–9; David Cohen and Carol Barnes, "Pedagogy and Policy" in *Teaching for Understanding,* ed. David Cohen, Milbrey McLaughlin, and Joan Talbert (San Francisco: Jossey-Bass, 1993), pp. 204–239. Richard Elmore

and colleagues have studied District #2 in New York City since the early 1990s where Anthony Alvarado put into practice many of these ideas. See Richard Elmore and Diane Burney, *The Challenge of School Variability: Improving Instruction in New York City's Community District #2* (New York: National Commission on Teaching and America's Future: Consortium for Policy Research in Education, 1998).

9. Wong and Shen, "Does School District Takeover Work?"

10. See David B. Tyack and Larry Cuban, *Tinkering toward Utopia* (Cambridge, MA: Harvard University Press, 1995).

11. Karla Reid, "Chicago Chief Named amid Urban Turnover," *Education Week,* 11 July 2001, p. 3.

12. For conclusions that can be drawn from test score data and other outcomes of standards-based reform in states, see Susan Fuhrman, ed., *From the Capitol to the Classroom: Standards-Based Reform in the States* (Chicago: National Society for the Study of Education, 2001), Part 2, pp. 5–8.

13. Robert Linn, "Educational Assessment: Expanded Expectations and Challenges," *Educational Evaluation and Policy Analysis,* 15 (1): 1–16 (1993); Lorrie Shepard, *Measuring Achievement: What Does It Mean to Test for Robust Understanding?* Third Annual William Angoff Memorial Lecture (Princeton: Educational Testing Service, 1996); Craig Bolon, "School-Based Standard Testing," *Education Policy Analysis Archives,* 8 (23): *http://129.219.89.99/epaa/v8n23* (2000).

14. Nicolas Lemann, *The Big Test* (New York: Farrar, Straus, and Giroux, 1999), pp. 227–229, 273.

15. See Michael Klonsky, "Small Schools: The Numbers Tell a Story," paper at Small Schools Workshop, University of Illinois at Chicago, 1996; Deborah Meier, *The Power of Their Ideas: Lessons for America from a Small School in Harlem* (Boston: Beacon Press, 1995); Bruce Fuller, ed., *Inside Charter Schools: The Paradox of Radical Decentralization* (Cambridge, MA: Harvard University Press, 2000).

16. Christopher Jencks and Meredith Phillips, eds., *The Black-White Test Score Gap* (Washington, DC: Brookings Institution, 1998).

17. Dorothy Shipps, Joseph Kahne, and Mark Smylie, "The Politics of Urban School Reform: Legitimacy, City Growth, and School Improvement in Chicago," *Educational Policy,* 13 (4): 518–545 (1999).

18. For Baltimore, see Marion Orr, "The Challenge of School Reform in Baltimore: Race, Jobs, and Politics" in *Changing Urban Education,* ed. C. Stone (Lawrence: University Press of Kansas, 1998), pp. 93–117. See also James Cibulka, "The City-State Partnership to Reform Baltimore's Public Schools" in Cuban and Usdan, eds., *Powerful Reforms With Shallow Roots: Improving America's Urban Schools.* New York: Teachers College Press (this volume).

19. Researchers have shied away from archival or even contemporary histories of school districts, urban or suburban. Exceptions are Jeff Mirel, *The Rise and Fall of an Urban School System: Detroit, 1907–1981* (Ann Arbor: University of

Michigan Press, 1993); Louis Smith, David Dwyer, John Prunty, and Paul Kleine, *Innovation and Change in Schooling: History, Politics, and Agency* (New York: Falmer Press, 1988); Diane Ravitch, *The Great School Wars, New York City, 1805–1973* (New York: Basic Books, 1974).

20. For Boston, see Peter Schrag, *Village School Downtown* (Boston: Beacon Press, 1967); J. Anthony Lukas, *Common Ground: A Turbulent Decade in the Lives of Three American Families* (New York: Alfred Knopf, 1986); John Portz, Lana Stein, and Robin Jones, *City Schools and City Politics* (Lawrence: University Press of Kansas, 1999).

21. Mark Strichez, "Philadelphia to Scrap 'Cluster' Plan in Bid to Save Money," *Education Week*, 20 (9 May 2001), p. 10. In Memphis, after 8 years of getting each school in the district to choose a whole-school reform that each staff would implement and after test scores in elementary schools had improved, Superintendent Gerri House resigned. Within 3 months, House's successor had suspended these efforts and moved the system away from mandatory whole-school reform. Aimee Edmondson and Michael Erskine, "School Reform Put to Test, Now to Rest," *The Commercial Appeal, http://www.gomemphis.com/newcal/o62001/20reform.htm* (2001). Positional leaders often dismantle programs of their predecessors in corporations, churches, hospitals, and so on.

22. Gary Yee and Larry Cuban, "When Is Tenure Long Enough? A Historical Analysis of Superintendent Turnover and Tenure in Urban School Districts," *Educational Administration Quarterly*, 32 (Supplement): 615–641 (1996).

23. Richard Elmore and Milbrey McLaughlin, *Steady Work* (Santa Monica, CA: Rand, 1988); L. Cuban, *How Teachers Taught* (New York: Teachers College Press, 1993); James Spillane, "Challenging Instruction for 'All Students': Policy, Practitioners, and Practice" in *From the Capitol to the Classroom: Standards-Based Reform in the States*, ed. S. Fuhrman (Chicago: National Society for the Study of Education, 2001), Part 2, 217–241; Frederick M. Hess, *Spinning Wheels: The Politics of Urban School Reform* (Washington, DC: Brookings Institution, 1999).

24. The gap in achievement scores between Whites and Blacks has been a persistent issue. In September 2001, when results from the state test again revealed a large discrepancy between minority and White scores, the local NAACP threatened to sue the district on grounds that Black students have been denied equal protection under the 14th amendment. Keith Ervin, "NAACP May Sue Seattle Schools," *Seattle Times*, 28 September 2001 (*http://seattletimes.nwsource.com/html/localnews/134347108_naacp28m0.html*).

25. Lawrence Cremin, *The Transformation of the School* (New York: Vintage, 1961); David Tyack and Elisabeth Hansot, *Managers of Virtue* (New York: Basic Books, 1982); Paul Peterson, *The Politics of School Reform, 1870–1940* (Chicago: University of Chicago Press, 1985); Ira Katznelson and Margaret Weir, *Schooling for All* (New York: Basic Books, 1985).

26. See Ray Rist, *The Urban School: A Factory for Failure* (Cambridge, MA: MIT Press, 1973). Ray McDermott, "Achieving School Failure" in *Education and the Culture Process*, ed. G. Spindler (New York: Holt, Rinehart, and Winston, 1974).

27. See, for example, David Tyack, Robert Lowe, and Elisabeth Hansot, *Public Schools in Hard Times: The Great Depression and Recent Years* (Cambridge, MA: Harvard University Press, 1984).

28. Katznelson and Weir, *Schooling for All,* pp. 210–222.

29. For different views on reforming high schools, see Evans Clinchy, *Creating New Schools* (New York: Teachers College Press, 2000); Milbrey McLaughlin and Joan Talbert, *Professional Communities and the Work of High School Teaching* (Chicago: University of Chicago Press, 2001); Michelle Fine, ed., *Chartering Urban School Reform: Reflections on Public Schools in the Midst of Change* (New York: Teachers College Press, 1994).

14

State Departments of Education*

editor's introduction:

Setting State-Level Policies. In addition to local communities, state governments also are charged with overseeing, supporting, and implementing American school systems. States can establish educational standards (see Selection 15), define assessment tests and procedures, and implement a broad variety of policies affecting such conditions as teacher training, teacher certification and recertification, the instructional time to be devoted to different academic subjects, and the course requirements for graduating.

Because of states' roles in education, statewide "reform" of education can be a potent force for improving schooling and student performance. The case study represented by this selection covers the initiatives undertaken by two states, Kentucky and Vermont. Following the passage of major state legislation, the states' departments of education reorganized themselves and attempted to define a coordinated or aligned group of policies and actions. Combined, these policies and actions formed each state's "reform" efforts.

The specific selection for this anthology does not cover these substantive issues but addresses the design of the case study. The author presents the rationale for selecting the two states and tells you how other design choices were made, including the selection of the local districts to be site visited and the persons to be interviewed within each state. Included also are a sample of the field protocols used and the general data analysis strategies. These procedures all deserve emulation by your own case study.

---

*Lusi, Susan Follett. (1997). "Methodology." In *The Role of State Departments of Education in Complex School Reform* (pp. 183–192). New York: Teachers College Press.

Relevance of Case Studies: Including Two Complementary Cases as Part of the Same Case Study. This selection shows another version of a "two-case" case study (also see Selection 9, "Low- and High-Performing Schools Serving Native American Students"). Such a case study collects data about two cases, which may have been chosen for any number of reasons (all represent examples of "purposeful sampling")—for example, because the two cases provide strong contrasts with each other (as in the earlier selection), are complementary, are replications, or represent important variations on a general topic. In the present selection, the two cases were chosen for this last reason, with one case representing a far-reaching effort in state-level education reform and the other case representing a "critical case."

The more that you may be trying to draw general lessons from your case study, the more that a "two-case" case study may be preferred over a "one-case" case study. A second case can go a long way to reducing some of the common criticisms of single cases—for example, that the single case might have been unique or benefited from some special circumstance, such as your access to the informants in the case. The second case also forces you to show how your data collection and other research procedures are robust, again going beyond what might have been the good fortune of completing a single case only. Finally, findings supported by two cases are stronger than those supported by a single case only. In this spirit, covering even more cases, as in multiple-case studies, can be even better. However, the main rationale for the present selection is to show how a "two-case" case study was designed.

This chapter explains the research decisions I made and the research approaches I used. These issues are addressed under the categories of state selection; research approach, sample, and sample selection within each state; and data analysis.

State Selection

I chose the states of Kentucky and Vermont using "purposeful sampling." "The logic and power of purposeful sampling lies [sic] in selecting *informa-tion-rich cases* for study in depth" (Patton, 1990, p. 169, emphasis in original). Specifically, I searched for states engaged in complex school reform. In addition, while no states had been involved in this type of reform for extended periods of time, I searched for states where reform implementation had been underway long enough to expect at least beginning changes in local practice. In addition, I took the issues of state scale and personal capacity into account at the margins of my selection process. By this I mean that I recognized that I was but one researcher and consequently had limited capacity for collecting and analyzing information. These capacity limitations would have made adequate study of extremely large states, such as California or New York, difficult to accomplish.

Within the above criteria, I chose Kentucky and Vermont based on the recommendations of knowledgeable observers of and participants in state-level education reform. I consulted with education policy researchers affiliated with the Consortium for Policy Research in Education who had been studying systemic school reform, as well as other researchers who had been examining the efforts of particular states. In addition, I spoke with people at the Education Commission of the States and the Coalition of Essential Schools—the partner organizations in the Re:Learning initiative. Finally, I talked with people in the recommended states, both SDE [State Department of Education] staff and others, trying to gain a basic understanding of the nature of the reform efforts taking place and to determine whether or not a particular state met my sampling criteria.

I ultimately chose the cases of Kentucky and Vermont because they met my sampling criteria, were interesting cases in their own right, and made an interesting and informative pair. Kentucky is an interesting case because it is the most far-reaching state-level reform effort in the country. . . .

Vermont is interesting because it is what Patton refers to as a "critical case":

> Critical cases are those that can make a point quite dramatically or are, for some reason, particularly important in the scheme of things. A clue to the existence of a critical case is a statement to the effect that "if it happens there, it will happen anywhere," or, vice versa, "if it doesn't happen there, it won't happen anywhere." (Patton, 1990, p. 174)

Vermont exemplifies the latter statement; it is being looked at as a "best-case scenario" by researchers around the country. Complex reform will be difficult in Vermont, to be sure, but it has the advantages of being a small, homogeneous state without the added complications of large urban areas, extreme poverty, or extremely low levels of local capacity.

Kentucky and Vermont are an interesting and informative pairing of cases because while the two states are attempting similar reforms, they are using very different implementation approaches. Kentucky's reforms are legislated, and participation is mandatory. The majority of Vermont's reforms are not legislated, and participation is voluntary. Vermont relies on making a convincing argument to bring about participation. I thought that local responses to these differing approaches would reveal much about the potential of state-level reform to bring about school change.

Research Approach, Sample, and Sample Selection Within Each State

I spent just over four weeks in each state doing on-site data collection. These site visits were spread over the period of approximately a year. Site visits to Kentucky took place in July and November 1992 and February 1993. Site visits to Vermont took place in March and July 1992 and January and April 1993. Additional telephone interviews were done in each state between site visits.

I used open-ended interviewing and some limited observation as my primary methods of data collection. In addition, I collected and read numerous documents from each state.

My cases are based on a total of 195 interviews, 102 in Kentucky and 93 in Vermont. I interviewed SDE staff members, local practitioners, and knowledgeable others in each state. "Knowledgeable others" included members of the state board of education, legislators, university people, and others in some way involved in the reform efforts. The distribution of interviews in each state is as follows: In Kentucky, 38 interviews are with SDE staff, 48 are with practitioners in three districts, and 16 are with knowledgeable others. In Vermont, 37 interviews are with SDE staff, 46 are with practitioners in four districts, and 10 are with knowledgeable others. The criteria I used to select my sample in each category and the questions I asked are outlined below.

SDE Staff. Within each state's SDE, I interviewed people who worked in areas engaged in changing the whole department, for example, leadership, personnel, department restructuring, and people who worked on the reform initiatives most likely to directly impact teaching and learning for all students, for example, curriculum, assessment, school restructuring, and decisionmaking. Within these targeted groups I interviewed people at all professional levels of the department, from top leadership to program consultants.

My earliest interviews with SDE staff were designed to orient me to the activity in each state and the history of that activity, beyond what I could learn from existing documentation. I also sought to learn how each department had changed in general terms. My subsequent interviews focused on how the individual's job had changed and how the department had changed as a result of the reform initiatives. In addition, I asked what the individual's sense was of the reform activity taking place in local schools and districts, and how he or she would describe the role of the department in reform implementation.

My generic interview protocol for SDE staff was as follows:

I. General information
   - Mind if I tape?
   - Please tell me if you wish to speak on or off the record.
   - Name?
   - Position?
   - How long in this position?
   - How long in department?
   - Previous positions? Where did you come from?

II. Your job
   - Has your job changed over time as the reforms have taken place and the department has restructured?
   - How do you and your staff spend your time?
     - What proportion in schools and districts/with practitioners?
     - What proportion on reporting to higher-ups?
   - How do you work with schools in your job? Exactly what do you do?
   - Does this differ in any way from the way you worked with schools in the past? How?
   - Is the way you work with schools indicative of how this division/office as a whole works with schools? Please elaborate.

III. Department
   - Is there a vision that guides this department? What is it?
   - What has restructuring the department meant for you?
   - How does the new department differ from the old?
   - How does your division/office work? How do you work together?
   - Does your division/office work with other divisions/offices? How?
     - How much do you know about what other offices and divisions dealing with other areas of the reform are doing—curriculum, assessment, etc.?
     - How does communication occur?
     - What kind of information is shared?
     - How do you get this information?
   - Are there connections between the work of the different divisions?
   - How does your division work with other divisions doing trainings and working with schools?

- How are decisions made in the department? What is the process?
  - What kinds of decisions can you make yourself and what kinds have to be passed upward?
  - If a problem is raised by a school or district, how quickly can you give them an answer/help them resolve it?
  - If you make what might be a controversial decision do you worry afterward, or generally assume that you will be supported?
  - What kinds of decisions can the people who work for you make on their own?
- How does planning occur in the department?
  - What is the process?
  - If it becomes clear to you and others in your office that an aspect of some plan needs adjustment, what do you do?
  - Can plans be adjusted fairly easily? What is the process?
- Is it easy to hire the people you need and want to work with?
- Are there ways for people in the department to learn new knowledge and skills—professional development?
- Do you have the information and technology you need to do the job?
  - Computers?
  - Easy access to information on the state education system?
  - Easy access to other parts of the system, e.g., schools, universities, other people involved in this kind of assessment and training?
- What is the Commissioner's role in the department?
  - What is he like to work for?
- What are the norms that exist in the department?

IV. Schools
- What do you hear from people in schools and districts?
  - What challenges are they facing in trying to implement KERA [Kentucky Education Reform Act]/Vermont's reforms?
  - What are they struggling with?
  - What would help them in meeting these challenges?
  - Where could/should this help come from?
- What changes have you seen in these districts as you've been working with them?
  - Concrete examples?

V. How would you describe the role of the department in implementing the reforms?
- How would you describe the way the department as a whole works with schools?
- Does the current relationship with schools differ from the relationship that the old department had?
- Do you/how do you work with others doing trainings in schools, e.g., universities, private consultants?

The reader should bear in mind while reading this protocol that in open-ended interviewing, unlike in survey research, questions are not asked of each individual in the same order and in exactly the same manner. The answers to some questions emerge in the discussion of others, and the interviewer follows up on pertinent topics mentioned, even if they do not directly address one of the questions in the protocol. In addition, I adjusted the protocol in light of the individual's particular position and areas of expertise, and also as needed to meet with his or her time constraints. I generally asked informants for an hour of their time, but if they only had 30 to 45 minutes available, I took it and adjusted my questions accordingly. All of this is to say that this interview protocol should be viewed as a rough guide to the conversations that took place.

District and School Practitioners. I chose three districts to visit in each state that represented something of the range of districts that SDEs are trying to change: (1) an "early adopter" district that was engaged in reforms similar to the current state-level reforms, prior to the state's involvement; (2) a "status quo" district that had delivered a more or less average traditional education to its students for years; and (3) a "low-performing" district that the state had been concerned about for some period of time due to its below-average delivery of educational services. This sampling strategy falls under Patton's category of "stratified purposeful sampling" (Patton, 1990, p. 174).

I also visited a fourth district in Vermont, to add a larger district to my sample. My findings in this district, however, did not vary significantly from those in the other districts. Consequently, I used the data from this district as supplemental information, rather than developing a fourth category for it in my Vermont sample.

I selected the districts in each state based on the recommendations of people both inside and outside the state department who were closely acquainted with numerous schools. I chose districts on which there was some consensus as to the category they fell into. In addition, I chose districts in different regions of each state.

I spent approximately three days in each district. I visited the elementary, middle, and high school that district personnel felt were furthest along in their reform efforts. I interviewed the principal and three teachers in each school, in addition to the superintendent and at least one other district-level staff person in each district. I asked principals to select teachers who had been the most involved in the state's and the school's reform efforts.

There were a few exceptions to this strategy. In one or two schools, I interviewed less than three teachers due to scheduling difficulties, and in one district there was only one administrator (the superintendent). Also, in some cases districts only had one elementary, middle, or high school to choose from. In addition, given the exigencies of school schedules, it is probably fair to say that principals chose teachers on the basis of their availability to talk as well as their involvement with the reforms.

I chose schools and personnel with the greatest involvement in the state's reform efforts due to the relative newness of the reforms. I reasoned that because the reforms were so new, I would need to look at the best-case scenario in order to see many signs of change. Even using this selection strategy, there was still wide variation in levels of involvement and change.

My interviews with practitioners focused on how the state's reforms had affected their own activity and practice, as well as the activity and practice in the given school and/or district, the relationship between practitioners and the SDE, and the role of the SDE. In addition, I asked district-level staff about the role of the district in these state-level reforms. My interview protocol for Vermont practitioners is listed below:

I. General information
   - Mind if I tape?
   - Anonymity is promised.
   - Name?
   - Position?
   - How long in this position?
   - Previous positions?
   - How long in Vermont?

II. History
   - When do you consider the current Vermont education reforms to have started?
   - Describe what was occurring in your district/school prior to that time.
     - Were there reforms already under way/in place? Please describe.
   - Are there local goals for education in your district/school?
     - What are they?

III. District/school's relationship to DOE [Department of Education]
   - How often do you or anyone else at your district/school interact with the SDE in any way?
     - What are the occasions for these interactions?
     - How would you characterize these interactions—attitude, tone, purpose, substance—what exactly have you been doing with the Department?
     - Have your interactions with the SDE changed in any way over the past few years?
   - Vermont has a number of education reforms under way. Which if any of these reforms have affected what takes place in your district/school?

(In terms of governance, teaching and learning, working with the community, expanded opportunities for children, integration of services, etc.)
  – Assessment?
  – Common Core of Learning?
  – Professional Standards Board?
  – Reinventing Vermont Schools
  – Carnegie Middle Schools Initiative
  – Deregulation
  – SDE Restructuring?
  – Governance?
  – Teaching and learning?
  – Act 230
- Has your own teaching been affected by these reforms in any way?
- Have you, as a practitioner, had any input into the shaping of these reforms? Have others that you know of?
  – Do you feel that you could have input and/or be involved in their planning if you wished to?
- Do you see any relationship between these reforms?
- How do all of these reforms fit with your local goals?
- What are the goals of these reforms collectively? [ONLY ask if see a relationship]

IV. Role of district (Ask district staff)
- What is the role of the district and district office in all of these reforms?
- How do you and the district office work with the SDE?
- How much input have you had into the shaping of these reforms?

V. Effects of the state reforms
- How has your district/school been affected by these reforms?
  – What has changed?
  – What is in the process of changing?
  – How have these state efforts affected your district/school's earlier reform efforts—pushed them ahead, slowed or stopped them?
- What key challenges/problems are your district/school facing in implementing these reforms?
  – What could help you to address these problems?
  – Where would you see this help coming from?
- What successes are you most proud of thus far?

VI. Role of the SDE
- What role(s) does (do) the SDE play in Vermont?
  – Has the role of the SDE changed in Vermont over the past 4–5 years? How?

- What could the SDE do that would be most helpful to you?
- What do you as a practitioner think of the SDE overall? What do you think the majority of school people in Vermont think of the SDE?
- If you had the opportunity to give the department advice, what would it be?

In addition to these general questions, I also asked questions about particular aspects of the reforms that the individual had direct experience with. For example, if the informant was a 4th or 8th grade teacher, we tended to discuss the portfolio assessment process at some length. My Kentucky practitioner protocol focused on similar issues but asked about various Kentucky, as opposed to Vermont, reforms. As with the protocol for SDE staff, this protocol should be viewed as a rough guide to the conversations that took place.

Knowledgeable Others. I chose the knowledgeable others whom I interviewed in a couple of ways. First, some were obvious choices due to role. Legislative leaders and members of state boards of education, for example, fell into this category. Second, there were individuals who were recommended to me by other informants as people who were knowledgeable about and active in various pieces of the reform.

Interviews with these individuals varied according to their roles and expertise. They generally focused on aspects of the reform they were involved in, as well as their overall impression of the work of the SDE, changes in the SDE, and changes in education in general that had occurred as a result of the reforms.

Data Analysis

The vast majority of my interviews were tape recorded, and all that were recorded were transcribed. I took copious notes on those interviews that could not be recorded and those notes were also transcribed.

I analyzed my data through coding, reflections, memos, and shorter papers. I analyzed each case individually in its entirety prior to doing my cross case analysis, although I did keep track of common issues through writing memos (described below).

I started by coding all of my interview data. My codes emerged from the interviews themselves, from the particular state's reforms, and from my analytical framework presented in Chapter 2. Examples of codes in each of these categories are "customer"—which emerged from interview data on Vermont's Total Quality process; "SBDM"—which referred to Kentucky's school-based decision-making reform; and "SDE decision-making"—which came from my analytical framework. I coded all of the information in my interviews for easy retrieval, even though I did not foresee using all of the codes in this analysis. I ultimately used the subset of codes needed to answer the questions generated by my framework. I used a data analysis package called HyperResearch for the coding and sorting of my data.

I also analyzed the data within each of the codes I used in the following manner. I generally had a large amount of data under each of my codes, due to my large number of informants. I consequently read through all the data under a given code and wrote a brief summary statement of the viewpoint expressed by each informant and the page number(s) where these data were located. These data summaries allowed me to weigh confirming and disconfirming evidence and also to pick out representative quotes relatively quickly. I also analyzed the data within codes to see if the variation in viewpoints expressed was systematically related to some other factor shared by a number of informants—their position in the SDE hierarchy or the type of district they worked in, for example.

I worked to ensure the validity of my analysis by analyzing my data in this way and by triangulating my interview data with the information contained in state documents and gained through the limited observation of SDE activity that I was able to do. I also checked my understandings and preliminary interpretations with various informants at the end of interviews and on occasion asked for feedback on pieces of written work.

In addition to the data analysis described above, I also tape-recorded reflections on my field work, the data I was gathering, and emerging hypotheses while I was in the field. These reflections were transcribed and coded as appropriate. They sometimes became the subject of longer memos.

I wrote memos to myself on a host of topics throughout my research and data analysis. Memoing is an informal method of recording reactions, fleshing out emerging analysis, and tracking ideas. I have a total of 33 memos. Their topics range from my selection strategy for districts and schools and thoughts for my concluding chapters to work plans and reactions to presentations I gave on this work.

Finally, I wrote shorter papers and presented them at conferences to further portions of my analysis. One of these papers presented the argument that I later developed into my analytical framework (Lusi, 1994). The other presented my analysis of the SDE portion of my Kentucky data (Lusi, 1993).

References

Lusi, S. F. (1993). *Systemic school reform: The changes implied for SDEs and how one department has responded.* Paper presented at the annual meeting of the American Educational Research Association, Atlanta.

Lusi, S. F. (1994). Systemic school reform: The challenges faced by state departments of education. In R. F. Elmore & S. H. Fuhrman (Eds.), *The governance of curriculum* (pp. 109–130). Alexandria, VA: Association for Supervision and Curriculum Development.

Patton, M. Q. (1990). *Qualitative evaluation and research methods* (2nd ed.). Newbury Park, CA: Sage.

15

State Education Standards*

editor's introduction:

The "Math Wars." This case study covers a specific instance of a longstanding and sometimes emotional debate on how to teach mathematics, including the role of computers and calculators in the learning process. The debate continues to this day, and the case study tries to present the competing views.

The first, embodied by a state commission's issuance of mathematics standards, tends to favor conceptual understanding and problem-solving ability, with less priority given to rote mathematics skills. In fact, as shown in the case study, the commission's version actually contained mathematical errors. The second, embodied in a board's revision of the state commission's original standards, was mathematically correct but was accused of only covering basic skills and therefore not representing world-class standards—which have come to include conceptual understanding and problem-solving ability, among other "higher-order" cognitive skills, in doing mathematics. You may agree that an obvious resolution to this debate is that both approaches are relevant to students.

Relevance of Case Studies: Reporting About Controversy. The selection shows how case studies also can report on a controversial topic—rather than just a concrete object such as a school, a teacher, or a superintendent. In this selection, the immediate case study is about changes in mathematics standards in a specific state at a specific time. However, the case study reflects the broader and still ongoing (and possibly never-ending) controversy about how to teach mathematics.

*Wu, Hung-Hsi. (2000). "The 1997 Mathematics Standards War in California." In Sandra Stotsky (Ed.), *What's at Stake in the K–12 Standards Wars: A Primer for Educational Policy Makers* (pp. 3–31). New York: Peter Lang.

The author writes with a mild level of passion, making the text more interesting to read, although simultaneously alerting the reader that the presentation of the case may not be considered fair or unbiased to all interested parties. Paradoxically, much of the analysis is based on examining documents as the main source of data. Just think of whether the text could have been more inspiring had the author devoted more attention to interviews with key educators.

The controversy discussed in this chapter has its origin in the 1992 Mathematics Framework for California Public Schools (the 1992 Framework).[1] Published three years after the Curriculum and Evaluation Standards of the National Council of Teachers of Mathematics (the NCTM standards),[2] the 1992 Framework [came] to symbolize the more extreme of the practices of mathematics education reform initiated by the NCTM document. Its overemphasis on pedagogy at the expense of mathematical content knowledge spawned several new curricula that so enraged the parents of schoolchildren that grassroots revolt against the reform within California spread like wildfire on a hot summer day. Eventually, the California legislature bowed to the inevitable and called for an earlier-than-expected writing of a new framework. It was also decided for the first time in the history of California that there should be a set of mathematics standards. By law, these standards have to be set at a level comparable with the best in the world. The California Academic Standards Commission (the Commission) was created by the California legislature for the purpose of writing the standards.

In October 1997, the Commission submitted to the State Board of Education (the Board) a draft of Mathematics Content Standards which took the Commission more than a year to complete.[3] Under normal circumstances, the Board would approve such a document with no more than minor changes. However, a preliminary review of the Commission's standards by several well-known research mathematicians was so devastating that the Board broke precedent by commissioning a group of Stanford University mathematics professors to revamp the Commission's draft. Within ten weeks, the Board issued the revised standards, first the portion on grades K–7 and then that on 8–12.[4] The reaction to the new version was swift and violent:

> [The Board's set of Standards] is "dumbed down" and is unlikely to elicit higher order thinking from the state's 5.5 million public school students.
>
> Delaine Eastin, Superintendent of Public
> Instruction as reported in the *New York Times*

I will fight to see that California Math Standards are not implemented in the classrooms.

> Judy Codding, Member, Academic Standards Commission as
> quoted at a National Council on Educational Evaluation conference

The critics claimed the Board's "back-to-basics" approach marked a return to 1950s-style methods . . . Opponents characterized the [Board's] Standards as a "return to the Dark Ages."

> as reported in the *San Diego Union*

The interest engendered by these two sets of standards remained unabated in the ensuing months. For example, in the February 1998 issue of its *News Bulletin,* NCTM weighed in with unflattering comments about the Board's standards.[5] Because education is a very political issue, it is expected that opinions would be delivered without relation to facts. However, a set of *mathematics* standards for schools also deserves a critical inspection from a mathematical as well as an educational perspective, one that is based on facts, not hyperbole. With this in mind, this chapter proposes to take a close look at both sets of standards from a scholar's perspective. . . .

Why the California Mathematics War Is of National Interest

It may be asked why a dispute within the state of California should be of interest to the rest of the nation. There are several reasons. One is that California, the most populous state of the nation, has been [at] the forefront of the current mathematics education reform. In the opinion of people outside California, "as California goes, so goes the nation." A second reason is that the inadequacy of mathematics education in this country has held a firm grip on the public's attention in the recent past, and the very visible act of groping for a solution in California adds enormously to cement this grip. Also the timing is just right: the Californian squabble came right in the midst of the revelation about the non-performance of American students in the Third International Mathematics and Science Study (TIMSS). The California situation thus offers other states a glimpse of what to look forward to in their own battles to save mathematics education.

A third reason that makes the dispute between the two sets of standards interesting to other states lies in the very nature of the dispute. The pervasive lack of precision in the Commission's standards is symptomatic of a larger trend in contemporary mathematics education, which is to minimize the technical precision inherent in the discipline in order to make it more accessible to a wider audience. Would a state be fulfilling its basic mission in mathematics education if it promotes such a modified version of mathematics in order to reach out to a higher percentage of its students? California answered this question in the negative in 1998 when the Board's revision restored the precision and the technical materials. This very likely ensures California's ability to continue to produce a robust corps of scientists and engineers. Whether or not it will also succeed in raising the mathematical achievements of the lower 50% of its students will be a matter of intense public interest. Other states would do well to look at the details of this dispute before they too fight the same battle in the near future.

The fourth and final reason is perhaps the most important because of its enormous practical consequences: the Board's standards [would] generate a completely new set of mathematics textbooks by 2001. According to the latest information (December 1998) from the California Department of Education, there was more publisher interest, by far, in this new round of textbook adoption than in any other that has ever been conducted in this state. This means that by 2001 the nation would have a plethora of alternative textbooks that heed the call, not of the NCTM standards but of the California Mathematics Standards and Framework. The debate within California would become a national debate in a matter of two years.

An Overview of the Two Sets of Standards

No critical inspection of the two sets of standards, the Commission's and the Board's, should engage in hairsplitting in order to search for perfection. Social documents generally do not fare too well when subjected to this kind of treatment. We expect flaws in both versions, and we shall find flaws aplenty. Yet, there is a fundamental difference between their flaws, and it is this difference that is our major concern.

The Commission's standards is a thoughtful document. In both the Interim Report from the Commission Chair to the State Board and the Introduction to Mathematics Standards, one sees clearly the care that went into the enunciation of the goals, the work that had been done to achieve them, and the work that was envisioned in their implementation. Even if one disagrees with some of the details, one can applaud the overall soundness of purpose and the conscientious effort that went into the writing. The good intentions, however, are not abetted by flawless execution. Some parts of the document are controversial, such as the omission of the division algorithm in the lower grades,[6] the omission of the Fundamental Theorem of Algebra in the upper grades, or the mixing of pedagogical statements with statements on content.

There is also a pervasive ambiguity of language that makes the document unreadable in many places, e.g., the word "classify" has a precise meaning in a mathematical context which is not consistently respected. Or, what is a 7th grade teacher to make of "identify, describe, represent, extend and create linear and nonlinear number patterns"? But the most striking impression it makes on a mathematically knowledgeable reader would likely be the numerous mathematical errors that almost leap out of the pages.

The Board's standards do not suffer from mathematical errors.[7] Mathematical accuracy thus assured, one can proceed to find fault from a higher perspective. It should be fairly obvious to experienced eyes that the standards for each grade are not very "idiomatic": They are more like marching orders from an outsider than sure-handed utterances by a veteran of the classroom. There are occasional (though very rare) linguistic ambiguities. There is an overemphasis on pure mathematics in grades 8–12. The geometry curriculum in grades 8–12 is too much tilted towards synthetic Euclidean geometry. And so on. But perhaps the one quality of the document that stands out is its overall jaggedness; the various standards don't fit together too well. Is there an obvious explanation?

According to R. James Milgram—one of the Stanford mathematicians who helped revise the Commission's standards—the revision was carried out under many constraints. The goals had been set for them: to rid the Commission's standards of all the mathematical errors, to re-arrange the existing standards to make better sense of them, and, above all, to clarify what was in there. There was also a strict order not to add anything new unless it was *absolutely* necessary because the Board itself was under the same pressure. Milgram also added that, in fact, the Stanford mathematicians would not have minded if the standards were a little less inclusive, but the choice of deleting the existing standards was not open to them or to the Board. Retrofitting a set of standards is much more difficult than writing a new one, and it showed.

In spite of the controversy surrounding these two standards, the verdict among mathematicians has been overwhelmingly in favor of the Board's version.[8] Could this be no more than a case of closing of ranks behind their own colleagues? At least one mathematician would venture the opinion that such is not the case, and that it is more a matter of triumph of substance over form, and clarity over vagueness.

The Board's standards have the unmistakable virtue of being clear, precise, and mathematically sound overall. They describe clearly and precisely what is expected of students' mathematical achievement at each level, and the mathematical demands thus imposed conform to the conception of mathematics of most active working mathematicians. The qualities of clarity, precision, and correctness are the *sine qua non* of any mathematical standards worthy of the name, but the sad truth is that very few of the existing mathematics standards of other states can lay claim to any of them.[9]

Even the influential NCTM standards are no exception.[10] These qualities will come to the fore in the comparison between the Commission's and the Board's standards in the next two sections. At the end, there should be little mystery as to why, notwithstanding its flaws, the Board's set of standards is the preferred version by far.

It may be puzzling to some as to why there is this great emphasis on the soundness of the mathematics in a set of mathematics standards. No doubt part of the puzzlement comes from a belief that the experts in mathematics education should be able to get the mathematics right. We know that such is not the case . . . and this discrepancy between perception and reality points to a serious problem in contemporary mathematics education: the divorce of mathematics from education. Too often mathematics educators and administrators lose touch with mathematics. Perhaps the publication of the Board's standards and the publicity engendered by the accompanying fracas will inaugurate a new era of reconciliation between the two disciplines.

The large number of mathematical errors in the Commission's standards also points to an intellectual problem far removed from the political fray. As the errors begin to pile up, they send out the unmistakable message that these standards were written by people whose mathematical understanding is inadequate for the task, and whose vision is therefore unreliable as a guide to lead students of California to a higher level of mathematical achievement. Such being the case, the so-called conceptual understanding embedded in this document is thus of questionable value at best.[11] The politicians and educators who rallied around the Commission's standards and praised it for its emphasis on "conceptual understanding" were most likely unaware of this fact. [Editor's note: There follow several pages detailing the mathematical errors in the Commission's standards.]

The Board's Standards

Now a brief look at the Board's standards.[12] . . . The main aim of this section is to contrast the mathematics here with the Commission's standards. Let us first start with grades K–7. This portion is *very* close to the Commission's standards, and the only difference between the two is that the Board's version eliminates the ambiguous and superfluous, corrects the erroneous, and deletes the *Clarifications and Examples* in the right-hand column of the original. I will have more to say about this last concern presently, but let us sample some of the differences. It was mentioned that in grade 4 the Commission's set of standards incorrectly asks for "the relationship between the concepts of perimeter and area." By comparison, the Board's version now reads:

Grade 4 Measurement and Geometry

1. Students understand perimeter and area.
    1.1 measure the area of rectangular shapes, using appropriate units (cm^2, m^2, km^2, yd^2, square mile).
    1.2 recognize that rectangles having the same area can have different perimeters.
    1.3 understand that the same number can be the perimeter of different rectangles, each having a different area.
    1.4 understand and use formulas to solve problems involving perimeters and areas of rectangles and squares. Use these formulas to find areas of more complex figures by dividing them into parts with these basic shapes.

It is clear, and it is correct. More than that, 1.2 and 1.3 anticipate students' possible confusion, and 1.4 emphasizes the importance of applications and the general principle of progressing from the simple to the complex.

Another example is the Board's correction of the error committed in the Commission's version regarding the introduction of coordinates in the plane in grade 4. Now it is accorded a standard all its own and is placed correctly in the strand on Measurement and Geometry.

Grade 4 Measurement and Geometry

2. Students use two-dimensional coordinate grids to represent points and graph lines and simple figures.
    2.1 draw the points corresponding to linear relationship on graph paper (e.g., draw the first ten points for the equation $y = 3x$ and connect them using a straight line).[13]
    2.2 understand that the length of a horizontal line segment equals the difference of the x coordinates.
    2.3 understand that the length of a vertical line segment equals the difference of the y coordinates.

Note that Standard 2.1 pays special attention to the *tactile* aspect of learning mathematics: use graph papers and draw ten points (by hand). We should be grateful that it does not say: "Enter these data in a graphing calculator and watch the graph emerge on the screen." Moreover, Standards 2.2 and 2.3 again anticipate students' confusion by singling out two key points for discussion. There is no question that this is an education document that truly tries to educate.

As a final example, let us look at how the Board's version discusses in one instance the issue of mathematical reasoning:

Grade 4 Mathematical Reasoning

3. Students move beyond a particular problem by generalizing to other situations.
    3.1 evaluate the reasonableness of the solution in the context of the original situation.
    3.2 note method of deriving the solution and demonstrate conceptual understanding of the derivation by solving similar problems.
    3.3 develop generalization of the results obtained and extend them to other circumstances.

In plain, readable English, this standard lays out a step-by-step method of doing mathematics. Educational writing can be no better than this.

It is improvements of this nature that make the Board's standards a superior document over the Commission's standards in grades K–7. Yet, intense criticisms were already pouring in as soon as the K–7 portion of the Board's standards appeared. Looking at the facts, how does one presume to claim that this set of standards is "basics only," or that it "cuts out almost everything that is not related to computation and the memorization of formulas"? Obviously not on account of the standards themselves. But one explanation is that some people reacted strongly to the deletion of the *Clarifications and Examples* that are in the Commission's standards. [Editor's note: There follow several pages claiming the Board's more rigorous standards for Grades 8–12, too.]

The New Framework

What are the problems with the Board's standards? Without trying to be comprehensive, I will describe a few obvious ones and, at the end of the section, will look into how the new framework addresses them.

First, the terse statements of the Board's standards need examples to clarify them. For example, Standard 4 in Geometry (grades 8–12)—"Students prove basic theorems involving congruence and similarity"—means many things to many people. Should one only assume *SAS* and prove *SSS* and *ASA*, or should all three be assumed for simplicity? Should the *AA* theorem for similar triangles be proved? Or take the case of the introduction of negative fractions and decimals in elementary school: Exactly when should this take place?

The preamble of the standards in grade 5 states: "Students increase their facility with the four basic arithmetic operations applied to positive and negative numbers, fractions, and decimals." Is this to be taken literally so that "fractions" and "decimals" mean (as usual) *positive* fractions and *positive* decimals, or does it mean "positive and negative numbers, positive and negative fractions, and positive and negative decimals"? It does not help that this linguistic ambiguity persists in the subsequent enunciation of the detailed standards in both grades 5 and 6.

We must remember that these standards are pioneering something new in California, and pioneers have to be transcendentally clear at each step or they run the risk of having no followers on their trail. I wish to drive home this point by comparing with what I consider a very admirable set of mathematics standards, the 1990 mathematics standards of Japan.[14] There the statement about similarity (in grade 8!) is equally terse:

> To enable students to clarify the concepts of similarity of figures, and develop their abilities to find the properties of figures by using the conditions of congruence or similarity of triangles and confirm them.
>   a. The meaning of similarity and the conditions for similarity of triangles.
>   b. The properties of ratio of segments of parallel lines.
>   c. The applications of similarity.

There is a big difference, however. The Japanese change their standards every ten years and, because they already have a well-established tradition, the changes are gradual and minor by comparison with the kind of sea change we have over here. Moreover, they have excellent textbooks already in place, so there is no great need to spell out everything.[15] By contrast, we are almost starting anew in California, especially in these turbulent times in education. There is, therefore, a very great need for the Board's standards to be absolutely clear.

Second, the Board's standards intentionally eschew any prescription on how to teach students in grades 8–12, whether in the traditional way or the "integrated" way. The intention for greater flexibility was admirable, except that, in the absence of a tradition, the added flexibility could be a curse. For example, the standards specify that each discipline (Algebra I, Geometry, etc.) need not "be initiated and completed in a single grade." It would appear that this specification makes it possible to describe the desirable content of each discipline without undue regard to the time limitation of fitting everything into exactly one year. Perhaps for this reason there are more topics in Algebra II than can be reasonably completed in a single year. How to teach this material in more than two semesters then becomes a challenge which few schools could meet. Also, Algebra I asks that "students [be] able to find the equation of a line perpendicular to a given line that passes through a given point." No matter how this is done, it would involve theorems about similar triangles. Does it then imply—contrary to the traditional curriculum—that Geometry may be taught simultaneously with Algebra I?

Third, the forthcoming tenth or eleventh grade statewide mathematics test was to include some statistics. The Board's set of standards does not suggest ways of teaching statistics in the early part of secondary school if the traditional curriculum is followed.

Fourth, considerations of this nature bring out the fact that the traditional method of offering year-long sequences for algebra and geometry is too rigid to be educationally optimal. While none of the current "integrated" models in this country seems to be entirely successful, the argument cannot be ignored that we should pursue the kind of integrated mathematics education that has been in use in Japan or Hong Kong for a long time.[16] The framework might fulfill its basic function if it could nudge California in this direction in a forceful manner.

Fifth, an idea that undoubtedly occurred to many people is how much the Board's standards for grades 8–12 read like a "Manual for Pure Mathematics." One almost has the feeling that this document could not bring itself to face the relationship between school mathematics and practical problems. Thus, the framework needed to restore the balance between the pure and applied sides of school mathematics. While it is true that the reform exaggerates the role of "real-world" problems in mathematics, ignoring them altogether is for sure not a cure either. We would do well to remember that the overwhelming majority of school students will be *users* of mathematics, and that as future citizens they need to be shown the power of mathematics in the context of daily affairs. But all through grades 8–12, I seem to see only three explicit references to applications:

Algebra

15. Students apply algebraic techniques to rate problems, work problems, and percent mixture problems.

23. Students apply quadratic equations to physical problems such as the motion of an object under the force of gravity.

Trigonometry

19. Students are adept at using trigonometry in a variety of applications and word problems.

I hope I am not overusing the Japanese model if, again, I look at the corresponding situation in the 1990 Japanese standards. The description of the *content* of the Japanese standards is every bit as abstract and "pure" as the Board's standards, but *The Construction of Teaching Plans and Remarks Concerning Content* after each of grades K, 1–6, 7–9, and 10–12 pays careful attention to the bearing of "daily affairs" on the curriculum. For example, here is what is said after grades 7–9:

> In the [8th and 9th] grades, problem situation learning should be included in a total teaching plan with an appropriate allotment and [implementation] for the purpose of stimulating students' spontaneous learning activities and of fostering their views and ways of thinking mathematically.

Here, "problem situation learning" means the learning to cope with a problem situation, appropriately provided by the teacher so that the content of each domain may be integrated or related to daily affairs. The tone makes it abundantly clear that this is no mere lip service to applications, but that the applied component is central to the whole curriculum.

A final problem concerns the contentious subject of technology. From K–12 in the Board's standards, I could detect only the following two references to technology:

Grade 6 Algebra and Functions

1.4 solve problems using correct order of operations manually and by using a scientific calculator.

Grade 7 Statistics, Data Analysis and Probability

1. Students collect, organize and represent data sets . . . both manually and by using an electronic spreadsheet program.

This reticence is a *de facto* confession that we, as educators, do not know what the proper role of technology is in mathematics education. The reality is that computer and graphing calculators are here to stay, and the younger generation is besieged on all sides by them. It would not be an effective education policy to retreat and abdicate responsibility exactly when we were supposed to come forward to provide guidance. We do not want any kind of technological debauchery in the mathematics classroom, but neither do we want to make technological prudes out of our students. What we want are students who are technologically informed, especially about the role of technology in mathematics, but we won't get them if we continue to pretend that technology does not exist. I am being intentionally suggestive in my use of language in order to force the comparison with sex education. In both situations, it is better to keep our students informed than to let them pick up the wrong information in a state of prevailing ignorance.

Allow me to cite for the last time the 1990 Japanese standards. Part of *The Construction of Teaching Plans and Remarks Concerning Content* also deals with the technological issue after each of grades K, 1–6, 7–9, and 10–12. Here is what is said after grades 1–6 and 10–12, respectively.

> At the 5th Grade or later, the teacher should help children adequately use "soroban" or hand-held calculators, for the purpose of lightening their burden to compute and of improving the effectiveness of teaching in situations where many large numbers to be processed are involved for statistically considering or representing, or where they confirm whether the laws of computation still hold in multiplication and division of decimal fractions. At the same time, the teacher should pay attention to provide adequate situations in which the results of computation may be estimated and computation may be checked through rough estimation.
>
> In teaching the content, the following points should be considered. The teacher should make active use of educational media such as computers, so as to improve the effectiveness of teaching. In the teaching of computation, the teacher should have students use hand-held calculators and computers as the occasion demands, so as to improve the effectiveness of learning.

The Board had already wisely decided that no standards-based state test in grades K–12 would use calculators. This general policy on technology, sensible as it is, needed to be supplemented by a more comprehensive one which gives guidance not only on when *not* to use it but also on *when* to use it. For example, encouraging teachers to use problems with more natural—and therefore more unwieldy—numerical data by enlisting the help of calculators is a beginning. In the presence of the no-calculator-in-tests rule, students would get a clear perspective on what they need to know regardless of technology, and on how they can use technology to their benefit when the need arises. Encouraging students in calculus to use a calculator to estimate the limits of sequences while also holding them responsible for proofs of convergence is another example. Doubtlessly, thoughtful educators could formulate similar specific recommendations in other situations. As the preceding passages from the Japanese standards indicate, we need to make *active* use of calculators and computers to improve the effectiveness of teaching and learning.

With all this said, it is time to look at the new framework to see how it managed to address the foregoing problems in the Board's standards. In this context, the foremost accomplishments of the new framework would seem to be as follows: It gives a detailed guide on how to teach the standards in each grade of K–7, and for each discipline in grades 8–12. In particular, the ambiguities regarding the introduction of negative fractions and negative decimals have been cleaned up. It also adopts a policy on the use of technology in the classroom that is as comprehensive as the available research allows. For example, it essentially recommends against the use of calculators in grades K–5, but encourages its judicious use starting with grade 6. Further, a conscientious attempt is made in the new framework to emphasize applications in grades 8–12.

Thus, almost all the major concerns regarding the Board's standards have been removed. *Almost,* except for two of them. It fails to directly address the issue of how to teach statistics in the traditional curriculum before grade 11. More seriously, it does not even take up the question of how to give Californian high school students a more integrated kind of mathematics education along the line of the Hong Kong or Japanese model. These failures are blemishes in the new document to be sure, but considering how far it has outdistanced its 1992 predecessor in terms of mathematical coherence and accuracy, one can afford to be philosophical about these blemishes. Social changes are rarely accomplished all at once. They take time.

What Have We Learned?

It is often forgotten in the war of words that mathematics education has a substantive component: mathematics. We have seen how a choice between the two versions of the Mathematics Content Standards in California came down to a mathematical assessment of the documents. The scant attention given to this component in the mathematics standards of an overwhelming majority of the states, as pointed out in the Fordham Foundation monograph, is nothing short of scandalous.

One positive outcome of the current mathematics education reform may very well be the revival of the idea that mathematics is important in discussions of mathematics education. The battle over the standards is a stunning illustration of this fact.

If there is anything that the Californian experience can teach policymakers in the other states, it is that without solid mathematical input, it would be impossible to have a sound policy on mathematics education. California happened to benefit from such input through entirely fortuitous circumstances. The accidental confluence of a group of enlightened state board members and a group of knowledgeable mathematicians who are also educationally informed led to the writing of a set of quality standards and a framework that is equally promising. So, what can other policymakers do in order to bring about comparable results?

One can try to seek out mathematicians who are dedicated to the cause of education, but by itself this is not without risk. It suffices to recall that the New Math of the sixties was spearheaded by a small group of well-intentioned mathematicians.[17] A safer recommendation would be that policymakers cultivate standard channels of communication within the mathematical community as a whole and seek consensus in that community at each major step of decisionmaking. Back in the age of the New Math, much anguish and frustration would have been avoided had this guideline been followed.[18] The mathematical community, especially research mathematicians, should likewise do their share and make an effort to stay informed about mathematics education. Fortunately, recent events have proven that at least the latter seems to be taking place. Let us hope that in the near future, mathematicians will be alongside educators in formulating major decisions in mathematics education.

It goes without saying that having a set of good standards and curriculum framework is only the first step towards improvement in education. The far more difficult issues of getting qualified teachers and administrative support for the implementation of the standards lie ahead in California. However, these would be subjects of a different essay.

Finally, let us return to the battle of the standards for a moment. Few would disagree that this so-called math war is entirely senseless, but in the context of human affairs, it may be necessary. Destruction often has to precede progress. Needless to say, not everybody shares this view. When news of the U.S. twelfth-grade performance on TIMSS was released on February 34, 1998, the President of NCTM at the time, Gail Burrill, made the following comment on the TIMSS result: "What's important is that we are working together toward a common goal of excellence in mathematics. The recent math wars have done nothing to improve mathematics education." These are sobering statements. On the one hand, Ms. Burrill's optimistic view that we are already working together toward a common goal in mathematics education could not have been based on the reckless public condemnations of the Board's standards that had just transpired. NCTM's editorial did not exactly contribute to promoting harmony either. On the other hand, the math war in California did manage to reverse the disastrous trend initiated by the 1992 framework.

While much work remains to be done to achieve a balanced mathematics education in California, this achievement disproves the assertion that the math wars have done nothing to improve mathematics education. When all is said and done, educational reconstruction should be the common goal of all parties at this juncture, and the battle over the standards is, in this light, nothing but a distraction. In his address before the Joint Annual Meeting of the American Mathematical Society and the Mathematical Association of America on January 8, 1998, [U.S.] Secretary [of Education] Richard W. Riley sounded the same theme of reconciliation: "This leads me back to the need to bring an end to the shortsighted, politicized, and harmful bickering over the teaching and learning of mathematics. I will tell you that if we continue down this road of infighting, we will only negate the gains we have already made—and the real losers will be the students of America."

In all our education activities we should think of our children first. No, we *must*. If there is a main lesson to be learned from the battle of the standards, it is that we should all learn to look at the facts and keep in mind the welfare of the students before we air our opinions.

Notes

1. *Mathematics Framework for California Public Schools,* California Department of Education, Sacramento, CA, 1992.

2. *Curriculum and Evaluation Standards for School Mathematics,* National Council of Teachers of Mathematics, Reston, 1989 (http://www.enc.org/online/NCTM/280dtoc1.html).

3. California Academic Standards Commission, *Mathematics Content Standards,* October 1, 1997 (http://www.ca.gov/goldstandards).

4. *The California Mathematics Academic Content Standards* as adopted by the California State Board of Education, February 5, 1998 (http://www.cde.ca.gov/board/board.html).

5. "New California Standards Disappoint Many," *NCTM News Bulletin,* Issue 7, 34 (1998), 1 and 5.

6. According to Commissioner Williamson Evers, "the omission of long division with two or more digit divisors was a conscious decision" by the Commission. See *California Mathematicians Respond* (http://www.mathematicallycorrect.com).

7. Unless one counts editorial howlers such as "1 square foot = 12 square inches" in standard 2.4 of Grade 7, Measurement and Geometry.

8. There was some dissent, of course, but on February 2, 1998, an open letter to California State University Chancellor Charles Reed signed by over 100 mathematicians was released to the public; it expresses sentiments in support of the Board's standards. See *California Mathematicians Respond* (http://www.mathematicallycorrect.com).

9. See the survey of mathematical standards of 47 states in R. Raimi and L. S. Braden, *State Mathematics Standards*, Fordham Report, Volume 2, No. 3, Thomas B. Fordham Foundation, Washington D.C., 1998.

10. H. Wu, "Invited Comments on the NCTM Standards" (http://math.berkeley.edu~wu).

11. Mathematicians are only concerned with whether students *understand* mathematics, *i.e.*, whether they know why something is true, why it is of interest, how to apply it, what its implications are, and whether something more general is still true. However, educators introduce the term "conceptual understanding" and make it one of the three pillars of a so-called balanced curriculum (the other items being "problem solving" and "basic skills"). To my knowledge, the meaning of "conceptual understanding" is as yet unclear.

12. The Commission's standards are published in a two column format which displays the mathematics standards on the left and the *Clarifications and Examples* on the right.

13. There is an unfortunate linguistic slip here: "draw ten points" is undoubtedly what is meant. Subsequently this error was corrected.

14. *Mathematics Programs in Japan*, Japan Society of Mathematics Education, 1990.

15. Cf. K. Kodaira, ed., *Japan Grade 7 Mathematics, Japan Grade 8 Mathematics, Japan Grade 9 Mathematics*, The University of Chicago Mathematics Project, Chicago 1992; K. Kodaira, ed., *Mathematics 1, Mathematics 2, Japan Grade 11 Mathematics*, American Mathematical Society, Providence 1997; and K. Kodaira, ed., *Algebra and Geometry, Basic Analysis, Japan Grade 11 Mathematics*, American Mathematical Society, Providence 1997. The publication date of the Japanese original of these texts is 1984.

16. Cf. e.g., the texts cited in the preceding endnote.

17. However, the common perception that mathematicians were solely responsible for the New Math debacle is wrong. In fact, NCTM was also behind the New Math.

18. See, for example, "On the Mathematical Curriculum of the High School," *American Mathematics Monthly*, 69 (1962), 189–193. This open letter was co-signed by 75 of the foremost mathematicians in this country.

PART V

Community and
School Board Action

16

An Urban Youth Program*

editor's introduction:

Education as One of Several "Youthwork" Projects. K–12 education is not limited to the formal K–12 system. Critical education-related opportunities also exist in the community (e.g., after-school programs and also subsequent postgraduation employment). This case study covers both the evaluation and a controversial program that was evaluated—an urban youth program taking place in Atlanta, Indianapolis, New York City, and other cities, known as "Cities-in-Schools" (another example of a "case" within a "case"—also see Selection 6, "School Inequality: Federal Courts").

The evaluation was conducted by a prominent investigator (Charles Murray) who has since published best-selling social science books on U.S. education policy. The case study is about Murray's evaluation ("the story of the evaluation study," p. 294) and how it covered the "Cities-in-Schools" program (a "social services reform effort," p. 294). The case study and the present selection were written by an equally eminent evaluator of education programs (Bob Stake).

By tracing Murray's evaluation, Stake's case study presents a not uncommon example of the struggles in documenting how innovative education programs are implemented—and whether they indeed have been implemented as originally intended. "Cities-in-Schools" was an attempt to have caseworkers coordinate K–12 education as part of "street academies," aimed specifically at youth at high risk of dropping out of school. Similar conditions in evaluating innovative programs routinely exist in education research, although the author of the selection explicitly notes that he has "tried to emphasize the uniqueness of this case more than its generality" (p. 293).

---

*Stake, Robert E. (1986). *Quieting Reform: Social Science and Social Action in an Urban Youth Program* (pp. ix–xvii and 3–15). Urbana: University of Illinois at Urbana-Champaign.

Relevance of Case Studies: Acknowledging Methodological Predispositions.
The selection shows how authors can take advantage of all of the different parts of
their case studies, to acknowledge methodological predispositions. In this selection, the general methodology used in the case study appears in the preface, portions of which have been extracted as a "prefatory note." The selection, which
appears as part of the book's opening chapter, then gives an overview of the case
study.

Unlike most methodological discussions, the material is easy to read and should
quickly engage you with the author's realm of interest. The author candidly shares
his individual preferences and style, which leans toward a "responsive-naturalistic"
evaluation that has "not tried to eliminate subjectivity" (p. 294). In the hands of a
senior evaluator such as Robert Stake, the approach is credible and possibly even
refreshing, compared to the more staid work of many evaluators.

Prefatory Note

This is a case study; actually it is a case study of social scientists doing a
case study. They were studying a program with the odd title of "Cities-in-
Schools" (CIS). It involved some people trying to help several hundred
severely disadvantaged ghetto youth in trouble—youngsters not behaving
the ways teachers, officers of the law, and other members of society wanted
them to. . . . By government reckoning, it was necessary to have a formal
evaluation study, to see if Cities-in-Schools was doing any good, to see if it
should be supported in other cities. A research corporation, the American
Institutes for Research (AIR), got additional government money to do a
three-year study. That study ended in 1981.

Of course by 1981 . . . the money was gone, the program was almost
gone, and the youngsters still had pretty much the same problems—as did
we all. It is not unusual to find that social problems survive our best remedial efforts, nor that we did not learn as much from the efforts as we expected.
But it is unusual to become aware that the research is contributing to a feeling that perhaps reform is futile, that in some situations social research may
be an enemy of reform.

This case study does not prove that social research is ever the enemy of
reform. As did Ibsen's *An Enemy of the People*, it presents an instance where
an idea needs to be considered. What I have done here is to examine the
many pressures upon the evaluation researchers, noting the multiplicity of
interests, the differences in perception of what constitutes success, and the

increasing incompatibility between what the youthworkers see as progress and what the evaluators count as impact. Even though aware of their organizational shortcomings, the Cities-in-Schools people felt increasingly estranged and unrewarded for dogged, even valiant efforts. What primarily resulted was not a greater wisdom about social services but a lessening, a quieting, of reform.

Methodological Notes

This case study of the evaluation of Cities-in-Schools was designed and carried out as a responsive-naturalistic study. It is "responsive" in that I concentrated largely on themes and issues actually found in the work of the evaluators. I tried to orient to the concerns and vulnerabilities of those who had a "stake" in the evaluation, hoping to add to their understanding of what happened. It is "naturalistic" in that ordinary events, witnessing and documentation, are featured, not so much to instruct readers as to enable them to add to their own experience.

This approach to educational research has been described by Louis Smith (1978), Egon Guba (1978), and myself (1978). I probably have been most influenced methodologically by the writings of Lee Cronbach (see 1982), though I have taken some ideas to extremes he has not sanctioned.

In recent years the case study approach has become increasingly popular in educational research. But many researchers object to various aspects of the case study as I did it here. Briefly in the paragraphs below I will try to identify and justify those aspects.

I have tried to emphasize the uniqueness of this case more than its generality. I have paid less attention to what in this AIR work is common to other evaluation studies, more to its special context and meaning. Believing that each reader will generalize to sites and circumstances about which I know little, I have tried to provide great detail about particulars that facilitate those reader-made generalizations. I have sought what Mary Kennedy calls "working knowledge" (1982).

I have tried to tell the story in "their own words," using AIR and CIS documents and quoting the people involved. The quotations and descriptions herein are too long and too uninterpreted, especially for readers who would like to be told just what it all means. Not all the narrative "leads somewhere," but I hope it all helps portray the action and the context.

A special aspect of this particularization is my rather personal presentation. Most evaluation writers avoid emphasis on personalities. I examine them closely. Education and educational evaluation are greatly determined by spontaneity and intuition, and "the particular" cannot be well understood, I believe, without a personal dimension.

Most of my colleagues would grant anonymity to as many people, programs, and places as they could. Exposure often leads to undervaluing. To an important extent, personal detail such as I have provided is demeaning. I regret that. My model is not the journalistic exposé. Nevertheless, I have avoided pseudonyms because they limit a reader's opportunity to combine new information with that already held. And here, where millions in public money were spent for a small program, and three-quarters of a million more for the evaluation, arguments for privacy for key figures seem unpersuasive.

Perhaps the most objectionable feature of their case study is a pervading presence of the biases expressed above. In examining Charles Murray's work [the AIR project director], I have not been a dispassionate reviewer. Even in describing it, and certainly in interpreting it, I have applied *my* standards. I have noted other standards. I have tried to be fair. But I have not tried to eliminate subjectivity (see more of this argument in Stake, 1981). Rather, I have tried to make subjectivity more apparent. I have tried to remind the reader that my investigation, too, is personal.

What I am makes a difference that should not be masked. I have often been an advisor to the [U.S. Department of Education's] National Institute of Education (NIE) and would like to be in the future. [Editor's note: NIE was a supporter of CIS and sponsored the AIR evaluation.] I was an advisor to this AIR work. In the last year I have been an advisor to the possibly continuing CIS national program. I argued for responsive-naturalistic evaluation on those several occasions, and before and after, and am arguing for it again in this case study, both by example and indirectly in interpretation. . . .

Since Murray's work was largely completed before I began the study, I relied heavily on interviews and document review. For correction, validation, and further data collection I asked key interviewees to confirm what I was hearing from them and to react to what I was saying about them. With Charles Murray this required an inordinate amount of his time, which for months he gave generously. . . .

There are several stories told here. The main one is the story of the evaluation study. It is not meaningful without the story of the social services reform effort. Nor is it meaningful without descriptions of a community of evaluation researchers called upon for assistance. These in turn need explication of an evolving federal and political scene, with particular attention to the National Institute of Education.

One cannot tell all these stories effectively in a single chronology or make history simple by telling the stories separately. On numerous occasions I have sacrificed chronology to theme, and I beg the reader's tolerance with confusions in sequence. Also, I tell too little of the actual work with urban youth; it was pretty much completed before I began the meta-evaluation. . . .

The Evaluation Study of Cities-in-Schools

In October 1977 Charles Murray of the American Institutes for Research began a federally sponsored evaluation study of the Cities-in-Schools program in Atlanta, Indianapolis, and New York City. He believed that the CIS program had a good chance of coordinating youth services in each city and of drawing the most intransigent or estranged young people into ordinary, desirable educational and social behaviors. He further believed that his study would provide good evidence of CIS program success and failure—and additionally provide policy-relevant generalizations for program administrators in cities, school districts, and funding agencies across the country.

Three-and-a-half years later a final draft of Murray's evaluation report was circulating among various "stakeholder" groups. The report said that the project had provided sustained face-to-face assistance to the most troubled youth of certain urban neighborhoods but had not succeeded in coordinating social service agencies, or in delivering an improved educational program, or in permanently uplifting the youth. Murray was able to say a lot about what went wrong. He even concluded that no such program could succeed given existing government regulation and the pressures of urban culture. He was unable to provide substantial documentation of how much work and how much good CIS had done, but he was certain that the Cities-in-Schools program had fallen far short of its promises.

The story of the evaluation of Cities-in-Schools is informative because it reveals not only the political nature of program evaluation (especially with an evaluation designed for "stakeholders") but also the elusiveness of knowledge useful to educators and social planners. The story is unique in many ways but reflects on evaluation research generally.

Here was a program with noble intent. It would seek out the most troubled and troublesome youth in the most troubling neighborhoods, upgrade their schooling, keep them out of trouble, lay the groundwork for more productive lives. It had money and political clout. The Lilly Endowment had been one of many early sponsors, and later [President] Jimmy Carter personally "found room" in the Executive Office Building for a national CIS office. Cities-in-Schools was not merely an educational program but a human service. Whatever these youth and their families needed, the program aspired to procure. Educational and social services integration was a major part of the plan.

The evaluation study itself was distinguished. It was undertaken by an eminent educational research group, the American Institutes for Research. Its conception began with Secretary of Health, Education and Welfare, Joseph Califano and Director Patricia Graham of the National Institute of Education. . . .

AIR researchers found this expensive national program in a number of schools in the three cities. At the onset fewer than a thousand youngsters were enrolled. The program would lose and replace many of these youngsters. It would treat them individualistically in uncommon circumstances. Much of this special attention would limit the opportunity for quantitative data aggregation.

Both program and evaluation study were unique—but perhaps not more unique than any federally funded program and its evaluations.

As to ordinary features, there was the need for evaluation feedback for decisions that had to be made before the study was completed and the need to start the evaluation work before the program was ready to be evaluated. Such an evolving, organic character is common among the few social and educational programs which get formally evaluated. Attention to the contextual restraints and opportunities of each individual application of a general program was needed here and is commonly recognized as necessary for understanding the workings and quality of innovative programs.

In the eyes of federal officials and applied social scientists, Cities-in-Schools was a "demonstration" project. If its effectiveness, productivity, and impact could be adequately documented, it would be considered for expansion into other cities.[1]

The Cities-in-Schools Program. Cities-in-Schools was a collection of urban "youthwork" projects. The first were started as street academies for school "dropouts" by Harv Oostdyk and William Milliken in New York City. With slowly increasing support from corporations, philanthropic foundations, and federal agencies—and with increasing tolerance by school districts— the projects grew and multiplied. In different circumstances each took on unique characteristics, but an ideology was shared.

The goal was to find the most estranged youth of the urban ghetto and to bring them into the mainstream of urban society—ultimately to become

---

[1]Indirectly this "meta-evaluation" review of CIS program evaluation also was funded by NIE. Part of a larger study of stakeholder evaluation utility and productivity, my case study was supported through subcontract with the Huron Institute. My collaborators in the larger work were Anthony Bryk, David Cohen, Eleanor Farrar, Ernest House, Grady McGonagill, Stephen Raudenbush, and Carol Weiss.

educated and employed, legally respectable and humane. According to the ideology, zealous staff members, most of them "outstationed" from a city agency or institution, would work intensively, "personalistically," with the youth. The many institutions and agencies of the city having responsibility for youth support would be brought together, even in certain ways "integrated," to work together on schoolgrounds. The design called for "families," often 40 students and four adults per family. The tasks of the day would be academic, decided by the schools, mainly centered on reading skill improvement. But "family life" would be rich with the cultural, athletic, and social activities of ordinary schools. Interpersonal communication and personal commitment were points of emphasis.

Consider briefly one of the sites. In the autumn of 1978 at Atlanta's Smith High School Project Propinquity (the name Cities-in-Schools was less used there), 98 ninth, tenth, and eleventh-graders were assigned to three "families." Each of the students was enrolled in science, math, reading, English, and social studies, all taught by district teachers in rooms for CIS students only. Two program specialists arranged trips, tours, and speakers. During that quarter there were 75 "caseload outings" and 32 field trips, including a five-day camping trip to Alabama, programs at Halloween, and two plays, "The Wiz" and "Tambourines to Glory." Each case manager provided emotional and physical care, making referrals to social service agencies as needed. One-on-one counseling and tutoring were common.

The image conveyed abroad of the CIS student was sometimes "the rebellious youth." There were some, but passivity and deprivation were more common than contentiousness and villainy. Education and health problems were seen more than legal problems. A 14-year-old girl, a chronic absentee, came herself to one CIS office to ask for help. She had multiple physical disorders—eyes, skin, malnutrition, arrested maturation. Her parents also were in extremely bad health, and unreceptive. Her CIS caseworker visited her home (squalor was not an overstatement) at least once a week for an extended period—never gaining admittance. The caseworker arranged for medical care, tutoring, professional counseling, and got her a job at a nearby Burger King where she could eat with regularity. The caseworker later served as pallbearer at her father's funeral.

A "program" at each CIS site was developed to fit within school requirements, personal interests, and the cultural opportunities at hand. In a sense these were not "programs," sometimes merely collections of activities. They shared something of a common history, funding, and ethical standing, yet operated individualistically and rather spontaneously within the demands of school and other civic authorities. Once CIS became federally funded, it was decided that generally shared activities flowing from the common ideology should be evaluated. It was decided that Cities-in-Schools should be evaluated as a single program.[2]

Each city, each street academy, each family had its own history. The earliest projects were located in New York City, Atlanta, and Indianapolis. Gradually adaptations were set up at numerous schools. By 1979 the buildings, enrollment, and staffing in all CIS projects were as shown in Table 16.1.

Table 16.1   Enrollment and Staffing in CIS, 1978–79 and 1979–80

CIS Components	Number of Caseload Students[a]		Number of Caseworkers[b]	
	1978–79	*1979–80*	*1978–79*	*1979–80*
ATLANTA				
Smith High School	98	101	11	14
Carver High School	125	105	12	13
Academy A	110	96	11	8
Academy B	96	133	10	9
Academy T	100	163	10	8
St. Luke's Academy	90	88	9	8
Craddock Elementary	120	128	10	6
Total	739	814	73	66
INDIANAPOLIS				
Arsenal Tech High School (Plan A)	643	634	65	53
Arsenal Tech High School (Plan B)	310	144	39	14[c]
Arlington High School	60	—	6	—
Crispus Attucks High School	71	—	8	—
Indy Prep	29	36	5	6
School No. 101 (Jr. High School)	124	—	13	—
School No. 26 (Junior High School)	74	40	8	4
School No. 45 (Elementary)	74	71	12	7
Total	1,385	925	156	84

(Continued)

---

[2]Problems of treating evangelical movements as programs within federal guidelines are discussed more directly by Eleanor Farrar and Ernest House (1983) in a case study evaluation of Jesse Jackson's Project PUSH-to-Excellence.

Table 16.1 (Continued)

NEW YORK				
Julia Richman High School	162	199	19	29
IS-22 (Junior High School)	120	134	22	19
PS-125 (Elementary)	80	—	6	—
PS-180 (Elementary)	60	—	3	—
PS-53 (Elementary)	—	70	—	—[d]
Total	422	403	50	48

	Number of Caseload Students[a]		Number of Caseworkers[b]	
CIS Components	1978–79	1979–80	1978–79	1979–80
HOUSTON				
M.C. Williams Junior High School	—	77	—	7
OAKLAND				
Hamilton Junior High School	—	78	—	15
WASHINGTON, D.C.				
Terrell Jr. High School	—	157	—	9

a. The exact number of caseload students fluctuated from month to month. These figures represent approximate levels during the first semester.

b. These figures do not include project directors and secretarial staff in 1979–80. Service staff who do not maintain caseloads are included only for the elementary and junior high programs.

c. Represents those Plan B staff with specific caseloads only.

d. Missing data

Source: *The National Evaluation of the Cities-in-Schools Program. Report No. 4, Final Report* (1981), p. 11.

What the program was and how it worked in the three cities are amply described in Charles Murray's evaluation reports. . . . During the four years the evaluators' views of the program were well documented. The major evaluation reports were:

	REPORT DATED	TITLE OF REPORT
1	February 1978	*Program Descriptions*
—	May 1978	*Evaluation Design*
2	May 1979	*The Program and the Process*
3	October 1980	*Program Impact*
4	1981	*Final Report*

These reports made clear that CIS staff members were concentrating on the plight of their young people. It became apparent that building an organization, creating a philosophy, participating in a scientific study, and demonstrating for others elsewhere what *they* might do were not as important to that staff as being face-to-face with youngsters day-by-day. The three criteria emphasized by the evaluators were: improvement in reading, staying in school, and staying out of trouble with the police. These particular aims were important to the program people, too.

Personalistic Youth Help. The action differed from the rhetoric. In the field CIS was seen as a service delivery program more than a services coordination or demonstration program.[3] It was a program characterized by charismatic leaders and missionary zeal. William Milliken, one of the co-founders of Cities-in-Schools, spoke at great length about the commitments needed:

Out on the streets I came spiritually to believe that you find your life by giving it away. I didn't understand it because all my life my culture told me, "You're incomplete. You need one more thing." If you get one more thing you're still incomplete.

Spiritually, to say "you get your life by giving it away" goes contrary to the whole thing. I thought "if that is true, then the poorest ought to have the opportunity to give. I'm not doing them any good unless they have the opportunity to give." How do you create an environment where that happens? We got them in a small-enough environment, the first step, to get an eyeball-to-eyeball relationship, keep remembering their name, etc. But that is the beginning. I've thought about it so many times since. It sounds so simple—simplistic. It's not a simple process.

I may have more skills, born in the right place or whatever—but internally, put me in that same situation, I could be that junkie, too. And I am a junkie of a different type.

What's the difference between the kids that make it and the kids that don't? I wonder whether it was the teacher or the socialworker or somebody else who broke through the hatred, the hostility, the anger, the mask. Sometimes the walls were too thick. That person didn't want you in. They were not going to let you in at any cost. The ones that did let you in found what *they* had to give. Then life began for them. Which meant that the only way that the young

---

[3]The Cities-in-Schools plan of action called for "an experiment leading to an integrated human service delivery system. . . . The Integrated System coordinates local institutional personnel into a new management configuration. This configuration is comprised of small units of multi-disciplined staff who deliver coordinated services to consolidated units of named service consumers on a consistent and personal basis" (Cities-in-Schools, 1977, p. 5).

person could give something away is for that other person to know how to receive—not necessarily "help" them, but to receive. (Interviewed by Stake, Atlanta, May 1982)

As Charles Murray and other AIR evaluation planners saw it, the idea that drove the Cities-in-Schools program forward was: personal assistance drawing the youngsters into "investments." In order for CIS to have the opportunity to assist kids in investing (or "receiving," as Milliken put it), an elaborate promise of services integration evolved. This is how Murray once described the complexities of CIS. He was opening a meeting with his ERS Technical Review Panel:[4]

We are evaluating an effort which got its first federal funding in the '77–'78 school year, but which had been operating in different forms since 1970 when the street academies started in Atlanta, earlier actually with Bill Milliken and Harv Oostdyk in New York City. The actual Cities-in-Schools notion started in 1974–75 in Atlanta and Indianapolis. The only site we have watched since its beginning has been New York City, but even there a rudimentary program of sorts was at Julia Richman (high school) in '75 through '77. So it is wrong to think of this as a program designed and sprung full-blown as the evaluation started. It has a long history.

As I tried to suggest in the "issues paper" it came about because a couple of really impressive entrepreneurs, caring an awful lot about helping kids, seized on an idea they thought made sense. It was sort of "We want to help kids. What kind of structure can we come up with to serve that purpose?" It later took on a life of its own, institutionally, whereby you do whatever needs to be done to get the bucks.

You now have this huge variety of activities which all fall under the label of Cities-in-Schools. The reports you are looking at, #2 and #3, focus on one component we call the "pure form." But in Report #2 we do describe the street academies, the elementary school and the junior high school programs, the delinquency programs . . . After initial intention to evaluate all those things, we decided that would not be the intended evaluation study because most of those cases were ad hoc, put-some-folks-in-the-school, put-some-folks-in-the-street-academy, kinds of efforts. They did not have the distinctive character of CIS in its "pure form."

Pure form, to reiterate, is to consist ideally of a set of caseworkers having four different specialities: (1) the social service specialist, from, for example, a Department of Family and Children Service, who has lots of experience with

---

[4]Murray said these things more articulately, more formally, and in greater perspective in the *Final Report*. This informal statement indicates how things were being vocalized.

the ways of bureaucracies, what the different municipal agencies are, and how you deal with them to get help; (2) the programmatic specialist, say from the Boy Scouts or the YMCA, who has skill in organizing trips, special events, athletic teams, drama groups, . . . (3) an educator, ideally a special education teacher, to deal with the kinds of educational problems these kids have, and remedial education in general; and (4) a youth worker, a street worker, someone who hangs out on corners, gets to know the kids, and does for them what needs to be done.

Each of these four would have a caseload of ten kids. With each kid they would develop what CIS called "personalism," a very close relation with both family and youngster. The caseworker was supposed to know what the family situation was in great detail. (Transcript, Chicago, 1980)

The work of CIS was quite different in the three cities, and at different sites within them, and continued to evolve at each site. Indianapolis had the largest participation, with a high in 1978–79 of 643 students in "pure form" at Arsenal Tech and another 742 in variations at Arsenal and six other participating schools. That same year CIS in Atlanta worked with 739 students at two high schools, four street academies, and an elementary school. The CIS people in New York City listed 162 high school, 120 junior high, and 140 elementary school students. Approximately 280 caseworkers were made available to CIS in the three cities to work with 2,546 students that year.

A Continuing Appeal. Across three long years, from 1978 to 1981, CIS project personnel tutored and counseled the youngsters and did the "streetwork." They appeared to win more admirers among business people and parents than among education and social service agency personnel. The programs grew larger, then cut back to concentrate on the more eligible youngsters.[5] They encountered management problems, particularly in coordination and continuity. They were obstructed by the problems of education generally (such as an Indianapolis teachers' strike delaying fall opening two months), received increased national publicity, saw CIS offshoots begin in Houston, Oakland, and Washington, D.C., and faced disruptive delays in funding. The number of optimistic advocates of Cities-in-Schools appeared to diminish as all this happened.

In February 1981 . . . the national coordinating staff lost its office space in the Old Executive Office Building. It continued its advocacies from Atlanta. Political and financial support was waning and internal problems

---

[5]At Arsenal Tech in Indianapolis, for example, it was finally decided that youngsters eligible for Tech 300 would be those with high absenteeism (some were out over 140 days of a 180-day year), who were below 5.9 grade level in reading, and who met Title XX poverty criteria.

were many, but the national board of directors showed no inclination to give up. . . .

In late 1981, after the "demonstration" period was over, CIS programs in the three cities found dissimilar future prospects in their communities. In New York City people from the mayor's and chancellor's offices took little note of Murray's not-very-supportive evaluation report. They listened to the pleas of Milliken, CIS Board Chairman Howard Samuels, and the chancellor's consultant Ronald Edmonds, and, with city funds, contemplated a new and larger CIS operation in the Bronx. In Atlanta's Carver High School activities were at a standstill, but elsewhere in that city CIS continued modestly. The Indianapolis project started the fall 1981 term with but eight caseworkers and 80 students, all at Arsenal Tech. Federal funding essentially had ended.

But winter 1981 was not a winter of discontent for everyone. CIS Executive Vice-President Burton Chamberlain continued to find a few people in the new [federal government] administration willing to listen. The "not evaluated" projects in Houston and Oakland were reputed to be vigorous, with credit regularly attributed to their superintendents. Not contemplating the demise of CIS, the national board of directors actually worried more about fending off bids from "fad followers." The board discouraged efforts to begin projects in new cities (with the possible exception of Chicago, whose Superintendent Ruth Love—the immediately previous superintendent at Oakland—was a member of the board).

During these years the Cities-in-Schools program had evolved from a small scattering of activities to a large but loose aggregate of projects. It had burst into fresh variations in a few additional places but diminished, at least temporarily, as federal funding diminished. Formal evaluation research on this program in the three original cities found little evidence of success. Generally, people interested in the program and in the problems it attacked showed little interest in the evaluation report. The remaining caseworkers and field managers were disheartened and did not presume that corrections and new vigor could come from studying it. One puzzling result was that many intelligent, responsible, caring people granted the correctness of the report and reiterated their faith in evaluation studies, but ignored the report's findings and recommendations. . . .

In the *Final Report* of the Cities-in-Schools evaluation study Charles Murray wrote: "If the question is 'Is the program *as it exists* a good investment of public funds?' the answer from the three sites that we examined is 'No.'" He went on to identify several unlikely but not impossible correctives.

In contrast, six months after circulation of the AIR *Final Report*, Howard Samuels, chairman of the CIS national board, told me, "The CIS concept has emerged as a sound basis for turning around urban education. It was administered poorly in the three cities, as the evaluation study showed. When managed by competent program directors and school administrators the program works, as is being shown in Houston and Oakland." Two years later, in mid-1983, Atlanta, New York City, Houston, and Washington appeared to have vigorous projects. New ones had opened in Los Angeles and Bethlehem. *State* plans were under consideration in North Carolina and Georgia. The national coordinating staff had dispersed, the office closing its doors in Atlanta, but Milliken was working to open a new office in Washington. . . .

References

Cities-in-Schools. 1977. "An Integrated System of Human Services Delivery" (a.k.a. the "Blue Book.") Washington, D.C.

Cronbach, Lee. 1982. *Designing Evaluations of Educational and Social Programs.* San Francisco: Jossey-Bass Publishers.

Farrar, Eleanor, and Ernest House. 1983. "The Evaluation of PUSH/Excel: A Case Study." In *New Directions for Program Evaluation.* No. 17. San Francisco: Jossey-Bass Publishers.

Guba, Egon. 1978. *Toward a Methodology of Naturalistic Inquiry in Educational Evaluation.* Los Angeles: Center for the Study of Evaluation, UCLA Graduate School of Education, University of California.

Kennedy, Mary. 1982. *Working Knowledge.* Cambridge, Mass.: Huron Institute.

Smith, Louis. 1978. "An Evolving Logic of Participant Observation, Educational Ethnography and Other Case Studies." In Lee Shulman, ed., *Review of Research in Education,* vol. 6. Chicago: Peacock Press.

Stake, Robert. 1978. "The Case Study Method in Social Inquiry." *Educational Researcher* 7, no. 2.

———. 1981. "A Needed Subjectivity in Educational Research." *Discourse* 1, no. 2.

17

School–Community Collaboration in Starting a New School*

editor's introduction:

The Dynamics of Local School Systems. Few people realize how dynamic a school system can be. Old schools may be closed and new schools started. The grade levels covered by a school can change over time, and changes in a school building (including construction of a new building) can alter school programs. Some systems may shift from a preference for separate K–5 elementary and Grades 6–8 middle schools to a K–8 configuration. Many of these changes reflect how school systems must adapt to shifting enrollments, new residential housing patterns, the normal aging of the physical plant, and new academic practices.

Within this dynamic condition, starting a new school—and especially an urban high school with high academic expectations—is no mean feat. This case study traces the planning for the school, its initial (and difficult) startup, and then its early years. As noted by the author, the case study covers the "extreme challenges" presented in getting a new high school from "a proposal on paper" to a "smoothly functioning school."

By the end of the case study, the school seems to have established itself, and the initial graduating classes have performed well. How these events transpired, given the confluence of such conditions as local district policies and the need to increase

---

*Stuart, Lee. (2000). "The Bronx Leadership Academy High School: The Challenges of Innovation." In Diane Ravitch & Joseph P. Viteritti (Eds.), *Lessons From New York City Schools* (pp. 117–137). Baltimore: Johns Hopkins University Press.

parental involvement, form the basis for the lessons learned from the case study. The experience seems highly relevant if you are interested in charter schools—which have become an increasingly popular type of public school across the country.

Relevance of Case Studies: Describing Organizational Collaborations. This selection describes the extensive collaboration and relationship between a school district and a major community organization—the South Bronx Churches. Such collaboration is a somewhat more abstract topic than those covered by the earlier selections (especially in Parts I, II, and III). The case therefore shows how case study methods can be useful in covering a broad range of topics, not just concrete situations.

The case study shows you how group interactions can be the subject of study. Unlike earlier selections, the case study gives little attention to the actions or thoughts of individual people. Rather, the case study continually discusses the ways that the organizations interacted—and their continuing involvement with the school even after it had been successfully started. Because the case study is about the work of these organizations (and not about the high school), the range of issues raised deals with changing the entire education system. For instance, the case study concludes with the alluring possibility that the same combination of organizational forces might turn to expanding the high school to include the middle school grades.

This chapter traces the origin, formation, growing pains, successes, and challenges facing the Bronx Leadership Academy high school. The Bronx Leadership Academy (BLA) is a collaborative project between the New York City Board of Education and South Bronx Churches (SBC), which is a broad-based organization of religious institutions that has been instrumental in rebuilding the South Bronx, especially in the areas of housing development, education reform, and increased citizen participation in public life. The Bronx Leadership Academy began in 1991 as a dream of SBC parents and clergy who were deeply frustrated at the lack of quality public education in the South Bronx and angry at their inability over four years of effort with the local school districts and principals to gain even basic recognition as stakeholders in the education of their children.

SBC leaders worked for nearly two years to build the necessary relationships within the Board of Education to establish the new high school. The school opened in 1993 and immediately suffered from a crisis in leadership that threatened its very existence. Two-and-a-half years in temporary quarters strained the ability of the faculty and staff to form a coherent educational community. Now, strong leadership from the current principal, a staff united behind high expectations and standards, and a new building complete with art studio, music room, and science laboratories have motivated the students to produce impressive results. Of students admitted in 1993 when the school opened, 93 percent graduated in four years. Of students admitted in 1994, all graduated on time. Forty-one of the forty-three students in this class applied to and were accepted into college, with a total of approximately $200,000 in financial aid awards.

Despite this success, systemwide conditions continuously threaten the school. Among the threats are the lack of policies developed specifically for small schools, a pressure to increase enrollment to or beyond the maximum capacity of the building, centralized budgeting at very low levels, politically motivated "mainstreaming" of psychologically troubled children, and lack of concerted action on the part of the board to correct the "Dead Zones"— local school districts where fewer than 35 percent of the children in elementary and intermediate grades read at grade level. Ultimately a failure on the part of the chancellor [head of the New York City public school system] to exercise his newly granted powers to remove principals for persistent educational failure and to hold principals accountable for the standards of education in their schools is responsible for the persistence of a two-tiered educational system in New York City, where, by an accident of birth, nearly 100,000 children in the South Bronx do not receive adequate education in the lower grades to prepare them for academic success in high school and beyond.

Origin and Vision

In order to understand the existence of the Bronx Leadership Academy, it is necessary to understand its development as an outgrowth of one of the primary issues of the public agenda of South Bronx Churches.[1] SBC was organized in 1987 as an affiliate of the Industrial Areas Foundation,[2] the nation's oldest and largest community organizing network. Clergy and lay leaders from over thirty congregations—Baptist, Catholic, Lutheran, Episcopalian, Presbyterian, Disciples of Christ, United Church of Christ, and United Methodist—came together to form the organization. They spent thousands of hours getting to know and trust one another, raising hundreds of thousands of dollars from their judicatories and bishops, pledging annual dues from each congregation to sustain the organization, analyzing the political and economic realities of the community, learning to build the power to participate fully in that political and economic reality, and developing an agenda for action on the most important issues facing their constituents. Not surprisingly, in the South Bronx, which at the time was a prime example of the nation's poverty, these issues included, in addition to improving public education, the development of new and renovated housing, providing better health care, increasing the availability of day care, and improving the economic life of families through increasing the minimum wage and a program of job development. Over 100,000 adults in the South Bronx signed petitions in support of SBC's agenda.

Unlike many community-based organizations before and since, SBC claimed the entire public domain as its own. With broad geographic representation throughout the South Bronx (and thus minimally limited by neighborhood turf boundaries), not at all limited on the range of issues on which they claimed the authority to act, and based in the only permanent institutions that had survived the decimation of the South Bronx, SBC was and is ethnically, religiously, and politically diverse. Inherent in the philosophy of SBC's leaders was a commitment to "stand for the whole" rather than for a narrow special interest, to practice the iron rule of never doing for others what they can do for themselves, and to hold both themselves and the public and private institutions of New York City to high standards of accountability. SBC leaders developed the power, both in terms of organized people and in terms of organized money, to engage those public and private institutions not as a supplicant, client, or victim but as a force to be reckoned with.

It was the attitude of self-determination that gave SBC leaders the courage and perseverance first to rid the local public hospital of a highly corrupt local political strongman, then to fight for control of abandoned land on which to build 750 new homes, and then to engage the local school boards and principals in order to have them do something to improve the dismal state of public education in the Bronx. Entrenched resistance to change, and in many districts, long-term corruption at the district level which starved resources from the classrooms, were formidable barriers.[3]

After being brushed off by principals and physically threatened by school board officials from one of the local districts, the leaders of SBC decided that it was impossible to work within the existing educational structures and personalities of the South Bronx. To get any change in education they would have to build their own school, as politically remote and impractical as this seemed. Then three young men were shot in a Brooklyn public high school, and their deaths forced the political moment that allowed the citywide new schools initiative under Chancellor Joseph Fernandez. When Chancellor Fernandez announced the formation of new, smaller high schools in collaboration with community groups as a way to reduce violence, improve education, and provide better links between the community and the schools, South Bronx Churches and its sister organization, East Brooklyn Congregations, decided to participate. Ultimately, East Brooklyn Congregations was successful in starting two high schools, one for Bushwick and one for Brownsville. South Bronx Churches started the Bronx Leadership Academy.

A group of about twenty-five parents and clergy constituted the Education Task Force of South Bronx Churches. They engaged the members of SBC in one-on-one and small-group meetings regarding the vision for a new school. The vision was shockingly simple, and therefore radical: SBC wanted an academically focused high school, which would admit students of varying abilities and train them for college and leadership in public life. The reason an academic, college preparatory emphasis is radical is that fewer than one-third of high school freshmen in the South Bronx graduate in four years and only 2 percent to 4 percent of graduates typically receive Regents diplomas. In all but one of the six local school districts in the Bronx (District 11), fewer than 35 percent of the students read at grade level.[4]

SBC's internal organizing to create the new school was comparatively simple compared to the need to organize the Board of Education itself for the creation of the school. The process was new for both sides, and the advantage that SBC had internally over the board was that it had no preset ideas, traditions, patterns, habits, bureaucracy, or procedures for dealing with educational issues. SBC could start with (comparatively) a *tabula rasa;* the board could not. The first step in the process was building the necessary relationships and respect between board personnel and SBC leaders. The early exchanges, which went on for about six months, were almost anthropological in nature: two cultures, both good-willed but very different, encountering each other. Attempts by SBC to engage professional educators as consultants in the process, however, were rarely successful or helpful. Eventually, a subcommittee comprised of the lead organizer of South Bronx Churches and ten members of the Educational Task Force carried out the bulk of the early negotiations.

This group researched new and effective models of school reform in New York City and beyond. They met with educators from Fordham University and Columbia, visited innovative schools throughout the city, and slowly developed their capacity to judge what made a good school and the qualities they wanted theirs to have. Early in the process, the group met with Joseph N. De Jesus, the Bronx superintendent of high schools, and gained his wholehearted support of the effort. His support was key for the establishment of the school and for meeting the challenges of the early years.

During the early stages of the formation of the new schools throughout New York City, a program called "New Visions" was established to provide financial and technical assistance to new school initiatives. SBC applied to New Visions but, upon learning that one of the requirements was collaboration with a local school district, did not pursue the relationship. Thus, the funding for SBC's efforts came from its core budget, supplied by congregational dues and grants from religious groups and private foundations. The educational expertise also came internally from teachers, principals, and other educators who were members of SBC congregations.

SBC, as do all the affiliates of the Industrial Areas Foundation, seeks to build "relational" rather than "dominant" power, both internally and between itself and public and private institutions.[5] Whereas dominant power is characterized by unilateral control, a position of one side over and against another, and expansion of the strength of the dominant at the expense of the subordinate, relational power is characterized by mutuality, a position of "power with" rather than "power over," and the expansion and growth of both sides as they develop a mutually beneficial strategy for action. The nearly eighteen months of negotiations and relationship building prior to the formal establishment of the school in February of 1993 were required to build sufficient relational power between the Board of Education and South Bronx Churches. This relational power was necessary to overcome the extreme challenges encountered in getting the Bronx Leadership Academy from a proposal on paper to a smoothly functioning school.

The people most responsible at the level of the central board for the successful formation of the Bronx Leadership Academy were Cesar Previdi, Pat Haith, and John Farrandino. These three met over many months with delegates from SBC. They guided the writing of a sound proposal that would both meet SBC's objectives and board requirements for the establishment of a school. Both sides learned to compromise. At no time were the discussions hostile in any way, though there was mutual struggle to come to a meeting of the minds on some kind of reasonable time line. The guarded approach of the board representatives was appropriate in light of the absolute need to know and trust their collaborators from SBC. The last thing New York City needed was a narrow political or religious interest forming pseudo-public schools with an agenda other than quality education. The religious diversity of SBC allayed fears of violation of church and state separation: the Board of Education personnel realized that SBC would tear itself apart over the question of which doctrine to teach (if such had ever been the intent).

Learning by Doing: Early Obstacles and Successes

Neither the Board of Education nor South Bronx Churches had a track record of establishing new schools. It is only in retrospect that some of the processes and procedures of the early days can be seen as deeply flawed. The experience of playing out ideas that appeared worthy at the time, particularly ideas about staff selection and training, curriculum development, support for new principals and project directors, and the all-important issue of a building, has yielded significant changes in the approaches taken in more recent school start-ups.

The Bronx Leadership Academy developed along a path that now appears designed for a disaster. This is not to say that the planners were not intelligent, committed people but that they nevertheless made decisions which yielded great hardships down the line, and which proved to be nearly fatal to the endeavor. One example of this is the general sequence of events in the school's formation. Growing out of the immediate self-interest of SBC member congregations, the initial proposal for the school was developed in conjunction with the highest levels of the NYC Board of Education. Then, again with the help of people high in the board's bureaucracy, the political work of chartering the new school, namely, getting it past the vote of the Board of Education and officially recognized as a school, was accomplished.[6] The next step was to find the staff, and the final step was to find a building. The problem was that the initial staff had no part in the years of predevelopment work and relationship building that the board and SBC had undertaken together. It was as if a machine had been designed with no involvement of those who would be most responsible for making it run. The second problem was that a very important issue with respect to a school, its physical location, was left to the end of the process. Both staff issues and site issues nearly delivered a fatal blow to the Bronx Leadership Academy in its first two-and-a-half years. These problems would not have had nearly the destructive potential had they been addressed earlier.

Although the initial project director was selected jointly by Board of Education and SBC leaders, and the director and the global studies teacher attended the national training of the Industrial Areas Foundation to become familiar with the work of broad-based organizations such as SBC, the relationship between the school staff and SBC quickly turned sour. At issue was what was meant by "collaboration"—whether that meant passive involvement on the part of SBC or whether the leaders of the Educational Task Force would be an integral part of the next stage in the school's formation such as curriculum development, particularly in the area of leadership for public life, internal practices and environment, and setting academic standards. The professional educators felt that SBC's involvement in these areas violated their professionalism; SBC leaders felt their exclusion to indicate lack of respect for the years of work already spent on the school. They felt that what had been "theirs" was now being "taken over" by people who had not participated in the struggle.

Also at issue was accountability. SBC leaders felt perfectly free to ask, and expected to get answers to questions such as: how will the mathematics curriculum be enhanced so that students weak in math can achieve Regents standards? How can we be assured that special education and ESL [English as a Second Language] students make acceptable progress toward graduation? What support structures will be in place to build a sense of community and shared endeavor among students? Unfortunately, time and time again, such questions were interpreted as challenges to the authority of the project director and teachers. SBC leaders were concerned that even when given a blank slate to start a new school, the professional educators would reproduce the same structures and culture that had already failed the children of the Bronx.

The simple fact was that SBC leaders had spent far longer, years longer in fact, wrestling with the question of what makes a good school than had the initial staff. Complicating the situation was the fact that the project director had no experience at the high school level, was unfamiliar with the high school curriculum, and had a weak relationship with the Bronx superintendent of high schools. The stage was set for a series of highly damaging disagreements as SBC began working with a brand-new staff under enormous pressure to bring together all elements of a new school. It had taken eighteen months for SBC and the high school division to develop a collaborative relationship in the school's formation. The timing of the opening of school allowed only one summer for the far more complicated task of turning the vision of one group (SBC) into action by another (school staff).

Space, Parents, and Race. As early as November of 1993, the tension between SBC and the staff was acute. Furthermore, efforts on the part of the superintendent's office to support the collaboration with SBC met stiffening resistance from school staff. Although a good effort had been made by both SBC and the Board of Education to find separate space for the new school, nothing had been found and the school opened in a wing of Samuel Gompers High School. The principal of Gompers made every effort to be welcoming, and most of the staff of the Bronx Leadership Academy [BLA] made the same effort. Nevertheless, some Gompers students resented the presence of the BLA students. The BLA students felt both threatened by the far more numerous Gompers students and resentful that, having been promised their own school, they were now guests at another. The necessity of shared space became a wedge issue used by the staff of BLA to further discredit SBC's involvement; SBC was portrayed as having failed to live up to its obligation to find space for the school, a failure which now put the students at risk of physical harm.

Sadly, the parents became pawns in the struggle between SBC and the staff and board. SBC had always assumed that it would assist in organizing the parents' association along the lines being undertaken by the Texas affiliates of the Industrial Areas Foundation.[7] This had been one of the core premises of the school. The Board of Education, however, has very set rules for establishing a parents' association, most of which are completely impossible to fulfill in a start-up situation where no relationships exist. For example, the first order of business, according to the *Blue Book*,[8] the bible of parents' associations, is to adopt by-laws and elect officers. SBC wanted to postpone this part until parents had a chance to meet one another, decide collectively on their goals and strategies, and take part in leadership training appropriate for building a relational model of a parents' organization. The people from the central board responsible for parents' associations held firmly to the traditional approach, and therefore the issue of the role of parents in the school was divisive. The picture was painted that SBC, in proposing a relational rather than a bureaucratic model for the parent association, was somehow denying parents their rights to organize!

The South Bronx is essentially a segregated society, in that Whites make up less than 2 percent of the population.[9] The first student body of the high school was entirely African American, Caribbean American, or Hispanic. The staff included Whites, but they were in the minority. Most of the leadership of SBC is likewise Black or Hispanic, but the lead organizer was White, as were some, but not all, of the clergy. Some of the staff of the Bronx Leadership Academy repeatedly and publicly challenged SBC's participation in the school on the basis of the organizer's race and on the presence of White clergy in the organization's leadership.

In short, SBC was painted by some of the staff as, variously, threatening racial domination by Whites, posing a sectarian takeover of public education, meddling in the work of educational professionals, and intentionally putting the safety of the children at risk by failing to provide a separate school building. That's a lot of freight for any organization to bear, and it was particularly hard on the SBC Education Task Force, which had worked so hard and long to establish the school.

As the polarization between the staff and SBC increased, SBC turned to the superintendent of high schools and requested support to reestablish a collaborative relationship. A series of meetings, retreats, workshops, discussion sessions, and so forth did nothing to ease tensions. Eventually it became obvious that collaboration was impossible with the existing leadership in the school, and in March of 1994, the project director was removed by the Board of Education.

Even six years doesn't give 20-20 hindsight on the first year of the Bronx Leadership Academy. What is clear is that the leaders selected for a new school should be among the most serious and seasoned professionals, with previous administrative experience at the level required for the job. It is entirely unclear whether, had the opening of the school been delayed from September 1993 to September 1994 to allow for the staff and SBC to work together on the next stage of the school's development, the extra time would have resulted in an atmosphere of collaboration.

The fact remains that the first year of the Bronx Leadership Academy was painful to all involved. The students were hurt educationally and emotionally by the turmoil and, perhaps worst of all, by the failure of the staff to provide a curriculum that met the requirements for New York City high school freshmen.

The job of the new project director, Katherine Kelly, was to stabilize the situation for the remaining months of school, evaluate staff for transfers and training needs, win back the trust of parents and students, set up the appropriate structures and curriculum, and somehow build a collaborative relationship between the school and SBC on the wreckage of the first seven months of the school's life. For its part, SBC was willing to take a back seat until things calmed down. The SBC leaders were nearly worn out because of the bitterness of the struggle, but they were confident in Mrs. Kelly's credentials and vision for education. All SBC had ever wanted was a good school, with high academic standards and a commitment to train students for full participation in public life. Endorsing Mrs. Kelly's plan for the academic curriculum and staff adjustments, SBC began working in earnest on the other vexing issue facing the BLA: a permanent home.

This took years. For most of the 1994 and 1995 school years, BLA was housed in a church education building. There were no labs or cafeteria, the classrooms were too small, the gym was the banquet hall, and the elevator was shared with the church. Sometimes this proved awkward. Due to the topography of the site, it was easier for funeral directors to bring the caskets in through the school and down the elevator to the sanctuary than to climb the stairs from the street to the sanctuary. Mrs. Kelly made heroic efforts to boost morale and set the school on a good course. She brought in young, talented teachers, and provided the leadership required to produce a truly outstanding school. The parents voted to establish a dress code, over the protestations of their children. The teachers began considering school-based options in their contract which would help them meet the demands of a new school. SBC kept looking for a building.

Finally one was identified—a cinder-block shell, which could be remodeled from within to form a school. Lease and construction negotiations took months, and the school was ready for occupancy in February 1996. Finally the students had well-equipped labs, an art studio, a music room, and a gym. The design of the school was not perfect: Board of Education architects had allowed ventilating duct work to cross through the safe room where state-administered exams were to be stored. This nearly caused a denial of certification of the school because of the inability to protect the exams from theft. Eventually a type of jail cell was built which isolated the ducts from the safe room. In another mistake, the architects designed the gym with the outside dimensions of a basketball court, with no space between the boundary lines and the walls, much less for any spectators. Through months of design review, this error was not caught, even though, had it been, it could have easily been corrected because the site was large enough to accommodate a full gym.

During the construction of the school what became known as the school lease scandal hit the media.[10] In an effort to rapidly expand classroom space, the Board of Education and various landlords entered into highly unsatisfactory and exorbitant leases. The BLA lease was not part of the scandal, but nevertheless was highly scrutinized.

What Was Learned? The Board of Education now requires staff educators to participate in the formation of new schools. While this might be seen as an attempt to co-opt the initiating role of the community group proposing the school, it avoids the situation encountered by SBC and BLA when the first staff were not adequately aligned with the vision of the school. It does place an additional burden, however, on community groups wishing to start schools, requiring them to organize carefully so that their views are not overwhelmed by people used to working within the system. Additional staff support and mentoring is now available for teachers and administrators in new schools, and the small schools have developed their own constituency.[11] It is now Board of Education policy that the leaders of new schools have the appropriate experience, and are not thrown into situations or administrative relationships entirely new to them. Many of the small schools started at the same time as BLA suffered from lack of permanent space. This has proven to be such an obstacle that current school start-ups require the designation of a site prior to the school's being established. While this can add years to the start-up process, it is probably wise because it provides for decent instructional space from the very first day of classes.

Establishing a Culture for Education and Learning. Most visitors to the Bronx Leadership Academy are instantly struck by two things: the cleanliness of the building and the focused order of students, both within the classrooms and when moving around the halls. Many New York City high schools have metal detectors; BLA has none. The school is rated above average in terms of safety. A standard design specification for New York City high schools is that the classroom doors be made of metal, because otherwise the students would destroy them. BLA has wooden doors. There is no trace of graffiti, either in the building or on its exterior. The students have their own committee to deal with anyone who defaces the building. Daily attendance is greater than 90 percent.[12] In many New York City public schools parents struggle to meet with teachers and principals. At BLA, there is an open door policy for parents. Without a playing field or standard gym, and with a small student body, BLA will probably never field a championship football, baseball, or basketball team. It does, however, field an excellent fencing team, coached by one of the judges in the most recent Olympics. Students win trophies in citywide debate.

Upon entering high school, many freshmen have studied literature only through excerpts. At BLA, there is an extensive summer reading list for all students, and novels, both classics and modern, are part of every year's curriculum. To make formal learning a year-round activity, all students in all grades have summer assignments in social studies, law, science, and mathematics in addition to the summer reading and writing requirements. Summer assignments are well integrated so that all teach vocabulary, writing, and reading as well as the content of the particular discipline. Students are responsible for summer work, and the work counts toward the first marking period grades.

BLA has a broad academic curriculum considering its size. French, Spanish, and Latin are taught. Advanced placement classes are offered in English, social studies, mathematics, and physics. General education and special education students are taught in the same classroom. The school has a band and a chorus and a spacious art studio. Extra ESL is offered after school for those who need it. Computers are accessible to students throughout the day, in the computer lab, in the library, and in some classrooms. With help from the Bronx borough president, BLA was one of the first high schools in the Bronx wired for the Internet.

The students contribute to the emphasis on academic achievement. In 1998, a student court was implemented as a means of self-discipline. Under the supervision of an adult, all students serve as jurors on a rotating basis. The students and staff collaborated to determine what would constitute a violation of the school community. Anyone in the school—staff or student—may give out violations for any breach of conduct, whether it is related to discipline, being late, being rude or disrespectful, being out of the dress code, defacing the building, or violating some other standard. Students with violations are given a "court date" and must appear before the jury to explain what happened. The students themselves decided that failing more than one subject should be considered a violation, particularly since tutoring is widely available and teachers are in the building at virtually all hours to help students with their courses.

Richard Baresch, a participant in the board's Principal of the Day program, came to BLA by the luck of the draw in 1995. He has continued his participation through the establishment of scholarships, additional financing for programs, and hiring graduates. Four attorneys are on the teaching staff; they have developed a curriculum theme of law as a way to promote leadership in public life and to integrate many academic skills. Each year the school sponsors trips to the traditional Black colleges and to schools throughout the region so that students can gain a better understanding of what is available to them in terms of higher education. And then there's the dress code: white shirts, with blue, gray, or black trousers or skirts. Ties are required for the boys; Bloomingdale's has contributed ties so those who forget can borrow one for the day. In a noteworthy gesture of solidarity, the principal and many of the faculty adhere to the dress code. The school has gained the public's attention: 4,000 students applied for the 125 available seats in the ninth grade in 1998.

The key to this remarkable enterprise is the school's principal, Katherine Kelly, and the able and dedicated staff she has gathered around her to provide the very best education to the students. The entire focus of the school is on learning and education. The grown-ups are clearly in charge. Antisocial behavior is simply not tolerated. Pride in one's self, one's school, and one's community is stressed. Hard work is the order of the day. Academic achievement is expected. Admission to BLA is by the board's "educational option" process. Students wishing to attend the school designate it in the standard articulation process used in middle schools throughout the city. Half of the entering students are selected randomly by computer from all applicants to provide a broad range of academic ability; the other half are selected by the school staff. It took weeks to comb through the 4,000 applicants for the 1998 entering class (the process is not computerized at the school level), with staff placing a priority on attendance, reading scores, the presence of a sibling already in the school, and recommendations from the middle school.

What is important to realize is that nothing done inside BLA is in any way contrary to or an exception to the general high school policies of the New York City Board of Education. The quality of education and the educational environment at BLA are available within all existing regulations of the board. What is special about BLA is the absolute political will to make those regulations work to their limit for the sake of the students. The staff has the full support of South Bronx Churches and the Bronx superintendent of high schools to do whatever it takes to create a good school. For example, the United Federation of Teachers' contract allows for many school-based options if supported by 75 percent of the teachers in the school.[13] BLA faculty voted for a school-based hiring policy which does not allow automatic seniority transfers when staff openings occur. This allows for substantial transmission of the school's culture to any incoming faculty member. Vision and commitment to a particular quality and style of education must override tradition, the ease of following standard practice, and the inevitable bottom-seeking behavior of huge bureaucracies with histories of low accountability.

Measures of Success. The Bronx Leadership Academy was established to provide a rigorous academic program that would prepare all students to pass the Regents exams and attend college. Whereas the college admission rate is high, performance on Regents exams and the SAT is disappointing, and these scores are still below the city average. Most of the students entering BLA come from districts in which a third or more of the students do not read at grade level; thus, current expectations are higher than they have been prepared for. The staff of BLA is not complacent or resigned, however, and various programs have been instituted to overcome educational deficiencies. As each year passes, student scores are expected to increase. The administration and staff are willing to be held accountable for their results.

Good progress is being made in certain areas. The state has recently set new standards that 90 percent of a school's eleventh grade students must meet in reading, writing, and mathematics. In the academic year 1995–96, BLA had nearly achieved the new state standards in reading (89.8 percent) and writing (87.8 percent), but was still low in math (77.6 percent). Therefore, all students began receiving double math instruction. Moreover, BLA is serious about students' learning to speak and write English, refusing to see LEP (limited English proficiency) as a permanent way of life. In 1995, 1996, and 1997, the percentage of LEP students achieving English proficiency was higher than the citywide average. In response to lower than average SAT scores, in 1998 BLA started Latin instruction for ninth-graders, taught by a Ph.D. candidate in classics from Fordham University.

The results from the first marking period of 1998–99 are encouraging. The percentage of students achieving the honor roll (80–89 average) has more than tripled, from 8 percent at the end of the 1997–98 school year to 26 percent now. Similarly, the number of students achieving averages between 70 and 80 increased from 13 percent in 1997–98 to 27 percent in the first period of 1998–99. Fifty-five percent of the student body is passing all classes; 22 percent are failing one class, and 23 percent are failing more than one. Those who are failing are targeted for special support. Is BLA at its desired level academically? No, not yet, but the school personnel have implemented and will continue to implement programs to reach their goals.

Parents: Still an Unmobilized Resource. Parental involvement at BLA, while significantly higher than in many high schools in terms of school volunteers and accessibility, is still far below the potential envisioned by school staff and South Bronx Churches. The original by-laws of the parent association, adopted in the first year of the school, state a quorum of five for conducting business. While this is horrifying enough in a small school such as BLA, it is fairly standard for even much larger schools to have a parent association quorum of less than ten. The expectation in high school is low parental participation, and this expectation is usually fulfilled.

The problem is rooted in a basic lack of understanding. In particular, no one knows exactly what "parental involvement" means. Involvement is generally considered a good thing, but how it works and what it is meant to achieve are questions that usually remain unasked. Obviously parents are important in helping to create the environment in the home that fosters learning, and clearly parents are important in helping with a wide assortment of tasks within the school. Parents should care about their children's education, but how does this translate into action? Bake sale fundraising for school trips, chaperoning dances, signing report cards, getting the kids to school on time—all are important common tasks of parents. But, then what? If, as seems logically correct, parents are key stakeholders in education, what does that mean?

In New York City, as mentioned above, the sanctioned parent associations are bound by the *Blue Book,* a manual devised by the board to provide "legitimate" parental involvement in the school. In labor organizing, this would be anathema, the equivalent to a company in-house union. The distribution of power within New York City's educational system is dominated by the teachers' union (the United Federation of Teachers, or UFT), the principals' union (the Council of Supervisors and Administrators, or CSA), and—though to a lesser degree than previously—unions representing the custodians and other service workers. These are the groups that organize to shape most of what happens in the school. The groups wield tremendous power in the state legislature: in the first six months of 1996 the UFT reported $900,000 in lobbying expenses and political contributions. The UFT in New York City has an annual budget of $68 million, of which $8 million (12 percent) comes from the Board of Education.[14]

There is simply nothing comparable for parents, no union with any clout and no financing. The Board of Education allocation for the parent association at BLA is $100 annually. Because the rules for parent associations are written by "management," it is clear that accommodation of parents is the goal, rather than inclusion based upon an independent base of power. Even when a nod is given to the Presidents' Council (the presidents of all parent associations within a district), the fact remains that the presidents of parent associations are presidents of groups that require a quorum of five to ten out of a membership of hundreds or thousands to operate. School-based parent associations are not designed for power; they are neither representative, democratic, nor accountable to a constituency, and the heads of these powerless associations are not, by extension, either. A constitution does not make an organization: organizing and relationships make an organization.

The issue of parental involvement at BLA, then, is not simply a local issue, but a systematic failing of the New York City Board of Education. SBC has proposed a different model of parental involvement that has grown out of years of work by the Texas affiliates of the Industrial Areas Foundation. The Texas program, the Alliance Schools Initiative, is a joint project of the Texas IAF affiliates and the Texas State Education Department. One hundred forty-six schools are now part of the Alliance Schools Initiative. Although test scores are only one method of evaluation, of the 89 Alliance schools serving over 60,000 students in 1996, nearly 90 percent increased the percentage of students who passed all sections of the state tests. The increase in 71.3 percent of the schools was higher than the state average increase.[15] In 1997, the Texas state legislature committed $8 million to support Alliance school campuses and to support the innovations developed through their interaction with the local IAF organizations. At the heart of the Alliance Schools Initiative, as defined by Dennis Shirley in his recent book, *Community Organizing for Urban School Reform,* is the engagement of parents "as citizens in the fullest sense—[as] change agents who can transform inner city schools."[16]

After four years of watching the *Blue Book* approach to building a parents' association falter and fail, SBC and the staff of BLA have just embarked on a new approach. With support from the Donors Educational Collaborative and the Public Education Association, SBC has hired a full-time organizer to build a model of parental "engagement," not parental "involvement." The organizer has begun a three-month campaign of individual meetings with staff, parents, and community leaders to find leaders, develop relationships, and exchange views and ideas related to issues in the school. As leaders surface, meetings of small groups of ten to fifteen will be held to find which issues are most important to the parents, and to develop an agenda for action on these issues. SBC expects that the organizer will know and be known by at least 150 of the parents through individual meetings, and even more through the small group meetings. A coherent issue agenda and a range of ideas, approaches, and viewpoints will have been developed, not through the ideas of the five or six who are the nominal heads of a typical parents' association, but through hundreds of give-and-take conversations on what is important about BLA. A later step will involve Neighborhood Walks, whereby parents, teachers, and community members go door to door to solicit views on community issues that affect both the school and the broader community. Eventually, just as the parents, teachers, and staff develop an agenda for internal issues in the school, the school and community residents will develop an agenda for external issues. The effort is to link school and community again, and to engage both the school and the neighborhood in collective action that will improve education.

This is a work in progress. SBC, however, has also begun one-on-ones with principals of intermediate schools in the South Bronx, looking for principals who would welcome a new approach to parent organizing. When a principal is open to it, SBC will attempt to raise funds, along with the principal, to develop an Alliance School prototype for New York City. Despite the high expectations for school-based management committees, as long as the educational establishment in New York City sees parents as passive participants, with only a consultative role, parents will continue to be an under-mobilized force in the reformation of New York City education.[17]

Pressures Against Success

Although by most measures, BLA is a proven success, there are current and pending challenges that threaten the very nature of the place.

Enrollment. The school was intentionally designed for a maximum enrollment of 550. This small size allows for students to know one another and for each student to be known personally by faculty, and it also makes the school eligible for the addition of staff, including administrators, teachers, and guidance personnel to provide better student-staff ratios. Limiting size was also a factor in selecting the site. The square-footage allotment per student required a building of about fifty thousand square feet for a student body of 500 to 550. SBC knew that if the building they found was significantly larger, they would be under continuous pressure to increase enrollment.

Even with these precautions, however, there is pressure on BLA to increase its size. The 1998 registration was 613. Although this is somewhat over capacity, many schools in the Bronx are at 150 percent capacity, and so BLA is seen as an "undercrowded school," which can easily accommodate more students. This pressure to pack in more students raises an important question: what is the point of creating innovative, smaller schools if Board of Education policies work to undo the educational environment that makes them special and to turn them into replicas of the larger schools, which are better known for their problems than their successes?

Arbitrary Assignment of Students Based on Political Criteria. SBC would be one of the first groups in the city to demand quality public education for all students, but recent decisions by the mayor and chancellor to eliminate special schools for emotionally troubled students are potentially damaging, both for the students themselves and for the schools to which they are "mainstreamed." For example, BLA is a target school for the transfer of so-called 'SIE-7' students (for Special Instructional Environment). These students, while not having academic problems, are prone to emotional outbreaks. The original plan was for BLA to receive ten SIE-7 students, who would not be selected until well into the academic year—which would make any attempt at normal integration impossible. The students and their parents would have participated in none of the orientation sessions, the dress code would be a surprise, and the students themselves would be behind the BLA students, whose first weeks are spent on reviewing work that was part of the summer assignment. They would miss the all-important first days when the faculty and staff set the tone of the entire year.

Fortunately the principal of BLA was able to convince the board to make substantial revisions in their plan in order to make the inclusion of SIE-7 students as smooth as possible. Only four SIE-7 students were assigned to BLA, and they were enrolled at the start of school. What is instructive in this example is that the original decision to implement the SIE-7 transfers was made with incomplete analysis. Only one part of the picture was considered: how to close special schools and mainstream students. The impact on the receiving schools, or even on the students themselves, was not considered. Students are not things or pieces to be moved around at political whim. BLA has turned out to be a good place for its SIE-7 students, but if the original plan had been implemented, the situation could have been very different.

Budget. The non-personnel budget for BLA was $40,000—less than $80 per student—for the 1998–99 academic year.[18] This includes state allocations for textbooks ($12,096), as well as local allocations for science equipment ($2,549), software ($899), and general education ($8,153). Coincident with the budget is a board-ordered switch to world history from area studies, and with the switch, new texts are needed; a single copy costs $35. It is ludicrous to run a school on such a shoestring. It is only through the external fundraising ability of the principal, various corporate leaders and corporations, and to a lesser extent SBC that the school has adequate resources to function. Obviously the question of budget is not unique to BLA but is a systemwide travesty.

Complicating the budget shortage is its restriction. Funds may only be used for designated purposes; there is no freedom on the part of the principal to move funds from one category to another. Although the principal of a high school, even a small school, is analogous to a CEO of a $5–$10 million corporation, the principal has no discretion with regard to the budget. While this might make sense to a system dedicated to central control, it does restrict local flexibility and innovation. School-based budgets would be a worthy improvement, even with budgets as tiny as $40,000 for 500 students. The principal is the front line: he or she knows where resources should go.

Another budgetary practice of the board is a closed system of vendors. The reason for this is obvious, in that it limits the potential for corruption and has the potential of delivering the best prices for goods and services systemwide. However, the lack of competition does allow some prices (on books and computers, for example) to be available through board-sanctioned vendors at a cost significantly higher than the market price. Again, the principal's hands are tied. When every penny counts, the principals should be able to make the best deals they can for their schools.

The Heart of the Matter: Accountability for Education Results

Although the statistics from BLA are encouraging relative to other Bronx high schools, and even throughout the city, many of the students are poorly prepared when they enter, and few graduate competitively at the highest level. At best, graduating classes from BLA will number 125–150. While educational "oases" are wonderful, they dramatize, rather than diminish, the need for systemic reform.

The changes in state education law in 1996[19] gave the New York City schools' chancellor new powers to control local districts and to replace principals for persistent educational failure. Not until September 1998 was a definition of "persistent educational failure" forthcoming from the chancellor. Newly promulgated evaluation standards for principals state that the principals must have a plan to improve educational standards, but do not hold the principals to account for implementation of the plan or achieving the standards.[20] Newly set standards for "essential elements of exemplary schools" include monitoring of student achievement, collection of data, program development based on the data, distribution of diagnostic information to teachers, students, and parents from the data, and organizing student groupings based on the diagnostics. There is not one word about having students achieve some measurable level of ability in reading or mathematics.[21]

For the two years, the Public Education Association [PEA] and the metropolitan area Industrial Areas Foundation [IAF] affiliates urged the chancellor to use his powers, particularly to hold principals accountable for results in their schools. The PEA-IAF definition of persistent educational failure is robust: persistent educational failure exists in any school when, under the same principal, reading scores have failed to reach 35 percent for five or more years. The PEA identified 14 school districts throughout the city in which persistent educational failure exists in the majority of the district's schools. PEA calls these districts "Dead Zones."

These districts, mostly in the Bronx, Harlem, Washington Heights, East New York, and Bedford-Stuyvesant, are attended primarily by Black and Latino students. Many of the districts have been a dumping ground for what the chancellor himself calls the "Dance of the Lemons."[22] All of the districts commonly sending students to BLA are in Dead Zones. Although some have gained marginally in reading scores in recent years, the Dead Zones are still far below the city average. At the recent rate of increase, it will take seven years for Dead Zone schools to reach the present citywide average reading levels. Using as a model the widely acclaimed "COMPSTAT" approach credited with reducing crime in New York City through holding captains of police precincts accountable for crime in their precincts, the PEA and IAF have urged a similar approach in schools with persistent educational failure. Both the chancellor and the CSA [Council of Supervisors and Administrators] have rejected this suggestion out of hand. Instead, the chancellor fought a losing battle in Albany to eliminate principal tenure, claiming that tenure, rather than performance, was the problem. At this moment the chancellor has the power to remove the principal from any school. Chancellor Crew chose, however, not to exercise this in the case of persistent educational failure. Admittedly, these are hard calls, but until a systemwide demand for accountability and such standards as are exemplified in schools such as the Bronx Leadership Academy, too many children will fail to receive the education they require for adult success. Creating a good school is not magic nor does it occur by chance: it takes firmness of purpose, a commitment to education, a willingness to make hard political decisions, and the good judgment to eliminate what does not work and to use what does. It takes leadership. While SBC and BLA can provide this kind of opportunity for five to six hundred students, a much larger effort is necessary.

This gets back to the question of "culture." The current Board of Education culture is still inherently bureaucratic and controlled by the interests of the teachers' and principals' unions rather than by the interests of the students. Occasional openings in this culture allow for the creation of schools like the Bronx Leadership Academy. What is required is a dramatic opening of the culture throughout the system.

What's Ahead?

Recognizing the need for the same kind of approach in lower grades as in the Bronx Leadership Academy, SBC leaders worked for two years with District 9 to create a middle school. Until recently, the lack of involvement by potential staff of the school and the lack of an available building have thwarted this effort. In October 1998, the district identified a potential site for a "school within a school" and several middle school administrators have joined the team working to create the new school.

On another front, the Bronx superintendent of high schools expressed interest in making BLA a grade 7–12 school. SBC and the current school staff have jumped at the opportunity. Available land exists immediately behind BLA, and the owner is interested in the site's being used for a school. SBC has relationships with alternative funding sources for school construction and with reputable private construction firms interested in doing the work in the most timely and cost-effective manner. SBC and BLA have formed a new Education Task Force, and meetings are beginning to make the middle school a reality.

Again, it is the opening of culture, not a Board of Education systemwide initiative that is at work. A few more children will be provided a decent shot at education. Most of their peers will continue to be trapped in Dead Zone schools. Glacial improvements will be celebrated. Throughout the city, in spite of tremendous odds, individual principals have shown what it takes to "turn a school around," and in some districts there has been significant improvement. What is needed is more of that same level of commitment to "turn a system around." The local energy for the transformation exists. What is lacking is central leadership. In this, the most politically willful of cities, it is nonetheless the lack of political will that leaves the schools so far behind.

Notes

1. Jim Rooney, *Organizing the South Bronx* (Albany: State University of New York, 1995).

2. Industrial Areas Foundation, *IAF: The First 50 Years—Organizing for Change* (San Francisco: Sapir Press, 1990).

3. Special Commissioner of Investigation for the New York City School District, "Preliminary Report: Corruption in Community School District 9," 1996.

4. Public Education Association, *Futures Denied: Concentrated Failure in the New York City Public School System* (New York, 1997).

5. Bernard M. Loomer, "Two Forms of Power," *Criterion* 15, no. 1 (1976).

6. The Board of Education resolution officially chartering the Bronx Leadership Academy was passed on February 17, 1993.

7. Texas Industrial Areas Foundation, *Alliance Schools Concept Paper* (Austin: Interfaith Education Fund, 1997); Dennis Shirley, *Community Organizing and Urban School Reform* (Austin: University of Texas, 1997).

8. New York City Board of Education, *Parents Associations and the Schools: The Blue Book,* June 17, 1998.

9. U.S. Census, 1990; Citizens Housing and Planning Council, *Preliminary Assessment of Community Redevelopment in the South Bronx* (New York, 1998).

10. Special Commissioner of Investigation for the New York City School District, "Background Investigation into Board of Education Leased Properties," September 1996.

11. Leanna Stiefel et al., *The Effects of Size of Student Body, School Costs, and Performance in New York City High Schools* (New York: Institute for Social Policy, Robert F. Wagner Graduate School of Public Service, New York University, 1998).

12. New York State Education Department, *Summary of Findings, Bronx Leadership Academy High School,* March 16, 1998.

13. *Board of Education of the City School District of the City of New York and United Federation of Teachers, Local 2, American Federation of Teachers, AFL-CIO Covering Teachers,* October 16, 1995–November 15, 2000. Article 8, sec. B.

14. Sherry Giles, Public Education Association (unpublished report).

15. Texas Industrial Areas Foundation, *Alliance Schools Concept Paper.*

16. Shirley, *Community Organizing and Urban School Reform.*

17. Andrew Page, "Crew's Control," *Brooklyn Bridge* 4, no. 1 (1998).

18. New York City Board of Education, "FY 99 Preliminary OTPS Allocation to High Schools. Bronx Leadership Academy 72X525," 1998.

19. *An Act to Amend the Education Law,* December 17, 1996 (S. 1).

20. New York City Board of Education, "Principal Performance Review," 1998.

21. New York City Board of Education, "New York City Performance Assessment in Schools Systemwide (PASS)—Essential Elements of Exemplary Schools," 1997.

22. "Lemon Tree Not So Pretty," *New York Daily News,* October 31, 1997.

18

Educational Programs and the Local Community Power Structure*

editor's introduction:

Dismantling a 20-Year-Old Bilingual Program. The case study is about the dismantling of a local school's nationally recognized, 20-year-old bilingual education program. Such programs have existed across the country to accommodate the numerous language-minority children that are part of U.S. schools. Whether such programs help to integrate these children into the educational mainstream—and therefore provide a strong foundation for their future success in the school system and in society—has been one of the hot topics of debate in public education.

Because of its local setting, the case study shows the close relationship between this education debate and the power structure within a local community—an industrial city in Pennsylvania (anonymously named "Steel Town"). In this case, the community's dominant, White majority has seemingly ignored the needs of an important Puerto Rican segment of the community, both by dismantling the bilingual program and by busing Latino and Latina students to schools outside of their neighborhood.

Such an outcome was made possible by the fact that, by design, the governance of the country's public schools has largely been a local, not state or federal, affair. School systems are overseen by school boards, in turn usually elected to their

---

*Soto, Lourdes Diaz. (1997). "Media Accounts." In *Language, Culture, and Power: Bilingual Families and the Struggle for Quality Education* (pp. 65–81). Albany: State University of New York Press.

positions by their communities. Heated policy controversy is not uncommon at the local level, and the present selection covers one such controversy. The case study also shows you how educational issues can be embedded within a community's history, culture, and politics (for a related case, see Selection 4 of this anthology).

Relevance of Case Studies: Bringing Multiple Sources of Evidence to Bear. The selection is from a book that represents the entire case study. The author drew from varied sources of evidence, including participant observation, ethnographic interviews, a pilot study of a group of informants, relevant documents (three key documents appear in the book as appendices), and an analysis of local newspaper accounts. Such breadth of evidence enables the author to intersperse local dialogue with detailed description of specific events as well as different perspectives or opinions about the controversy.

Possibly because of the diversity of evidence, the overall effect differs from case studies that might only have relied on one type of evidence. For instance, case studies based on direct observations tend to focus intensely on the set of events that have been observed—but correspondingly cannot easily cover events that were not directly observed. At possibly the opposite extreme, case studies based mainly on documentation tend to cover a wider scope of events but are seemingly remote with regard to the actual behavior of specific people. In contrast, the present selection, by using a variety of evidence, produces a blended effect: a close, if not intimate, feeling for a local community and specific individuals within the community, combined with an understanding of the broader set of events that marked the controversy.

The "Blue E"

Listeners heard about the "Blue E" on the local radio station. The "Blue E" referred to a proposed city ordinance encouraging local merchants to post a "Blue E" on their doorways to signify their support for the English-only ordinance. The ordinance provided store owners with the ability to price goods based upon the English language proficiency of their prospective buyer. For example, if the store clerk detected an accent or felt that the buyer's English was not up to par, they were expected to pay an additional 10 percent to 20 percent on their purchase since this signified additional paperwork and expense for the merchant.

Supporters of this ordinance called the radio talk show, expressing views such as: "Send all the spics back to their country"; "This is America . . . for whites only"; "Our city was better off without all this trash"; "English is the language my grandparents had to learn"; "One state should be set aside for these people . . . but not Pennsylvania." Only one caller opposed the city ordinance and felt that diverse languages would enhance the tourism industry and the economic well-being of the city. Many of the callers communicated in non-standard American English varieties and dialects. The xenophobic and racist fears described by Crawford (1992) were expressed by most of the callers to the "Blue E" radio talk show.

The manager of the local radio station assured the community that comments and discussions centering on the "Blue E" were a media hoax. "The community need not be alarmed by that discussion," he stated. "Besides, Mr. Jones no longer works for the station and is currently residing in New Jersey." It could be argued that one isolated incident would not be responsible for creating a climate of distrust. Yet to piece many similar incidents together is to gain insights into the many faces of racism and the cumulative effects of oppression in this community. Ultimately, for example, the companion city of Post Town passed an English-only city ordinance while in Steel Town the bilingual program became the center of controversy.

I analyzed the local newspaper accounts (from 1992 to 1993) that reported information on Steel Town's bilingual controversy. These accounts helped uncover how the particular players brought their own meanings to the community context. In many ways the political battles were partially fought through the media as the different players rallied support for their position. Three sets of players represented three major perspectives: English-only proponents, bilingual proponents, and neutral parties. Included in this analysis is a public meeting with over 650 participants.

English-only proponents were comprised of the school superintendent, school board decisionmakers, and third-generation immigrant citizens who called for the dismantling of the bilingual program. *Bilingual education proponents* were comprised of school personnel, community organizations, community leaders (including clergy), national/local experts, and bilingual families struggling to maintain the bilingual program; and *neutral parties* were comprised of editors, Raggae School parents, institutions of higher learning, common citizens, and a mediation-type organization that sought to maintain an impartial position.

A timeline of the events will guide the reader in understanding how the circumstances evolved in the Steel Town school district.

Account of Events

March 1992

(a) the school board initiates a one-way busing system of 150 mostly Latino/a children from their South Side home school to a second school and ultimately to a third school

(b) a petition drive is initiated by bilingual families requesting a school for the South Side children and voicing concerns about the education of Latino/a children

November 1992

(c) school-appointed committee report entitled "Bilingual Program Recommendations" supporting the existing bilingual program is released

(d) public attacks on the bilingual are initiated by the school district superintendent, including the document entitled "Superintendent's Response to Bilingual Committee's Report," and some school board members

(e) Steel Town's Action Committee petitions the Office of Civil Rights

(f) the school board decides to delay discussions about the bilingual program until after the holidays

(g) opinions are disseminated in the media indicating support for the bilingual program from experts, educators, families, and children; and support for the school superintendent from school board and selected individuals

(h) the space allocation needs to the school district are discussed as a part of the bilingual program's viability

January 1993

(i) the school board holds an open meeting on the bilingual program with over 650 community participants and security guards

February 1993

(j) the school board votes to dismantle the bilingual program

(k) the school initiates an English-immersion planning committee

June 1993

(l) the report of the school district's English-immersion program titled "A Ticket for Tomorrow" is revealed

November 1993

(m) the school board votes unanimously to demolish and rebuild the Raggae School located on the West Side of Steel Town (not the South Side).

The district's choice of construction projects can be seen as a part of the historical context. In 1969, for example, the district agreed to sell a South Side elementary school to a local corporation. The district talked about using the $1.43 million proceeds from the sale of construction of a new school for the South Side, which was approved by the court. Years later there was no new school. Instead, the district sought and received permission from the courts to use the money for other construction projects.

Mr. Berrios, a Puerto Rican doctoral candidate at a local institution of higher learning, summarized his perceptions of the educational controversies:

> When I lived in Puerto Rico, a friend told me about the marvelous schools and educational system the United States has. Moreover, the richness in ethnicity and bilingualism was presented as an integrated fact within the school system. After living in Steel Town for six years and participating as a father of a school-age kid, I regret to say that my friend was wrong; nothing of what he stated happens in Steel Town. Maybe this is personal, but my school district sleeps. In Steel Town the current crisis in education has been defined by color and tone. The words "diversity" and "bilingual" have been used (as) an appropriate tool to politically and aggressively alienate a community that is culturally different. The school district has decided to step backwards and ignore that language, born of culture and ethnicity, which gives voice to the hearts and minds of the individuals who speak it. The educational crisis is characterized by the common causes of power in politics and a clear defiant challenge toward the citizens that do not have access to play the political game as they do.

The "political game" Mr. Berrios described was initiated by the school district superintendent and school board members, who mandated and implemented unilateral decisions impacting the education of bilingual children. Superintendent/board (busing, space allocation, resource allocations, dismantling of the program) led to the political struggle that permeated and divided the community. Bilingual families continued to express frustrations about the quality of education their children were receiving.

The historically "silent ones," the bilingual families of Steel Town, entered the political arena. They first protested decisions to bus their children, requested an additional school in the South Side to alleviate crowding, and opposed the dismantling of a twenty-year-old, award-winning bilingual program. The families' struggle for a quality education included initiating petition drives; expressing concerns at school board meetings; holding meetings with local and state citizens; contacting local, state, and national experts in the bilingual education field; filing a complaint with the Office of Civil Rights; and running for political office. The major concern expressed by families and community leaders was the educational welfare of bilingual (Latino/a) children.

The March 1992 petition drive against one-way busing garnered over seven hundred signatures with a call for "no more silence" ("se terminó el silencio"). The families asked that a neighborhood school be built for the children of the South Side. They expressed concern about busing young children, overcrowding, and continuing demographic evidence showing increasing numbers of culturally and linguistically diverse children. They indicated that they were willing to temporarily compromise their request if portable classrooms were placed at one of the local schools. The school board, nevertheless, voted to bus the children from their home school to a second school in the fall and ultimately to a third school in the spring. Don Jacinto expressed his sentiments about the school district's continued disregard for bilingual/Puerto Rican children: "build additions to Stony Garden, tear down and rebuild the Raggae School, but can't build a school on the South Side. Why? Because that would be for Puerto Ricans."

The school district appointed a committee comprised of monolingual and bilingual teachers, school administrators, and community leaders to examine the efficacy of the bilingual program. The committee's thirty-four-page report indicated that, with some modifications, the bilingual program should be maintained. The school superintendent and members of the school board, however, publicly attacked their own program. An article in the local paper (Martin, November 10, 1992) reports the events:

> One thing is clear: Change is coming to the bilingual program in the Steel Town school. But what kind of change—and how it will impact the program's nearly 1,200 students—only grew cloudier after last night's Steel Town Area School Board meeting. Ten months after it began assessing bilingual education, a committee last night recommended some changes but generally urged the board to keep the current model that groups Spanish-speaking students at a few sites and gradually assimilates them into the regular education program by high school.
>
> But the committee's 34-page report drew an immediate challenge and criticism from an unlikely source: the school superintendent. "I have had and continue to have a deep concern about the length of time we keep children in this program and out of regular education," he said. "I do not see a need to maintain any one particular ethnic group's culture via the school system."
>
> He heard no dispute from the board.
>
> In a possible sign of the future, the directors almost uniformly expressed concerns about the program and recommendations. "I think we need to make a concerted effort to get the students out of the program as soon as possible," said director Johnson. About 94% of this year's bilingual program students speak Spanish; the remaining students speak a total of 18 other languages.
>
> The board vice president called the current model "overkill." The school superintendent said he has his own recommendation for the bilingual program, but that he will present them to the board at another time.

Another newspaper article (Schnur, November 10, 1992) also documented the superintendent's and the school board's public comments at this time. The headline read, "[School superintendent] criticizes bilingual program," and continued:

> The Steel Town superintendent told the school board Monday the district's bilingual program doesn't move students into regular English-only classes quickly enough, despite findings in a report that mostly supports the current system. "We've got to throw them into the pool. They'll swim," the school superintendent said. "With a little help from us they'll swim."
>
> On Monday, the board was presented with a report from a committee of community members, teachers, and administrators that supports the current system with some modifications. . . . But the school superintendent disagreed with the report. The superintendent advocates a system where students go directly into classes taught in English by bilingual teachers who can translate something into Spanish if a student is confused . . . while the board vice president indicated that "he agreed with the school superintendent '100 percent.'"

A local Spanish-speaking newsletter found humor in the superintendent's remarks, disseminating a cartoon depicting the superintendent literally "throwing" children off a dock and into a lake. His statements became a "red herring," a clear signal to the bilingual program proponents about his intent. His perspective was translated as supportive of a "sink or swim" philosophy outlawed by legal statutes, including the U.S. Supreme Court (Lau v. Nichols, 1974). I found it intriguing that the school superintendent's ethnic origin is Portuguese. It was not possible to obtain information about how he feels about his own ethnicity, language knowledge, and his family's immigration process. My repeated requests for meetings with the superintendent were denied. I suspected that he clearly understood my opposition to his philosophy and was reluctant to discuss issues dealing with bilingualism.

The bilingual controversy was burning brightly with supporters and opponents. Graduate students in a summer course I taught examined the controversy. The students collected and critiqued the ongoing media discussions. We invited and informally interviewed reporters, community representatives, and school district leaders well versed on the bilingual controversy.

I have not shared those interviews here since complete confidentiality was assured all of our invited guests. My students continued their own fact finding, however, and reported many more community groups and individuals who supported the bilingual program than opposed it. My students indicated that the opponents—the local superintendent, school board members, and several individuals—were ultimately the privileged power brokers.

Newspaper reporters who tried to make sense of the controversy included the following:

> Both sides in the debate over the future of bilingual education in city schools say they have the best interest of the children at heart. The superintendent and some members of the school board say the Latino students need to learn English faster. The Latino community, bilingual teachers, and school administrators say the current program is working just fine. (Schnur, November 14, 1992)

After the Bilingual Committee's report, the school superintendent announced the four options he planned to offer the school board: (1) accept the recommendations of the Bilingual Committee; (2) accept the school superintendent's philosophy and develop a new bilingual program; (3) develop a pilot program to test how effectively the school superintendent's ideas work; or (4) hire an objective consultant to evaluate the district's program.

The school superintendent indicated to the press that he was "surprised" at the Latinos' response, but that he had a great deal of support for his position.

> "I'm surprised. I know it's a very emotional issue, and I know there are very strong advocates for it," said the school superintendent. "I know there are people in our community who don't agree with the program."
>
> The school superintendent said he has turned the prospect of a civil rights complaint over to the district's solicitor, who was unavailable for comment yesterday. (Hall, November 14, 1992)

> At the next school board meeting, the school superintendent described his program plans, indicating that he proposed an intensive program that would have children learning English in a year, if possible. He could not say how that would be done. "I'm not an expert," he said. "That's for people to design."
>
> In other business, the school superintendent received a 5.5 percent raise with a one percent merit bonus, raising his salary to $95,024. (Schnur, November 17, 1992)

The following day the school superintendent confessed his (lack of) expertise in the field of bilingual education: "I'm not an expert on bilingual education," he said. "I just know that we need to shorten the time line of the program" (Snyder, November 18, 1992).

In subsequent newspaper articles the week of November 20, monolinguals' community support for the superintendent's position appeared with the typical "when my grandparents came to this country" argument, reflecting third-generation immigrant perspectives:

When my grandparents came to this country from their native land, they did not speak English. They did not expect anyone to cater to them and change everything into their native tongue. In fact, they did not even teach their children their native language; they believed their children were Americans and so should speak the language of America. Perhaps it is time for people who intend to make America their homeland to adopt this philosophy also.

A local school principal interviewed by reporters indicated his perspective:

The district has no statistics comparing the Latino bilingual program and the non-Latino program. "Stony Garden Elementary School didn't have a teacher to give English lessons to its German and Arab students until early this month," the school principal said. The school principal thinks Latino students should take classes in English (only) rather than Spanish. "I'm supportive of what the superintendent is saying," said the school principal, a Greek-American. He said he learned English more quickly by being immersed in the language. "We got by," he said. (Schnur, November 21, 1992)

An outsider and invited guest at a local college was also willing to speak to the issue by attempting to draw comparisons among ethnically diverse populations:

William Andersen isn't sure how well bilingual education is working. (The) Director of (a) national office spoke about bilingual education facing the Steel Town Area School District. "The Asian community has found ways to succeed through cultural barriers by simply working harder at it. . . . I think we must find a way to create a support system to encourage the same results for the Hispanic and African American communities." (Williams, January 24, 1993)

Supporters of the bilingual program and the Bilingual Committee's report included community organizations, bilingual families, community leaders, and experts in the field of bilingual education. The Community Council, a grassroots organization, was concerned with educational issues impacting language-minority speakers. The president of the council supported the committee's report:

These are recommendations that were thoughtfully, thoroughly discussed by teachers who instruct these students and many of whom have had special training in educating second language students. We believe their recommendations are sound and worth listening to. (Schnur, November 13, 1992)

The organization denounced the superintendent for his "negative comments regarding the bilingual education program and his belief that the use of Spanish as a language of instruction is un-American." The superintendent was also criticized for his support of an "immersion" approach that expected students who speak little or no English to be taught in English, thinking they would learn the language faster.

> The school superintendent objects to the teaching of the culture of Hispanic students even when they comprise 21.4 percent of our school population, and indications are that this number will increase. (Kupper, November 13, 1992)

Steel Town's Action Committee, an advocacy group, indicated that they were prepared to file a federal civil rights complaint if the district changed the bilingual program. They stated:

> Our organization takes exception with his [superintendent's] comments that our schools need not teach Latino culture. Since by the superintendent's own admission the bilingual education program works, well, then the Steel Town Action Committee is prepared to insure that the civil rights of our Latino youth are not violated by eliminating a portion of a program solely based on the biases toward a particular ethnic group, in this case Latino children. (Hall, November 14, 1992)

The complaint to the Office of Civil Rights became a reality:

> Latino leaders living in the Steel Town Area School district have filed a complaint with the federal Office for Civil Rights, charging some members of the district administration with illegal and discriminatory practices. "It is our belief that the district through the actions of some of the members of the present administration have engaged in acts that are morally indefensible and clearly illegal. . . . This is indicative of the view that somehow schools on the Southside and students who go to them are less than anyone else."
>
> The Action Committee is asking the Philadelphia OCR [Office of Civil Rights] to conduct an independent investigation. The complaint was filed Thursday. The committee was represented by (an) attorney of Steel Town. The Committee cited the U.S. Constitution, the Equal Opportunity Education Act of 1974, the 1964 Civil Rights Act, Title VI, the Lau v. Nichols case guidelines, and federal case law as standards to measure the district's alleged shortcomings. (Politi, November 16, 1992)

The issues cited in the OCR complaint included unequal treatment of students, harassment, disproportionate suspensions, the "proposed dismantling of the bilingual program linked to the school superintendent's personal bias against primary language instruction and to not wanting to provide equitable space in the Southside schools which are operating at near functional capacities," and mistreatment of the 1,200 bilingual students (94% Latino/a).

The night the committee's report was presented, the bilingual coordinator stated:

> A lot of nurturing takes place. . . . The committee really believes this is the best program. . . . Studies show children need five to seven years before they speak a new language well enough to do well in academic classes in that language. (Schnur, November 14, 1992)

Bilingual experts also came to the defense of the bilingual children and families:

> James Lyons, a national proponent for bilingual education, also slammed the school superintendent's proposal yesterday. "I don't know of a single educational authority that has said it's even a plausible goal for a child in a year," said Lyons, the executive director of the National Association for Bilingual Education. "A year is just poppy-cock." He said the district should continue with bilingual education classes. "Students who receive instruction in their native language learn English better, and they do not lose valuable time in other subjects, such as math and science," he said.
>
> "In the school district of Annville, students in bilingual classes drop out of school less than students in any other program in the district," said the Annville district program coordinator. "The dropout rate is about 5 percent in the bilingual program," he said. "Students who participate in the bilingual program perform equal to or better than other students on standardized tests," Lyons said. "It's certainly proven itself in this district." (Snyder, November 18, 1992)

At the time, I was an associate professor of education at a local university and indicated to the press that much research supports having classes taught in the native language:

> The very best way to teach children English is to make sure their home language and home culture is intact. Dr. Soto called the school superintendent's proposal "educationally unsound." (Snyder, November 18, 1992)

The children and families spoke on their own behalf at meetings and in the media. Bilingual students and families appeared in newspaper stories and in photo essays, for example:

Latino students begged the school board not to change the district's bilingual program. Some students carried signs saying things like, "Inequity = academic failure = high dropout rates." (Schnur, November 17, 1992)

Education shows love, Latino father says. Chevere's two sons are among the 1,200 non-English-speaking students enrolled in the Steel Town District's bilingual education program, 94 percent of them Latino. (Hall, November 22, 1992)

High school students' voices were heard at school board meetings and from local reporters. Maria Rivera organized groups of students, who carried banners at meetings, spoke at the school board's "courtesy of the floor," and were represented in the media accounts:

The superintendent's plan of "English immersion" shouldn't be tried, according to several students. When Maria Rivera arrived in Steel Town from Puerto Rico 16 months ago, she knew very little English and very little about politics. Maria, a junior at Steel Town High School, speaks English clearly now and sometimes she speaks it fiercely, defending a program that she believes is helping her and her younger sisters and brother succeed in the United States. She and several of her classmates in the high school's English as a Second Language program have been fighting the school superintendent in his bid to change the bilingual education program.

Felipe Rodriguez is a Steel Town junior, who came to Steel Town from Puerto Rico 2½ years ago. He says that without a program like the one he's experienced, "I would be completely lost. . . . It's like you have lions in a cage and you put in a little goat," he says. "It's so hard to come out of that cage and break out." (Mulligan, January 28, 1993)

The nearby twin city of Post Town passed an English-only ordinance in 1994, but its Latino leaders showed support for families struggling with the bilingual controversy in Steel Town.

Bilingual education is a community wide issue, Dr. Rodriguez said. He feels the Hispanic community, which already has a high dropout rate among students, will suffer even more if the bilingual program is removed. (Williams, January 23, 1993)

Where were the neutral parties and possible mediators throughout the bilingual controversy? One community organization comprised of mostly Anglo citizens held a series of meetings in an attempt to act as mediators. Basic information about the field was shared in an informal manner. When I presented information to this group, one of the members accused me and the bilingual families of Steel Town of having a "hidden agenda." It was not clear to me what they meant by these attacks. The only hidden agenda I understood was an agenda that would provide access to quality programs for children. Unfortunately these efforts were only helpful to the English-only proponents. Individuals in the group with noble intentions were silenced by more fearful and suspicious elements.

It probably makes more sense to group the neutral parties with the English-only advocates because historically a neutral philosophy can ultimately lead to tragic losses. Those of us who grew up as baby boomers can relate many national and international examples that have ultimately resulted in the loss of life, including the Civil Rights Movement, the Holocaust, Native American genocide, and ethnic cleansing in Bosnia.

In this study, various dynamics were observed among the neutral persons. For example, local university administrators who appeared to support the bilingual proponents at the onset of the bilingual controversy declared their neutrality after receiving telephone calls from the local superintendent. It was difficult for me to understand the rationale and thinking of my colleagues and my own educational leader, who confessed to me in whispered tones, "You know, I just don't want to be seen as supporting the Latinos." What does that mean? Does danger lurk somewhere for those who support "the Latinos"? How much courage does it take for an educator to stand up on behalf of equity? Are the conservative opinions of a superintendent czar more important than children's well-being? Whatever happened to freedom of speech?

There were two additional sources in the media that could also be portrayed as neutral mediators but whose well-intentioned efforts were also not helpful to the bilingual families and children struggling to have their voices heard. First, a columnist, and then an editor of a local newspaper:

Bilingual education debaters both want what's best.
  Neighborhood Column:
  Nobody is using the "c" word, but it's just below the surface of conversation in Steel Town these days. Coddle. The Bilingual Coordinator says the bilingual program is taking the rap for the failure of Latino students who were never enrolled in it. "The public is being led to believe the program is the failure," the Bilingual Coordinator says. "These (bilingual students) are the ones who are actually faring better."
  But the school board has difficult questions to ask itself before making a decision. For example, if the bilingual program doesn't work, why does the Latino community want to keep it? Latinos have been vocal and organized about other issues like a police substation for Southside and improvements for Jefferson Elementary School. If the bilingual program was failing them and preventing them from getting better jobs, wouldn't they be the first ones to demand change? (November 19, 1992)

Editorial

The debate over bilingual education does not have to tear Steel Town apart. It is true that decisions about how to teach children for whom English is a second language carry with them a great deal of emotional baggage. And, they get tangled with other complicated issues, such as overcrowding and the fairness with which the Steel Town Area School District allocates its resources. But the best hope to resolve this matter—and to make the schools better for everyone—is to be careful about defining the issues. We must start not with the bilingual program itself, but with the widespread belief in the Latino community that the school district puts its children second. The uneven application of discipline, a lack of new texts for Hispanic students and overcrowding of schools that serve neighborhoods where Hispanics pre-dominate are only part of their grievances. There is also the perception that some principals and other Steel Town administrators are prejudiced against non-white and Hispanic students. A task force on school space acknowledged that one way to reduce crowding at Jefferson and Vineyard schools is to end the bilingual programs, which bus children from around the district to those buildings. It will be the school district's shame if, in effect, it tells Latinos, you can have a bilingual program or you can have less-crowded schools, but you can't have both. (November 22, 1992)

The debate continued in the community with the school board announcing that it wanted to resolve the bilingual program question by January. Two of the school board members voiced opinions unlike their counterparts: "It's more than just a bilingual curriculum issue," said a school board member. "This is an ethnic issue. This is, in some people's mind, a race issue." A second board member indicated: "I sense a distrust of our schools in relation to Latino children" (Martin, November 30, 1992). Three of the school board members would later vote for keeping the bilingual program.

The struggle continued as two possible dates for the public informational meeting regarding the bilingual program were announced by the board. The meeting would be scheduled for either January 12 or January 25, depending on the board's scheduling conflicts. A separate public hearing was scheduled for January 28 (Kopacki, January 5, 1993). The superintendent was quoted as saying, "I want to nail this one and I want the best for our students" (Mulligan, January 12, 1993). The superintendent wrote the following column:

Express Yourself

by the School District Superintendent

Proposal for bilingual education stresses acquiring English early.

I oppose many of the committee's recommendations and have stated my reasons publicly. I have received an overwhelming number of letters and calls from people supporting my position. In a nutshell, the debate hinges on three central issues: The length of the program; maintenance of culture for Latino students in the bilingual program; lack of social integration of Latino students into the English-speaking student population. On Nov. 16, I recommended to the school board an outline for a new program. Its main premise is early English acquisition, which would ensure success equipping students with the ability to communicate in the language of this country—English! The fact is that English immersion programs are legal and have been implemented successfully all over the United States for many years. The question of building a new elementary school on the Southside has nothing to do with bilingual education. As super-intendent, please know that my single motivation for changing the current bilingual education program is my deep and sincere belief that the earlier children master the English language, the better their chances for success. (January 27, 1993)

This opinion piece was published just prior to the public hearing and reflects issues of power and the conservative agenda sweeping institutions of learning. Aronowitz and Giroux (1985) have described the conservative vision in a book entitled *Education Under Siege,* while Cummins (1994) refers to the "new enemy within." The superintendent's letter reflects this agenda.

Prior to the public hearing, teachers were asked to provide information about their bilingual students. Some of the teachers indicated that they were "ordered" to rate individual student performance without any instructions as to the purpose of the data gathering. "We were told that either the teachers do the evaluations or they would be done by an administrator," a middle school teacher said. A Jefferson teacher commented, "I assumed it was to place the kids, group them for next year." The teachers felt left out of the whole decision-making process about the bilingual education program. "Quite honestly, I don't think that any of us know what's going down," said a middle school teacher (Martin, January 28, 1993).

The January public hearing reflected anticipation, excitement, and preparation on the part of the speakers. Amid the cheers, boos, and flag waving, a nine-year-old silenced the crowd. The board seated at the front of the high school audi-torium became noticeably frightened when a congregation knelt and prayed on behalf of the bilingual children in Steel Town. The board's fear of the bilingual participants was unwarranted, but board members supportive of the bilingual program were confronted at a subsequent meeting by white males who shouted and gestured, "You people don't understand what's happening." They called the board members "incompetent" and added that "white middle class people end up bearing the cost of education for Spanish-speaking students." (Mulligan, February 2, 1993)

Martin (1993), in one of the newspaper accounts, noted that at this meeting the decision to dismantle the bilingual program had already taken place. The bilingual proponents had been silenced, even before they spoke at this meeting. This was Martin's account of the public hearing:

> ### Steel Town High Crowd Urges Keeping Bilingual Program—Board Supports Immersion
>
> With flags, signs, emotion, and concern, about 650 people crowded Steel Town High School auditorium last night to deliver messages to the Steel Town Area School Board. "If you take away the bilingual program in Steel Town, you take away the Latino students' chances of learning," said a high school student, "and gradually they will become frustrated and drop out." For three hours the crowd hooted and howled, clapped and cheered. Pastors sermonized. Students testified. Others criticized in English and Español. But all may have been for naught. Four of the nine board members polled after the meeting said they would vote Monday to replace the current program.
>
> Said a teacher, "If we reject the student's language, we also reject the student's culture. What message are we sending?" A nine-year-old silenced the crowd with his soft, innocent voice. "When I started here, I did not know English," said the nine-year-old, an Argentinean who attended the bilingual program at Vineyard. "I also learned lots of English," he said, "as you can now tell."
>
> Toward the end a pastor called the crowd to the front of the auditorium. More than 100 people marched to the table of board members. Some handed the school superintendent a folder crammed with petitions signed by parents of students in the bilingual program. The pastor prayed. "Bless these administrators," he said, eyes closed. "Let them vote in our favor, in the favor of our kids." The vice president of the board said later he appreciated the blessing, but that he had seen the light before the hearing. "I've heard them all before," he said. (Martin, January 29, 1993)

The roles of the local pastor and a local priest were captured by Mulligan in the January 29, 1993, article:

> The pastor of the Church on Steel Town's Southside took the microphone off its stand and approached board members, speaking softly, "Bendito, please listen to the parents," he said. "I've seen too many kids suffer and too many kids don't make it. Let's give the kids a chance." Facing the audience, the pastor motioned Latino members to come to the front and began to pray as board members found themselves looking up at a solid wall of standing people. "Bless this administration. Let us love."
>
> The two security guards tensed.

> The priest of (the) Church called for a compromise, asking that the school board extend its Monday deadline and heed the recommendations of the committee that studied the program for 10 months to keep it intact and consider revisions. "It seems to me unfair to truncate their work," he said.

As the school board continued to discuss the decision regarding the bilingual program, some members of the board revealed their doubts while others requested additional information. The final 6 to 3 vote was cast in February, supporting the school superintendent's proposal calling for English by immersion for children who spoke little or no English to "become fluent in English in the shortest amount of time so they may experience maximum success in school" (Mulligan, February 2, 1993). The three school board members who dissented expressed their disappointment and faced confrontations with English-only proponents.

The high school students who had been so active in their support of the bilingual program were described by one of their teachers as feeling "depressed because they put a lot of time into it. They did a great job. They did all that they possibly could and there were things that they said and did that definitely had a positive effect in the community" (Mulligan, February 3, 1993). Maria Rivera, the student who organized her peers, continued to express optimism.

The English Acquisition Design Team appointed was comprised by a new set of players (largely monolingual and monocultural this time) and led by the school administration to begin its design of an English-immersion program. A consultant from a nearby state was asked to speak at an all-day meeting with the newly formed committee. The committee's report, presented in June, was entitled "A Ticket for Tomorrow." The program included a buddy system, pairing language-minority students with English speakers. At least one of the school board members (Mrs. Light) expressed concern about the programmatic implications of the report:

> I'm very concerned about the elementary school proposal. According to the report, most elementary school students who would have been placed in the bilingual programs . . . will now be placed in regular all-English classes in their home schools and receive 75 minutes a day of English for speakers of other languages instruction. They'll be frustrated when classes are totally in English. (Mulligan, June 14, 1993)

The design team released its report as the English-immersion plan for the school district. The plan outlined relates a program design acquired during a visit to a school district in a nearby state that had been previously successful in a court battle involving issues of English as a second language. A retired school district principal, who referred to Latino families as those "migrating birds" and Latino fathers as "sex offenders," was instrumental in initiating this contact. The fact that this district was successful in court prompted the district administration to reason that they, too, could stand up to the local leaders' existing Office of Civil Rights complaint.

The Steel Town school district continued to make decisions that disregarded the needs of the South Side bilingual families while at the same time they rewarded the West Side largely monolingual families. Initially during the controversy, bilingual families collaboratively reached out to the Raggae Parent and Teacher Association (PTA), who seemed supportive. One of the PTA leaders met me in a parking lot near my office, whispering that they could no longer support the bilingual families. Apparently the school superintendent met with parents of the Raggae School, offering to assist with a new building for their children. The message the monolingual parents received was that silence could prove valuable. In November 1993 the outcome was evident:

> The school board voted unanimously to raze the 75-year-old (Westside) Raggae Elementary School once another the same size is built behind it. The $3.4 million project won't begin for about a year, but the money is already guaranteed through a bond issue the board approved last summer. The state will reimburse the district for $620,300 of the cost.
>
> Also last night, the board decided by a 7–1 vote to give the school superintendent a raise from his annual salary of $94,732 to $98,152. The vote came after a glowing evaluation of the school superintendent's service was read into the record.
>
> Before the Raggae vote, the president of Parents and Teachers of Raggae School joined a parent in asking that the new building remain a neighborhood school of about 300 students. (Bronstein, November 16, 1993)

Whose education and whose schooling is reflected in Steel Town? Power became an important element during Steel Town's bilingual controversy. Issues of power continued to be evident in November 1993, when the school board voted to demolish and rebuild the Raggae School in a non–South Side neighborhood. The call for a neighborhood school for 300 students at Raggae begs the question: What about the 1,200 children represented by the bilingual education proponents? Why were 1,200 children's educational needs sacrificed in this political struggle? Will language-minority children in Steel Town live long enough to experience educational equity? What is the role of the Office of Civil Rights with regard to language-minority children in Steel Town?

One of the bilingual program supporters was so moved by the events that he wrote the following poem:

Under the Cover of Darkness

by Sis-Obed Torres Cordero

December 18, 1992

Under the Cover of Darkness driven men hitched horses
in preparation for rides pre-planned under the burning sun.
Targets were selected to use "as examples" or for retaliation
    for slights,
real or imagined.
Coordinated psychological terror.
When will they visit again? Today? Tomorrow?
Wood-shaped symbols of Eternal Salvation, ablaze, seared into
    the national
subconscious sending primal fears, goose bumps down, from
    the nape of
the neck to the small of the back.
Be quiet. Silence or death, night or day, open your mouth,
you are "free" to choose, but "remember your place."
Stillness imposed.
People were watched during the day while whispers fanned the
    winds.
We are going to get you, quietly, effectively,
creating doubt in the minds of others,
don't speak out.
The undercover Riders lived among neighbors, friends,
family who knew it was criminal,
UN-Holy, morally indefensible, unjust,
but the Riders quietly observed and controlled the watch.
Deep down in the hearts of many,
those "who knew" stood transfixed:
mannequin spectators,
the Christians and the lions,
minds encased, empty, shrouded in the knowledge
coffins are made to be filled with tongueless,
    welded mouths.
To stand up for the natural human rights of other means to

abandon zombie lives and risk shunning, death
   or excommunication from
the body politic.
The Eternal Order of "Don't Cross That Line"
replaces the Souls of the living.
Yesterday, Today and Tomorrow.
Under the Cover of Darkness,
"The Lynching Rope" is replaced by sophisticated
   jaws in the Coliseum.
In the name of the majority,
the devouring Lion of Public Opinion is
   primed to destroy humans in being.
Witness the spectacle.
They will try to discredit you, dishonor you,
   disrobe you in public, humiliate
you in the eyes of your peers, threaten
   you with unemployment so that you
will go away.
Death by Public opinion. The New Hanging Rope.
Shame.
Spectators suffer from paralyzed hearts
   pounding to conserve precious
blood.
Of what use is that blood when we
   continue to allow those under cover of
darkness
to operate freely?
The only power that defeats fear is the
   power that comes from the Soul.
Once fear is defeated, to live in silenced
   submission is no longer a viable
alternative.
It is within your power to choose.
Silence = Death. Choose wisely.

This defeat was personally difficult for children, leaders, and families who were proponents of the bilingual program. Threats, confrontations, and lost jobs resulted from Steel Town's bilingual controversy. The threatening phone calls I received late at night prompted my graduate students and colleagues to offer assistance on the matter, but other players were not as fortunate as I was. Ultimately the political struggle led to a variety of losses to children, families, and the community. . . .

References

Aronowitz, S., & Giroux, H. (1985). *Education under siege.* South Hadley, Mass.: Bergin & Garvey.

Bronstein, H. (November 16, 1993). School board votes to demolish Calypso, build new school. *Morning Call,* B3.

Crawford, J. (1992). *Hold your tongue.* New York: Addison-Wesley.

Cummins, J. (1994). Keynote speech at the National Association for Bilingual Education, Los Angeles.

Hall, M. F. (November 22, 1992). Education shows love, Latino father says. *Morning Call,* B9.

Hall, M. F. (November 14, 1992). Doluisio "surprised" at Latinos' response but he cites support for changes in bilingual program. *Morning Call,* B12.

Kopacki, J. (January 5, 1993). Bilingual education meeting set. *Express Times,* B1.

Kupper, T. (November 13, 1992). Hispanics object to BASD language plan. *Morning Call,* B1.

Martin, J. P. (January 29, 1993). Liberty crowd urges keeping bilingual program. *Morning Call,* B1, B5.

Martin, J. P. (January 28, 1993). Public to have say on bilingual issue. *Morning Call,* B1, B7.

Martin, J. P. (November 30, 1992). School ponders bilingual mainstreaming. *Morning Call,* B1.

Martin, J. P. (November 10, 1992). Bilingual program headed for change. *Morning Call,* A1.

Mulligan, B. (June 14, 1993). Board to decide on what to teach English-lacking. *Express Times,* B1, B5.

Mulligan, B. (February 3, 1993). Picking up the pieces after bilingual battle. *Express Times,* B1.

Mulligan, B. (February 2, 1993). School to immerse in English. *Express Times,* A1, A2.

Mulligan, B. (January 29, 1993). Cheers, boos, prayer at bilingual meeting. *Express Times,* A1, A2.

Mulligan, B. (January 28, 1993). Students defend Spanish program. *Express Times,* A1, A2.

Mulligan, B. (January 12, 1993). Doluisio pushes ideas on bilingual education. *Express Times,* B1, B2.

Politi, N. (November 16, 1992). Latino leaders file complaint against BASD. *Morning Call,* A1.

Schnur, B. (November 21, 1992). Bilingual program has many languages. *Express Times,* B1–B2.

Schnur, B. (November 17, 1992). Bilingual program to be studied. *Express Times,* A1, A2.

Schnur, B. (November 14, 1992). Bilingual program debated. *Express Times,* B1, B2.

Schnur, B. (November 13, 1992). Civil rights complaint threatened. *Express Times,* A1, A2.

Schnur, B. (November 10, 1992). Doluisio criticizes bilingual program. *Express Times,* A1, A2.

Snyder, S. (November 18, 1992). Bilingual education is questioned: Educators debate value of classes in Spanish. *Morning Call,* B1.

Williams, T. (January 24, 1993). Ethnic barriers not insurmountable. *Express Times,* B1.

Williams, T. (January 23, 1993). Latino leader wants 800 at hearing. *Express Times,* B1, B4.

19

School Board Leadership*

editor's introduction:

School Boards at Work. Nearly every school district in the country has its own school board. Because there are more than 15,000 districts, there are about the same number of school boards. Although most of these school boards consist of elected officials who have governing powers (e.g., the power to raise levies) and who clearly can affect the quality of education offered by our public schools, little formal research exists about board actions and interactions.

A major function of the school board is to hire and oversee the work of the school superintendent, and the present case study extends over the tenure of three superintendents in Houston. The selected excerpt focuses on the school board's decision to appoint one of these three superintendents, Rod Paige. The appointment and Rod Paige's tenure were later recognized as major accomplishments in the reforming of the district. The district gained a distinctive reputation within the entire state, if not the country, as an exemplar of urban district reform. Moreover, Rod Paige subsequently went on to become the U.S. Secretary of Education, from 2001 to 2005.

Relevance of Case Studies: Capturing Group Dynamics. Case studies also can be about groups of people and their interactions. In fact, such situations are common topics of case studies. In education, a significant group, whose behavior and actions are not always appreciated, is that of the school board, and the present selection is excerpted from a book by a longstanding member of the school board in Houston, Texas.

The selection shows how you might report group conflict, convergence, and consensus. The point of view is clearly that of an author who also participated in the

*McAdams, Donald R. (2000). "The Wonderful Cacophony of a Free People Disagreeing." In *Fighting to Save Our Urban Schools . . . and Winning! Lessons From Houston* (pp. 104–121). New York: Teachers College Press.

events. Though a participant and not an external analyst of events, the author increases his credibility through repeated citations to published news stories as well as ample use of direct quotations attributed to specific individuals. In this sense, directly quoting what people say demands greater accountability on your part than writing in vague generalities or making indirect references to actual events. You then have a good example of the "triangulation" of evidence when the quotes and the news accounts, along with the author's direct observations, appear to present a consistent picture of the course of events.

The selection's quotes and reported events cover about a 1-year period. They are but part of a larger case study of the Houston school board's actions during the years 1989 to 1997, covered by the entire book. The book also includes considerable description of the reform actions taken by the Houston school district, so the book also serves as a record of the educational progress made by the district during those years, in addition to focusing on the board's work.

The reelection of all five of the reform leaders on the [nine-member] board of education in November 1993 confirmed that the reform of the [Houston Independent School District] HISD would continue. And there was reason for optimism. Shared decision making was beginning to take hold in schools. School attendance boundaries had been rationalized without controversy. School accountability was becoming a reality. Accountability for employees was increasing, at least a little. Test scores were up, at least a little.

On the down side, though the 32 percent tax increase had made possible a significant raise for teachers, it had left a bitter taste in the public's mouth, and Frank [Petruzielo, the HISD superintendent who had started in August 1991] was stonewalling attempts to decentralize the district. Decentralization was the board's next priority, and a public battle between Frank and the board seemed inevitable.

Suddenly there was a new priority. The board might have to elect a new superintendent.

What If HISD Needs a New Superintendent?

Petruzielo Might Go to Florida. It was Sunday evening, November 28, 1993, the end of a pleasant Thanksgiving weekend. The phone rang. It was Frank: "I've got some news for you. I've been asked to consider the superintendency in Broward County [Florida]. For most of the years I worked in Dade County, I actually lived in Broward County. I've got family in Broward County, and my wife wants to move back to Florida. Professionally it's a good move. If the position is offered, I'll probably take it. The story will probably be in tomorrow's newspapers."

The next day everyone was talking about the possibility that Frank Petruzielo might leave HISD. HISD employees could talk of almost nothing else. Few seemed unhappy with the prospect. Privately most board members, school employees, and business leaders hoped he would go.

I had mixed feelings. I liked Frank, and on balance I believed he had been good for HISD. But ever since the great tax battle of 1992, except for a few bursts of energy, he seemed to be a reluctant reformer. Replacing him would be problematic, but if the new superintendent quickly earned the trust of the employees and the respect of the business leaders and moved forward aggressively with decentralization, Frank's departure would be a plus. HISD was better for Frank's coming. It would also be better for his leaving.

HISD Needs Paige. Broward County was supposed to make a decision early in 1994. Frank might be gone by March. The scenarios for replacing Frank ran through my mind. A search process like the one that brought us Frank? The only upside was that under an interim superintendent the board would have the opportunity to decentralize the district. No traditional superintendent, some of us had concluded, would ever voluntarily relinquish power.

The downside was huge. We would have to appoint an interim superintendent, select a search firm, and then wait for up to six months for the politically correct short list of finalists. Then the ethnic politics, which would have been going on from day one, would break into the open. We had been lucky to escape open ethnic conflict when we hired Frank. We would probably not be lucky a second time.

And even if we were lucky and avoided ethnic conflict, the new superintendent, whatever he or she said, might not embrace *Beliefs and Visions* [HISD's vision statement approved by the board in 1990]. (I recalled Frank's *Blueprint.*) What would happen to decentralization? The new superintendent would also have to build relationships with Houston's business, political, civic, and ethnic leaders, something Frank had never done; and last but not least, manage a large, complex organization. The task was monumental. No outsider would be able to sustain the reform momentum. I was certain of it.

HISD needed an insider, someone who already understood the complexity of HISD, someone who already had the trust of administrators and teachers, someone who already had the respect of Houston's business, political, civic, and ethnic leaders, someone who had already embraced

Beliefs and Visions and would move quickly to decentralize the district. HISD needed Rod Paige! [Editor's note: Paige was then on the HISD board and had led the development of *Beliefs and Visions*.]

It hit me sometime in mid-December. Rod was perfect for the job. He had coauthored *Beliefs and Visions* and had been its heart and soul for three years, constantly reminding the rest of us where we had promised to go. He had been a civic activist for more than a decade and was widely respected by Houston's business, political, civic, and ethnic leaders. And as dean of the Texas Southern University School of Education he had been active for years as a teacher and scholar. Rod had been in most of HISD's schools. He read almost everything. He was smart. He was strong. He had courage and integrity. He was an effective public speaker. He radiated warmth and sincerity. Why not?

The Do Little Strategy. Rod would be a great superintendent, but did he want the job, and could he be elected? A few days later on the phone I just dropped it on him. "Rod, let me tell you who I think would be the ideal person to replace Frank as superintendent."

"Who?"

"You."

There was a moment of silence. "Don, we shouldn't talk about this."

That was all I needed. Rod had not said no.

A few weeks passed. Board members talked a lot about whether Frank would go or stay. We recalled our experience with the search firm when Frank was hired. We speculated about interim superintendents. We talked about the stalled decentralization process. One day [HISD board member] Cathy Mincberg called: "Don, I have been thinking about our conversations. The only way we're going to maintain our reform momentum, especially with decentralization, is to make Rod superintendent."

I told her about my phone conversation with Rod.

"We need to talk," Cathy said with urgency.

A few hours later we met in my office. We agreed there was a good chance Rod would take the position if offered, though we suspected he would be a reluctant candidate. We thought through all the pros and cons. We thought through all the possible scenarios. Would it look like the board was trying to put one of its own in the superintendent's chair so it could directly manage the district? How would the Hispanic activists respond? [Paige is African American.]

We decided to call Ron Franklin [another board member]. Ron's initial reaction was cool. He feared that Rod's election might spark controversy. "I'll give it some thought," he promised. A few days later he concurred.

From that moment Cathy, Ron, and I knew there was a good chance Rod would be HISD's next superintendent. We could count. Arthur Gaines and Carol Galloway [two other board members] were African Americans. Arthur for certain, and probably Carol, would support Rod. That made five [out of nine] votes.

We also knew we needed to speak and act with great caution. Any decision made by the board outside of a duly posted open meeting would be a violation of the Texas Open Meetings Act. If five or more board members met to discuss HISD issues, or if in groups of less than five we consciously went back and forth to predetermine the outcome of a meeting, we could go to jail. Also, a huge public controversy was almost certain if word got out that several trustees wanted to elect Paige superintendent. The less said, the better.

There was just one call that I felt I had to make. When and if the time came, I wanted Arthur to put Rod's name before the board. Arthur had lived through the desegregation of HISD. He and Rod were close friends. If anyone was going to put Rod's name before the board, it should be Arthur. A few days later I called him. Arthur was enthusiastic.

That was it. There was nothing more to do but keep quiet and wait. If Frank resigned there would be numerous complex issues to manage. It would be a mistake to try to manage them in advance.

It was against state law for a school board member to solicit employment with the district on whose board he or she served. And a school board member continued to be the legal trustee until his or her successor had been chosen and taken the oath of office. If Rod were to become superintendent, he would have to resign his board seat and wait until a successor was appointed or elected before he could even apply for the job. The voters in his district might insist on an election. That could take months and be very problematic. Also, Rod could not serve as superintendent unless he had a Texas superintendent's certificate. I did not know whether he had one or not. On top of all this, Frank might not get an offer from Broward County. No, there was no way to manage the process, and one would have to skirt the edges of the law to try.

The Desire of the Board of Education

Preparations for a Big Day. Meanwhile, there were other issues to manage. On December 7, [board member] Felix Fraga was elected to an open seat on the Houston City Council [and would have to relinquish his board seat]. HISD was going to get a new trustee. Once again there was discussion in the Hispanic community: an appointment or an election? This time the community, organized as the Hispanic Education Advisory Committee, chose the appointment of a caretaker, who would be appointed on January 20, 1994, and the election of a replacement on the next regularly scheduled election day, May 7.

The caretaker was to be José Salazar, a Houston Community College mid-level administrator with an M.S. in ESL/bilingual education from the University of Houston. José was a young man with sharp features, a big smile, and a fiery temper when provoked on Hispanic issues. He had been very active in Hispanic education issues, and just six months earlier had served as president of the grassroots group that officially adopted Rusk [Elementary School] following Frank's [reconstruction of it].

On January 6, Frank was offered the Broward County superintendency and immediately left for Fort Lauderdale. If he and the Broward County Board agreed on a contract, he would resign, effective almost immediately.

So, at the January 20 meeting the board would appoint José Salazar to fill the vacancy created by Felix's election to the city council; elect a new board president, who everyone agreed would be Ron Franklin; and most likely go into closed session to select an interim superintendent. January 20 would be a very big day for HISD.

What would happen in the closed session? None of us knew. The board might select an interim superintendent and defer other decisions to a later date. It might launch a full search or a search limited to Houston candidates. It might offer the superintendency to Rod Paige. The key person was Carol Galloway. I believed Carol would support Rod, but maybe not. Carol was a full-time HFT [Houston Federation of Teachers] employee. Her boss, Gayle Fallon, and Rod Paige were on the opposite side of the fence on many issues.

The Board Makes a Decision. The January 20 board meeting opened to a full gallery buzzing with anticipation and rumors. Over the past several days I had shared with a few business leaders and parent activists my belief that Rod should be HISD's next superintendent. I knew Cathy, Ron, and Arthur had done the same, and leaks were inevitable.

The public meeting went as expected. José Salazar was appointed to fill Felix's seat [as a seventh board member], sworn in, and seated at the board table. Ron Franklin was elected board president and took the gavel. Then, after a presentation by the Houston Business Advisory Committee on decentralization, we went into closed session.

Frank was expected to sign a contract with Broward County within a day or two and be gone by February 1. The first agenda was an interim superintendent. But should we not settle on the process for selecting a superintendent before we selected an interim superintendent? A short-term interim could be almost anybody. A long-term interim superintendent would need to be selected with great care. Then Arthur spoke: "Mr. President, in my opinion Rod Paige would be an outstanding superintendent for HISD."

Discussion followed. (About this time Rod left the room.) I do not remember the order in which board members spoke, but when Carol Galloway said she supported Paige, we all knew the board had made a decision.

José Salazar erupted. "It looks like it's already been decided. This is outrageous." José was leaning forward in his chair, shaking, practically shouting. A cabal had conspired to elect Rod superintendent. No one had talked to him about Rod. No one had talked to [the eighth board member] Olga [Gallegos]. The Hispanic community had been purposely excluded, insulted, humiliated.

[The ninth board member,] Paula [Arnold,] was upset. She had passed off comments to her in recent days by Arthur and Cathy in support of Rod as off-the-cuff comments, not firm commitments. She had no idea Rod was a serious candidate and already had such strong support. She agreed that Rod would make an excellent superintendent. But, she insisted, it would be unfair to the Hispanic community to select him without an open search process.

The discussion went back and forth. What should we do? Could we keep it a secret that five board members wanted Rod to be superintendent? If a search were held and Rod resigned his board seat and applied, would anyone else apply? Was there any process we could launch that ended in Rod's selection that would not rightly be called a sham? The fact was, no state law, no HISD policy, no board promise committed us to a search.

Finally it was decided. We would tell the public the whole truth: a majority of the board wanted Rod Paige to be the next superintendent of HISD. We could not offer him the job. He was a sitting board member. If he wanted the job, he would have to resign his board seat and apply for it.

The great sliding door dividing the board table from the gallery slowly rolled open. Arthur read the motion: "Mr. President and Board, I move that we express the desire of the Board that Dr. Rod Paige consider becoming the next superintendent of the District. We express this desire with the recognition that he would have to resign and have a successor sworn in prior to our being able to negotiate with him for the position" (HISD, January 20, 1994, p. 244). Five board members voted yes. Paula, Olga, and José voted no. Rod abstained.

All Hell Breaks Loose

Hispanics Object to the Process. The public was stunned. No one had seen it coming, but initial reactions from HISD employees were positive. Rod's famous sacred cow letter had not been forgotten. Employees had passed it around and quoted it ever since. Business leaders also seemed pleased.

Hispanic leaders, as expected, were angry. The board had discriminated against the Hispanic community. The problem was not that five board members wanted Paige to be superintendent. It was the process. A formal search was mandatory. Hispanics had been "shut out." It had nothing to do with race. The Hispanic Education Committee, the group that had come together to nominate José Salazar for appointment to the board, claimed they would protest the appointment of anyone, even a Hispanic, elected directly by the board (*Chronicle*, January 22, 1994, p. A1).

The next day, Friday, January 21, board members gathered at a beautiful old bed and breakfast in Columbus, a small country town about one hour west of Houston, for our annual board retreat. . . . The argument began at once.

José was furious. We had contrived to exclude the Hispanic community from the process. We had insulted them, humiliated them. They would fight.

Paula was hurt and mad. She used the f-word a lot when she was mad. We heard the f-word a lot that evening. Cathy, Ron, and I, her friends, her partners in school reform, had shared their thinking with each other, but not her. "How could you f-ing do this to me?" she stormed, glaring around the large, old oak table covered with drinks and snack food. "Have I not always been loyal to you? Have I not always worked with you since the Joan Raymond [the HISD superintendent prior to Petruzielo] deal? You'd better never, ever do this again to me. Do you f-ing hear me. I swear if you do, I'll f-ing create hell."

We continued late into the night over dinner, interrupting each other, shouting on occasion, going around and around over the same points. Once Rod reminded the group how he had been out of the loop two-and-a-half years earlier when the decision had been made to hire Frank. Once José called me a racist, a man who wanted to hold minorities down because of my own personal insecurities.

Discussions continued all day Saturday. Meanwhile Ron, our new board president, José, Paula, and others were continually called away for phone calls. The press was insatiable. And the Hispanic Education Committee, meeting at Velia's Cafe, was organizing for a fight.

For the next few days the newspapers were full of the Paige controversy. Readers were shown headlines like, "Did HISD exclude 3 dissenters? Talks held in private some allege"; "Members divided on superintendent"; "Hispanics not happy with way HISD recruited a new leader"; "Hispanics decry input on Paige pick"; "Walkout, sickout mulled as protest"; "Hispanics threaten HISD suit"; "Group protest superintendent selection process"; "Paige's HISD backers defend choice." An editorial in the Saturday *Post* called on HISD to "Do it again." The board's action was called "appalling," "arrogant," and "bizarre" (January 20, 1994, p. A28).

A big showdown was planned by the Hispanic Education Committee for Sunday evening. Between 175 and 200 people packed into Velia's Cafe.[1] For nearly two hours Ron and Cathy were queried, challenged, sometimes insulted, and almost continuously hissed and booed. "Shame on you," said one speaker. "Our children are not for sale," said another. "There is a deep rage in us," said a third.

Paula made it clear to the group that she did not approve of the process, but she affirmed that Rod would make an outstanding superintendent. There were five votes committed to him, she said. It made no sense to fight for a search. If Rod applied for the position, she would vote for him. Now the crowd directed its anger at Paula. She was a turncoat.

Apparently some had thought they could pressure at least two board members into reconsidering their support for Rod, but when it became clear that Ron and Cathy would not yield, the crowd became even angrier. Committees were formed: one to press a lawsuit against the board; another to collect signatures on a petition for a recall election against Paula; a third to manage a public relations campaign to pressure the board into launching a search process; and a fourth to look into possible school walkouts, boycotts, and other protest measures. Checks were collected. Lists of volunteers were started. Roman Martinez, who was a candidate for the Texas Senate, said several HISD employees had promised "to sing like canaries" about how the Paige selection was illegally stage-managed by the board (*Post*, January 24, 1994, p. A1; *Chronicle*, January 24, 1994, p. A9).

Two days later, on January 25, Ron responded to the *Post* editorial with an op-ed defending the offer to Paige. The board went into closed session prepared to consider all options, he said. After two hours of discussion it became apparent that a majority of the board wanted Paige to consider becoming superintendent. "The *Post* criticizes us for this process being 'secret,'" he concluded. "Would the *Post* prefer that instead of voting on this issue, we should have kept this information to ourselves? That we should have embarked on a selection process that would intentionally mislead the public and candidates for the superintendency?" (p. A15).

African Americans Respond. On the same page, Robert C. Newberry, a regular columnist for the *Post* and an African American, took his shot at the Paige selection. He concurred with the board that Paige was an excellent choice, though like everyone else he damned the selection process. Then he concluded, "[I]t's a race issue. Pure and simple."

The controversy in the media continued. Every day the television stations had another story on the Paige selection. Columns, op-eds, letters to the editor expressed the full range of opinions. More and more the central issue was race. Most letter writers were strongly supportive of Paige and disgusted by the ethnic politics.

The inevitable Black backlash came almost immediately. On Monday, January 24, at a news conference, the Rev. J. J. Roberson, president of the Baptist Ministers Association of Houston and Vicinity, praised the board for its swift invitation to Rod. Hispanics, he said, were only upset because the board did not choose someone from their community. They once "thought they were White folks," he said. "Then they found out they were minority groups like ourselves. They've never really been with us. We fought our battles and they fought theirs. My suggestion to them is let's unite and have a united front. It's our time now; it may be theirs the next time." Blacks, he continued, would not sit idle while Hispanics challenged the hiring of Paige. "If all of us get in our pulpits and start talking, the Hispanics may as well start walking. We are going to talk about it in our pulpits. Our members are going to be talking about it on their jobs. Everywhere we go, we are going to have somebody talking about Rod Paige being superintendent of this school district" (*Chronicle,* January 26, 1994, p. A17; *Post,* January 26, 1994, p. A1).

That afternoon 25 Black children picketed outside the HISD administrative office headquarters in support of Paige.

Throughout all this controversy, Rod kept his composure. His comments to the media were humble and conciliatory. He was meeting with everybody, including Hispanic leaders. "I respect the cordial way they've received me," he said. "Some were supportive, some less so, but all were respectful. . . . I think this is going to run its course, and then I think there will be peace and we'll work together in harmony" (*Post,* January 26, 1994, p. A1).

The next day he said he was "considering what is the path to take, because I don't want to be a part of a disruptive situation" (*Chronicle,* January 27, p. A18). A few days later, on Thursday, January 27, Rod announced his resignation from the HISD board and stated that he would consider the position of HISD superintendent if it were offered.

Important Appointments Required. Immediately a new set of wheels started turning. A person to replace Rod as the district nine trustee had to be found and sworn in before Rod could begin negotiations with the board. Also, Rod had to obtain a Texas superintendent's certificate. Meanwhile the board had to select an interim superintendent. On January 24, following just a few days of negotiation, Frank and the Broward County board agreed on a contract and Frank submitted his letter of resignation. The effective date was February 1.

A special executive meeting of the board was posted for January 31. José Salazar came prepared with a recommendation. He wanted Yvonne Gonzalez, an assistant superintendent in the campus management department, to be interim superintendent. I was opposed. There were easily a dozen or more school administrators who outranked Yvonne and by experience and ability deserved the honor of being named interim superintendent. Two of them were Hispanic, one a Panamanian and the other a Mexican American woman married to an Anglo. If we had to appoint a Hispanic, which everyone agreed we did, why not one of them? No, said José, they were not *real* Hispanics. Being Hispanic, apparently, was not enough. One had to be Mexican American and politically active. So Dr. Gonzalez was elected interim superintendent.

Poor José. He thought he was doing the right thing. But the Hispanic Education Committee was upset. Wednesday night at Velia's Cafe he was given a tongue-lashing. He was supposed to show his displeasure with the board by voting against everything.

"I am not a puppet," he told the group at Velia's. "Just because you are angry, I am not going to sit here and be vilified just because you want revenge."

Marcia Olivarez, co-chair of the committee, retorted: "All I am hearing is an elitist attitude: 'The masses are asses and I can do it better'" (*Chronicle*, February 3, 1994, p. A19).

Replacing Rod on the board, which could have been difficult, turned out to be simple. Within days the Black leadership of Houston had united behind Robert Jefferson. Jefferson, a short, heavy man with a very round head and almost no hair, was pastor of the Cullen Missionary Baptist Church. He had been active in his community for years and received the NAACP [National Association for the Advancement of Colored People] Unity Award for founding Ministers Against Crime, a coalition of Black and Hispanic ministers established to combat violence in public schools. Jeff, as he was called, had been a PTO [parent-teacher organization] president, served on numerous school and civic committees, and was known by almost everyone. His endorsement letters were numerous and came from all the right people.

At the regularly scheduled February 3 board meeting, Rod officially resigned his position on the board and Robert Jefferson was elected trustee for District Nine. Paula voted no. José and Olga abstained. There was applause from a packed gallery, but not from the members of the Hispanic Education Committee, who sat together as a group and looked on in angry silence.

Paige Hired. Contract negotiations with Rod began immediately. On Monday, February 7, at another specially posted executive meeting, the board approved a contract with Rod. He would serve out Frank's term, which ended June 30, 1995, and receive the annual salary the board had been paying Frank, $147,000 plus benefits and perks. The vote was 6–2. Paula voted yes. José and Olga voted no. Members of the Hispanic Education Committee, watching from the gallery, told the press, "It's not over yet" (*Post,* February 8, 1994, p. A13).

Confrontation With the TEA and a Lawsuit

The TEA Investigation. Unfortunately Rod was not able to assume the superintendency immediately. The Texas Education Code required superintendents to be certified. Rod was not certified, but a 1984 statute allowed the commissioner of education to grant certificates to "outstanding educators." Rod certainly qualified, and no one expected Commissioner Meno to delay the issue of a temporary superintendent's certificate pending Rod's passing of the superintendent's examination.

Commissioner Meno, however, said he did not have time to examine Rod's credential before leaving on a 10-day vacation. Then, on his return, he requested that the board formally request a waiver. TEA [Texas Education Agency] rules, he said, conflicted with the statute. He did not have the legal authority to act without a formal board request. So on February 17, the board voted to ask a the commissioner to apply the law. "Normally we don't have to ask a state official to follow the law. They just do," said Cathy (*Post,* February 18, 1994, p. A25).

The next day, Friday, Commissioner Meno granted Paige a two-year superintendent's certificate, contingent on his passing within one year the state test to qualify as a superintendent. (Subsequently Rod passed the test on his first attempt with a very high score.) But at the same time, Meno announced that he was sending a TEA assessment team to Houston to investigate complaints about the Paige selection.

A week earlier the Hispanic Education Committee had filed an official complaint with the TEA asking for an investigation. The committee charged that the board had violated the Open Meetings Act, acted unethically by excluding three trustees and their largely Mexican-origin constituents from the process, and ignored affirmative action laws by failing to conduct a national search.

It seemed obvious. Meno had stalled on the Paige certificate to test the political waters. Then he responded, as bureaucrats frequently do, with a compromise. Paige got his certificate. The Hispanic Education Committee got its investigation.

But the Hispanic Education Committee was not satisfied.[2] And Sunday the League of United Latin American Citizens (LULAC) announced that it would ask the U.S. Department of Education's Office of Civil Rights to investigate Paige's appointment. LULAC also said because of the "continued insensitivity and arrogance on the part of the board," it was forming a blue-ribbon panel to study creating a separate school district of mostly Hispanic students (*Chronicle,* February 22, 1994, p. A13).

Tuesday, February 22, was Rod's first day on the job. He spent most of his day in schools and meeting with rank-and-file employees. "I felt good being out in the schools," he told the press. "I'm in my element, and I can see what my job really is" (*Post,* February 23, 1994, p. A13). "The highlight of any day is when I can spend it in school with the teachers and the children who seem to reinforce your energy" (*Chronicle,* February 23, 1994, p. A17).

That same day the TEA assessment team began its investigation. The team was led by Ruben Olivarez, executive deputy commissioner for accountability. Assisting him were James Vasquez, senior director and head of the TEA division that reviewed board actions, and Walter Chandler, recently retired as associate commissioner for accreditation and investigation. Chandler, an African American, was pulled out of retirement to give the team ethnic balance.

The team began its work by meeting Rod and Ron. That evening they met with the Hispanic Education Committee. About 75 people were present when Martha Almaguer pointed at the TEA officials and said, "If we have a walkout, and some child kills another child because it looks like a Black-Hispanic issue, I'm not taking responsibility. It's going to be your responsibility" (*Chronicle,* February 23, 1994, p. A17).

The next day the assessment team met with board members. My meeting was in the morning. Olivarez bore in like a prosecuting attorney. He asked leading questions, inferred ulterior motives. He suggested that Ron had voted for Rod as superintendent in return for Arthur's vote for him as board president and that Cathy had supported Rod in order to obtain the support of Houston's Black leaders for her husband David, who had declared his candidacy for chairman of the Harris County Democratic Party. I almost laughed.

The assessment report and any actions by the commissioner, said Olivarez, would not be announced for several weeks. Most board members concluded that the news would not be good. Olivarez came across as an angry Hispanic activist. It looked like he had already made up his mind.

Meanwhile Rod's credentials had become public documents. Now it was not just the process. Hispanic activists charged that Rod was unqualified.

Because his doctorate was in physical education, charged Tatcho Mindiola, a professor at the University of Houston, Rod was "the least prepared person to become superintendent in the history of HISD." Paige and the African American community were "being used by the White members of the board to pursue their own agenda." We were pitting Mexican and African Americans against each other to achieve our goals. We were willing to "flout the law and publicly scoff at the Mexican American community." We—Ron Franklin, Cathy Mincberg, Don McAdams, and Paula Arnold—suggested Mindiola, were *gringos*—"vicious manipulators who would do anything to gain their way" (*Post,* February 25, 1994, p. F2).

The Lawsuit. On March 3, the Hispanic Education Committee filed its long-threatened lawsuit against the board in state district court. The plaintiffs, the Hispanic Education Committee, the Texas Association of Chicanos in Higher Education, and four individuals—Marcia Olivarez, Guadalupe San Miguel, Alfredo Santos, and Rosemary Covalt—alleged that the board had violated the Texas Open Meetings Act and requested a permanent injunction enjoining Paige from serving as superintendent. There was another flurry of news stories and editorials, and then, for the rest of March, relative quiet.

The TEA Report. The assessment report of the TEA investigation team was released on March 30 (TEA, February 22–24, 1994). The main conclusion was that there was no evidence that the Open Meetings Act was violated. "However, given the number of meetings and contacts with most of the board members involved at one time or another, the facts do indicate a potential violation of the Open Meetings Act."

The report also concluded that Rod violated the Texas Education Code by applying for and soliciting the position of superintendent while serving on the board. The evidence? At the January 27 press conference where he announced his decision to resign his board seat and respond positively to the board's invitation, Rod said to the entire city of Houston: "By accepting the offer of the school board, I also extend my hand to my friends and colleagues on the board to work cooperatively with them. I am hoping they will advise me about the best forum for soliciting input from their individual constituencies."

Finally the report concluded that though the board had not violated any of its own policies or procedures, "the board's action does call into question whether or not they violated their affirmative action policy which is under the jurisdiction of the Office of Civil Rights."

Based on these conclusions, Commissioner Meno announced that he was referring the possible Open Meetings Act violation to the Harris County

District Attorney and the possible civil rights violation to the U.S. Department of Education, Office of Civil Rights. He was strongly encouraging the board "to immediately develop and implement an open and appropriate search process for selecting an individual to serve as superintendent beginning July 1, 1995." He was revising Rod's temporary superintendent's certificate so that it would expire on June 30, 1995. And he was assigning James Vasquez to monitor HISD. "He will report to me on the board's progress in implementing my recommendations and provide technical assistance if requested by the district" (Meno, March 30, 1994).

I was stunned. Ron was outraged. He characterized the report as "bizarre" and "influenced by political pressure." "This is a sad day for the TEA, and for everyone who believes in local control of schools."

Rod told the press the report hit him "like a ton of bricks," but he knew he had done nothing wrong and intended to keep his focus on students and schools.

The Hispanic Education Committee was delighted. "What the TEA has done is prove we've not been frivolous with our allegations," said Marcia Olivarez. She went on to charge board members with "race-baiting" (*Post*, March 31, 1994, p. A1).

The Commissioner Backs Down. The next few days were tense. The newspapers were once again full of stories about the HISD mess. It seemed that everybody had an opinion, most of them unfavorable to the board of education. A *Post* editorial put the full blame for the "mess" on the board, saying the board had exhibited poor leadership, insensitivity, and arrogance (*Post*, April 1, 1994, p. A30). Board attorney Kelly Frels informed us that it would be wise for us to begin thinking about hiring personal lawyers. Meanwhile, we determined among ourselves that we would not comply with the commissioner's directive. We would not begin a search. We would ignore Mr. Vasquez. And we might file a lawsuit against the commissioner.

The dark clouds began to part almost immediately. The very next day, March 30, Harris County District Attorney John B. Holmes, Jr., announced that his preliminary review of the TEA findings turned up no evidence of wrongdoing by either the board or Paige. "If this is all they have to show that he solicited that job," he said, referring to Rod's acceptance statement, "I am unimpressed. Somebody might want to point out to these folks, the TEA, that they are not immune from libel and slander" (*Chronicle*, April 1, 1994, p. A1).

At least I would not need a lawyer. But there was still the matter of Rod's certificate and Commissioner Meno's requirement that HISD conduct a search for a new superintendent. It was time for political action.

We had information that Houston Hispanics, including at least one highly placed HISD Hispanic administrator, were in direct contact with TEA officials. We knew several Hispanic elected officials and office seekers were making as much out of the issue as possible. We were convinced Meno was acting politically and that he, and maybe Governor [Ann] Richards, had made a bad mistake. How stupid! It was an election year. Two traditional Democratic constituencies were on either side of a complex issue. Meno could have, should have, politely stayed out. Instead he had attacked HISD's first Black superintendent.

The phone calls and meetings began immediately. Rod told the press he was getting so many calls he had put his phone in the refrigerator. The Reverend Bill Lawson, pastor of the Wheeler Avenue Baptist Church and perhaps Houston's most respected Black leader, said the issue was "like a lynching because it does look like there is some kind of concerted attempt to get him out at all costs" (*Chronicle,* April 1, 1994, p. A1).

I do not know the details of this part of the story. The work in the Black community was managed by Robert Jefferson and Arthur Games. They kept me informed and told me not to worry. They were going to inflict serious political damage on Governor Richards if Meno did not reverse himself.

Governor Richards really was on the spot, as *Chronicle* political columnist Jane Ely pointed out on April 3. After making fun of the school board as a bunch of political incompetents, she pointed out that George W. Bush [the next governor of Texas] might make an election-year issue of the HISD mess. Ann Richards was between "a really big political rock and a superhard political place." She either had to chew out Meno or "swallow whole" her commitment to local control of education. And she had to "walk an especially careful line among the minority voters vital to a Democrat's political fate" (p. E2).

The Black offensive continued. On April 4, the Houston branch of the NAACP announced that it would intervene in the lawsuit filed against the HISD board by the Hispanic Education Committee. "The board's actions," said President Al Green, "were not only lawful, but also in keeping with its established policies" (*Chronicle,* April 5, 1994, p. A15). Also, a group of Black ministers was organizing to demand the resignation of Commissioner Meno and possibly the abolishment of the TEA.

State legislators were also hammering Meno. Sue Schecter (D-Houston) sent a strongly worded protest to Meno with copies to Richards, the Harris County legislative delegation, and others. Debra Danburg (D-Houston) also sent Meno a letter decrying his "overreaching power play" and defending local control of schools. Harold Dutton (D-Houston) said he was drafting a letter to Meno and thought maybe it was time to "Make TEA DOA" (*Chronicle,* April 8, 1995, p. A25).

Two days later Commissioner Meno crumbled. On April 6, he sent a letter to Ron Franklin to "clarify" his letter of March 30. No, Mr. Vasquez was not a "monitor" under section 35.121 of the Texas Education Code. He was just available to observe and be helpful. And no, reducing the time of Paige's temporary superintendent certificate did not preclude Paige from qualifying for permanent certification or having his contract renewed. He said, "Any other interpretation of my previous correspondence would be incorrect." And finally, "I have no interest in influencing who the board selects [as superintendent] from a pool of qualified applicants." In other words, do whatever you wish.

The same day District Attorney Holmes announced that he had found no evidence of misconduct by the board and was discontinuing his investigation. "I think they're wrong," he said of the TEA allegations. "It's D.O.A." (*Post*, April 7, 1994, p. A1).

It was public humiliation for Commissioner Meno. A source in the governor's office said, "We relayed our feelings to him that this was a local school board issue. We had no business being in there, and he agreed." Richards's press secretary, Bill Cryer, said that any possible role the state might have played in the HISD superintendent selection was eliminated when Holmes found that no laws had been violated. "We believe it's over. All the questions have been answered. There's nothing left for the TEA to do." Was Meno pressured? asked a reporter. "I would not say that he was pressured," said Cryer. "I'd say we let him know what we thought" (*Chronicle,* April 7, 1994, p. A1).

The Paige selection controversy was over. Houston's Black leaders, however, wanted to fire one more shot to show the TEA, Governor Richards, the Hispanic Education Committee, and anyone else who might have doubts that Paige was their man and that he better be left alone. A huge rally for Paige was scheduled for April 13 at the Mt. Hebron Baptist Church.

It was wonderful. The church was packed. A drill team of young people marched up and down the aisles, executing complex drills in perfect unison. A large choir filled the church with powerful gospel music. Minister after minister thundered against the TEA and the great injustice done to Rod Paige. Board members were introduced to sustained applause and allowed to say a few words. And Governor Richards's recently appointed secretary of state, Ron Kirk, an African American, assured everyone that Governor Richards was taking a personal interest in the situation.

A week later Commissioner Meno came to Houston and shared breakfast with Rod at one of HISD's elementary schools. Cordiality prevailed. The media gave the breakfast major coverage and then dropped the issue. The controversy was over.

The Lawsuit Dismissed. All that remained was the lawsuit. The Hispanic Education Committee, of course, did not go away. They had built their reputation as great fighters. They could not surrender now. So the lawsuit dragged on and on. It was moved to federal court at the request of HISD. Documents were produced and interrogatories answered by the defendants in May. Depositions were taken in July. Finally, in December, United States District Judge Lynn N. Hughes ruled. HISD's request for summary judgment was granted. All charges against the board were dismissed (*Hispanic Education Committee v. HISD,* December 27, 1994).

Judge Hughes's opinion was a complete vindication of the board. He pointedly noted that the undercurrent of complaint was that the board did not select a Hispanic: "Paige does not represent in a meaningful way all Black people any more than the committee can claim to represent all Hispanic people."

He ruled that there was no discrimination, and informal discussions by trustees were not cabals to subvert public view of the selection decision. "Important decisions require preparation as well as visible decision, and the individual members of the board did not evade Texas law by conferring with one another, staff members, interest groups, and other individuals."

The complaint that segments of the community had been denied the right to speak was also rejected: "During the whole gaggle of events from the occurrence of the vacancy through to the appointment of the new superintendent, the board was subjected to the buffeting of letters, press conferences, speeches, meetings, and the rest of the wonderful cacophony of a free people disagreeing."

The Hispanic Education Committee, of course, appealed to the United States Fifth Circuit Court of Appeals. The case would drag on a little longer. The documents generated by the lawsuit already made a stack of paper five inches high. More briefs would be written. Legal fees would go even higher. But it was over. Everyone knew it was over. Except for a short story when the Fifth Circuit Court rejected the appeal in August 1995, the newspapers never mentioned the lawsuit again. Neither did anyone else.

José Salazar resigned from the HISD board on April 8 as he had promised. He was succeeded by Esther Campos, who was elected in a runoff election on May 31 by a very low turnout.

George W. Bush defeated Ann Richards in the November 1994 election, and soon after his inauguration as governor of Texas, Skip Meno was replaced as commissioner of education.

Rod, meanwhile, proved to be a brilliant superintendent. Within three months he had intervened in three schools. Within a year he was transforming the district. In time, nearly everyone acknowledged that Rod was an outstanding superintendent. Still, just as universally, the board members who selected him were damned for arrogance, stupidity, and worse for selecting him the way they did.

Notes

1. The leaders had worked the phones for two days to get this turnout. I had to attend a wedding and was spared the event.

2. "It's unscrupulous of the TEA to immediately certify him," said Guadalupe San Miguel, a spokesman for the committee. "It's quite clear they really don't care about the process" (*Post,* February 19, 1994, p. A28). Marcia Olivarez, co-chairman, said, "I think that by sending out the assessment team, they are just trying to appease us. Why grant a waiver and send an assessment team at the same time? Why bother? If they had truly wanted to do the right thing, they would have sent the assessment team out weeks ago" (*Chronicle,* February 19, 1994, p. A1).

20

A Post-9/11 Perspective
on U.S. Education*

editor's introduction:

Worldly Knowledge. This engrossing selection appears as the afterword to a case study of an upper-middle-class, White suburban U.S. high school (named Prior Lake High School in the case study). Having completed the case study (which traced events over an academic year at the high school), the author was in a Central Asian country (Kyrgyzstan) on what happened to be September 11, 2001.

The tragic events of that date stirred the author to think again about the (limited) worldly knowledge of the U.S. students whom she had recently studied. The average student's knowledge—much less understandings of—international geography, politics, and history all seemed deficient. The author also notes how the deficiencies appeared even in comparison to students from as modest a country as Kyrgyzstan.

The author then traces the potential roots of U.S. students' education, providing sharp but possibly accurate commentary. The "vast majority" of the students "still indulged themselves in the reassuring belief that, like them, most people on the planet were Christian" (p. 371). Most "couldn't name even two of the rights they enjoyed under the United States Constitution" (p. 371). More than complacency, the author reports, Americans may actually take pride in knowing nothing about the rest of the world. The author goes on to attribute this state of affairs to shortcomings in U.S. educational policy, national and local. She discusses how much, much more needs to be taught to American students . . . and learned by them.

---

*Burkett, Elinor. (2001). *Another Planet: A Year in the Life of a Suburban High School* (pp. 323–332). New York: HarperCollins.

Relevance of Case Studies: Reflecting. Case studies also provide opportunities for authors to reflect about a subject that has been studied. Such reflections need to be carefully distinguished from the actual case study, as in an afterword. (An afterword typically gives the author a chance to update an original text, bringing into play some new or updated set of events.)

You also could use such reflections to reexamine the case study and the possible "filters" or "lenses" that might have been at work. Realize, too, that such filters or lenses exist in using all other social science methods—including the design of experiments and surveys—and that they are not merely creatures of case study research. A possible beneficial future procedure might be to have all investigators give written reflections on their studies at the end of their research, regardless of the method used.

One evening, six months after completing *Another Planet*, I found myself sitting in an outdoor café at the feet of a forty-foot statue of Lenin in the center of Bishkek, Kyrgyzstan, talking about the education I'd gotten at Prior Lake High School.

It was a prosaic scene that night, September 11, 2001. The sunset had turned the snow-capped peaks of the Pamir Mountains a soft pink, and scores of couples lingered outside to savor the mild weather, their serenity broken only by the percussive cacophony of bleating buses that is the music of Third World streets. Our kabobs hadn't been overcooked and the ice cream made no concession to the sensibilities of the butterfat-averse. We were eight Americans relaxing at the end of a long day, grousing, as expatriates tend to do, about the ignorance, even the indifference, of friends back home to anything beyond American borders.

I had arrived in this Central Asian Republic just a month earlier and was still reeling from how thoroughly the region was defying expectation. I'd been cautioned that the infrastructure was crumbling, that every corner of society was rife with corruption, and that the people ached for the security and stability of the old days of Communism and the Soviet Union.

No one, however, had warned me about what I would find in the classroom where, as a Fulbright professor, I was teaching journalism. My students at the Kyrgyz-Russo-Slavonic University were literate in two, if not three or more languages. They spoke knowledgeably not only about Pushkin, Tolstoy, and Dostoyevsky but also about Shakespeare, Thornton Wilder, and Eugene O'Neill. Working with no computers at home, with university Internet access that exemplified the speed of molasses, and classrooms without functional blackboards, they were nonetheless well versed in European history and American politics, geography, and philosophy.

I ached at the comparison to the young people I'd met in Prior Lake.

"It gets worse every generation," I remarked to my friends, recounting the story my parents, Ivy League graduates, had told me about having to race to the atlas when they'd heard that Pearl Harbor had been bombed. The lesson of World War II seemed to have been lost by the time my generation came of age. We learned about Pearl Harbor, Hiroshima, and Nagasaki, but we were clueless when faced with Dien Bien Phu and Hue—or the hatred of Cubans. We were saved—if you can characterize political activism as a form of salvation—by our backgrounds in history, geography, and politics, by the fact that we actually knew how to read. It wasn't nearly enough, but it provided us with a starting point to formulate questions and organize our own teach-ins. The next generation, however, more disempowered still by ignorance, lacked even enough knowledge to begin formulating questions about the world beyond the borders of school and the mall.

It wasn't just that the Prior Lake students I'd interviewed and tested didn't know the simplest geography: what body of water lapped onto Jamaica's beaches or what quadrant of the planet Pearl Harbor was in. Despite years of "diversity training," the vast majority still indulged themselves in the reassuring belief that, like them, most people on the planet were Christian. These suburban students—upper-middle-class White students—couldn't name even two of the rights they enjoyed under the United States Constitution.

"Americans have long been complacent in their ignorance about the rest of the world," I continued, regaling my dinner companions with stories about Prior Lake: about the English teachers who argued that it wasn't important that their students learn French if such acquisition demanded that they subject themselves to the rigors of memorization, about the parents who insisted that Band was as vital a course as American Government or that geography was "passé"; and about the world cultures course which pretended to teach Eastern and Western civilization (read that as Asia, Africa, and Latin America) in a single trimester.

"It's not complacency," one of my companions interrupted. "It's more willful than that. Americans *love* knowing nothing about the rest of the world. It's a badge of honor, a symbol of our insulation, our invulnerability."

That conversation was replaying itself in an internal loop in my head when I staggered into my tiny classroom the next morning. As was often the case, the electricity in the building wasn't working. My students didn't seem to notice its absence.

"Do Americans understand that their opposition to the Russian war in Afghanistan contributed to the rise of the Taliban and Osama bin Laden?" one girl asked me even before I could sit down.

"It's more than that," one of her nineteen-year-old classmates added. "You created these people. You gave them weapons and training, so you really have yourselves to blame."

I was bleary-eyed from a sleepless night firing off frantic e-mail messages to friends back home in New York and parrying their equally frantic messages to me, the pleas for reassurance—"Are you all right? Are you safe?"—careening in both directions. When my server crashed, as it did with infuriating frequency, I'd taken refuge in television. It wasn't just a hunger for news that had kept me riveted to Fox News, the only American station on my cable. It was a need for community, no matter how electronically illusory.

The next morning, then, as the questions came at me, fast and furious, I wasn't at my professional best.

"Don't you think that we're seeing a modern version of the Crusades? Aren't the Muslims trying to do to the West what the Christians tried to do to the East?"

Interspersed among the questions, the students offered words of comfort and sympathy. The Kyrgyz people honor family and, in their eyes, my family had been attacked and maimed.

"I think that a better parallel is to the Enlightenment," one boy remarked. "That the Islamic world feels assaulted by new ideas, by secular ideas, and some people are trying to turn the clock back."

For people in this Muslim country sandwiched in among the other disintegrating fragments of failed Russian expansionism, the attacks on New York and Washington weren't a distant catastrophe, an abstract horror about which they were bantering idly. They'd been living on the front lines of Muslim fundamentalism for three years, their country suffering repeated attacks by the Islamic Movement of Uzbekistan, which is bent on carving a Taliban-like nation out of the valley where Kyrgyzstan meets Tajikistan and Uzbekistan.

There was no doubt in their minds that a U.S. strike against Afghanistan was imminent. And, living less than 400 miles from Afghanistan, the pending war felt perilously close to home. Everyone was imagining hordes of refugees fleeing north, bringing yet more poverty, and more militant Islam, into this already teetering young republic.

"Why are Americans calling this Islamic terrorism?" one girl asked. In this moderate Muslim country, where young women walk around town in miniskirts and bustiers on even the most important religious holidays, that link was a sensitive subject. "That makes it sound like Islam and all Muslims are to blame."

A boy, usually shy and quiet, interrupted and commented, "Americans don't call the people who bomb abortion clinics 'Christian terrorists.'" The class erupted. "They act as if all Muslims were the same. We know that you have all kinds of Christians—fundamentalists and Catholics, Protestants and Orthodox. So why do Americans act as if Islam doesn't have similar divisions?"

While Central Asian students were busy memorizing irregular verbs in English and German, American public-school kids were missing classes for pep rallies and decorating the gym for homecoming. Teachers in local high schools in Bishkek drilled teenagers on the shape of every corner of the globe as the sine qua non of any understanding of geopolitics. Back home, they assigned them short stories for Creative Writing or lip-synching presentations for Public Speaking. In this country, even college students studied five hours each day, six days a week, putting in more hours at home each night in preparation for their comprehensive exams. In the corner of U.S. public education I know best, the suburban high schools where most of our children are educated, teenagers were out partying because parents grouse if their children receive too much homework and testing. Being held accountable might damage adolescent egos.

I'd surveyed the results while I was at Prior Lake. They were chilling. More chilling still were the e-mails I received from alumni over the next few days. "I say, nuke the bastards," several read. When I responded by asking precisely which bastards they were referring to, the only response I received was, "The ragheads." I pressed on. "Which ragheads are you talking about?" The answer: "An Arab's an Arab, so why should we care whether they're from Afghanistan or Egypt?"

A few went beyond racist jingoism. "What the hell is going on in the world?" one boy queried me. "Why is everyone suddenly talking about bombing Afghanistan when none of the terrorists are from Afghanistan? And where in the hell is Afghanistan, anyway? And what's going on there?"

A girl who'd graduated at the top of her class wanted to know, "What's a jihad? What do Muslims believe? What are they so angry about? Aren't the Saudi Arabians our friends? What does any of this have to do with us? Or does the Muslim bible preach hatred of Christians?"

Those reactions were hardly surprising since for years we've allowed the deterioration of our public education system to become a political football, leaving our schools with the unenviable task of trying so hard to be something to everyone that old-fashioned education has been squeezed into the short time slot left between study hall and lunch. In the process, knowledge has been reduced to a series of facts that you don't need to learn and retain because in this new world of electronic libraries you can simply tap into the Internet, that great unwashed source of data that is utterly useless if you don't know enough to cull through the crap.

The major debates in education, whether among professionals or among parents, are no longer about knowledge, about what information one generation should impart to the next, but about values and emotions. What children should be taught to feel has replaced old arguments over what they should be taught to know.

So instead of struggling to decide how much foreign-language training kids should receive, teachers and school boards grapple with whether sixteen-, seventeen-, and eighteen-year-olds should be graded on the quality of their work, or if effort and quantity should be taken into consideration . . . lest those who work hard, but poorly, feel bad.

Rather than debate how to ground young people in European history without breeding ethnocentrism, we argue over tracking, over whether we should segregate kids according to ability . . . lest teenagers be scarred by being told what they already know.

We shun all discussion of how powerless the next generation will be without a solid foundation in geography and civics because, among educators and a surprising number of parents, memorization has been discarded as a worthless pursuit, replaced by an emphasis on reasoning and self-expression . . . lest young people's creativity be trampled. Indeed, our teachers are trained never to correct wrong answers but to "lead students to the right ones" instead . . . lest their young charges become demoralized.

In comfortable places like Prior Lake, where, by dint of social class, virtually everyone went to college and where, by dint of connections and a booming economy, hardly anyone had to worry about finding a decent job, it has been seductively easy to bask in the illusion that we were having all the right debates. After all, knowledge—old-fashioned commodities like reading, geography, and history—wasn't all that critical, especially if gaining it meant that Johnny's homework would cut into football practice or a part-time job that paid the car insurance or affected some other activity he needed to be "well-rounded." Anyway, it wasn't like kids from other suburbs knew all that much more.

In light of September 11, however, that attitude seems dangerously self-indulgent.

Does it make sense to insulate young adults, most of whom are already working, from the reality that, say, a journalist who writes dozens of poorly reported and clunkily written stories will not advance as rapidly as one who crafts fewer, but harder hitting, more accurate, and more eloquently moving chunks of prose? Or to treat them as if they are too dim-witted to comprehend that some people are simply smarter than others? To expect them to reason and create without a base of knowledge on which to build? Do any of the new educational fads give young people power—the power to ask questions, to spot convenient presidential lies or historical half-truths, the power to decide for themselves?

In the weeks following the World Trade Center cataclysm, Americans struggled to come to grips with a new world still choked by the ashes of almost three thousand dead. As we discovered that the price of business as usual was that semiliterate thugs could walk into our airports and hijack our country, or that people don't have to yell "Death to the Infidels!" for us to be in peril, our reality shifted. We almost instantly accepted that we could no longer be quite as complacent about our safety, that we might have to put up with long lines at airports, that the Statue of Liberty might have to become somewhat less welcoming, that we might well have to live, perhaps for a very long time, with a level of insecurity that is the norm elsewhere and from which we, for the most part, had been blessedly immune.

I couldn't imagine, then, that the catastrophe that turned Manhattan's morning into the nation's night wouldn't provide the same wake-up call in education that it had in so many other arenas of life, both public and private. After all, the price of turning out young people woefully underprepared to understand what had happened and what was going to happen had been thrown into the starkest relief.

I was painfully naive. In fact, I was completely and utterly wrong. On September 30, in a piece written for the *Washington Post,* Judith Rizzo, deputy chancellor for instruction in New York City schools, used the attack as leverage in her long-standing crusade for greater sensitivity to multicultural education. "Those people who said we don't need multiculturalism, [that] it's too touchy-feely, a pox on them. I think they've learned their lesson. We have to do more to teach habits of tolerance."

Lynne Cheney, the former chair of the National Endowment for the Humanities and wife of Vice President Dick Cheney, responded by accusing Rizzo and her cohorts of blaming the victim. "The deputy chancellor's suggestion . . . implies that the United States is to blame for the attack of September 11, that somehow intolerance on our part was the cause," she said in a speech in Dallas on October 5. "But on September 11, it was most manifestly not the United States that acted out of religious prejudice."

Rather than underlining the need for more multicultural education, she said, the horror of September 11 demonstrated how much our children need to be taught America's ideals. "We need to understand how fortunate we are to live in freedom. We need to understand that living in liberty is such a precious thing that generations of men and women have been willing to sacrifice everything for it. We need to know, in a war, exactly what is at stake. These are things our children should know. And I don't think it would hurt a bit when we teach them about the Constitution to use the word 'miracle.'"

As I followed that repartee from my vantage point seven thousand miles from home, my heart sank. At a turning point in history that demands new questions and new ways of thinking, two of the nation's leading educational voices replayed the same old script by repeating the same debate that has framed public education for decades and just repackaged it for the consumer in the wrapping paper of 9/11 destruction.

Today's young people don't need to be taught tolerance any more than they need to be schooled in patriotism. Does anyone really believe that the lessons of patriotism can stick if not backed up by a firm grounding in American history and politics, or that tolerance can take root without a thorough understanding of the history of the price of intolerance? Isn't uninformed tolerance as dangerous as informed intolerance, and blind patriotism its own brand of ignorance?

Rizzo and Cheney were revisiting an argument that has long torn apart our social studies and literature programs: the inane dispute over whether teachers should emphasize multiculturalism or, as they put it, a "common narrative." As New York's firefighters culled through the wreckage searching desperately for human remains, we all witnessed the answer to that question firsthand. No matter the divisions of race, religion, ethnicity, and class that separated them in life, in the end, the victims of the World Trade Center attack wound up buried in a communal grave.

Certainly, we cannot be indifferent to the emotional and moral development of our children. But we've expended so much energy debating how schools should train them to feel, how much patriotism they should learn, how much tolerance they must be taught, how sensitive they should be to our diversity, that we've ignored how terrifyingly little they know. It is knowledge they need. They need enough knowledge about history, geography, politics, and world affairs to understand the price of intolerance and the value of what America offers, enough knowledge to make sense out of what they saw on September 11, enough knowledge to be the kind of informed, questioning citizens who guarantee our nation's future.

In the months since the nature of our collective reality shifted on a single morning, Americans have hungered for a return to normalcy, for the days when televised FBI alerts were the stuff of bad Hollywood thrillers, when there was so little real news that we could max out on Chandra Levy and JonBenet Ramsay, perhaps even for the days when middle-class young people could live in blissful ignorance of the history of Israel, of the geography of Central Asia, of names like bin Laden, Al Qaeda, and Camp X-ray.

But we can't afford it. The richest country in the world can't afford middle- and upper-middle-class kids who can't even locate an island in the

Caribbean, not to mention who don't know why so many foreigners are proud of being anti-American.

The reform of our education system was at the top of the national political agenda before global terrorism seized center stage. Both houses of Congress had passed their own versions of a reform bill, and President Bush was stumping for immediate, and drastic, action. However, before we even had a chance to get to the major issues, rather than the ones politicians were debating, education was overwhelmed by the events of September 11. But as we consider with a new seriousness the concept of homeland defense, let us not forget that, in the long run, beefed-up airport security, guards at our tunnels, and more stringent visa requirements will be meaningless gestures if our citizenry isn't fluent in world history and foreign policy, if our young people can't find Afghanistan, and every future Afghanistan, on a map.

Appendix: Doing Case Studies in Education*

editor's introduction:

The Case Study as a Major Method for Doing Educational Research. Educational research remains one of the most challenging forms of research. Is it a form of psychology, susceptible to the designs in psychological experiments? Is it a philosophy, with the need to express visions, beliefs, and values? Or is it something else, possibly involving a range of methods from case studies to statistical analyses to economics research?

The selection does not address these issues directly. However, regardless of the response, case studies are likely to continue as one of the major methods for doing education research. This appendix covers a broad range of practical issues that you will confront in doing case studies. You may especially find the five common "worries"—along with their remedies—to be a helpful and succinct set of reminders.

Practical Guidance in Doing Case Studies in Education. This appendix provides practical guidance on doing case study research in the education field. The selection, originally appearing in a handbook of research methods published by the American Educational Research Association, assumes that you are someone desirous of either doing case studies or interpreting case study research. The methodological

---

*Yin, Robert K. (2005). "Case Study Methods." In Judith Green, Gregory Camilli, & Patricia Elmore (Eds.), *Complementary Methods for Research in Education* (3rd ed.). Washington, DC: American Educational Research Association. The author extends sincere thanks to Profs. Chris Clark (University of Delaware) and Bob Stake (University of Illinois at Urbana-Champaign) for their helpful comments and to the volume editor, Gregory Camilli, for his methodic encouragement and feedback in reviewing earlier versions of this manuscript.

approach is based on earlier works by the author but has been customized to specific issues in education.

Narrower than some of the other approaches presented in the rest of this anthology, and also narrower than other forms of qualitative research more generally, the selection favors an evidence-based approach to case studies. You will find helpful discussions on

- designing your case study,
- choosing your "case,"
- using various sources of data, and
- analyzing case study data.

The goal is to increase the quality of case study research by emulating methods from the natural sciences, although you should recognize that case study research to this day remains a social science.

In doing case study research this way (other ways not being precluded), your challenge is to show that you (a) followed empirical research procedures, (b) considered whether a two- or multiple-case study would have been appropriate, and (c) tried hard to distinguish evidence (data) from interpretation (and conclusions) in your analyses. Over the past 20 years, this orientation to case studies appears to have been welcomed by a wide audience of students and scholars in many fields, not just education (Yin, 2003).

To make the appendix more helpful, you might want to read the text without initially attending to its endnotes and references. That information delves into important methodological issues but does not necessarily contain practical guidance.

Reference

Yin, R. K. (2003). *Case study research: Design and method* (3rd ed.). Thousand Oaks, CA: Sage.

By now, the case study method has attained routine status as a viable method for doing education research.[1] Other methods include but are not limited to surveys, ethnographies, experiments, quasi-experiments, economic and statistical modeling, histories, research syntheses, and developmental methods.[2] Summary Point No. 1: *Compared to other methods, the strength of the case study method is its ability to examine, in-depth, a "case" within its "real-life" context.*

This chapter gives you a running start in knowing how to use the case study method, highlighting a few basic considerations. The main considerations have been condensed even further, into a series of "summary points," the first having just been noted above. The chapter then concludes with discussion guides for five common "worries" about using the case study method. However, the compactness of the chapter should not mislead you about the real challenges in doing case studies. For more help and greater detail on the method, you need to refer to other, more extensive works.[3] As an aid, key terms in this chapter have been *italicized*, to enable you to refer to particular parts of these other works.[4]

When to Use the Case Study Method

Case study research enables you to investigate important topics not easily covered by other methods. Conversely, other methods cover many topics better than does case study research. The overall idea is that different research methods serve complementary functions. Your study might even use multiple methods that include a case study.[5]

The distinctive topics for applying the case study method arise from at least two situations. First and most important (e.g., Shavelson and Towne, 2002, pp. 99–106), the case study method is pertinent when your research addresses either a descriptive question (*what* happened?) or an explanatory question (*how* or *why* did something happen?); in contrast, a well-designed experiment is needed to begin inferring causal relationships (e.g., whether a new education program had improved student performance), and a survey may be better at telling you *how often* something has happened.

Second, you may want to illuminate a particular situation, to get a close (i.e., in-depth and first-hand) understanding of it. The case study method helps you to make direct observations and collect data in natural settings, compared to relying on "derived" data (Bromley, 1986, p. 23)—e.g., test results, school and other statistics maintained by government agencies, and responses to questionnaires. For instance, education audiences may want to know about a high school principal who had done an especially good job, or about a successful (or unsuccessful) collective bargaining negotiation with severe consequences (e.g., a teachers' strike), or about everyday life in a special residential school. You could use other methods, but the case study method will go far in serving your needs.

Box 1 lists some typical examples of case study topics in education. To begin understanding the case study method, for each topic you should ask: what is the "case" (*unit of analysis*), and what related subtopics need to be

Box 1   Examples of Possible Case Studies in Education

1. How a Limited-English-Proficient student struggles to do well in school, also preserving relationships to family and friends outside of school

2. How teachers form and make use of informal planning groups to improve instruction

3. Implementing a 5th grade violence prevention program and tracing the results

4. The actions taken by a low-performing school, over the course of only a few years, to improve its performance markedly

5. Why a school-business partnership helped improve student performance by providing challenging out-of-school opportunities

6. What happens in a pre-school program that prepares children for their later schooling and education

7. How a school "choice" policy (whereby parents can choose the school their children will attend) works in a school system

covered as part of the related case study? Take the first topic in Box 1 as an example. The "case" would be the single student. The related subtopics would include the student's school, family, and friends. You might think of these subtopics as key contextual conditions, for this first topic. Continue defining the "case" and the relevant subtopics for the other topics listed in Box 1.

Summary Point No. 2: *The case study method is best applied when research addresses descriptive or explanatory questions and aims to produce a first-hand understanding of people and events.*

An Essential Skill for Case Study Investigators

In many ways, doing case study research will not be different from using other research methods.[6] All methods require reviewing the literature, defining research questions and analytic strategies, using formal data collection protocols or instruments, and writing good research reports. However, case studies call for at least one additional skill on your part.

Unlike most other methods, when doing case studies you may need to do data collection and data analysis together. For instance, a field interview of one person may produce information that conflicts with that from an earlier interview. Doing the interview is considered data collection, but surfacing the conflict is considered data analysis. You want that analysis to happen quickly, so that you can modify your data collection plans while still in the field—either by re-interviewing the earlier person or by seeking to find a third source to resolve the conflict.

The need to do data analysis while still collecting data produces huge differences compared to using other methods. With both surveys and experiments, for instance, data collection is likely to occur as a formal stage separate from data analysis. One stage usually gets done before the other starts. The data collection also may be delegated to a research assistant or a trained interviewer, neither of whom may have anything to do with the later data analysis. Similarly, data analysis may be in the hands of a senior investigator who had little direct involvement with the data collection.

Do not take for granted the ability needed to do data analysis while collecting data. The implications, compared to other methods, are huge. You, as a case study investigator, need to master the intricacies of the study's substantive issues while also having the patience and dedication to collect data carefully and fairly—potentially hiding (if possible) your own substantive thoughts. For instance, in case studies you might have to ask questions, during a field interview, whose answers you believe you already know. Do you think you can ask the questions fairly? Summary Point No. 3: *A key demand of the case study method is the investigator's skill and expertise at pursuing an entire (and sometimes subtle) line of inquiry at the same time as (and not after) data are being collected.* A good case study investigator may even appear to mimic the role of a good detective. You ought to know whether you have the requisite ability and also know how to build even further your skills in this direction.

Three Basic Steps in Designing Case Studies

The first step, already discussed in relation to Box 1, is to define the "case" that you are studying. Arriving at even a tentative definition helps enormously to organize your case study. Generally, you should stick with your initial choice, because you might have reviewed literature or developed research questions specific to this choice. However, a virtue of the case study method is the ability to redefine the "case," after collecting some early data. Beware when this happens—you may then have to backtrack, reviewing a slightly different literature and possibly revising the original research questions.

A second step calls for deciding whether to do a single case study or a set of case studies. The term "case study" can refer to either *single-* or *multiple-case studies*. They represent two types of *case study designs*. You also can choose to keep your case *holistic* or to have *embedded* sub-cases within an overall holistic case. For example, your holistic case might be about why a school system had implemented certain student promotion policies, and the system's classrooms could serve as embedded "sub-cases" from which you also collect data. Holistic or embedded case studies represent another two types of case study design, which can exist with either single- or multiple-case studies—so that you should think of the two-by-two combination producing four basic designs for case studies.

Of these combinations, the most intriguing are the ones contrasting single- and multiple-case studies. Focusing on a single case will force you to devote careful attention to that case. However, having multiple cases might help you to strengthen the findings from your entire study—because the multiple cases might have been chosen as *replications* of each other, deliberate and contrasting comparisons, or hypothesized variations.

A third step involves deciding whether or not to use *theory development* to help to select your case(s), develop your data collection protocol, and organize your initial data analysis strategies. An initial theoretical perspective about school principals, for example, might claim that successful principals are those who perform as "instructional leaders." A lot of literature (which you would cite as part of your case study) supports this perspective. Your case study could attempt to build, extend, or challenge this perspective, possibly even emulating a hypothesis-testing approach. However, such a theoretical perspective also could limit your ability to make discoveries—i.e., to discover from scratch just how and why a successful principal had been successful.

In general, the less experience you have had in doing case studies, the more that you might want to adopt some theoretical perspectives. Without them, and without adequate prior experience, you might have trouble convincing others that your case study had produced findings of any value to the field. Conversely, highly experienced case study investigators may deliberately avoid adopting any theoretical perspectives, hoping to produce a "break the mold" case study.

Summary Point No. 4: *A good case study design, at a minimum, involves defining your case, justifying your choice of a single- or multiple-case study, and deliberately adopting or minimizing theoretical perspectives.*

Choosing Specific Persons, Groups, or Sites to Be Your "Case"

Your case study will be about one or more actual real-life cases. While you already may have defined your case conceptually, as in the seven examples previously presented in Box 1, you may still need to select the actual real-life case(s) to be studied. Selecting the case(s) serves as possibly the most critical step in doing case study research (Stake, 1994, p. 243). The process poses common problems that you can nevertheless overcome with adequate thought and effort. One of the most common misconceptions for you to overcome is believing that case studies are to represent a formal "sample" from some larger universe, and that generalizing from your cases depends on statistical inference (*statistical generalization*); instead, generalizing from case studies reflects substantive topics or issues of interest, and the making of logical inferences (*analytic generalization*).[7]

When doing a single-case study, you may have chosen to study an *extreme or unique* case, or even a *revelatory* case—e.g., the workings of a school-based gang—and you may have been poised to study this case from the outset. Or, you already may be aware of the case to be studied because of some special access that you have for collecting data about that case. However, in other situations (e.g., in studying the *typical case*, the *critical case*, or a *longitudinal case*) there may be several if not many qualified candidates, and you have to select from among them. Under this circumstance, you should conduct a formal *case study screening* procedure. The screening can be based on reviewing documents or querying of people knowledgeable about each candidate. Useful screening criteria include the willingness of key persons in the case to participate in your study, the likely richness of the available data, and preliminary evidence that the case has had the experience or situation that you are seeking to study, even if the case is to be a *typical* case. Summary Point No. 5: *The case selection or screening goal is to avoid the scenario whereby, after having started the actual case study, the selected case turns out not to be viable or to represent an instance of something other than what you had intended to study.*

When doing a multiple-case study (even a *two-case* case study), all of these considerations are relevant, plus certain cross-case issues. These have to do with your logic of inquiry. You should decide whether the two (or more) cases are to represent confirmatory cases (i.e., presumed replications of the same phenomenon), contrasting cases (e.g., a success and a failure), or theoretically diverse cases (e.g., a primary school case and a secondary school case).[8] With three or more cases, audiences also like to see some geographic, ethnic, size, or other related variation among the cases. None of the cases should be considered "controls" for each other, in the same sense of the term "control group," because in case study research you do not manipulate "treatments" or control any real-life events.

Despite these complications and extra work, multiple-case designs have important advantages for you to consider. First, you will be able to show your audience that you can practice the complete cycle of case study research (e.g., design, selection, analysis, and reporting) with more than a single case, reducing suspicion that your skills were limited to a single case that also might have been personally special to you in some way. Second, you would be able to respond to a common criticism of single-case studies—that they are somehow unique and idiosyncratic and therefore have limited value beyond the circumstances of the single case. Third, you will have a modest amount of comparative data, even if the cases were chosen to be confirmatory cases, helping you to analyze your findings.

Varieties of Sources of Case Study Data

Case study research is not limited to a single source of data, as in the use of questionnaires to carry out a survey study. In fact, good case studies benefit from having *multiple sources of evidence*. Box 2 lists six common sources of evidence. You also may use focus groups and other sources besides these six. The main concern is not that any particular source be used. Rather, Summary Point No. 6: *In collecting case study data, the main idea is to "triangulate" or establish converging lines of evidence to make your findings as robust as possible.*

How might this *triangulation* work? The most desired convergence occurs when two or more independent sources all point to the same set of events or "facts." For example, what might have taken place at a school's faculty meeting might have been reported to you (independently) by both the teachers and the principal, and the meeting also might have been followed by some documented outcome (e.g., issuance of a new policy that was the presumed topic of the meeting). You were not able to be at the meeting yourself, but having all these different sources gives you more confidence about concluding what transpired than had you relied on a single source alone.

Triangulating is not always as easy as the preceding example. Sometimes, as when you interview different teachers and the principal, all appear to be giving corroborating evidence about how their school operates—e.g., how assistant teachers are used in the classroom. But in fact, they all may be

Box 2   Common Sources of Evidence in Doing Case Studies

1. Documents (e.g., newspaper articles, letters and e-mails, and reports)

2. Archival records (e.g., student records)

3. Interviews (e.g., open-ended conversations with key informants)

4. Direct observations (e.g., observations of classroom behavior)

5. Participant-observation (e.g., being identified as a researcher but also filling a real-life role in the scene being studied)

6. Physical artifacts (e.g., computer printouts of students' work)

echoing the same institutional "mantra," developed over time for speaking with outsiders (such as parents and researchers).

This collective "mantra" may not necessarily coincide with the school's actual operations. Reviewing the literature may help you to anticipate this type of situation, and making your own direct observations also may be extremely helpful. However, when relying on direct observations, note another problem that can arise. Because you may have pre-scheduled the classroom observations, a teacher may have decided to change the instructional practices just for your visit. So, getting at the actual role of assistant teachers in the classroom, or at some other school operations, may not be as easy as you might think.

Nevertheless, you always will be better off by using multiple rather than single sources of evidence. This methodological preference again raises the need for certain capabilities in using the case study method: your ability to work skillfully with multiple or varied sources of evidence and to be expert at handling different kinds of evidence.

Some researchers, either by training or preference, can only deal comfortably with a single type of evidence—e.g., interviews. Such persons may give too much weight to what they hear others saying, may not be able to conduct thorough searches for other relevant evidence, and may not pay sufficient attention to other forms of evidence. In this example, the ensuing case study is likely to be based on "verbal reports"—e.g., what the principal says happened rather than what actually might have happened. You should avoid relying on such a narrow evidentiary base. Your study in this example would actually be an open-ended interview study (a variant of a survey), not really a case study. One way of telling how skilled you are in collecting multiple sources of evidence is to observe your interest in different data collection techniques—do you keep up with the state-of-the-art on more than a single technique?

Regardless of its source, case study evidence also can include both *qualitative and quantitative data*.[9] Qualitative data may be considered non-numeric data—e.g., categorical information that can be systematically collected and presented; quantitative data can be considered numeric data—e.g., information based on the use of ordinal if not interval or ratio measures. Both types of data can be highly complex, demanding analytic techniques going well beyond simple tallies.[10]

As with your ability to handle different sources of evidence, you also should be comfortable and adept at working with both qualitative and quantitative data. For example, some case studies—e.g., a case study of a school district's student achievement trends over time—might be heavily quantitative. Other case studies—e.g., the strategies underlying a superintendent's initiation of a combination of all-day kindergarten, early literacy programs, and advanced placement courses to spur education reform—might be heavily qualitative. Yet other case studies—e.g., showing how student achievement had improved in conjunction with the preceding combination of initiatives—might be heavily quantitative and qualitative.

A final but essential comment on case study evidence: You need to present the evidence in your case study with sufficient clarity to allow the reader to judge independently your interpretation of the data. Older case studies frequently mixed evidence and interpretation. This practice may still be excusable when doing a unique case study or a revelatory case study, because the descriptive insights may be more important than knowing the strength of the evidence for such insights. However, for most case studies, mixing evidence and interpretation may be taken as a sign that you do not understand the difference between the two, or that you do not know how to handle data (and hence proceeded prematurely to interpretation).

In doing your case study, you should follow the classic way of presenting evidence: arraying data through tables, charts, figures, other exhibits (even pictures), and vignettes. Footnotes, quotations from interviews, chronologies, and narrative questions-and-answers also are suitable—as long as these are set apart from your interpretive narrative. Whatever the way of presenting the data, the structure or format of the array needs to reflect an overarching concern for presenting data *fairly*. A brief description of how the evidence was collected, including use of a formal data collection tool (*case study protocol*), also is helpful. Summary Point No. 7: *Case studies should present their data formally and explicitly, in a variety of data arrays set apart from the case study narrative.*

Ways of Analyzing Case Study Data

If selecting your case(s) to be studied is the most critical step in doing case study research, analyzing your case study data is probably the most troublesome. Much of the problem relates to false expectations: that the data will somehow "speak for themselves," or that some counting or tallying procedure (e.g., "Q-sorts," regression models, or factor analyses) will be sufficient in producing the main findings for the case study. Wrong.

You actually made some key assumptions for your analysis when you defined your research questions and your "case." Was your motive in doing the case study mainly to address your research questions? If so, then the techniques for analyzing the data might be directed at those questions first. Was your motive to derive more general lessons for which your case(s) (is) are but (an) example(s)? If so, the techniques might be directed at these lessons. Finally, if your case study was driven by a discovery motive, you might start your analysis with what you think you have discovered.

Now comes a "reverse" lesson. Realizing that key underlying assumptions for later analysis are in fact made at the initial stages of the case study, you could have anticipated and planned the analytic strategies or implications when conducting those initial stages. Collecting the actual data may lead to changes in this plan, but having an initial plan that needs to be revised (even drastically) may be better than having no plan at all.

Several analytic techniques can help and can be planned during the case study design. One possibility is to stipulate some pattern of findings at the outset of your case study. Your analysis would then consist of the analytic technique of *pattern-matching* the collected evidence against the initially stipulated pattern. For example, studies of educational reform can start with some hypothesized patterns: schools must implement improved (e.g., "standards-based") curricula and instruction; school systems must redesign their tests or assessments to cover the concepts in the new curricula and instruction; new inservice opportunities must be provided to teachers and principals that coincide with the new curricula and instruction; and the preservice training of new teachers also must incorporate these conditions. Your case study would collect data to determine whether this pattern of educational conditions had actually occurred—and the degree to which the conditions were substantively aligned.

Other analytic techniques include *explanation-building, time-series analysis,* the use of *logic models,* and *cross-case synthesis.* None of them comes with any formulas, although statistical calculations can be part of them. For instance, one form of logic model is a hypothesized sequence of events that should occur over time. In this example, suppose your case study of school improvement stipulated the following five-stage sequence: (a) mentor teachers receive training on an academic subject; (b) the mentor teachers lead new training sessions for other teachers; (c) the mentor teachers provide classroom assistance for the other teachers; (d) the instructional practices of the other teachers subsequently change; and (e) student performance improves. If you were studying the sequence as part of your case study of an entire school district, your analysis would trace the actual sequences and assess the reality of the predicted behavioral changes. Depending upon the available data, part of your analysis could be represented by a structural equation model representing the five-stage sequence—representing a statistical calculation within your case study.

For case study research, the challenge of doing analysis stretches one important step further—and well beyond selecting and planning for a particular analytic technique: The presentation of your analysis can interact with the structure or composition of your case study report. In the preceding example, the assumption was that your report would present the data and then carry out the analysis, including the structural equation model. Such a *linear sequence* mimics the reporting of most quantitative research (i.e., hypotheses → method → data analysis → findings → interpretations and conclusions). However, for case study research, the linear sequence is not the only way. You also might present your analysis throughout the reporting of your case study—as a history is presented or as much sociological fieldwork has been reported.

Although he writes about doing ethnography (not case studies), Van Maanen (1988, p. 30) succinctly captures the essence of this latter type of reporting. He says that, while a report may be

> ... *crammed with details and facts, it also conveys an argument and an informing context as to how these details and facts interweave.*

An obvious example would be to tell your story in chronological sequence: "in the beginning. . . ." You would present (fairly) and discuss the data about this initial period of time. You would then present data and discuss the next period of time. You would repeat the process as many times as needed. For each period of time, the underlying themes might have been developed from your research questions, stated at the outset of your case study and now being used as the interweaving themes. Following this iterative process, be aware that you are building an argument, hoping to convince the reader that your rendition of reality is correct. As a final note, your ability to be convincing increases the more that you also incorporate *rival explanations* or *alternative perspectives* into your analysis.

Summary Point No. 8: *Case study analysis can rely on several techniques whose use might even be anticipated during the initial design of the case study; the analysis can be presented throughout a case study, as you gradually build an argument that addresses your research questions.*

Composing Case Study Reports

As you have just seen, the structure of a case study report can be heavily influenced by your analytic strategies. More generally, because the report does not have to follow any particular form, the opportunity to compose case studies can be more exciting and call on greater creativity than reporting about research that has been based on most other methods. The other side of the coin is that if you have difficulty composing, the opportunity can heighten any uncertainty you might have had in doing case study research in the first place, leading to writer's cramps and eventually even despair and desperation. Make no mistake about it: if you want to do case studies, be sure that you also enjoy composing. In doing any given case study, you can and should test your compositional skill early: Try to compose some substantive material *even before completing your fieldwork.*[11] Is the composition easy and smooth? Do your colleagues think the composition is promising?

To get some idea of the varieties of *case study compositions,* Box 3 contains an extensive list of books readily accessible to most of you. Covered are 44 individual case studies (mostly about schools and school systems; equally large lists could have been amassed on curricula, student learning, teaching and instruction, leadership, and other topics). Keep this list as a quick future reference, whether you end up doing your own case study or not.

For Further Discussion

Five common worries about doing case study research (not including the composing of the case study report) serve as a summary of this entire chapter (see Box 4). Engaging in the discussion points at the end of each worry will help you overcome it. You will then be well on your way to doing a successful case study.

Box 3   Varieties of Case Studies on Schools and School Systems

---

Single Case Studies of Schools or Local School Systems

Anyon, Jean, *Ghetto Schooling: A Political Economy of Urban Educational Reform*, Teachers College Press, New York, NY, 1997—student equity in the Newark (NJ) school system.

Bryk, Anthony S., et al., *Charting Chicago School Reform: Democratic Localism as a Lever for Change*, Westview Press, Boulder, CO, 1998—7 chapters, one containing a statistical analysis.

Bryk, Anthony S., David Kerbow, and Sharon Rollow, "Chicago School Reform," in Diane Ravitch and Joseph P. Viteritti (eds.), *New Schools for a New Century: The Redesign of Urban Education*, Yale University Press, New Haven, CT, 1997, pp. 164–200—a shorter and earlier version of the same case study.

Gross, Neal, et al., *Implementing Organizational Innovations: A Sociological Analysis of Planned Educational Change*, Basic Books, New York, NY, 1971—implementing a new instructional method in a single elementary school.

McAdams, Donald R., *Fighting to Save Our Urban Schools . . . and Winning!: Lessons from Houston*, Teachers College Press, New York, NY, 2000—extensive citations to local news articles help to offset potential biases of author, who was a key participant in the case study.

Single Case Studies of State Education Systems or of Educational Programs

Whitford, Betty Lou, and Ken Jones (eds.), *Accountability, Assessment, and Teacher Commitment: Lessons from Kentucky's Reform Efforts*, State University of New York Press, Albany, NY, 2000—14 chapters include 6 subcases inside schools and classrooms, 2 of accountability systems, and 6 other chapters on the state system.

Zigler, Edward, and Susan Muenchow, *Head Start: The Inside Story of America's Most Successful Educational Experiment*, Basic Books, New York, NY, 1992—extensive interviews by the second author help to offset potential of the first author, who was a key participant in the case study.

"Two-Case" Case Studies

Elmore, Richard F., Charles H. Abelmann, and Susan H. Fuhrman, "The New Accountability in State Education Reform: From Process to

(Continued)

Box 3 (Continued)

Performance," in Helen F. Ladd (ed.), *Holding Schools Accountable: Performance-Based Reform in Education*, The Brookings Institution, Washington, DC, 1996, pp. 65–98—comparative discussion of 2 state departments (MS and KY) throughout the chapter, to appreciate contrasting experiences on a topic-by-topic basis.

Lusi, Susan Follett, *The Role of State Departments of Education in Complex School Reform*, Teachers College Press, New York, NY, 1997—separate case studies of 2 state departments (KY and VT), with commonalities and differences discussed in a closing chapter.

Multiple-Case Studies

Cuban, Larry, and Michael Usdan (eds.), *Powerful Reforms with Shallow Roots: Improving America's Urban Schools*, Teachers College Press, New York, NY, 2003—6 case studies of school systems presented in separate chapters and separately authored, with 2 additional chapters providing a cross-case introduction and conclusion; Yee, Gary, and Barbara McCloud, "A Vision of Hope: A Case Study of Seattle's Two Nontraditional Superintendents," pp. 54–76—one of the best documented among the 6 case studies.

Hill, Paul T., Christine Campbell, and James Harvey, *It Takes a City: Getting Serious about Urban School Reform*, The Brookings Institution, Washington, DC, 2000—main text is a cross-case analysis of 6 case studies, with the 6 case studies presented in an appendix and not separately authored.

Perrone, Vito, and Associates, *Portraits of High Schools*, The Carnegie Foundation for the Advancement of Teaching, Princeton University Press, Lawrenceville, NJ, 1985—13 case studies of different kinds of high schools, each presented in a separately authored chapter.

Sirotnik, Kenneth A., and John I. Goodlad (eds.), *School-University Partnerships in Action: Concepts, Cases, and Concerns*, Teachers College Press, New York, NY, 1988—2 chapters are on "concepts" and 2 on "concerns," all separately authored; the other 6 chapters are case studies of individual partnerships, also separately authored.

Willie, Charles V., Ralph Edwards, and Michael J. Alves, *Student Diversity, Choice, and School Improvement*, Bergin & Garvey, Westport, CT, 2002—of 10 chapters, 3 are case studies of success stories (Boston, MA; Cambridge, MA; and Lee County, FL).

Box 4   Five Common "Worries" in Using the Case Study Method

1. **How do I know if I should use the case study method to do my study?**

   There's no formula, but your choice depends in part on your research question(s). The more that your questions are descriptive ("what has been happening?") or explanatory ("how or why has it been happening?"), the more that the case study method will be relevant. *What other reasons might you cite for using or not using the case study method?*

2. **How should I select the case to be studied?**

   You need sufficient access to the potential data, whether involving people to be interviewed, documents or records to be reviewed, or observations to be made in the "field." Given such access to more than a single candidate, you should choose the one(s) that best illuminate(s) your research questions. Absent such access, you should consider changing your research questions, hopefully leading to new candidates to which you do have access. *Do you think access should be so important?*

3. **I am studying a school. What is my case: Is it the teachers? The reading program? The whole school?**

   The specific definition of your case again depends upon your research question(s). The least desirable question is to want to know "everything that happened." Your literature review should help lead to more specific questions of interest and they, in turn, should readily point to the appropriate definition of the case. *As a further part of defining your case, do you think you should identify a particular time period, before and after which events will be deemed irrelevant to the case, or is your case timeless?*

4. **How much time and effort should I devote to collecting the case study data? How do I know whether I'm finished collecting the data?**

   Unlike other methods, there is no clear cut-off point. You should try to collect enough data so that: (1) you have confirmatory evidence (evidence from two or more different sources) for most of your main topics; and (2) your evidence includes attempts to investigate major rival hypotheses or explanations. *What do you think are some of the cut-off points for other methods, and why wouldn't they work in doing case study research?*

5. **How do I start analyzing my case study data?**

   You might start with questions (e.g., the questions in your case study protocol) rather than with the data. Start with a small question first, then identify your evidence that addresses the question. Draw a tentative conclusion based on the weight of the evidence, also asking how you should display the evidence so that readers can check your assessment. Continue to a larger question and repeat the procedure. Keep going until you think you have addressed your main research question(s). *Discuss the benefit of starting with questions rather than starting with the data.*

References

Bock, Edwin A., and Alan K. Campbell (eds.), *Case Studies in American Government: The Inter-University Case Program,* Prentice-Hall, Englewood Cliffs, NJ, 1962.

Bromley, D. B., *The Case-Study Method in Psychology and Related Disciplines,* John Wiley, Chichester, Great Britain, 1986.

Campbell, Donald T., "'Degrees of Freedom' and the Case Study," *Comparative Political Studies,* 1975, 8:178–193.

Christensen, C. Roland, and Abby J. Hansen, *Teaching and the Case Method: Text, Cases, and Reading,* Harvard Business School, Boston, MA, 1981.

Cook, Thomas D., and Monique R. Payne, "Objecting to the Objections to Using Random Assignment in Educational Research," in Frederick Mosteller and Robert Boruch (eds.), *Evidence Matters: Randomized Trials in Education Research,* Brookings Institution Press, Washington, DC, 2002, pp. 150–178.

Gomm, Roger, Martyn Hammerlsey, and Peter Foster, "Case Study and Generalization," in Roger Gomm, Martyn Hammerlsey, and Peter Foster (eds.), *Case Study Method: Key Issues, Key Texts,* Sage, Thousand Oaks, CA, 2000, pp. 98–115.

Hammerlsey, Martyn, and Roger Gomm, "Introduction," in Roger Gomm, Martyn Hammerlsey, and Peter Foster (eds.), *Case Study Method: Key Issues, Key Texts,* Sage, Thousand Oaks, CA, 2000, pp. 1–16.

Keeves, John P., *Educational Research, Methodology, and Measurement: An International Handbook,* Pergamon Press, Oxford, England, 1988.

Mitchell, J. Clyde, "Case and Situation Analysis," in Roger Gomm, Martyn Hammerlsey, and Peter Foster (eds.), *Case Study Method: Key Issues, Key Texts,* Sage, Thousand Oaks, CA, 2000, pp. 165–186. Originally published in *Sociological Review,* 1983, 31:187–211.

Pigors, Paul, and Faith Pigors, *Case Method in Social Relations: The Incident Process,* McGraw-Hill, New York, NY, 1961.

Platt, Jennifer, "'Case Study' in American Methodological Thought," *Current Sociology,* Spring 1992, 40(1): 17–48.

Shavelson, Richard J., and Lisa Towne (eds.), *Scientific Research in Education,* National Academy Press, Washington, DC, 2002.

Sieber, Samuel D., "The Integration of Fieldwork and Survey Methods," *American Journal of Sociology,* 1973, 78:1335–1359.

Simons, Helen, "The Paradox of Case Study," *Cambridge Journal of Education,* 1996, 26:225–240.

Stake, Robert E., "Case Studies," in Norman K. Denzin and Yvonna S. Lincoln (eds.), *Handbook of Qualitative Research,* Sage, Thousand Oaks, CA, 1994, pp. 236–247.

Stake, Robert E., "Case Study Methods in Educational Research: Seeking Sweet Water," in Richard M. Jaeger (ed.), *Complementary Methods for Research in Education,* American Educational Research Association, Washington, DC, 1988, pp. 253–300; 2nd edition, 1997, pp. 401–427.

Stenhouse, L., "Case Study Methods," in John P. Keeves (ed.), *Educational Research, Methodology, and Measurement: An International Handbook,* Pergamon Press, Oxford, England, 1988, pp. 49–53.

Van Maanen, John, *Tales of the Field: On Writing Ethnography,* University of Chicago Press, Chicago, IL, 1988.

Yin, Robert K., *Applications of Case Study Research,* Sage, Thousand Oaks, CA, 2003a, 2nd edition.

Yin, Robert K., *Case Study Research: Design and Methods,* Sage, Thousand Oaks, CA, 2003b, 3rd edition.

Yin, Robert K., "The Abridged Version of Case Study Research," in Leonard Bickman and Debra J. Rog (eds.), *Handbook of Applied Social Research,* Sage, Thousand Oaks, CA, 1998, pp. 229–259.

Yin, Robert K., "Rival Explanations as an Alternative to Reforms as 'Experiments,'" in Leonard Bickman (ed.), *Validity & Social Experimentation: Donald Campbell's Legacy,* Sage, Thousand Oaks, CA, 2000, Vol. 1, pp. 239–266.

Yin, Robert K., *The Case Study Anthology,* Sage, Thousand Oaks, CA, 2004.

Yin, Robert K., "Evaluation: A Singular Craft," in Charles Reichardt and Sharon Rallis (eds.), *New Directions in Program Evaluation,* 1994, pp. 71–84.

Notes

1. Hammersley and Gomm (2000, p. 1) have noted that interest in case study research had eclipsed by the late 1970s and early 1980s. Platt (1992, p. 18) made a similar observation, also noting that the case study method had all but disappeared from the popular textbooks of that time. Both works acknowledge the ensuing resurgence of interest from that time to the present (over 20 years). The method is now commonly used and cited in mainstream education publications (e.g., Shavelson and Towne, 2002, pp. 99–106).

2. How the case study method is to be categorized among other social science methods has been the subject of extensive writing, especially in education research. For instance, an international handbook divides the various methods into scientific and humanistic research, placing the case study method under the latter (Keeves, 1988, p. 7). While no method of social research, by definition, can replicate the scientific method in the natural sciences, the present chapter is written from the perspective that *emulating* the principles of scientific research—e.g., starting with explicit research questions, using a research design to address these questions, collecting and fairly presenting evidence to support interpretations, and referencing related research to aid in defining questions and drawing conclusions—will produce stronger case study research. The humanistic tradition offers other strengths, such as emphasizing participant-observation and prolonged engagement in the field, celebrating the particular rather than the general,

and becoming "experientially acquainted" with the case (e.g., Stake, 1994; and Simons, 1996).

Despite the terms 'scientific' and 'humanistic,' which are too stereotypic, the two orientations to doing case study research are not necessarily conflicting. They may be seen as differences in emphasis (e.g., Stenhouse, 1988; and Yin, 1994). However, in designing a new case study, you should be sensitive to these different orientations and whether key members of your audience have particular preferences.

3. These works include comprehensive texts (Yin, 2003a and 2003b), an earlier and abbreviated version on the case study method (Yin, 1998), a paper on rival explanations (Yin, 2000), and an anthology of classic examples of case study research (Yin, 2004). You also should consult the contributions on case study methods (Stake, 1988; and 1997) that appeared in the earlier editions of *Contemporary Methods*.

4. See Yin (2003b) for further clarification of the italicized terms.

5. For instance, the complementarity between case studies and surveys has long been appreciated (e.g., Sieber, 1973). The recent focus on using experimental methods in education research has pointed to additional complementarities. As noted by two proponents of experimental designs using randomized assignment, case study methods can be valued ". . . as adjuncts to experiments rather than as alternatives to them" (Cook and Payne, 2002, p. 168).

6. A brief reminder is that this entire chapter is devoted to case study *research,* even though case studies enjoy extensive use as a *teaching* tool (e.g., Bock and Campbell, 1962; and Christensen and Hansen, 1981) and as a way of improving *practice* (e.g., Pigors and Pigors, 1961).

7. The distinction, together with the broader question of whether the main value of case studies is to render the individual case or to arrive at broader generalizations, is critical to doing case study research. Where generalization is an important goal for your case study research, and to understand more clearly the strong preference for using analytic generalization (also noting that different writers use different labels for the same concept), consult Mitchell (1983) and Gomm et al. (2000). To understand why the statistical view is possibly an inappropriate way of generalizing from case studies and may lead to misunderstanding the value of case study research, see an incisive but little known article by Donald Campbell (1975).

8. The motive underlying the selection of multiple cases is not different from that used by scientists initially defining a series of experiments. As with multiple experiments, multiple-case studies are not selected to represent some universe but instead to pursue a logical framework of inquiry.

9. This treatment of qualitative from quantitative research as two types of data comes out of a unitary vision that challenges the view of qualitative and quantitative research as opposing types or even philosophies of empirical research (see Yin, 1994).

10. Bob Stake (see acknowledgments) has continually emphasized the complexity of the situations and phenomenological accounts that can be represented by

qualitative data. I have taken the liberty of attributing the same feature of quantitative data, which can assume the form of complex quantitative models. In both situations, the complexity is not necessarily with the analytic techniques or their mechanical operations—but rather with the logical thinking that is needed.

11. Chris Clark (see acknowledgments) reminded me of this excellent practice in his review of an earlier draft of this manuscript.

Index

Abbott v. Burke (1990), 104, 105, 106, 107, 108, 109, 112, 113, 115

Academic failure, of Mexican-origin children, 64–67
  See also Mexican immigrant families, attending American schools

Accountability, school, 165
  See also Probationary schools

Achievement, of Mexican-origin children, 64–67
  See also Mexican immigrant families, attending American schools

Achievement, student. *See* Probationary school

After-school programs, 291

Alternative schools, 178–179

An Enemy of the People (Ibsen), 292

Analytic generalization, 385

Analytic techniques, 389–391

Appointment, of superintendents. *See* School board leadership, appointment of

Atlanta Public Schools. *See* High school perspective, urban

Baltimore, MD, 233, 235, 248

Basic skills curriculum reforms. *See* State legislative educational reforms

Bilingual programs. *See* Mexican immigrant families, attending American schools; Power structure, within local community

Boston, MA, 233, 235, 246, 247, 249

Brandt, S. D., 105

Bromley, D. B., 381

Bronstein, H., 344

Bronx Leadership Academy (BLA) project
  accountability for education results, 323–325
  conclusion, 325
  introduction, 306–307
  obstacles and successes, 310–321
  origin and vision, 307–310
  pressures against success, 321–323
  relevance of case studies, 306

Brown v. Board of Education (1954), 89–90

Burrill, G., 286

Califano, J., 296

California Achievement Test (CAT), 210–211

California Public Schools. *See* Mathematics education, in California Public Schools

Canadian education, 150
  See also School effectiveness, perspectives on

Carter, J., 295

Case study compositions, 391, 392–393

Case study design methods, 383–384

Case study investigator skills, 382–383

Case study methodology. *See* State Departments of Education, methodology in

Case study research methods, in education
  analytic techniques, 389–391

basic steps in designs, 383–384
case study compositions, 391,
    392–393
essential skills for investigators,
    382–383
five common worries, 391, 394
introduction, 379
practical guidance, 379–381
selection of real-life cases, 385–386
sources of data evidence, 387–388
typical examples of topics, 381–382
Case study screening procedure, 385
Centolanza, L. R., 104, 105, 106
Change process, components
    of, 29–32
    See also Reconceptualization, of
        teaching and learning
Charter schools, 177, 306
Chicago, IL, 233, 235, 248
Choice tracking. *See* Public school
    choice, in New York City
Chubb, J., 185
Cities-in-Schools (CIS) program
    evaluation study of, 295–304
    introduction, 291
    methodological notes, 293–295
    prefatory note, 292–293
    relevance of case studies, 292
Civil Rights Act of 1964, 336
Classroom culture. *See* International
    comparison, of teaching/learning
Classroom management, 10–22
    See also Motivation and
        management, in the classroom
Classroom unity models, in Japan,
    39–43
Coleman, J., 184
Commitment, to change, 30
Community and School Board action
    post-9/11 perspective, 369–377
    power structure within local
        community, 327–348
    rebuilding the South Bronx,
        305–326
    school board leadership, 349–367
    urban youth program, 291–304
Community-district relations. *See*
    Rebuilding the South Bronx

*Community Organizing for Urban
    School Reform* (Shirley), 320
Community power. *See* Power
    structure, within local community
Comprehensive Educational
    Improvement and Financing Act
    (CEIFA) of 1994, 114, 115
COMPSTAT approach, 324
Constitution, U.S., 90, 92, 94, 101, 102
Constructivist philosophy, of teaching
    conclusion, 32
    grades and knowledge, 25–26
    initial novelty, 27–28
    introduction, 23–24
    knowledge construction, 28–29
    real-life context, 24–27
    reconceptualization, components
        of, 29–32
    relevance of case studies, 24
Cooperative learning, 27–28, 30
    See also Constructivist philosophy,
        of teaching
Cooperative teamwork, 41
Cordero, S. T., 345
Core curriculum standards. *See* State
    legislative educational reforms
Corporal punishment, 11
Corporate/political model, of urban
    district governance. *See* Reform
    initiatives, of urban districts
Council of Supervisors and
    Administrators (CSA), 319, 324
Crawford, J., 329
Cronbach, L., 293
Cultural environment, 30–31
Cummins, J., 68, 341
Curricular materials, 31
Curriculum guidelines, in Japan, 46–47

Data sources, examples of, 386–398
De Jesus, J. N., 309
Dead Zone schools, 324, 325
Desegregation, school, 212–213, 218
Dewey, J., 31, 45
Difficult student, 10–15
Discipline practices, 10–22
District-level policy changes.
    See Districts and states

Districts and states
    reform initiatives of urban districts,
        233–259
    state education standards,
        273–288
    state-level policies, 261–272
    superintendent profiles, 207–231
Diversity, of educational life
    culturally diverse families and
        schools, 59–68
    school inequality: federal courts,
        83–100
    school inequality: state courts,
        101–117
    special education programs, 69–81
Dropout rates, 121

Edmonds, R., 303
Education Under Siege (Cummins), 341
Educational reforms, in Seattle Public
        Schools, 217–223
    See also Reform initiatives, of urban
        districts; State legislative
        educational reforms
Educational research, doing. See Case
        study research methods, in
        education
Educational resources, equitable
        distribution of. See Inequalities
        among U.S. schools
Educational standards. See
        Mathematics education, in
        California Public Schools
Effective schools. See School
        effectiveness, perspectives on
Engaged effort, value of, 45
English language development. See
        Mexican immigrant families,
        attending American schools
English-only ordinance. See Power
        structure, within local community
Equal Opportunity Education Act of
        1974, 336
Equal Protection Clause, 91, 93
Equality, of school finance. See
        Inequalities among U.S. schools
Evaluation research. See Cities-in-
        Schools (CIS) program

Evidence, forms of, 386–398
Explorers Program, 141

Federal legislative educational reforms.
        See Inequalities among U.S.
        schools, federal courts
Ferguson, R., 185
Fifth-grade teacher, vignette of
    conclusion, 32
    constructivist perspective, 26–27
    grades and knowledge, 25–26
    initial novelty, 27–28
    introduction, 23–24
    knowledge construction, 28–29
    real-life context, 24–25
    reconceptualization, components of,
        29–32
    relevance of case studies, 24
Firestone, W., 104, 105, 111

Goertz, M. E., 104, 105, 106,
        110, 111
Governance reforms. See Reform
        initiatives, of urban districts
Grades and knowledge, 25–26
Graham, P., 296
Group learning, 27–29
Guba, E., 293

Hall, M. F., 334, 336, 338
Hanushek, E., 185
Hemphill, C., 179
High-performing schools, contrasting.
        See School effectiveness,
        perspectives on
High school perspective, urban
    catalyst of change, 126–132
    challenges at the top, 122–124
    contrast across the tracks, 124–126
    the internal orientation, 137–147
    introduction, 121
    relevance of case studies, 121–122
    shaping a new image, 132–137
Higher-order cognitive skills, 273
Hispanic Education Committee v.
        HISD (1994), 366
Home and school relationships, in
        Japan, 47–48

Houston Independent School District
(HISD). *See* School board
leadership, appointment of

IEP conferences, 75
Industrial Areas Foundation (IAF),
307, 310, 324
Inequalities among U.S. schools,
federal courts
the foundation program, 84–87
introduction, 83–84
landmark federal case, 89–99
local liberty and equity, 87–89
relevance of case studies, 84
state constitutions, 94
Inequalities among U.S. schools,
state courts
financial and educational disparity,
111–117
introduction, 101–102
relevance of case studies, 102
state educational reforms, 102–111
Instructional reforms. *See* Reform
initiatives, of urban districts
International comparison, of
teaching/learning
curriculum guidelines, 46–47
detail and process, 36–37
energy and engagement, 37–39
engaged effort, value of, 45
home and school relationships,
47–48
introduction, 33–34
real-life context, 34–36, 43–44,
48–55
relevance of case studies, 34
social lessons, 46
unity of equals, 39–43
Iowa Test of Basic Skills (ITBS), 211

Japan's educational practices,
American interest in
curriculum guidelines, 46–47
detail and process, 36–37
educational standards, 281, 284
energy and engagement, 37–39
engaged effort, value of, 45
home and school relationships,
47–48

introduction, 33–34
real-life context, 34–36, 43–44,
48–55
relevance of case studies, 34
social lessons, 46
unity of equals, 39–43

K-12 public education. *See* Schools
Kelly, K., 314, 317
Kendrick, W., 227, 228–229
Kennedy, M., 293
Kentucky, 262, 263, 264, 271
Knowledge construction, 28–29
Kohn, E., 41
Kopacki, J., 340
Kupper, T., 336

Labor-management trust agreement,
221–222
Ladd, H., 185
Lau v. Nichols, 336
Leadership behavior. *See* Reform
initiatives, of urban districts;
School board leadership;
Superintendent profiles, in Seattle
Public Schools
Lefelt, S., 89
LeVine, R. A., 67
Liberty and equity, contest between,
87–89
Lilly Endowment, 295
Local governance, in education.
See Inequalities among U.S.
schools
Love, R., 303
Low-performing schools.
See Probationary schools
Low-SES schools, contrasting,
151–153, 161–162t
See also School effectiveness,
perspectives on
Lusi, S. F., 271

Magnet school programs,
177, 178
Managerial reforms. *See* Reform
initiatives, of urban districts
Marshall, T., 92, 93
Martin, J. P., 332, 340, 341, 342

Maryland State Performance
    Assessment Program
    (MSPAP), 166
    See also Probationary schools
Math wars. *See* Mathematics
    education, in California Public
    Schools
Mathematics education, in California
    Public Schools
    the Board's standards, 278–280
    framework for, 274–275
    introduction, 273
    learned outcomes, 285–287
    national debate of, 275–276
    the new framework, 280–285
    overview of standards, 276–278
    relevance of case studies, 273–274
McLaughlin, J., 114, 115
Memorization and rote
    learning, 37–39
Mexican immigrant families, attending
    American schools
    academic failure of, 64–67
    introduction, 59–60
    real-life context, 60–64
    relevance of case studies, 60
Milgram, R. J., 277
Milliken, W., 300, 301
Moe, T., 185
Motivation and management, in the
    classroom, 39–43
Mulligan, B., 340, 341, 342, 343
Murray, C., 295, 299, 301, 303

National Institute of Education
    (NIE), 294
Native American (First Native)
    students, serving. *See* School
    effectiveness, perspectives on
Natriello, G., 104, 105, 111
Natural intelligence, 74
Naturalistic inquiry, in education
    evaluation. *See* Cities-in-Schools
    (CIS) program
NCTM standards. *See* Mathematics
    education, in California Public
    Schools
New building construction. *See*
    Rebuilding the South Bronx

New Jersey State Department of
    Education, 113
    See also Inequalities among U.S.
    schools
New York City Board of Education.
    See. Public school choice, in New
    York City; Rebuilding the South
    Bronx
No Child Left Behind Act (NCLB) of
    2001, 165

Odden, A., 102
Office of Civil Rights (OCR), 336, 344
Olchefske, J., 215, 216–217, 224–225,
    227, 228

Paige, R., 349
Patton, M. Q., 263, 267
Peer tutoring, 41
Performance, 36
Perturbations, in change, 30
Peterson, P., 186
Philadelphia, PA, 233, 235, 248
Physical arrangements, 42
Picus, L., 102
Politi, N., 336
Political reforms. *See* Reform initiatives,
    of urban districts
Portland Board of Education, 234
Post-9/11 perspective, on U.S.
    Education
    introduction, 369
    real-life context, 370–377
    relevance of case studies, 370
Powell, L., 90, 91, 92, 93
Power structure, within local
    community
    account of events, 329–347
    English-only ordinance, 328–329
    introduction, 327–328
    relevance of case studies, 328
    "Under the Cover of Darkness"
        poem, 345–346
Principal professional standards,
    220–221
Principles, 37
Probationary schools
    improvement strategies, 170–175
    introduction, 165

leadership and interactions, 167–170
low-performance label, 166–167
relevance of case studies, 165–166
summary, 175–176
Problem solving ability, 27–28, 273
Public Education Association
(PEA), 324
Public school choice, in New York City
choice in District 2, 196–198
choice in District 4, 181–184
conclusions, 198–200
examining student performance,
184–186
interdistrict choice programs,
178–180
introduction, 177–178
performance patterns over time,
186–196
relevance of case studies, 178
Public School Elementary and
Secondary Education Act (PSEA)
of 1975, 104, 106, 113

Qualitative-quantitative data, 388
Quality Education Act (QEA) of 1990,
110–111, 114

Real-life case selection process,
385–386
Rebuilding the South Bronx
accountability for education results,
323–325
Bronx Leadership Academy (BLA)
project, 306–307
conclusion, 325
introduction, 305–306
obstacles and successes, 310–321
origin and vision, 307–310
pressures against success, 321–323
relevance of case studies, 306
Reconceptualization, of teaching and
learning, 29–32
See also Teaching and learning
Reflection, 31–32
Reform initiatives, of urban districts
explaining mixed outcomes, 245–251
introduction, 233
reflections on urban district reform,
251–255

relevance of case studies, 233–234
six cities profiled, 234–245
Reynolds, D., 160
Riley, R. W., 287
Robinson v. Cahill (1973),
103, 104, 106
Roeock, E. C., Jr., 113
Rote learning and memorization, 37–39
Rouse, C., 186

Salmore, B. G., 110
Salmore, S. A., 110
Samuels, H., 303
San Antonio Independent School
District v. Rodriguez (1973),
83, 90, 94, 101, 102
See also Inequalities among U.S.
schools, federal courts
San Diego, CA, 233, 235, 247, 249
Sanders, W., 222
Schnur, B., 334, 337, 338
School accountability, 165
See also Probationary schools
School administrators. See
Superintendent profiles, in Seattle
Public Schools
School board leadership,
appointment of
Board of Education decision,
353–355
Houston Independent School District
(HISD), context of, 350–353
introduction, 349
objections to the process, 355–360
relevance of case studies, 349–350
Texas Education Agency (TEA)
investigation, 360–367
School choice. See Public school choice,
in New York City
School-community collaboration.
See Community and School
Board action
School culture. See High school
perspective, urban
School effectiveness, perspectives on
the Canadian school system, 150
conclusions, 160
the curriculum, 155–156
a day in the life of a child, 153–154

the headteacher/principal, 156–157
influence of parents, 156
inter-staff relations, 157–158
introduction, 149–150
low- and high performing schools,
    151–153
relationship with local authorities,
    158–159
relevance of case studies, 150
resources, 158
school image, 159
summary of differences, 161–162t
teachers' teaching style, 154–155
School finance. *See* Inequalities among
    U.S. schools
School reform. *See* Districts and states
Schools
    low- and high performing,
        comparison on, 149–163
    on probation, 165–176
    public school choice, 177–204
    urban high school perspective,
        121–147
Schools of excellence, drive for, 87–88
Sciarra, D., 114
Science teaching. *See* Teaching and
    learning
Scientific research, in education.
    See Case study research methods,
    in education
Seattle Education Association
    (SEA), 221
Seattle Public Schools. *See* Reform
    initiatives, of urban districts;
    Superintendent profiles, in Seattle
    Public Schools
Self-reliance, 36–37, 46
Serranno v. Priest (1971), 102
Shallow roots, 248–249
Shavelson, R. J., 381
Shirley, D., 320
Smith, L., 293
Snyder, S., 334, 335, 337
Social lessons, in Japan, 46
Social studies. *See* Post-9/11
    perspective, on U.S. Education
Special education programs
    introduction, 69
    methodology, 75–81

real-life context, 70–75
relevance of case studies, 70
Staff Training Assistance and Review
    (STAR) program, 221
Stanford, J., 213–215, 216, 223, 224,
    226, 227, 250
State aid, 86
State constitutions, 94
    See also Inequalities among U.S.
        schools, state courts
State Departments of Education,
    methodology in
    data analysis, 270–272
    introduction, 261
    relevance of case studies, 262
    research approach/sample methods,
        264–270
    state selection criteria, 262–264
State education standards, in
    mathematics. *See* Mathematics
    education, in California Public
    Schools
State legislative educational reforms,
    102–111, 217–218
    See also Inequalities among U.S.
        schools, state courts
State-level polices. *See* State
    Departments of Education,
    methodology in
States rights *v.* federal intervention.
    See Inequalities among U.S.
    schools, federal courts
Statistical generalization, 385
Student achievement. *See* Probationary
    schools
Student teaching science
    classroom discipline, 10–22
    introduction, 3–4
    real-life context, 4–10
    relevance of case studies, 4
    See also Teaching and learning
Students with disabilities. *See* Special
    education programs
Superintendent profiles, in Seattle
    Public Schools
    conclusion, 226–229
    context of, 210–213
    data analysis, 223–226
    educational reforms, 217–223

introduction, 207
leadership behavior, 208–210
leadership of present era, 213–217
relevance of case studies, 207–208
Systemic school reform. *See* State
   Departments of Education,
   methodology in

Teacher-student authority
   relationship, 41
Teaching and learning
   the constructivist perspective, 23–32
   international comparison, 33–55
   student teaching science, 3–22
Teddlie, C., 160
Towne, L., 381
Tractenberg, P., 102, 103

"Under the Cover of Darkness"
   (Cordero), 345–346
United Federation of Teachers
   (UFT), 319
Unity and harmony, Japanese
   pedagogies of, 39–43

Urban high school perspective. *See*
   High school perspective, urban
Urban school reform. *See* Reform
   initiatives, of urban districts
Urban youth work programs.
   See Cities-in-Schools (CIS)
   program
U.S. Constitution, 90, 92, 94,
   101, 102

Value-added performance measure,
   222–223
Vermont, 262, 263, 264, 268
Vision, for change, 30

Washington Essential Academic
   Learning Requirements, 217
Weighted Student Formula, 219–220
Weinberg, J., 86
White, M. I., 67
White, O. Z., 91, 95, 98
Whole child process, 70–75
Williams, T., 335
Working knowledge, 293

About the Editor

Robert K. Yin, Ph.D., serves as Chairman of the Board and CEO of COSMOS Corporation, an applied research and social science firm that has been in operation since 1980. Over the years, COSMOS has completed hundreds of projects for government agencies, private foundations, and other entrepreneurial and non-profit organizations. At COSMOS, Yin actively leads various research projects. For the past several years, the projects have focused on K-12 education, including studies of statewide reform in mathematics and science, whole-school reform covering all academic subjects, public school choice, informal science education, and university-school partnerships. These studies have been sponsored by the U.S. Department of Education, the National Science Foundation, education associations, and private foundations.

Yin has authored numerous books and peer-reviewed articles, including a chapter on "Case Study Methods as Applied to Education Research" in the 3rd edition of *Complementary Methods for Research in Education* (2005), reprinted as an appendix in this anthology. In 1998, he founded the "Robert K. Yin Fund" at M.I.T., which supports seminars on brain sciences, as well as other activities related to the advancement of predoctoral students in the Department of Brain and Cognitive Sciences. He has a B.A. from Harvard College (magna cum laude) and a Ph.D. from M.I.T. (brain and cognitive sciences).